ENTERPRISE INFORMATION PORTALS AND KNOWLEDGE MANAGEMENT

ENTERPRISE INFORMATION PORTALS AND KNOWLEDGE MANAGEMENT

JOSEPH M. FIRESTONE, PH.D.

KNOWLEDGE
MANAGEMENT
CONSORTIUM
INTERNATIONAL

Routledge
Taylor & Francis Group

LONDON AND NEW YORK

First published 2003 by Butterworth-Heinemann

This edition published 2011 by Routledge
2 Park Square, Milton Park, Abingdon, Oxfordshire OX14 4RN
711 Third Avenue, New York, NY 10017, USA

First issued in hardback 2016

Routledge is an imprint of the Taylor & Francis Group, an informa business

Library of Congress Cataloging-in-Publication Data

A catalog record for this book is available from the Library of Congress.

British Library Cataloguing-in-Publication Data

A catalogue record for this book is available from the British Library.

ISBN 13: 978-1-138-15879-5 (hbk)
ISBN 13: 978-0-7506-7474-4 (pbk)

For Bonnie—
Who waited for this

CONTENTS

Part Two—Benefits of Enterprise Information Portals and Corporate Goals

3
BENEFITS OF ENTERPRISE INFORMATION PORTALS   35

4
ESTIMATING BENEFITS OF ENTERPRISE INFORMATION PORTALS: CONCEPTS, METHODOLOGY, AND TOOLS   43

Part Three—Architecture of Enterprise Information Portals and Enterprise Artificial Systems Integration

5
EIP ARCHITECTURAL QUESTIONS AND APPROACHES: EASI AND THE TWO PROBLEMS OF IT   63

6
THE ROLE OF INTELLIGENT AGENTS IN EIPs

Part Four—On Knowledge and Knowledge Management

7
ON KNOWLEDGE

11
THE ROLE OF XML IN ENTERPRISE INFORMATION PORTALS 215

Part Six—EIP Frameworks, Portal Product Case Studies, and Applications to E-Business

12
A FORWARD LOOKING EIP SEGMENTATION FRAMEWORK 229

13
THE ENTERPRISE KNOWLEDGE PORTAL AND
ITS ARCHITECTURE   251

14
DECISION PROCESSING PORTAL PRODUCTS   269

15
CONTENT MANAGEMENT PORTAL PRODUCTS   275

16
COLLABORATIVE PORTAL PRODUCTS   313

17
DECISION PROCESSING/CONTENT MANAGEMENT AND ADVANCED PORTAL PRODUCTS   339

18
PORTAL TECHNOLOGY, E-BUSINESS, KNOWLEDGE PROCESSING, AND KNOWLEDGE MANAGEMENT   381

Part Seven—The Future of the EIP

PREFACE

My odyssey culminating in this book began in 1991, when, after an 8 year absence from analytical work, I joined a small database marketing firm located in Washington, DC and discovered the world of database marketing which later was one source of Customer Relationship Management (CRM). I was hired as the firm's Director of Statistical Services, and soon found myself immersed in data mining, fuzzy logic, survival analysis, neural networks, and customer retention and lifetime value models. That work led me to two discoveries that put me on the road to this book. First, I discovered client/server enterprise computing and soon after Object Technology and the work of Ivar Jacobson, James Rumbaugh and his co-authors, Grady Booch, and James Martin and James O'Dell. And second, I discovered data warehousing a field that coupled with database marketing, and data mining placed me back in touch with my career-long interest in Executive Information and Decision Support Systems (DSS).

As the 1990s passed and I became more deeply immersed in data mining and data warehousing, and as I observed the progress in enterprise computing, I began to realize that data modeling and data-centric approaches to data warehousing and DSS were not adequate for representing the complex systems models, causal models and process models that were necessary for sophisticated decision support. Also, as the data warehousing IT environment became increasingly more complex with diverse databases, application servers, and business process engines, I realized, as well, that the old data-centric approaches would not suffice to model the change processes characteristic of more complex data warehousing systems. That is, I perceived that a Dynamic Integration Problem (DIP) was developing in DSS systems based on data warehousing, and I believed that this problem was due to the data-centricity of data warehousing practices.

Spurred by this perception I set out to persuade others that an Object-Oriented (OO) approach to data warehousing was the right way to go and so, in August 1997, I wrote a White Paper called Object-Oriented Data Warehousing, that one can still find at www.dkms.com. I don't know whether that paper or my views on OO data warehousing were very successful in influencing that field, but they certainly made me develop a coherent distributed object/component view of computing, and a vision of Online Complex Processing (OLCP) that combined

DSS, Online Transaction Processing (OLTP), and Batch processing all coexisting in the same system. When I contemplated that system and realized that it would contain models that were validated by human investigators in the process of data mining, I concluded, further, that this distributed computing system would support the production of knowledge (i.e., validated knowledge models), and therefore could be considered a *Distributed Knowledge Management System* (DKMS). So later that same August, I wrote a White Paper called "Distributed Knowledge Management Systems: the Next Wave in DSS" (also available at www.dkms.com), a revised version of the OO Data Warehousing paper to record my new insight.

I don't know if that paper was any more successful than the first one. But it did one very important thing for me. It, along with some very current material from a special issue of CIO magazine, made me realize that I was working in a field broader than data warehousing, a field called Knowledge Management that had been developing very well during most of the 1990s, and whose development I had missed. So, I began to read everything I could about knowledge management, and also began a transition, by now complete, from someone practicing data warehousing to someone practicing knowledge management. I kept writing data warehousing material, of course, but more and more, as I moved forward, the material was slanted towards knowledge management.

And, really, this transition, suited my background and previous interests better than data warehousing had. My DSS and data mining, and data warehousing background were all still relevant, but, in addition, my previous work in General Systems Theory, Social and Political Theory, Philosophy of Science, Epistemology, Value Theory, Theory of Measurement, Operations Research, Sociology, Social Psychology and Conflict Theory were all enormously relevant as well. Who ever said, "you can't go home again"? Here I was, at home in knowledge management, at last.

Just about that time, in early 1998, the Knowledge Management Consortium (KMC), later to become the KMCI (I for International), was just getting started and I became a founding member. Soon, I found myself working on Knowledge Management Metrics and thereafter on basic knowledge management theory and on Artificial Knowledge Management Systems (AKMSs), a concept very closely related to my previous DKMS idea. My work on the AKMS/DKMS paradigm developed through the fall of 1998 and I produced first a paper on Enterprise Knowledge Management Modeling and the DKMS for a KMCI session at the KMWorld Conference in October 1998 in Chicago, and second, two working papers for a rather premature, but very exciting KMCI standards conference held in Silver Spring, MD in January of 1999. One of these papers was on a Knowledge Base Management System (KBMS) standard, and the other on an Artificial Knowledge Management System (AKMS) standard. Both helped me to develop the AKMS concept presented in Chapter 10 of this book.

At about the same time, however, in January of 1999, I encountered the Merrill Lynch Report on Enterprise Information Portals. The relationships between EIPs, DKMSs and AKMSs, were immediately apparent. Basically, an ideal EIP was just a DKMS system with a portal front-end and without the model validation element. The DKMS/AKMS, on the other hand was just a particular kind of portal, or at least would be if it had a portal front-end, to go with its middle-tier and back-end architecture, and that kind was obviously an Enterprise Knowledge Portal, a concept that had not yet been defined in the portal literature.

This inference led me to write the first article on Enterprise Knowledge Portals (EKPs) in March of 1999 (see "Enterprise Information Portals and Enterprise Knowledge Portals" at www.dkms.com). That article defined the EKP concept, and though I've often seen the term used since with other meanings entirely, and though I've specified the concept in greater detail myself in other publications, I've only seen one other attempt to formally specify the concept. That was by Jeff Grammer in an article in DM Review (2000), an article I critiqued (I hope successfully) in my "Enterprise Knowledge Portals Revisited" (see www.dkms.com).

At about the same time I published my first article on the EKP, I continued to be involved in significant work at the KMCI on the foundations of knowledge management. That work, done in collaboration primarily with Mark W. McElroy, now President of the KMCI, and my co-instructor in the KMCI Certified Knowledge and Innovation Manager (CKIM) program (but also involving the assistance of Edward Swanstrom, Douglas Weidner and Steven Cavaleri), led to the initial formulation of the Knowledge Life Cycle (KLC) framework. The KLC later became the basis for Mark's definition of the Second Generation Knowledge Management (SGKM) concept and its subsequent adoption as the KMCI orientation to KM.

Mark and I have continued to develop the KLC concept, and a knowledge management framework based on it, since then. Our publications on the foundations of KM are available at www.dkms.com, at www.macroinnovation.com, and at www.kmci.org., and Mark is also publishing a book called *The New Knowledge Management* in this KMCI Press series. This journey has further clarified the connection between knowledge management and the Enterprise Knowledge Portal construct that is developed in detail later in this book.

In addition to the work on the foundations of knowledge management and the EKP, I've also continued my work on Enterprise Information Portals and tracked developments in EIP products as the trend toward portal application frameworks accelerated and portal products added increased functionality. In December of 1999, Executive Information Systems, Inc. published my industry report called "Approaching Enterprise Information Portals." The report covered some of the same ground as this book, including the relationship of EIP products to KM, but in far less detail than this book, and without benefit of the case studies of portal products included below, and at an earlier stage of portal progress. My work on EIPs led, in 2000, and 2001 to many presentations on the subject at national and local meetings and to the design of seminars, workshops, and a segment of the KMCI Certification class on EIPs and their role in knowledge management.

All of my work on EIPs has been done against the backdrop of, and with an eye toward, the broader work in The New Knowledge Management (TNKM) being conducted in collaboration with Mark and the KMCI. That work now encompasses not only the foundations of knowledge management, and conceptual frameworks on the KLC and KM, but additional work on sustainable innovation, social innovation capital, The Open Enterprise, Knowledge Management Metrics, Knowledge Management Framework Methodology, and the relationship of EIPs and the full range of IT products to Knowledge Management.

All of the foregoing, represents the context for this work. From it, I've taken the view that EIPs have their place in the larger mosaic of knowledge management and that their purpose in this broader context, is to help organizations and

individuals adapt to the changing environment of the workplace and the organization. In particular I think that ultimately EIPs should be evaluated from the
viewpoint of the support they give to *organizational intelligence*, the ability of an
organization to adapt to its environment.

That ability accounts for new knowledge production and integration that
solves problems of business processing: i.e., innovation in business processing. And
it also accounts for knowledge process innovation, or new knowledge production
and integration relating to knowledge processing itself. In this book, I will be
concerned to analyze EIPs in general, and EIP products in particular, from the
viewpoint of the support they provide for new knowledge production and integration. And while I am also concerned to present a rounded and comprehensive
view of the EIP space as well, my bias in this book is to evaluate EIPs from the
knowledge processing and knowledge management viewpoint and even more
specifically from The New Knowledge Management viewpoint, that gives equal
weight to knowledge production and knowledge integration as primary concerns
of knowledge management.

Joseph M. Firestone, Ph.D.
Alexandria, VA
March 3, 2002

ACKNOWLEDGMENTS

There are many I would like to thank for contributing to this book. Some are other authors that greatly influenced my views. Others are friends or colleagues who read my work at one time or another, or heard one of my presentations and were kind enough to provide me feedback, or sometimes even training opportunities that I used to further develop my ideas. Others helped with production of the book, and still others provided permissions to use part of their work.

In the area of *permissions* I'd like to thank Brio Software, Inc., Hummingbird, Communications, Ltd., Netegrity, Inc., Open Text Corporation, Plumtree Software, Inc., Sun Microsystems, Inc., Sybase, Inc., and TheBrain Technologies, Inc., for their enlightened attitude in extending permission to use their graphics. I am particularly grateful to them for their cooperation in light of the surprising attitude of some other (unnamed) software vendors who evidently thought their interests were better served by not extending such permission and not providing the readers of this book easy access to the companies' own visuals of their portal architectures.

Among authors who have been most influential in shaping my views were Karl Popper, for his theory of knowledge and its generation, Charles Sanders Peirce for his "fallibilism" and open-minded pragmatism, Carl Hempel and Willard Van Orman Quine for their writings on theoretical networks, Ivar Jacobson, for his work on use cases and his ideas on their relation to business processes, James Rumbaugh for his account of how object models are related to data models, Grady Booch for his fundamental work on object technology, Thomas L. Saaty for his pioneering work on the Analytic Hierarchy Process (AHP) and on the theory of ratio scale measurement, Ralph Kimball for his great work on the virtual data warehouse and distributed data marts and for his generous invitation to participate in his Advanced Data Warehousing Workshop from which my DKMS ideas benefited enormously, John Holland for his work on complex adaptive systems and emergence, Paul Thagard for his work on scientific change and revolution, and Verna Allee for her recent work on value networks.

Among friends, some of whom are also authors, I'd like to thank my primary collaborator over the last few years, Mark W. McElroy for one of the most fruitful collaborations of my career. Together, we've worked through, and continue to work through the basic conceptual framework of The New Knowledge Management (TNKM). I've benefited very much from his various articles, and presentations, from our e-mail interactions, and most recently from reviewing his book manuscript on The New Knowledge Management for KMCI Press. Mark always challenges me to face objections to our theories of knowledge and knowledge management and to continually strengthen their foundations. We've had a good bit of help in developing our ideas on KM, most recently from Mark A. Notturno, the author of *Science and the Open Society* and other works, and over the period of the past three years, from Steven A. Cavaleri and Arthur J. Murray (our co-instructor in the KMCI Certified Knowledge and Innovation Manager – Government [CKIM – G]) program. I thank all three for the attention they've paid to our work and for their continuing support.

In the area of portals, object technology and intelligent agents, I've had help from many people. First, I thank my friend Ron Goodes for getting me involved with Template Software, a company that until its recent acquisition by Level 8 Systems was at the forefront of Object/Component-based development and business process engine technology with its SNAP Development Environment, Enterprise Integration Template (EIT), and Business Process Automation Template (BPA). I owe a lot to Template's conceptualization of Active Information Managers that lay at the base of its EIT and BPA products and that now provide the foundation for Level 8's Geneva Enterprise Integrator and Business Process Automator. That conceptualization provides part of the foundation for my own Artificial Information and Knowledge Servers and Artificial Knowledge Management Systems developed in this manuscript. I became conversant with Template technology due to the recommendation of Ron Goodes, and the kindness of Template's former Vice President Ben Martindale, who provided me with training on Template's Workflow Template (WFT) a forerunner of BPA, and on EIT. Both of these training experiences as well as access to Template's technical materials and some of its personnel contributed to developing my views on the AKMS. In particular, I'd like to thank Doug McPhaden, formerly of Template, for his efforts to explain the workings of SNAP, WFT, and EIT to me.

Following Template's acquisition by Level 8, I met Nancy Korpela, now KMCI's Director of Membership and Director of International Business Development at EM Software Solutions, the former Government subsidiary of Template Software, when she attended a presentation I gave at the KM in e-Gov conference in March of 2000. Nancy, instantly felt a kinship with my ideas on Enterprise Knowledge Portals and since then has introduced me to a number of former key Template developers who have been only too happy to help me increase my understanding of my EKP construct by discussing it with me from the Template point of view. This group included Laura Pels, Ed Sorensen, most recently Andy Schneider, and most importantly, Chuck Droz who exchanged views with me on a number of occasions, and who joined KMCI, became head of its Greater Washington Area Chapter, and my friend, before his life was tragically ended when AA Flight 77 crashed into the Pentagon, just a few miles away from his workplace at EM Software Solutions.

Others who have helped me with this book include Mark Potter. I met Mark at Ralph Kimball's Advanced Data Warehousing training class. He instantly responded to my ideas on the DKMS and has been a frequent correspondent, KMCI stalwart, and gentle critic during the time I developed and extended my ideas on EIPs and EKPs. I met Steve Tracy, now of Hartford Life, at the same training class I met Mark. Steve had read my work on OO Data Warehousing prior to that class and we talked about it a lot through that week of training. Afterwards, Steve also joined KMCI and he and I have corresponded at various times since then on data warehousing, the DKMS, and most recently on Enterprise Information and Knowledge Portals.

I also want to thank Robin Holland. Through the Spring and Summer of 2000, Robin became very interested in my work, did volunteer work as the Associate Editor of Knowledge and Innovation, the Journal I founded for the KMCI, and edited some of my published work during this period. She was helpful also in the development of my views on knowledge, knowledge management and the EKP during this time. Jay Karlin of Viable Systems and NASA, listened to my ideas on intelligent agents, read my sometimes very difficult papers, and helped me to understand better the importance of IAs and their applications. I thank him very much for his encouragement and help.

Others who helped me develop my ideas on portals include Marvin Scaff, Damien Miller, Stan Lockhart, and John Anderjaska. I'd like to thank Marvin and Damien, for sharing their ideas on Intelligent Agents with me during the Winter, Spring and Summer of 1999. Their concepts certainly contributed to the final form of my views on how IAs relate to EIPs.

For a time during the Summer of 1999 and extending into the late spring of 2000, Stan Lockhart and I shared the dream of beginning a venture around the EKP concept. Stan helped me to sharpen my views on how EKPs could contribute to business processes and knowledge management. He helped me greatly in thinking through what EKPs could mean to knowledge workers in the Enterprise. John Anderjaska, also shared the dream of beginning our EKP venture. In interactions with John, I was able to further develop my thinking about the role of IAs in EKPs. I thank him for his contributions to the views on CAS agents in the EKP expressed in Chapter 13.

Those who were important in producing this book include Steve Cavaleri, who as President of KMCI and KMCI Press, encouraged me to put a book proposal together, and brought my proposal to the KMCI Press Board. Jennifer Pursley of Butterworth-Heinemann was instrumental in beginning the negotiations that led to this book, and Nicki Kear was instrumental in completing them. As time wore on, however, I have worked most closely with Karen Maloney, who as Chairperson of the KMCI Press Board, showed unfailing good humor as I worked my way through the nooks and crannies of this work, and, particularly, as I researched my way through the survey of portal products. I thank you all for your help in producing this book.

Finally, I'd like to thank my wonderful wife and loving life partner, Bonnie, for this book. She (and I) waited a long time for this, my first book. Even though I've published many articles and many reports over the years, I never got around to doing a book, even though she always urged me to do one. Well now it's finally done, and I think it's Bonnie I have to thank the most for it.

INTRODUCTION

In November of 1998, a new "investment space" called Enterprise Information Portals (EIPs), was declared by Christopher Shilakes and Julie Tylman of Merrill Lynch's Enterprise Software Team (1998, p. 1). Merrill Lynch saw EIPs as the next big investment opportunity in the IT sector and believed that the EIP space would eventually reach or exceed the size of the Enterprise Resource Planning (ERP) Market. Indeed, Merrill Lynch estimated the 1998 total EIP market at $4.4 billion, and forecast "that revenues could top $14.8 billion by 2002, approximately 36% CAGR for this sector." While it is debatable whether this instance of a potentially "self-fulfilling prophecy" was accurate, the Merrill Lynch report, combined with software development trends in the second-half of the 1990s to create the forecasted new investment space, and, now, in 2002, it is certainly a multi-billion dollar market in size depending on the assumptions used in projecting it, and whether or not the applications of EIP technology in e-business are included in calculating the size of the space.

This growth, according to Shilakes and Tylman, is driven by three basic benefits provided by EIP systems (1998, p. 9). The first benefit is "competitive advantage" derived from the "competitive potential lying dormant in the information stored" in enterprise systems. The second benefit is that "packaged" EIP systems lead to increased ROI because they are less expensive, easier to maintain, and easier to deploy than customized systems. They also generate revenue through the well-informed actions they support. And the third is that "EIP systems provide access to all" in a convenient, reliable, and inexpensive delivery vehicle providing everyone a single point of access. To all data, content and applications in the enterprise.

A slightly different point of view on benefits is provided by Plumtree Software. (1998, p. 9) Plumtree, one of the pioneering EIP vendors, sees them as (1) increasing employee productivity by decreasing the amount of time employees spend searching the web, (2) increasing effectiveness by providing needed information that helps decision making, and (3) decreasing overall cost of information by lowering the cost of its delivery. Statements like these about the benefits of EIPs, begin to introduce the issues of the business context and justification of EIP introduction and their relationship to enterprise goals. I will return to this issue in Chapter Three, where I will show that some of the most important of the above benefits are actually EKP and not EIP benefits.

One benefit that is clearly an EKP, rather than EIP, benefit is that of supporting organizational intelligence, by which I mean, not business intelligence, as the term is commonly used in IT circles, but organizational intelligence in the sense of the ability of an organization to learn and adapt to its changing environment. Competitive advantage, increased ROI, greater effectiveness, etc. are all subordinate, from the point of view of the enterprise, to organizational intelligence, which is the fundamental property that allows an organization to maintain itself over time. The EKP is about *supporting innovation in business processes* through its support of enhanced knowledge production and integration processes. And it is also about better *knowledge process innovation* through its support for enhancements to knowledge management processes.

The Enterprise Information Portal (EIP) is still among the "hottest" current information technology subjects, four years after the Merrill Lynch report. With so many new vendors having entered the area, along with the inevitable hype accompanying any new packaging of Information Technology, it is difficult to arrive at an understanding of this new attack on the "islands of information" and "islands of automation" problems in context. Yet it is such an understanding that decision makers need in order to evaluate portal technology and to help them arrive at their own truth about portals and their utility for business.

Purposes and objectives: what this book is about

In this book I provide an approach to Enterprise Information Portals and an analysis of their relationship to Knowledge Management. This analysis is much needed, since EIPs have frequently been called the "killer app of knowledge management," and since the "killer app of knowledge management" promises to deliver the kind of support for organizational intelligence that enables organizations to adapt to change. That is, we need to know, have we reached the "Holy Grail" of IT support for organizational intelligence, or do we still have a ways to go? But, in addition to answering this central question, I have a multiplicity of other purposes in writing this book. These are to:

- immerse the reader in the EIP orientation and outlook and provide a feel for the issues involved in delineating the scope of the field (Part One);
- trace the evolutionary trends in Information Technology that culminated in EIPs (Part One);
- create an awareness of key issues relating to claims made about EIP benefits (Part Two);
- propose a new methodology for estimating EIP benefits that places monetary and non-monetary benefits on the same measurement scale and therefore is useful both for private and governmental enterprises (Part Two);
- provide a comprehensive approach to EIP systems integration and architecture that transcends Enterprise Application Integration (EAI) and clearly distinguishes the major dimensions of enterprise and EIP systems integration (Part Three);

- delineate the coming role of intelligent agents in fully-developed EIP systems architecture (Part Three);
- present a careful analysis of knowledge, knowledge processing and knowledge management that will provide an adequate foundation for evaluating whether EIPs are, in fact, the "killer app of knowledge management," and whether Enterprise Knowledge Portals (EKPs), in line with the claims made by some EIP vendors, exist yet (Part Four);
- apply the knowledge, knowledge processing and knowledge management framework to the definition and specification of Artificial Knowledge Management Systems (Part Five) and also to the definition and specification of EKPs (Part Six);
- describe and project the role of XML in EIPs (Part Five);
- provide a comprehensive and forward-looking, segmentation framework of EIP products and a simplified segmentation adequate for classifying the present group of EIP products (Part Six);
- provide brief case studies of a healthy sampling of portal products applying the framework to their classification and analyzing the support they provide for knowledge management (Part Six);
- outline the contributions that EIP/EKP technology are making and can make to e-business (Part Six), and finally;
- provide an analysis projecting the future of the EIP space and identifying major trends within it and their relevance for knowledge management (Part Seven).

Overview

I have divided the book into seven parts. Part One: Introducing Enterprise Information Portals: Definition and Evolution, introduces the EIP concept. In Chapter One, EIPs are defined and specified in detail. Different types of EIPs are distinguished from one another, EIPs are distinguished from Business Portals and Corporate Portals, and the extension of EIP technology to e-business is discussed. In Chapter Two, the origin and evolution of the EIP is discussed, and the relationships of EIP applications to Content Management, ERP, Data Warehousing, DSS, Data Mining, and Data Management applications (the main components of EIPs as defined by Merrill Lynch), and issues of EIP integration are analyzed. Finally, the prospect of further evolution of EIPs is introduced, the Enterprise Knowledge Portal (EKP) is proposed as the likely direction of EIP evolution. This issue is discussed at greater length in other parts of the book as well.

In Part Two, Benefits of Enterprise Information Portals and Corporate Goals, I place EIPs in the context of Corporate Goals and Benefits. Most discussions of EIPs and, for that matter, of benefits of other software alternatives, are not tightly coupled to corporate goals and business processes. They have not approached a systematic analysis of corporate goals, objectives and benefits in the context of IT alternatives, including the EIP. In Chapter Three, I consider how the various claimed EIP benefits are related to corporate goals, business processes, and to IT applications. I then make the case that the approach taken to benefit analysis is basically intuitive rather than analytical, and does not clarify the relationship of the claimed or envisioned outcomes of EIP adoption to corporate goals or business processes.

In Chapter Four, I present concepts, methodology and tools for producing improved EIP benefit estimates. My objective is to provide a framework for thinking about more comprehensive estimation of EIP benefits—estimation that is tightly coupled to corporate goals, and that distinguishes benefits whether monetary or non-monetary, according to their relative importance.

In Part Three, Architecture of Enterprise Information Portals and Enterprise Artificial Systems Integration, I present an analysis of the underlying architecture of enterprise information portals, both current and prospective. Chapter 5 begins with an identification of the two "islands" problems of Enterprise Artificial Systems Integration (EASI) and of the meaning of EASI itself. It then proceeds to consider 13 types of EASI as the basis for an analysis of the two islands problems and the architecture of enterprise information portals. The discussion covers Stonebraker's account of enterprise integration, the distinction between Natural and Artificial System integration, Enterprise Application Integration (EAI), the Data Federation approach, content integration, artificial information integration, and artificial knowledge integration. The results of this analysis is then used as the basis for proposing the Distributed Information Management System (DIMS) as a solution to the islands of information problem. In laying out the solution, I discuss: the Artificial Information Manager (AIM), connectivity services, application servers, object/data stores, Object Request brokers (ORBs) and other components, protocols, and standards supporting distributed processing. The consideration of the islands of information problem then ends by relating the DIMS solution to it to data federations and the Enterprise Information Portal.

Chapter 5 next moves on to consider the islands of automation problem. Here three of the 13 types of EASI, which together offer a solution to the islands of automation problem, are discussed: (a) user interface subject matter integration, (b) application integration through work flow, and (c) Information integration from application to application through ad hoc navigation while sharing information and maintaining a common view across them.

After completing its analysis of the two islands problems, Chapter 5 applies the results to portal architecture by developing a taxonomy of portal architectural types. First, EIP integration is related to architecture, then Passive Access to Content (PAC), Data Federation Integration (DFI), Structured Application Integration (SAI), Distributed Content Management (DCM) and Portal Application Integration (PAI) approaches to architecture are specified, considered and evaluated. The chapter then concludes with the recommendation that incremental PAI architecture is the appropriate architectural goal of EIP solutions.

Chapter 6 considers an important aspect of PAI architecture and EASI not covered in Chapter 5. That aspect is the role of intelligent agents in EIPs and in PAI architecture. Chapter 6 discusses definitions, agents in PAI architecture (including their role in in-memory proactive object state management and synchronization across distributed objects; component management; use case and workflow management; and transactional multithreading). Chapter 6 moves on to consider a view of agents as scaled-down business process engines and ends with conclusions on the role of intelligent agents in EIPs and in creating the virtual enterprise.

Parts 1–3 take us as far as we can go in analyzing the relationship of Enterprise Information Portals to Knowledge Management without engaging in an explicit consideration of what we mean by knowledge and knowledge management. It is commonplace, in these days of "industry" discussions about knowledge and knowledge management, to say many things about them while assuming that everyone knows what everyone else means by these words, but my own experience with the literature, clients, students, and other participants in various Web-based list serves, persuades me that the opposite is true, that everyone uses these words differently; and that there is even more difficulty in finding a common language here, then there is in finding it in discussions of EIPs.

Part 4, On Knowledge and Knowledge Management, provides the explicit consideration of knowledge and knowledge management needed to talk intelligently about the relationship of EIPs to knowledge processing and knowledge management. Chapter 7 is a somewhat lengthy consideration of the nature of knowledge. It begins with the problem of definition and contrasts the ideas of definition, specification, and cognitive mapping (or semantic networking). It then surveys alternative definitions of knowledge, including definitions of world 2 and world 3 knowledge. It discusses the distinctions between world 2 data, information, and knowledge (see Chapter 2 for distinctions among world 3 data, information, and knowledge). It provides a conceptual framework for understanding in broad outline how knowledge is produced and integrated in organizations. This framework views business processes as aggregated from decision cycles of individuals and groups. It views the knowledge processes of knowledge production and integration as responses to problems. These processes are arranged in a problem-solving life cycle called The Knowledge life Cycle (KLC) that produces and integrates knowledge in an organization for use in business processes and ad hoc activities.

After presenting the framework, Chapter 7 applies it to the analysis of tacit and explicit knowledge, reviews the ideas of Popper and Polanyi and the notion of implicit knowledge, discusses the relationship of the KLC to individual level knowledge and motivational hierarchies. Chapter 7 also discusses the relationship of the framework to the idea of culture, and ends with a critique of the Nonaka/Takeuchi knowledge conversion model and its relationship to the KLC.

Chapter 8 presents a much more detailed conceptual framework of knowl edge processing. It specifies information acquisition, individual and group learning knowledge claim formulation and knowledge claim validation, the sub-processes of knowledge production; and knowledge broadcasting, searching/retrieving, knowledge sharing, and teaching, the sub-processes of knowledge integration. All sub-processes are analyzed in enough detail to provide an understanding of what types of process activities an EIP would have to support in order to enhance knowledge processing. Chapter 8 ends with a discussion of the relationship of the KLC to accelerating innovation.

After the specification of knowledge and knowledge processing, Chapter 9 focuses directly on knowledge management. It presents my approach to KM, the notion of Complex Adaptive Systems (CAS), the idea of the Natural Knowledge Management System (NKMS), the distinction between hierarchical and organic KM, a survey of KM definitions, the difference between Information Management and Knowledge Management, the differences between knowledge processes and information processes, a definition and specification of KM and IM processes, more on how KM and IM differ, how culture relates to KM, and knowledge management impact and innovation. Chapter 9 provides the background needed to move on to analysis of Artificial Knowledge Management Systems in Chapter 10.

Part 5, Artificial Knowledge Management Systems and the role of XML, is composed of transitional chapters providing additional background necessary for understanding the later EIP segmentation framework and the Enterprise Knowledge Portal. In Chapter 10, I consider the question of how information technology applications may support knowledge processing and knowledge management, and more specifically the nature of the functional requirements of such technology applications. I begin by specifying the connection between the Natural Knowledge Management System, and a generalized IT construct called the Artificial Knowledge Management System. I show that the AKMS (in theory) partially supports the NKMS by partially supporting processes and tasks in the NKMS through use cases that specify the functional requirements of the Distributed Knowledge Management System (DKMS), a realization of the AKMS using present technology. The chapter also discusses AKMS/DKMS architecture including the Artificial Knowledge Manager and its relationship to Knowledge Claim Objects (KCOs) and intelligent agents.

Chapter 11 describes the role of XML in EIPs. XML is the *other* major trend in IT over the last few years. In this chapter I discuss XML in PAI architecture for EIPs, XML for messaging and connectivity in portal systems, XML on the client side, XML in databases and content stores, XML and agents, and finally, new developments in XML-related standards, including XML Resource Description Framework (RDF), XML Topic Maps (XTM) and Meaning Definition Language (MDL).

In Part 6, EIP Frameworks, Portal Product Case Studies, and Applications to e-Business, I present a comprehensive framework for segmenting portal products, specify a particular type of EIP of great importance to knowledge processing and knowledge management, the Enterprise Knowledge Portal (EKP) in more detail, and then apply both frameworks to an analysis of portal product case studies and to an analysis of the role of the portal in e-business. In other words, in this part, I answer questions about where the product EIP space is now, where many of its products fit into a forward-looking segmentation, what precisely, they contribute to knowledge processing and knowledge management, and what applications portal technology has in e-business.

Chapter 12 presents the forward-looking conceptual framework for segmenting portals and offers a simplified segmentation, which may be serviceable for the current crop of portal products. The chapter begins with a discussion of the first EIP product segmentation, then presents a forward-looking EIP segmentation framework including function, type of architecture/integration, portal scope, and data and content sources dimensions. Chapter 12 ends with consideration of the special importance of knowledge processing and knowledge management portals and with a simplified forward-looking segmentation.

Chapter 13 develops the EKP concept as a standard for evaluating the gap between actual portal products and solutions and this standard. It covers: a story contrasting windows desktops, EIPs, and EKPs; formal definition and specification of the EKP; EKP architecture and components; the adaptive, problem-solving essence of the EKP; the EKP, the AKMS/DKMS, and EKP functional requirements; EKPs knowledge sharing and corporate culture; e-business knowledge portals; whether there are any EKPs; and types of knowledge portals.

Chapters 14–17 provide 23 portal product case studies. Each product is described and analyzed in terms of its features, architecture, vision and direction, and touchpoints with knowledge processing and knowledge management. Chap-

ter 14 reviews two Decision Processing Portals. Chapter 15 reviews 9 Content Management Portals. Chapter 16 reviews 4 Collaborative Portals. And Chapter 17
reviews 8 Decision Processing/Content Management Portals. Each Chapter presents conclusions emerging from the analysis and Chapter 17 presents conclusions applying to all four chapters.

Chapter 18 looks at e-business from the viewpoint of the eKP it covers: EIP
technology and e-business applications; The DKMS, the knowledge portal, and
e-business applications; The KLC framework and e-business; The eKP and eCRM;
The eKP and eSCM; The eKP and eERP; The eKP and e-commerce; and the
DKMS, eKP applications, and the future of e-business.

Part 7, The Future of the EIP is the final chapter. It covers: pathways of development; increasing vendor consolidation, increasing multi-functionality of portals; verticalization of EIPs/EKPs/eKPs; more comprehensive integration of EIPs;
collaborative commerce; and an increasing focus on knowledge processing and
KM.

Who this book is for

The book as a whole is for EIP, Knowledge Management, Content Management,
DSS/Data Warehousing, Innovation Management, Collaborative Commerce, and
EAI Professionals and for Information Technology, Knowledge Management
and Business Students. The methodology for estimating benefits is targeted at
corporate executives and consultants. The treatment of systems integration and
architecture and the chapter on the role of XML in EIPs, should be important
for anyone concerned with building an EIP or an EKP. The analysis of knowledge, knowledge processing and knowledge management will, hopefully, stand
on its own as a contribution to knowledge management and as a foundation for
developing a benchmark EKP concept, and so, both should be of great interest to
knowledge managers and others interested in knowledge management. The
Chapters on the Artificial Knowledge Management System and on the EKP are
targeted at knowledge managers, knowledge workers, organizational learning
practitioners, R&D professionals, and innovation managers interested in the real
"killer app" of knowledge processing and knowledge management. And the segmentation, case studies and forecasts of the future of EIP technology and its
applications, while also of general interest, should be important to (a) executives
and (b) consultants who need to evaluate competing EIP solutions, (c) investors
who need to decide whether to invest in new EIP ventures, and (d) software companies looking to identify new product niches in the portal space.

How to use this book

Parts of this book can be read alone or in an order other than the linear arrange-
ment required by book form. Part One, the Chapters on definition and evolution
of EIPs may be read separately to get background on perspective on the EIP space.
Part Two, on benefits, also stands alone, and can be read with or without other
chapters or in any sequence. Part Three on architecture, including chapters 5 and
6 may be read alone, or in combination with Chapters 10, 11, and 13, on the
AKMS, the role of XML and the EKP. Part Four including Chapters 7–9, stand
alone as a conceptual framework for knowledge processing and knowledge man-

agement. The chapters in Part Five, don't stand alone however. Chapter 10 on the AKMS/DKMS is dependent on Chapters 5–9, while Chapter 11 on the role of XML is dependent on Chapters 5–6.

In Part Six the various chapters are dependent on all that has gone before. Some benefit may be gotten out of the chapters individually, particularly out of Chapter 13 on the EKP and the case studies in Chapters 14–17, but to get full benefit out of these chapters the earlier chapters are recommended. Finally, Part Seven, may prove interesting by itself to some, but it is likely that the issues discussed there will seem less significant to those who have not read the remainder of the book.

References

Plumtree Software, (1998). "Corporate Portals," Plumtree Software, San Francisco, CA.

Shilakes, C. and Tylman, J. (1998). *Enterprise Information Portals,* New York: Merrill Lynch.

PART ONE

Introducing Enterprise Information Portals: Definition and Evolution

In Part One, I introduce the enterprise information portal (EIP) concept. In Chapter 1, EIPs are defined and specified in detail. Different types of EIPs are distinguished from one another, EIPs are distinguished from business portals and corporate portals, and the extension of EIP technology to e-business is discussed. In Chapter 2, the origin and evolution of the EIP is discussed, and the relationships of EIP applications to content management, ERP, data warehousing, DSS, data mining, and data management applications (the main components of EIPs as defined by Merrill Lynch), and issues of EIP integration are analyzed. Finally, the prospect of further evolution of EIPs is introduced, the enterprise knowledge portal (EKP) is proposed as the likely direction of EIP evolution. This issue is discussed at greater length in other parts of the book as well.

CHAPTER 1

Introduction: Defining the Enterprise Information Portal

EIP definition is a political process

It is fortunate that the enterprise information portal (EIP) concept was introduced by two analysts with a concern for definition (Christopher C. Shilakes and Julie Tylman, 1998). Otherwise, given the sudden popularity of EIPs, there would be no restraint on the tendency of vendors to try to exploit the label by attaching it to their products. Even so, since the area is in a state of very rapid growth and differentiation, vendors and analysts with an interest in it are adding their own orientations and nuances to the EIP idea every day. Some do this by addressing the term EIP directly, others by defining related terms such as business portal, corporate portal, or enterprise portal.

Inevitably, the process of definition is a "political" business—an attempt to persuade the Investment/IT and ultimately the user community—to define EIP in a manner favoring one's own vendor or analytical interests. If a vendor gets its favored definition accepted, it gets to say that a competing vendor is not really an EIP vendor, or lacks this or that required EIP characteristic. If an analyst or consultant gets its definition accepted, it gets a boost for its mind share and all the rewards that accompany such a competitive advantage over other consultants or analysts.

But if the process of EIP definition is political, it is politics constrained by the reality that any successful EIP definition must offer strategic advantage to the community. It must provide an image of the scope of the EIP area that the community will accept as providing both a clear idea of what an EIP is and a vision of what it ought to be. In order to clarify the network of meanings surrounding the EIP concept, and to provide my own view about how the term should be defined strategically, I will:

- Survey some of the definitions and characterizations offered by the *early* commentators and vendors in the EIP field who established the primary variations in meaning.
- Follow with a classification of types of definitions.

- Provide a synthesis and proposal on how the term EIP should be defined.
- Provide some definitions of my own, extending the EIP concept into the e-business environment.

This examination will introduce some of the concepts and vocabulary I will need to support my discussion of history, benefits, and architecture in later chapters, but it will not produce the forward-looking segmentation I will ultimately need for characterizing EIPs, analyzing EIP products and solutions, and forecasting the future of the EIP space. That segmentation will be presented in Chapter 12 following consideration of the foregoing subjects, knowledge processing and knowledge management, and finally the role of XML in EIPs.

EIP definitions

Here are some views defining the EIP and related concepts from analysts and commentators. According to Shilakes and Tylman (1998, P. 1), "Enterprise Information Portals are applications that enable companies to unlock internally and externally stored information, and provide users a single gateway to personalized information needed to make informed business decisions." They are: "an amalgamation of software applications that consolidate, manage, analyze and distribute information across and outside of an enterprise (including Business Intelligence, Content Management, Data Warehouse & Mart and Data Management applications.)"

And here are the essential characteristics of EIPs according to the same authors (pp. 10–13):

- EIPs use both "push" and "pull" technologies to transmit information to users through a standardized Web-based interface.
- EIPs provide "interactivity"—the ability to "question' and share information on" user desktops.
- EIPs exhibit the trend toward "verticalization" in application software. That is, they are often "packaged applications" providing "targeted content to specific industries or corporate functions."
- EIPs integrate disparate applications including content management, business intelligence, data warehouse/data mart, data management, and other data external to these applications into a single system that can "share, manage and maintain information from one central user interface." An EIP is able to access both external and internal sources of data and information. It is able to support a bi-directional exchange of information with these sources. And it is able to use the data and information it acquires for further processing and analysis.

Content management systems process, filter, and refine "unstructured" internal and external data and information contained in diverse paper and electronic formats. They archive it and often restructure it and store it in a corporate repository (either centralized or distributed). Business intelligence tools access data and information and through querying, reporting, online analytical processing (OLAP), data mining, and analytical applications provide a view of information both presentable and significant to the end user. Data warehouses and data marts are integrated, time-variant, nonvolatile collections of data supporting DSS and EIS applications, and, in particular business intelligence tools and processes. And data management systems perform extraction, transformation, and loading (ETL) "tasks, clean data, and facilitate scheduling, administration and metadata management for data warehouses and data marts."

The Shilakes and Tylman definition of EIP is an attempt at a comprehensive definition, emphasizing both the basic functions of an EIP, and the subsidiary applications that are presently converging to produce EIP products and applications. It seems to leave little to the imagination, but it does have a stronger decision support rather than collaborative processing emphasis, and it also emphasizes the idea of the EIP as a gateway to wide-ranging data, content, and applications. In contrast, Gerry Murray of IDC (Gerry Murray, 1999) views the corporate portal as more than a gateway.

According to Murray, "portals that focus only on content are inadequate for the corporate market." Corporate portals must connect us not only with everything we need, but with everyone we need, and provide all the tools we need to work together. This means that groupware, e-mail, workflow, and desktop applications-even critical business applications—must all be accessible through the portal. Thus the portal is the desktop, and your commute is just a phone call."

Murray distinguishes four types of corporate portals. Enterprise information portals connect people with information by organizing large collections of content on the basis of subjects or themes they contain. Collaborative portals enable teams of users to establish virtual project areas or communities along with the tools for collaboration they offer, and to work cooperatively within these communities. Expertise portals link people together based on their skills and expertise, as well as their information needs. And knowledge portals do everything the first three types do and an unspecified something "more."

So Murray's emphasis is not so much on the corporate portal as a gateway to content, or even decision support, but rather on the portal as an application that may provide comprehensive support for the end user's job role. For Murray, the EIP is only the first and most limited stage of portal development, and it is only a gateway to content of all varieties. Much more important are the collaborative, expertise, and knowledge portals that promise to provide comprehensive job support.

The conflict between the Merrill Lynch and IDC definitions of EIP lies in Murray's restricting his EIP definition to applications providing a gateway to content alone. While the Shilakes and Tylman definition emphasizes decision processing more than collaborative processing, it is clearly meant to include collaborative, expertise and knowledge management (KM) applications as part of the EIP. This is implied by their statement that "EIPs provide "interactivity"—the ability to "'question' and share information on" user desktops. And it is made quite explicit that they mean to include collaborative applications in their ensuing discussion of the content-management segment of EIPs. There they explicitly endorse the development of KM applications in the content-management segment and also state (Shilakes and Tylman, 1998, p. 18) that they believe EIPs "will marry Knowledge Management with structured data management."

Colin White (1999, p. 1) defines an EIP simply, as providing "business users with a single web interface to corporate information scattered throughout the enterprise." Within this broad definition, he classifies EIPs into two main categories. Decision processing EIPs help "users organize and find corporate information in the set of systems that constitute the business information supply chain." This type of information is highly structured and comes from operational data and data warehouse information and from "external systems." Decision processing EIPs use business intelligence tools and analytic applications to create reports and analyses and then distribute them throughout the enterprise using a variety of electronic means. Collaborative processing EIPs help "users organize and share workgroup information, such as e-mail, discussion group material, reports, memos, and meeting minutes." This type of information is relatively unstructured and comes from individuals and work groups. It is processed with collaborative groupware and workflow tools.

White views decision processing and collaborative processing as connecting within the groupware and workflow systems where collaborative processing takes place, and decision processing reports and analyses are ultimately distributed. Indeed, he sees the distinction between the two types of EIPs as blurring over time. And he blurs the distinction somewhat himself by recognizing that decision processing EIPs employ collaborative processing to track decisions and actions taken based on the use of structured business information. "The combining together of corporate business information, user knowledge and collaborative processing is sometimes labeled knowledge management. Decision processing portals could be described as knowledge management portals, but given the number of different definitions in use for knowledge management, the term knowledge management portal is best avoided here." (White, p. 3)

White is apparently in basic agreement with the original Merrill Lynch definition of EIPs. His overall definition is open to different interpretations depending on how one defines "corporate information." But his segmentation into decision processing and collaborative processing EIPs, discussion of the process connections between the two types and his discussion of the likely evolution of EIP products to incorporate both classes of functionality together remove any ambiguity. They suggest that he sees the ideal EIP as providing a gateway to both collaboration and decision support as well as support for knowledge management. That is essentially the Merrill Lynch view as well.

A term closely related to EIP is business portal. In a report from The Data Warehousing Institute, Wayne Eckerson (1999, p. 1) defines a business portal as an application that "provides business users one-stop shopping for any information object they need inside or outside the corporation." He therefore emphasizes the gateway aspect of business portal applications as fundamental to the concept. He also emphasizes the importance of shared services such as "security, metadata repository, personalization, search, publish/subscribe," as well as a common look and feel to the gateway.

Eckerson places very little emphasis on collaboration or workflow applications in either his definition or his specification of the business portal concept. He points out that users can publish information to the business portal repository to foster collaboration and further indicates that document management vendors will have to convert or extend their workflow capabilities (Eckerson, p. 2) in order to enter the portal space. But this is the extent of his emphasis on collaboration as a primary business portal–based function. His business portal seems therefore to be most similar to Murray's concept of the EIP, an information gateway that supplies a variety of structured and unstructured content to users through a Web-based gateway for the purpose of decision support. It is not an

EIP from the standpoint of either the Merrill Lynch or White definitions, and it is quite distinct from Murray's collaborative, expertise, and knowledge portals.

Another term closely related to EIP is corporate portal. Hadley Reynolds and Tom Koulopoulos (Reynolds and Koulopoulos, 1999) emphasize the user-centric focus, and workflow and task-integrative functions of corporate portals. They see corporate portals as centralizing "enterprise information access in a graphically rich, application-independent interface that mirrors 'knowledge-centric' work-flow," and as providing "a single point of integration through the enterprise." (Reynolds and Koulopoulos, pp. 28–29) They, too, see corporate portals as integrating the "islands of automation" formed by today's application-based desktops and eventually creating an integrated business environment "providing information access, delivery, and work support across organizational dimensions."

The corporate portal and the public portal have fundamentally different purposes. (Reynolds and Koulopoulos, p. 32) Public portals have a unidirectional relationship with their viewers. Their purpose is to attract large numbers of repeat visitors and to build online audiences with compelling demographics and tendencies to buy what portal advertisers are selling. But the purpose of corporate portals is to "expose and deliver business-specific information in context to help today's computer workers stay ahead of the competition. Being competitive requires a bi-directional model that can support knowledge workers' increasingly sensitive needs for interactive information-management tools."

Reynolds and Koulopoulos provide the least emphasis on the decision processing/business intelligence, structured data aspects of portal applications and the strongest emphasis yet on the concept of the portal as support for tasks, work-flow, (implicitly) collaboration, and the creation and integration of knowledge. Some emphasis on this aspect is included in Shilakes's and Tylman's analysis and in White's (1999) collaborative processing portals. But Reynolds and Koulopoulos provide center stage to the user-centric, workflow view of portals.

Just as early analysts and commentators defined the EIP with differing emphases on decision versus collaborative processing, for the most part vendors also varied along this spectrum. An important early vendor in the EIP space that did not conform to this pattern was Plumtree Software, which treated the corporate portal extensively in a white paper (Plumtree Software, 1998, p. 5). It lists seven "defining characteristics" of corporate portals in relation to "Internet Portals" including

- Integrating access in a wider variety of data formats than a web portal (comprehensive)
- Organizing access to information for users to browse (organized)
- Assembling personalized views of key information and notifying users of the availability of new material via electronic mail and other media (personalized)
- Organizing access to data, but not storing the data itself (location transparent)
- Supporting extensions for cataloging new types of information (extensible)
- Automatically identifying and organizing access to new content (automated)
- Selectively brokering access to internal corporate information (secure

This definition is clearly oriented toward distinguishing corporate portals from public portals on the basis of the kind of access available in corporate portals. It is not focused on the types of applications supported by such access, however, and is consistent with decision processing portals with or without collaboration, collaborative/workflow processing portals, expertise processing portals, and knowledge portals.

Viador, another prominent early portal vendor, defined EIPs in a manner that is on the surface similar to Colin White (1999, p. 2). EIPs, according to Viador (1999), are

> . . . applications that enable companies to provide access to internally and externally stored information, and offer users within and external to the enterprise, a single window to personalized information needed to make informed business decisions. An Enterprise Information Portal is a browser-based system that provides ubiquitous access to vital business information in the same manner that internet content portals like Yahoo are the gateway to the wealth of content on the web.

Though on the surface similar to White's portal views, in fact the Viador view, as expressed in its product specification, is closer to Wayne Eckerson's business portal formulation, because, unlike White's, it provides little role for collaborative processing applications in its EIP concept. In effect, Viador takes the business portal concept and applies the EIP label to it.

According to Information Advantage (1999, p. 2), now Computer Associates, business intelligence portals should provide comprehensive intelligence for decision makers, allow an unprecedented level of accessibility, adapt to a changing and larger user population, deliver the right solution for your needs, and have a long record of success. Neglecting the last two requirements that are clearly non-definitional in character, there is again the same emphasis on business intelligence, broad accessibility, and adaptability seen in some of the other definitions. And there is also a similarity to the Eckerson and Viador views in that Information Advantage is strictly focused on decision processing without emphasis on the collaborative or workflow capabilities of portals.

Sqribe, Inc. (1999), now Brio.Portal, defined the EIP as an "automated information gateway that delivers information to users based on their level of security, job, and interests." (Sqribe, p. 4). Sqribe also viewed the EIP as able to provide access to any information, any time, regardless of the content of that information, and as providing the single point of access for all of the information in the enterprise. As with Eckerson, Viador, and Information Advantage, Sqribe placed little or no emphasis in its portal definition on collaborative or workflow processing. To Sqribe in 1999, an EIP was a decision processing EIP, excluding its collaborative component.

Types of definition and synthesis

The early positions on defining business-specific portals just reviewed can be categorized into a few types. First, there are definitions of *decision processing portals* without significant emphasis on workflow, task integration, or collaborative processing Eckerson's business portal, Murray's, Viador's, and Sqribe's enterprise information portal, and Information Advantage's business intelligence portal all fit comfortably within this category.

Second, there are definitions that define portals generally in such a way that both decision processing and collaborative processing portals, as well as syntheses of the two, would fit the general category. The original Merrill Lynch definition of EIP and Colin White's and Plumtree Software's definition of the term *corporate portal* all fit into this category. Murray's definition of knowledge portal also fits since it involves a combination of decision processing and collaborative portals (including expertise portals as explained subsequently).

Third, the Murray collaborative processing portal, and the Reynolds and Koulopoulos corporate portal concepts comprise a category of collaborative processing portals that do not emphasize decision processing. Add to this type Murray's expertise portal. It is distinguished from other collaborative portals because it ties together the skills of those who participate in it, with their information needs. Nevertheless it is still a subtype of the collaborative processing portal, rather than an independent type.

The variations in thinking represented in these types provide perspective on the question of how enterprise information portals should be defined, as well as on the question of how the term is currently being used. The original definition of Shilakes and Tylman envisioned a category of application that would integrate business intelligence based on structured data with collaboration, workflow, unstructured data, and knowledge management. The term "information" in enterprise information portals is being used here in a very broad way to encompass all kinds of structured and unstructured content, and the EIP was envisioned as an application that would also make available a broad range of applications, both analytical and collaborative, to end users. In spite of this comprehensiveness, the original definition of EIP does not lack clarity. Shilakes and Tylman specify EIPs in some detail, as does Colin White in taking a position similar to the Merrill Lynch report.

While the original EIP definition is specific and comprehensive, it also provides a vision. It makes clear that ideal EIPs synthesize both decision and collaborative processing orientations. It may not be clear at present what the full ramifications of such a commitment are. But this "openness of meaning" is an argument in favor of retaining the original definition of EIP as a useful strategic concept that can give rise to innovation. Developments in information technology may allow novel syntheses of these two areas. The possibility that this may happen is a good justification for continuing to adhere to the Merrill Lynch EIP definition as strategic. Since the Merrill Lynch EIP concept is clear and comprehensive and provides suggestions for future development, why should we accept using the term in a different sense?

The initial use of the term EIP by Viador, and Sqribe, reviewed earlier, is a case of vendors' license. The definitions offered by these vendors are just departures from the original use of the term, and they are departures made without benefit of strategic justification or because the original EIP definition lacks clarity or has some other significant shortcoming. Murray's use of the EIP term also represents a change from the original definition. Clearly he wanted to distinguish business portals from collaborative, expertise, and knowledge portals, and he used the term EIP—rather than "business intelligence" or "business portal"—as part of the process of making the distinction. In fact, the Viador, Sqribe, and

Murray EIP definitions actually correspond to the concepts of business portal offered by Eckerson and business intelligence portal initially offered by Information Advantage. The use of either term by Viador, Sqribe, and Murray would have maintained a useful distinction between these terms and EIP.

Reynolds and Koulopoulos use the term corporate portal to describe the same concept Murray calls a collaborative portal; but not the same concept used by Colin White when he uses the term collaborative processing portal. White's portals are viewed as EIPs with some decision processing capability and as adding more of this capability over time. This brings us again to Murray's expertise portal. As I indicated earlier, Murray's expertise portal is a type of collaborative processing portal. That it ties together skills and information needs of users doesn't change its collaborative character. Finally, Murray's knowledge portal, since it combines decision and collaborative processing (including expertise processing) in the same portal is actually a type of EIP. He should have used that term to describe it.

In sum then, we have the following situation based on analysis of these early portal definitions. There are three major categories of constructs used to describe EIPs: business portals, corporate portals, and enterprise information portals. *Business (or business intelligence) portals* were defined by Eckerson, Viador (their EIP), Sqribe (their EIP), Information Advantage, and Murray (his EIP). *Corporate (collaborative) portals* were defined by Reynolds and Koulopoulos, and Murray (his Collaborative and expertise portals). *EIPs* were defined by Shilakes and Tylman, White, Plumtree (their corporate portal), and Murray (his knowledge portal).

In addition, the analysis suggests the following subtypes within the major categories:

- *Business portals*—none
- *Corporate portals*—collaborative portals tying together peers, collaborative portals tying together skills and information needs
- *Enterprise information portals*—decision processing portals, collaborative portals, knowledge portals

As I will make clear in Chapter 12, this typology of enterprise information portals is far from complete and is not an adequate segmentation of the EIP space. But, together with the following section, it will be sufficient until I discuss EIP segmentation in detail.

EIP technology and e-business

Since the overnight appearance of EIP technology in 1998 and the early part of 1999, it has spread rapidly beyond the enterprise into e-business applications focused on supplier and customer relationships and on enterprise collaboration. This means that terms like "enterprise information portals," and "enterprise portals" are no longer fully descriptive of the area of application of "EIP technology," but, rather, reflect only inward-looking information portals focused on a single enterprise.

An EIP is an e-business information portal—that is, it uses EIP technology to support e-business processes that transcend the enterprise. There are two basic types of EIPs: Extraprise information portals (ExIPs) and Interprise information portals (IIPs).

The term "extraprise" seems to have evolved gradually during the past decade, reflecting the reality of increased corporate collaboration and the image of the "super-enterprise" evoked by increasing collaboration. But I will use the term, as it was introduced to me by my collaborator Mark McElroy in an e-mail communication in February 2000 (McElroy, February 2000). An "extraprise" is "an extended enterprise usually consisting of a community of trading partners revolving around a common host enterprise of mutual interest who do business with one another on a fairly predictable and repetitive basis." Stephen Haeckel in *Adaptive Enterprise* (1999, p. 46) provides a prime example of the creation of an extraprise in Dee Hock's Visa. The enterprise at the center of an extraprise system usually hosts the "extended intranet" (a/k/a, the "extranet"), of the extraprise. An extraprise information portal (ExIP) is an information portal supporting such a community.

The term "interprise" was introduced by Kenneth Preiss and his collaborators in a number of publications (S.L. Goldman, R.N. Nagel, and K. Preiss, 1991, 1995; Preiss, 1997) dealing with agility and its emergence in the context of inter-enterprise collaboration. They viewed the interprise as an extended enterprise, and did not clearly distinguish between the extraprise and the interprise. An interprise, as McElroy (2000) defined it, is a network of businesses whose members collaborate "on a fairly unpredictable and irregular basis in response to individual expressions of demand in marketplaces of mutual interest."

An example of an interprise is provided by the Merchants of Prato (Haeckel, 1999, pp. 43–44), a network of 8,500 small textile firms. These firms collaborate on an ad hoc basis to fulfill orders for custom fabrics for the fashion industry. The individual members of the network operate according to a simple set of custom-based rules. In response to individual behavior conforming to these rules, the Merchants of Prato system self-organizes to fulfill orders in a very efficient manner. The system produces more than $5 billion in annual revenue, and is the largest textile-producing integrate in Europe.

An interprise information portal (IIP) is an information portal supporting an interprise network. The members of an interprise can do business with one another through the IIP.

Conclusion

The remainder of this book will focus on enterprise information portals and, in Chapter 18, on the extension of EIP technology into e-business. I will not consider the typology of enterprise portals already presented any further because (1) business portal and corporate portal technology is covered within the EIP category, (2) the definitions of the business and corporate portal categories are somewhat vague compared to the Shilakes and Tylman definition of EIPs, and (3) as I shall explain later, knowledge processing and knowledge management, other central concerns of this book, are supported by a particular type of enterprise information portal called an enterprise knowledge portal.

So I will continue this examination of EIPs with an examination of their origin and evolution. According to the classification we have just examined, there should be five types of portals that have evolved:

- Decision processing portals
- Collaborative processing portals
- Knowledge portals

- Extraprise information portals
- Interprise information portals

References

Eckerson, W. (1999). "Business Portals: Drivers, Definitions, and Rules,"The Data Warehousing Institute, Gaithersburg, MD.

Goldman, S.L.; Nagel, R.N.; and Preiss, K. (1991). *21st Century Manufacturing Enterprise Study: An Industry Led View*, The Iacocca Institute, Lehigh University.

Goldman, S.L.; Nagel, R.N.; and Preiss, K. (1991, 1995). *Agile Competitors and Virtual Organizations* (New York, NY: Van Nostrand Reinhold).

Haeckel, S.H., (1999). *Adaptive Enterprise* (Boston, MA: Harvard Business School Press).

Information Advantage (1999). "MyEureka Business Intelligence Portal," *Information Advantage White Paper*, Information Advantage, Eden Prairie, MN.

McElroy, M.W. (February, 2000). "Marketing Concepts" (e-mail communication).

Murray, G. (1999). "The Portal and the Desktop." *Intraspect* (available at www.intraspect.com).

Preiss, K. (1997). "The Emergence of the Interprise." Keynote Lecture to the IFIP WG 5.7 Working Conference, Organizing the Extended Enterprise, Ascona, Switzerland, September 15–18, 1997.

Plumtree Software (1998). "Corporate Portal," Plumtree Software, San Francisco, CA.

Reynolds, H., and Koulopoulos, T. (1999). "Enterprise Knowledge Has a Face," *Intelligent Enterprise*, March 30, 1999, pp. 28–34.

Shilakes, C., and Tylman, J. (1998). *Enterprise Information Portals* (New York: Merrill Lynch).

Sqribe, Inc. (1999). "Sqribe Enterprise: Enterprise Reporting with Intelligence," Sqribe, Inc. Brochure, Sqribe, Inc., Redwood City, CA.

Viador (1999). "Enterprise Information Portals: Realizing the Vision of 'Information at Your Fingertips.'" A Viador, Inc. white paper, Viador, San Mateo, CA.

White, C. (1999). "The Enterprise Information Portal Marketplace," *Decision Processing Brief DP-99-01*, Database Associates International, Inc., Morgan Hill, CA.

CHAPTER 2

The Origin and Evolution of Enterprise Information Portals

Enterprise information portals (EIPs)

EIPs (Shilakes and Tylman, 1998) represent the coming together of a number of distinct classes of applications. The most visible of these is the Internet public portal and the corporate intranet. The idea of access to information and applications through a single desktop gateway is a compelling one to those who get information from corporate intranets already, or who have experienced "Yahoo-like" public portals with their meaningful hierarchical classifications of content and personalization capabilities. Public portals create the desire for an EIP that provides universal access to enterprise information.

When it comes to thinking about the content of such a portal, it is natural to divide this content into

- Structured data, information, and knowledge, and applications that produce, manage, and maintain such structured resources
- Unstructured or semi-structured data, information, and knowledge (including multimedia objects of various kinds) and applications that produce, manage, and maintain these

This distinction is natural because unstructured data has no standardized metadata structure. It has no standard facility for query, search, or analysis of it. So, there is an obvious difference between structured and unstructured resources in the techniques that can be used to manipulate them. The distinction is also natural since in the portal context, structured data applications tend to be used in decision processing or OLTP applications, while unstructured data applications tend to be used in collaborative processing applications.

The emergence of EIPs requires the emergence of capabilities to produce, manage, and maintain resources and applications in both structured and unstructured areas of information. The emergence of EIPs also requires the emergence of capabilities to manage the relationship between structured and unstructured resources and to integrate the EIP system and its set of diverse applications and data/content stores. It is the emergence of these capabilities, along with the desire for EIPs created by exposure to Web applications that explains the origin of EIPs. In turn, this origin is dependent on evolutionary changes during the past few years in IT applications in the structured, unstructured, "relationship," and integration categories.

Structured data/information/knowledge management

Evolution in this category has been rapid, as the two-tier client/server paradigm has given way to multi-tier enterprise networking architectures. The impetus has been the continuing quest to overcome the "islands of information" problem. There is a need to get rid of "stovepipes," both of legacy origin and of more recent vintage resulting from relatively closed enterprise resource planning (ERP) and proprietary database marketing applications along with independent, isolated data marts implemented for departmental decision support.

Indeed, from one point of view, the EIP movement can be seen as only the latest stage in a continuing trend toward achieving enterprise information or knowledge integration—a trend that has fueled data warehousing and enterprise resource planning (ERP) sales, and is now beginning to fuel enterprise application integration (EAI), knowledge management, and EIP implementations. There is an abiding drive on the part of enterprises to gain control over their data, information, and knowledge resources and over the processes that produce and integrate them. The drive exists because integration can produce competitive advantage, greater productivity, and realization of the full asset value of these resources. For these reasons, this drive will not be denied, even though successive generations of IT applications promise a solution to the integration problem and fall short of the goal.

Though Shilakes and Tylman (1998), separate business intelligence, data warehousing, and data management as separate areas within the EIP segment, this classification is not optimal for describing or analyzing the trend toward enterprise information or knowledge integration in the structured content sphere. While it is valid enough for differentiating companies, investment spaces, and even software products, it is not valid for differentiating information systems implemented for clients or for describing the trend toward increasing complexity and integration in those systems.

For example, data warehousing practitioners are one group that is hard-pressed to make these distinctions and, in fact, finds them counterintuitive, because they are based on a software application rather than an information system point of view. When a data warehousing practitioner talks about implementing a data warehouse system, she is talking about what Shilakes and Tylman call data management, data warehousing, and business intelligence, all implemented in the same system—which today is increasingly likely to be delivered over the intranet. Indeed, when data warehousing was first invented, the primary distinctive application products associated with it were extraction, transformation and loading (ETL) applications (data management) and querying and reporting (BI) applications.

There are two primary structured content areas in which one can see the drive toward increased integration in the face of the growth in complexity: Data warehousing and enterprise resource planning. Data warehousing systems are the primary current embodiment of DSS processing. They incorporate business intelligence and data management applications in a systematic way. ERP systems represent the current frontier of innovation in OLTP processing. They sometimes incorporate data management and business intelligence tools, but only in an attempt to extend their reach into the DSS sphere.

Data warehousing (business intelligence and data management)

In the beginning, there were only "islands of information," operational data stores, legacy systems needing enterprisewide integration, and mission-specific decision support systems. Then "along came Bill" (Inmon) and his concept of the data warehouse (DW), seen as the solution to the problems of information integration and redundancy, the embodiment of enterprisewide DSS for the 1990s.

Inmon (1995, p. 1) defined the DW as "a

- subject-oriented,
- integrated,
- time-variant
- non-volatile
- collection of data in support of management's decision making process."

This is the classic definition of the data warehouse. According to it, the DW is a type of database managed by a DBMS. Indeed, in its present form, the DW is a database that uses a relational DBMS. Inmon's definition is now undergoing change as the DW field evolves. Figure 2.1 depicts where DW began.

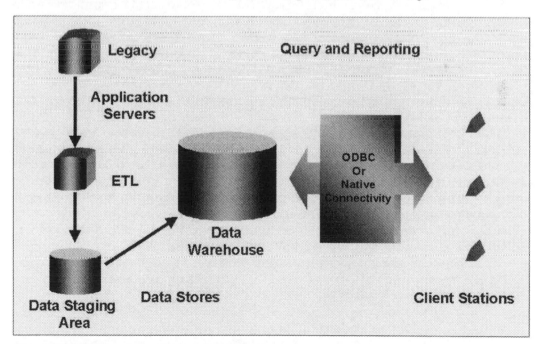

Figure 2.1. Where data warehousing began.

Data marts and data mining were not part of the vision reflected in Figure 2.1. At the beginning, there was only the DW. But the vision was too sweeping. DWs were too costly, often impolitic, took too long to implement, and their architecture turned out to be too simple to support growing customer requirements.

So evolution in data warehousing systems began with the introduction of

- *Data marts.* "A data mart is a subject-oriented, integrated, time-variant, nonvolatile collection of data in support of management's decision-making process focused on a single business process or department" (Firestone, 1998, p. 2).
- *Dynamic data staging areas.* A dynamic data staging area is an archival repository storing cleaned, transformed records and attributes for later loading into data marts and data warehouses.
- *Operational data stores.* "An ODS is a collection of data containing detailed data for the purpose of satisfying the collective, integrated operational needs of the corporation. . . . The ODS is: subject-oriented, integrated, volatile, current-valued, detailed." (Inmon, Imhoff, and Sousa, 1998, pp. 87–88).
- *Web and On-Line Analytical Processing (OLAP).* Clients in response to specific customer requirements.

Data warehousing evolved from its initial two-tier client/server model into its current multi-tier architecture in response to these additions. The movement to data marts created a market for multidimensional OLAP (MOLAP) servers, and these in turn generated a competing product, called the relational OLAP (ROLAP) application server, which was applied to both data marts and data warehouses (Anahory and Murray, 1997, p. 321; Berson and Smith, 1997, Ch. 13). Meanwhile the proliferation of independent data marts raised architectural issues about how these could be integrated into a single data warehousing system. One of the answers was to use dynamic data staging areas as a repository of conformed dimensions that could be used to populate related data marts having a shared, common architecture as time went on (Kimball, Reeves, Ross, and Thornthwaite, 1998, p. 345)

The ODS, designed to support operational, tactical decisions, involves four kinds of processing: loading data, updating, access processing, and DSS-style analysis across many records ((Inmon, Imhoff, and Sousa, 1998, pp. 95–97). A multi-tier architecture that will support both DSS- and OLTP-style processing is needed in order to optimally integrate a hybrid platform such as the ODS into the broader data warehousing architecture. The addition of Web clients adds further to the need for multi-tier architecture, since these require Web application servers to fulfill their thin client and Web architectural requirements.

In addition to the changes resulting from introducing these initial components, the most powerful current trends in integrating application servers into data warehousing are probably

- The introduction of "second generation" metadata exchange architectures based on a commitment to DCOM or CORBA, and object technology for improving metadata managers and integration of ETL, other application servers and DSS data stores

- The integration of knowledge discovery in databases (KDD)/data mining servers, along with "exploration warehouses" (Inmon, 2001, p. 58), providing yet another type of data store, this one optimized for data exploration and mining.

A variety of application servers were or are also being added to the ETL, legacy, and database servers in DW Systems, in order to fill a variety of other user needs. Currently, intelligent agent technology is being integrated into DW Systems, though we do not yet see a generalized use of agents.

The most powerful current trend in integrating new data into the data warehouse is the trend toward accessing and integrating data from ERP applications with other warehouse data external to ERP applications, including data external to the enterprise. This trend is so powerful that it has fueled enterprise application integration growth as well as growth in data warehousing. The trend has resulted from the desire of ERP users to use ERP-based data for decision support.

Initial attempts to use standard client or Web-based reporting tools on ERP databases resulted in poor performance and in dissatisfaction, because the ERP systems could not alone provide all the data end users needed to fulfill their information requirements. In addition, the ERP data involved had not gone through the ETL process. Thus, it was not always sufficiently clean from the viewpoint of DSS needs. Nor was it necessarily transformed into a form that was useful from a DSS requirements standpoint.

The response from DSS vendors, users, and some of the ERP vendors themselves was to apply data warehousing tools, methods, and methodologies to extract and warehouse ERP data, often in rapidly constructed data marts. SAP has released a data warehousing tool suite called Business Information Warehouse (BIW) to implement data warehousing combining SAP and external data, and Oracle has released its own data warehousing suite of tools called Oracle Applications Data Warehouse. In addition, vendors are rapidly producing packaged DSS applications targeted at vertical markets. These contain ETL tools to get data out of ERP and other data stores and to use data mart and analytical application templates to implement specific sales, forecasting, customer relationship management (CRM), business performance management (BPM), and many other specific applications.

The end result of the data warehousing approach to analyzing ERP data is to loosely couple ERP systems into a distributed data warehousing architecture containing both nonvolatile DSS data stores and ERP application servers. The end result of all of the changes and additions just summarized leads to Figure 2.2, which depicts where DW is now.

Note the great increase in functionality and complexity in the foregoing system and the correspondingly greater need for integrative mechanisms. In particular, the expanded and still increasing role of application servers in general—and Business Process Engines (BPE) in particular—is manifest in data warehousing. "Business Process Engines are application servers that maintain state in memory rather than in persistent storage". (Rymer, 1998, p. 1) An example is a stock trading server or a packaged analytical financial application that supports financial outcome simulations. ROLAP and KDD servers are also BPEs. As reflected in Figure 2.2, metadata is now heavily emphasized as an integrative mechanism.

Data warehousing used to focus on gathering data from legacy sources of various kinds, putting it through the ETL process, loading it into the data ware-

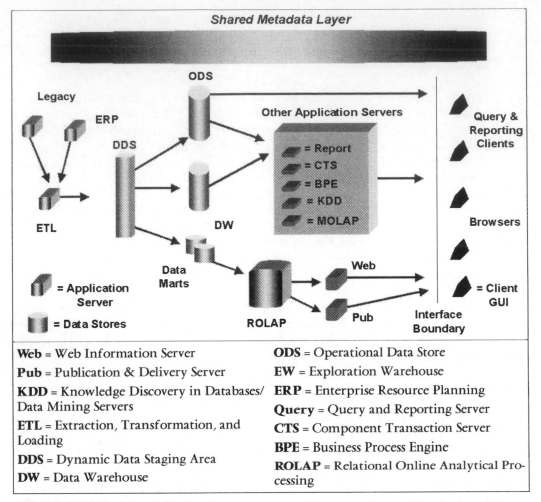

Web = Web Information Server	**ODS** = Operational Data Store
Pub = Publication & Delivery Server	**EW** = Exploration Warehouse
KDD = Knowledge Discovery in Databases/ Data Mining Servers	**ERP** = Enterprise Resource Planning
	Query = Query and Reporting Server
ETL = Extraction, Transformation, and Loading	**CTS** = Component Transaction Server
	BPE = Business Process Engine
DDS = Dynamic Data Staging Area	**ROLAP** = Relational Online Analytical Pro-
DW = Data Warehouse	cessing

Figure 2.2. Data warehousing now.

house, and providing reporting tools and report templates to access it conveniently. Given the changes in DW system complexity, data warehousing is now, increasingly, a problem of integrating a variety of distributed warehouse data stores with various specialized application servers and front end access devices that need warehouse data. The data warehousing system, which began as a low-volatility system, is now a system that can integrate DSS, batch and OLTP processing and that, therefore, may incorporate considerable volatility.

This description of evolution in data warehousing suggests clearly that certain decision processing EIPs are, in significant part, an extension of current trends in Web-based data warehousing (DW) systems. Web-based DW Systems now contain—and also amalgamate and integrate—Web-based interactive querying and reporting, business intelligence, data warehouses and data marts, and data management (ETL) applications. Data warehousing as a field has also exhibited a strong trend toward vertical market applications. And indeed, among the first entrants into the EIP space were corporations such as Viador, Information Advantage (since purchased by Computer Associates), and Sqribe (since purchased by Brio), previously active in the BI, DW, and data management segments. So what are the differences between current Web-accessed DW Systems and EIPs?

The big differences between EIPs and current Web-enabled data warehousing/data mart system applications are the

- Integration of content management systems
- Increasing emphasis on exchange of data with external data stores and applications
- Emphasis on sharing data and information among users
- Renewed emphasis on data mining and analytical applications
- Emphasis on integration of the disparate applications and data sources into a single, integrated, EIP application

Integrating content management leads to an explosion of potential data and information sources for EIPs. Whereas DW Systems have dealt mainly with structured legacy systems generally dealing with on-line transactional processing (OLTP); EIPs will integrate and amalgamate data and information from diverse sources. These include Web documents, research reports, contracts, government licenses, brochures, purchase orders, data warehouses, data marts, and other DSS/EIS systems, legacy systems, enterprise application servers (e.g., SAP, Baan, KDD/data mining servers, stock transaction servers), and any document with content relevant for some corporate interest.

A focus on such documents, applications, and data stores and the problem of capturing them and extracting and analyzing information contained in them also means a focus on technologies that have never been important to the field of DW. Technologies such as imaging and scanning, document management, workflow and groupware, COLD storage, business process automation, key word, phrase, or concept-based searching, text mining, OODBMSs, and Video streaming now become important to EIPs. Other technologies such as intelligent agents which have played a small role in DW Systems now attain major importance because of their important roles in optimizing focused acquisition, retrieval, analysis, and transmission of content.

The increased emphasis on exchange of data with diverse internal and external sources means that connectivity to a variety of servers is even more important in EIPs than in DW Systems. In EIPs, the problem is not just one of establishing connectivity to legacy systems, flat files, and relational and multidimensional databases. Instead, generalized connectivity to any data, application, or content source of interest to a user is the ideal for EIPs. This means that the EIP products with the broadest range of connectivity to data, information, and knowledge stores and to diverse applications will be favored as this market develops.

The emphasis on sharing ideas and information among users reinforces the concern in EIPs with workflow and business process automation technologies. Data warehousing systems have not emphasized business process automation and support. In particular, the DW approach to collaborative corporate planning has been somewhat informal and ad hoc. An EIP planning process, in contrast, would be much more focused on systematic workflow and group collaboration assisted by intelligent agents.

The renewed emphasis on data mining in EIPs comes from different elements within the EIP idea. First, data mining has not grown as rapidly as it might have in the DW Systems context. Part of this is that data mining has not generally been available through Web interfaces, as it is more frequently in the EIP context. Another reason is that data mining has not been fully integrated into DW Systems. It has been a "sister application," generally resident in a proprietary application, or an "exploration warehouse" (Inmon, 2001, p. 58). While it exchanges data with DW data stores, its integration with them is loose and constitutes a barrier to the use of data mining applications. The increased integration of the components of EIP systems, as well as the availability of Web interfaces, should act as a spur to data mining.

A second spur to data mining in EIP systems will come from their increasing emphasis on text mining in content management. Text mining will produce structured data (I will explain why later), which can then be data mined. So, the availability of new categories of structured data that have never been mined before will serve as a spur to data mining.

A third spur to data mining in EIPs comes from their overall emphasis on the full spectrum of BI applications. In DW Systems the emphasis is on querying and reporting and traditional "slice-and-dice" OLAP. Sometimes data mining applications are developed. But DW Systems have not emphasized analytical applications such as simulation and forecasting. They have not emphasized validation of patterns developed in data mining. The emphasis in EIP applications on the full spectrum of BI, highlights the status of data mining *as part of a broad knowledge production process* that includes data mining as a stage, but not as the be-all and end-all of the process. By placing data mining in a more meaningful context and lessening the skepticism about its legitimacy, the EIP orientation could, paradoxically, increase the use of data mining.

Finally, the explicit emphasis in EIPs on integration of disparate applications and data sources, along with the amalgamation of content management and the production of new structured data from content, mean that EIP applications will require a higher order of integration than has been characteristic of DW Systems. The biggest selling point of EIPs is their ability to present information from diverse sources through a common interface. Consequently, the most visible integration requirement for EIPs is to provide an integrated browser interface–based view of all (whether data store, content, or application server–based) of the information resources of the enterprise and the external information resources that are the target of the EIP application.

To this aspect of front-end integration, EIPs add the need for integration in the face of rapid change in EIP objects, data, and components. This is the dynamic integration problem (DIP) in EIPs. I have previously pointed out the increasing importance of the DIP in DW Systems as complexity in those systems has increased (Firestone, 1998a, p. 8). With the further complexity of content, application, and query-able data stores of diverse formats added to create EIPs, the need for integration and coordinated evolution in the face of change is further exacerbated by the sheer number of information-related entities subject to change. Without this coordination and integration, inconsistencies in data and information, in business rules and methods, and in metadata would be prevalent in an EIP, and its usefulness as an authoritative enterprise source would be severely compromised.

Enterprise resource planning (ERP)

While data warehousing has sought enterprise structured content integration through moving and transforming data into new, reengineered, logically and physically integrated data stores, enterprise resource planning has sought such integration by implementing comprehensive client/server–based OLTP applications using relational databases, a common business applications framework, and an integrated data model. These multi-functional applications support the reengineering of various business processes such as manufacturing, financial, human resources, distribution, and customer service processes, by implementing IT applications that were formerly implemented with far fewer features on "stovepipe" legacy systems.

The heart of the trend toward integration is in the reliance on the architecture of a selected ERP system, supplied by a single ERP vendor, as the "backbone" (Caruso, 1999, p. 20) of long-term integrative efforts. The backbone provides services to a range of business components that, together with it, constitute an integrated system for OLTP processing. Since the backbone can be taken for granted, enterprise application integration (EAI) applications can focus on integrating various component applications with the SAP, Baan, Oracle, Peoplesoft, or J.D. Edwards application that is providing the backbone of the system. This provides leverage to efforts to integrate various components with the core ERP application, and promotes the further evolution of integrated, feature-rich ERP applications.

As ERP has evolved, the addition of new components has led to a dramatic expansion of ERP capabilities into such fields as forecasting, business performance modeling and measurement, risk management, and customer relationship management (CRM). There has also been an increasing demand from ERP customers for decision support applications to supplement the traditional area of ERP expertise in OLTP processing. This trend has brought ERP into direct conflict with the other major expanding area in structured data management–data warehousing, and has presented the problem of integrating DSS functionality into ERP systems.

As I mentioned earlier, ERP data can be extracted from ERP systems and successfully integrated into data warehousing systems architecture. The approach of direct integration of DSS into ERP systems, however, is to apply the business intelligence tools used in data warehousing and DSS applications directly to ERP systems, without benefit of DW data management processing, or integration of the data into an optimized DSS data store. Reporting tools such as Brio and Actuate can directly access ERP data stores, produce formatted reports, and then store the data in this form on enterprise reporting servers. Other approaches, such as Cognos's, involve issuing queries to the relational database of the packaged ERP application and creating multidimensional data structures for desktop OLAP.

Direct integration of DSS into ERP systems has drawbacks. The heart of the matter is whether ERP OLTP applications provide components that will support DSS as well as OLTP processing. ERP vendors say that since ERP data is integrated as compared with older stovepipe applications and since they provide OLAP and reporting tools, their system of components can support DSS processing as well, or nearly as well, as a system constructed around data warehousing components. However, this is not true. Integrated data plus DSS tools still don't spell quality DSS.

First, ERP applications are built on normalized E-R models, and one of the primary lessons in data warehousing is that normalized E-R models (though optimal for OLTP) can't deliver good DSS performance. Given certain queries, they can degrade response time for all users or even tie up database servers for lengthy periods. To get adequate performance, you need dimensional models used with relational databases, or multidimensional database servers. Desktop OLAP tools will provide good performance, but only with limited (though growing) data sets.

Second, ERP OLTP applications don't incorporate the same data management (ETL) functionality as data warehousing data management applications such as Evolutionary Technologies, Informatica, Sagent, Informix, and others. As a result, the quality of ERP data doesn't equal DSS/data warehousing data. The result of using it will be an inferior foundation for DSS processing.

Third, you need more than reporting and/or OLAP tools used with ERP data for effective DSS. You also frequently need third-party data on customers and businesses that is not available in ERP OLTP packages. You also need time series data not recorded in ERP data stores, for trend and time-series analysis. And again, this data needs to go through an ETL process before it can be used in a DSS system for either querying/reporting or for KDD/data mining.

For these reasons, the desire to directly integrate DSS query and reporting capabilities in ERP systems is misplaced. On the other hand, if data warehousing tools and methods are applied to extract ERP data and analyze it; or if preconfigured packaged analytical applications are used with ERP and external data is consolidated into data warehouses or data marts, the promise of DSS for strategic enterprise management can be realized. But to realize this promise is to depart from the vision of integration through the ERP architectural backbone supported by a single vendor.

Once data warehousing tools and methods must be applied to ERP data, the ERP OLTP data model is no longer inviolate but must share the spotlight with DSS data models, and often with multiple DSS data models, integrated through conformed dimensions (See Kimball, Reeves, Ross, and Thornthwaite, 1998, Ch. 5) across related data marts. Also, the relatively tight integration of ERP applications must give way to the loose integration of the components of data warehousing applications. The array of application servers and data sources represented in Figure 2.2 comes to the ERP system. Or, more accurately, architecturally the ERP and the data warehousing system merge, and the complexity of the Web-based data warehousing system encompasses the ERP system as well. The result is a distributed information management system that is neither an OLTP ERP system nor a DSS data warehousing system, but both. It is a system that raises many conceptual and architectural as well as systems-integration issues.

Requirement: integration of data warehousing and ERP applications in EIPs

The integrative trends in both data warehousing and enterprise resource planning are accelerated by the movement toward enterprise information portals. Users want both DSS and OLTP applications available in their portals. And they want ERP data to be available for integration with data warehouse and other "external" data, now all "internal" to the portal. They do not understand that data warehouses and ERP systems are separate applications, because they see both of them in their personalized EIP, which they will, in turn, view as a single application. They want all types of data to be available in common views they can use to analyze and synthesize information and knowledge from wide-ranging sources. The evolution of data warehousing and ERP systems brings IT to the brink of such integration. The movement to EIP places IT over the brink and imposes the mission of incorporation of OLTP ERP and DSS data warehouse systems, along with the EIP front end, in the same, comprehensive, integrated, IT application.

Content management

Many writers have addressed the distinctions among data, information, and knowledge—see, for example, Allee, 1997; Bellinger, 1998, Beller, 2001; Murray, 2000; and Barquin, 2001. My own version will provide a necessary background to taking up future issues on the distinctions between data management and knowledge management, content management and knowledge management, and information management and knowledge management.

What are the differences among data, information, and knowledge in human organizations? Data, information, and knowledge all emerge from the social process. They are global properties of an organization, or its constituent agents, depending on the organizational level that is the focus of analysis. They are inter-subjective constructs, not personal data, information, or knowledge; they are organizational data, information, and knowledge.

A datum is the value of an observable, measurable or calculable attribute. Data is more than one such attribute value.

Is a datum (or is data) information? Information is always provided by a datum, or by data, because data is always specified in some conceptual context. And it is important to note that the conceptual context is one that expresses data in a structured format. Without that structured format we would not call it "data." So, *data is a type of information.* It is a type of information whose conceptual context provides it with structure and whose purpose is to represent observation.

Information, in more general terms, is data plus conceptual commitments and interpretations, or such commitments and interpretations alone. Information is frequently data extracted, filtered, or formatted in some way.

Organizational knowledge is a subset of organizational information. But it is a subset that has been extracted, filtered, and formatted and, in general, processed, in a very special way. It is information that has been subjected to and has passed tests of validation. It is information that has been enhanced by the record and experience provided by the validation process.

This brings us to the Case of the Misconceived Pyramid. In treating the distinctions among data, information, and knowledge, it is often assumed that these are arranged in a pyramid with data, the most plentiful type, at the bottom; information, produced from data, above it; knowledge, produced from information through the hard work of refining or "mining," above it; and wisdom produced from knowledge, the rarest of all, at the top. This makes a nice picture (Figure 2.3). But if data and knowledge are also information, what happens to the pyramid?

Figure 2.4 presents a new picture. In it, information is not made from data. Data and knowledge are made from preexisting information—that is, "just information," data, knowledge, and problems are used in the knowledge life cycle to produce more information, including new knowledge. In effect this figure is say-

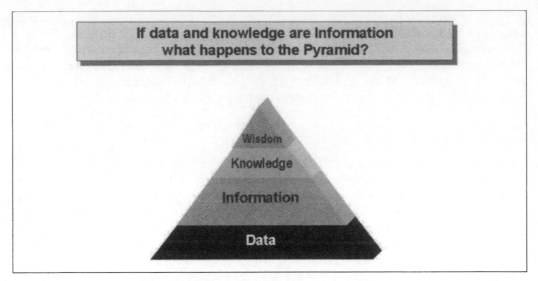

Figure 2.3. The case of the misconceived pyramid.

ing "Get rid of the pyramid, get on to the cycle." Later on, I will go into much greater detail about the nature of the knowledge life cycle (KLC)

What has happened to wisdom in this new image? Wisdom is knowledge of what is true or right coupled with "just" judgment about action to achieve what is right

Another definition is the application of knowledge expressed in principles to arrive at prudent, sagacious decisions about conflict situations. Both these definitions are consistent with the parable of Solomon, but they suggest that wisdom is ambiguous. It is (1) either a form of knowledge (i.e., also information) about doing what is right or (2) a kind of decision (in which case it's not information, but a

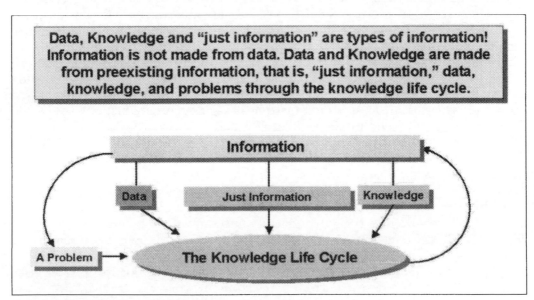

Figure 2.4. Get rid of the pyramid, get on to the cycle.

type of action in a business process). That is, depending on how it is defined, wisdom may not be the same kind of thing as data, information, or knowledge.

Unstructured content refers to media objects, or objects found in media, that are *not* described in terms of attributes and their values. Text objects such as documents and parts of documents, records, files, visual objects, electronic objects, e-mail messages, video files, and project plans are all examples of unstructured content. Since unstructured content has no attributes and no structure of attributes, or rules for manipulating them, it also has no metadata structure. Therefore, there is "no standard facility" for query, search, or analysis of it.

Content analysis is the transformation of unstructured content into data, information, or knowledge by describing it in terms of attributes of media objects, attribute structures, and rules relating attributes. *Content management* is the process of organizing, directing, and integrating content analysis and distribution efforts aimed at producing or distributing data, information, or knowledge. Content management systems acquire, process, filter, analyze, and distribute previously "unstructured" internal and external media objects contained in diverse paper and electronic formats. They also archive and often restructure these media objects so they can more easily be retrieved and manipulated. And they store the resulting data, information, or knowledge in a corporate repository (either centralized or distributed).

Content management systems are evolving from applications that primarily performed simple document management tasks focused on acquisition, retrieval, and delivery of unstructured documents to users, to systems that also manage transforming unstructured content in documents to structured data, information, and knowledge. That is, content management systems are becoming data, information, and knowledge production and extraction systems in the broader context of a content value chain that includes content acquisition (searching for, gathering, and receiving content), storage, content retrieval and content distribution activities. Figure 2.5 provides a view of this value chain.

The content chain is not a "knowledge chain," or a knowledge management process, even though it clearly supports these. It produces data, information, and even knowledge. These are important products used by knowledge processes, in particular by knowledge production and knowledge integration processes and their subprocesses. But the content chain that produces them is distinct from the knowledge chain and from the knowledge management process, because it is only one of the contributors to knowledge production, knowledge integration, and knowledge management.

The primary evolving capabilities in content management applications implementing the content chain include

- Search agents, called "spiders" or meta-crawlers, that track changes in content and use context in responding to queries
- Retrieval engines that automate content classifications, access and scan over 200 file types, and create searchable indices
- Increased ability to structure and describe unstructured content through use of text-mining engines and/or agents that construct semantic networks specifying and relating concepts
- Continuous content acquisition based on user profiles
- Content markup and metadata capabilities based on the eXtensible Mark-up Language (XML). (XML tagging creates the possibility of access

to arbitrary "chunks" of document content, which may be treated as objects.)

- Enterprise content object models providing a common view of all enterprise content assets, object relationships, and available methods for manipulating content
- Workflow capabilities for handling complex, nested workflows
- Ability to handle business rules and relationships as policy objects
- Versioning capabilities for both whole documents and document "chunks"
- Full text search and index management capabilities
- Web document creation and subscription/publication capabilities
- Complex routing and distribution capabilities
- Development tools for adding new applications to the content management package
- Profiling and change agent capabilities supporting personalizing delivery of content to users
- Distributed content management server capabilities to provide scalability to content management systems
- Security and access capabilities that can restrict access to individual objects in content repositories

The major content management vendors (Documentum, Hummingbird, OpenText, Filenet, and Ceyonique) are implementing these capabilities, at least in part, in their latest releases. The distributed nature of the new content manage-

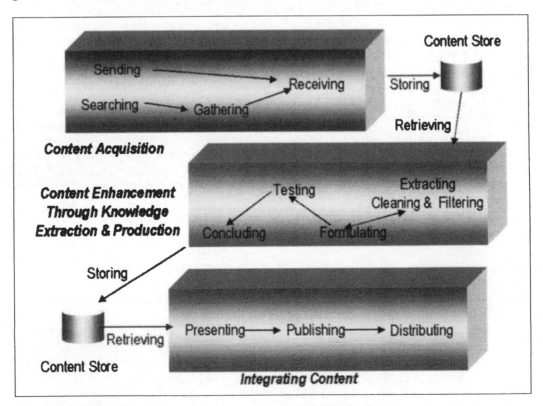

Figure 2.5. The content value chain.

ment systems, their broad connectivity to content expressed in a wide variety of formats, their connectivity to packaged applications such as SAP and Peoplesoft, and their use of object models to provide a common view of the distributed document management system all confirm that the trend toward integrative architecture, observed in data warehousing and ERP applications, is also driving content management applications. The obvious question is whether all three are coalescing into a single enterprise application architecture encompassing data warehousing, ERP applications, and content management systems?

EIPs: managing the structured/unstructured content relationship

The emergence of EIPs requires the emergence of capabilities to (1) produce, manage, and maintain resources and applications in both structured and content managed areas of information (already discussed), (2) manage the relationship between structured and less structured resources, and (3) integrate the EIP system. The evolving capabilities for managing the relationship between structured and "content" resources are, for the most part, themselves content management capabilities. I will discuss them before dealing more generally with the question of EIP capabilities for integration.

First, in EIPs an automated content classification process implemented by search engines, meta-crawlers, retrieval engines, and change agents distinguishes content categories and monitors change in these categories. The meta-crawlers and retrieval engines know the difference between structured and content resources based on their scanning of the metadata from all corporate repositories and on their recognition of the differences in metadata between resources in the two categories. Structured and content applications are also distinguished in the portal interface by explicit incorporation of separate publishing, search, and collaborative applications accessing both content and structured data as well as reporting, ERP, collaborative, and decision processing applications that access structured data alone. Many portal tools (e.g., Plumtree, Computer Associates CleverPath Portal, Citrix Sequoia XML Portal, Enfish Enterprise, Data Channel, Viador, and many others) have developed the capability for rapidly adding new, separate, content-based or structured data applications to the portal.

Structured data and content can also be related within the portal through workflow applications (provided in an increasing number of portal products). The portal's ability to handle collaborative workflow through its application servers creates the possibility of workflow using both types of content.

Second, at the middleware level in some EIP systems, distributed content management servers, guided by enterprise object models have appeared. Distributed content management servers balance the content management processing load and relieve pressure on structured resource application servers and database servers. They provide scalability to portal applications. In addition, in those portals that are fully integrated, these servers manage the EIP's metadata for content stores and applications, as well as for structured data, information, and knowledge stores.

They can manage secure access to content resources down to the object level. Using distributed object models including business objects, they express relationships between structured data and content stores used by the EIP application. The

EIP content management servers have the ability to interpret queries coming from the user and to direct them to the appropriate enterprise stores, whether they are of the structured data or content type. The servers also have connectivity to diverse file types and formats. They can access virtually any content or data store.

Third, a developing content management capability in portals is the ability to produce structured data from unstructured content. This is based on techniques of text mining whose use produces semantic networks through content analysis of text. The combination of these text-mining capabilities, along with widespread use of XML, and XML Topic Maps (XTMs) (Ahmed, et al., 2001) allowing access to small "chunks" of content, will facilitate this content analysis process in the future and make the ability to produce structured data from unstructured content a frequently used portal capability.

Fourth, if the choice is made to use an object-oriented database management system (OODBMS) as one of the data stores for an EIP system, structured data and content can be stored in the same distributed database. OODBMSs can distinguish structured data from unstructured content and manipulate both, as well as relations between them, *particularly when the OODBMS is one that stores XML objects, such as eXcelon's XML database*. Where an OODBMS is used, the portal's business object model will match its persistent store. Other things being equal, this will lead to a gain in performance involving the database. However, the typical situation in an enterprise will require EIPs to access legacy (hierarchical), flat file, relational and multidimensional structured databases. In that case, an EIP system will need to map its object model to the persistent data stores used by the enterprise.

Integrating EIP-based systems

"Central to the concept of Enterprise Information Portals is the assumption that disparate applications (content management, business intelligence, data warehouses/marts and data management) will: 1) access other internal and external sources of information and data, 2) exchange information (bi-directional) and 3) use that information within the application for processing and analysis. In other words, these applications must be integrated with each other and to other external systems. This is no small task as each of these software solutions was built by different vendors for different markets using different architectures. We believe the drive by EIP vendors toward full integration will initially fuel partnership arrangements and consolidation within industry groups. Further out, we believe that vendors from the unstructured (Content Management) and structured (Business Intelligence, Data Warehouse) sides will look to merge and acquire between industry groups to create Enterprise Information Portals. This will ultimately result in applications that share, manage and maintain information from one central user interface." (Shilakes and Tylman, 1998, p. 10).

The original formulation of the EIP idea by Shilakes and Tylman emphasized that the EIP would provide a single desktop interface to all enterprise resources. They also emphasized that application integration is central to the concept of the EIP. They did not address the question of how EIP components would be integrated with one another and with external application servers, however. Nor did they spell out how content management resources would be integrated with decision processing resources. Their primary graphic on the EIP (ibid., p. 8) identifies

- A decision processing workflow proceeding from structured data applications (ERP, point-of-sale) through a number of stages, including OLTP storage, ETL processing, data warehousing and administration, data marts and analytical application, OLAP, query and reporting, and data mining and ending in the enterprise information portal
- A less well-defined content management process proceeding from external content sources through documents and media of various types through a content management application, repository, and content database, and ending in the enterprise information portal.

What stands out about the representation of the EIP presented in the graphic is the absolute lack of interaction between structured decision processing and content management at any point in the process workflows. The graphic implies that the only relationship between the decision processing and content management realms is that both types of resources appear on the same portal interface—an idea that is inconsistent with their EIP vision.

Integrating the EIP system and its set of diverse applications and data/content stores is the most important problem in implementing EIPs, because without such integration, the EIP is just a frequently updated unrelated collection of data stores and applications with a pretty face. The capabilities discussed in the foregoing text for managing the structured/unstructured content relationship in EIPs are relevant for integrating EIPs. Portal interface capabilities provide integration on the desktop. More thoroughgoing integration of data and content stores and applications is provided by the workflow capabilities of EIPs and by the enterprise distributed object model capability available in some portals.

The workflow capability can provide portal integration by structuring patterns of systematic, serial use of structured data and content resources. This is task-based integration. It doesn't require tight integration of structured and content resources. It provides for phased access to structured and content resources rather than for ad hoc and perhaps simultaneous access to heterogeneous applications and stores.

The object model capability, on the other hand is the key to the dynamic integration problem (Firestone, 1999b, p. 4; Firestone, 1999a) in EIPs. I previously pointed out the importance of dynamic integration in both data warehousing and EIP systems as complexity in those systems increases. Without the coordination provided by dynamic integration, inconsistencies in data and information, business rules and methods, and metadata would be prevalent and the EIP's usefulness as an authoritative enterprise source would be severely compromised.

Note that an EIP is very different from a consumer Web portal in this respect. In MyYahoo, the responsibility for making sense of inconsistencies, conflicts, and incommensurabilities in queries, reports, and results can be left to the user. In an EIP, though, if its integrative services are inadequate and we query two different sources and they incorporate different meanings for the same term (for example, "Customer") or different business rules for calculating losses, the results of our query may be, at best, deceptive and, at worst, meaningless nonsense.

In the context of maintenance and evolution of EIPs, the DIP problem is three-fold:

- First, an integrated view of all enterprise server-based assets relevant to the EIP application is needed.
- Second, flows of data, information, and knowledge throughout this system need to be monitored and managed to maintain the common view of enterprise resources in the face of change in the form and content of any resource, and to distribute the system's data, information, and knowledge bases as required.
- Third, such management needs to occur automatically and without centralizing the system so that the authority and responsibility for adding new data and information to the system is distributed.

To solve the three-fold DIP, EIPs need an integrative software layer (i.e., an artificial information manager (AIM)) to perform (dynamic) integration in the face of change in data stores and applications in communication with the EIP. This integrative software layer can be implemented with portal metadata capabilities and procedural code, or it can be implemented much more easily with object modeling technology that encapsulates both metadata and methods (including business rules) in objects (Firestone, 1998a, 1999). The capabilities for implementing either of these types of integrative layer have been developed and are either present or may be integrated in EIP tools and solutions.

Further EIP evolution

EIPs, of course, are only at the beginning of their product life cycle. They are still evolving. As White (1999, p. 5) predicted and as the history of EIP development since 1999 has indicated, the dividing line between decision processing EIPs and collaborative processing EIPs is blurring with the passage of time. He also stated that a decision processing EIP that incorporates workgroup collaborative processing capabilities could be described as a knowledge management portal, since it combines business information, user knowledge, and collaborative processing (though he thinks the term knowledge management should be avoided because of the many definitions of the term) (White, p. 3). Murray, in turn, defined the knowledge portal as a combination of the enterprise information portal, the collaborative portal, and the expertise portal, plus "something more," he did not define (G. Murray, 1999, p. 4). Both, therefore, agree that there is something beyond the EIP still to appear. I think that something is the enterprise knowledge portal (EKP).

An EKP is a type of EIP. It is an EIP that is goal-directed toward knowledge production, knowledge integration, and knowledge management focused on enterprise business processes (e.g., sales, marketing, and risk management) (Firestone, 1999b) and also focuses on, provides, produces, and manages information about the validity of the information it supplies.

Knowledge portals, in other words, provide information about your business, and also supply you with meta-information about what information you can rely on for decision making. EKPs, therefore, distinguish knowledge from mere information. And they provide a facility for producing knowledge from data and information, in addition to providing mere access to data and information.

EKPs, moreover, orient one toward producing, acquiring, and transmitting knowledge as opposed to information. Intrinsically then, they provide a better basis for making decisions than do EIPs generally. Those who have knowledge have a competitive advantage over those who have mere information.

Since EKPs are types of EIPs, they share with them all of the differences distinguishing them from DW Systems. In the case of EKPs, however, the renewed emphasis on data mining and analytical applications will be particularly strong since these have a critical role in producing new knowledge.

In addition, the integrative layer in the EKP is different from that in the EIP. In the EIP, the AIM has no intrinsic requirement to manage or implement criteria used to test and validate information that is produced or acquired. In the EKP, in contrast, the integrative layer, called The Artificial Knowledge Manager (AKM) (Firestone, 1999, 1999b, 1999b), places a heavy emphasis on criteria used to test and validate the knowledge produced or acquired by the EKP. It is these criteria and their application that distinguish the AKM from the AIM and, derivatively, the EKP from the EIP.

There are no EKP products yet (in spite of the claims made by certain vendors that they are selling an EKP), but we can still project what their benefits would be based on the definition of an EKP. EKPs have the same benefits for the enterprise as EIPs, but they also provide a sharper focus for many of these benefits. Thus, the competitive advantage provided by EIP systems exists only because some of the information produced by such systems is valid information—that is, knowledge. If a particular EIP transmitted only invalid knowledge it would decrease and not increase competitive advantage.

Insofar, as an EKP can be expected to improve the efficiency and effectiveness of knowledge and knowledge management processes because of its explicit goal direction toward optimizing these processes, it can also be expected to produce increased competitive advantage and ROI in comparison with an EIP. The reason is simply that decisions based on knowledge provide a better basis for successful competition and higher ROI than decisions based on mere information. Again, the benefit of increased effectiveness can be expected to increase for EKPs, because acting on the basis of knowledge identified as such by EKP metadata and meta-information is more likely to be effective than acting on the basis of unvalidated or invalidated information.

References

Allee, V. (1997). *The Knowledge Evolution: Expanding Organizational Intelligence* (Boston, Butterworth-Heinemann).

Anahory, S. and Murray, D. (1997). *Data Warehousing in the Real World* (Reading, MA: Addison-Wesley).

Barquin, R. (2000). "From Bits and Bytes to Knowledge Management," January–February, 2000, www.e-gov.com; also available at www.barquin.com.

Beller, S. (2001). "The DIKUW Model," *National Health Data Systems*, April, 2001, available at www.nhds.com/toc.htm.

Bellinger, G. (1998). "Data, Information, Knowledge and Wisdom" at http://www.radix.net/~crbnblu/musings/kmgmt/kmgmt.htm.

Berson, A. and Smith, S. (1997). *Data Warehousing, Data Mining, and OLAP* (New York: McGraw-Hill).

Caruso, D. (1998). "Get a Backbone," *Intelligent Enterprise*, December, 1998, pp. 18–20.

Firestone, J.M. (1998). "Data Warehouses, Data Marts, and Data Warehousing: New Definitions and New Conceptions," *DKMS Brief*, **6**, *Executive Information Systems, Inc.*, Wilmington, DE, November 12, 1998. Available at http://www.dkms.com/White_Papers.htm.

Firestone, J.M. (1998a). "Architectural Evolution in Data Warehousing," *Executive Information Systems, Inc. White Paper*, Wilmington, DE, July 1, 1998. Available at http://www.dkms.com/White_Papers.htm.

Firestone, J.M. (1999). "Knowledge Base Management Systems and The Knowledge Warehouse: A Strawman," *Executive Information Systems Working Paper for Knowledge Management Consortium, International*, Wilmington, DE January 25, 1999. Available at http://www.dkms.com/White_Papers.htm.

Firestone, J.M. (1999a). "The Artificial Knowledge Manager Standard: A Strawman," *Executive Information Systems Working Paper for Knowledge Management Consortium, International*, Wilmington, DE January 25, 1999. Available at http://www.dkms.com/White_Papers.htm.

Firestone, J.M. (1999b). "Enterprise information Portals and Enterprise Knowledge Portals," *DKMS Brief*, **8**, *Executive Information Systems, Inc.*, Wilmington, DE, March 20, 1999. Available at http://www.dkms.com/White_Papers.htm.

Firestone, J.M. (1999c). "Enterprise Knowledge Management Modeling and Distributed Knowledge Management Systems," *Executive Information Systems White Paper*, Wilmington, DE, January 3, 1999. Available at http://www.dkms.com/White_Papers.htm.

Inmon, W.H. (1995). "What Is a Data Warehouse?" *Prism Tech Topic*, 1, no. 1, 1995.

Inmon, W.H. (2001). "What a Data Warehouse is Not," *DM Review*, 11, no. **7**, July 2001, 56–58.

Inmon, W.H., Imhoff, C., and Sousa, R. (1998). *Corporate Information Factory* (New York: John Wiley & Sons).

Kimball, R., Reeves, L., Ross, M., and Thornthwaite, W. (1998) *The Data Warehouse Life Cycle Toolkit* (New York: John Wiley & Sons).

Murray, A.J. (2000). "Knowledge Systems Research," *Knowledge and Innovation: Journal of the KMCI*, 1, no. 1, 68–84.

Murray, G. (1999). "The Portal and the Desktop," *Intraspect* (available at www.intraspect.com).

Rymer, J. (1998) "Business Process Engines, A New Category of Server Software, Will Burst the Barriers in Distributed Application Performance Engines," *Upstream Consulting White Paper*, Emeryville, CA, April 7, 1998.

Shilakes, C.C. and Tylman, J. (1998). *Enterprise Information Portals* (New York: Merrill Lynch).

White, C. (1999). "The Enterprise Information Portal Marketplace," *Decision Processing Brief DP-99-01*, Database Associates International, Inc. Morgan Hill, CA.

PART TWO

Benefits of Enterprise Information Portals and Corporate Goals

In this Part, I place EIPs in the context of corporate goals and benefits. Most discussions of EIP and, for that matter, of benefits of other software alternatives are not tightly coupled to corporate goals and business processes. They have not approached a systematic analysis of corporate goals, objectives, and benefits in the context of IT alternatives, including the EIP. In Chapter 3, I consider how the various claimed EIP benefits are related to corporate goals, to business processes, and to IT applications. I then make the case that the approach taken to benefit analysis is basically intuitive rather than analytical and doesn't clarify the relationship of the claimed or envisioned outcomes of EIP adoption to corporate goals or business processes.

In Chapter 4, I present concepts, methodology, and tools for producing improved EIP benefit estimates. My objective is to provide a framework for thinking about a more comprehensive estimation of EIP benefits—an estimation that is tightly coupled to corporate goals and that distinguishes benefits according to their relative importance.

CHAPTER 3

Benefits of Enterprise Information Portals

Enterprise innovation and justification

We live in a time of wave upon wave of innovation in Information Technology: client/server systems, distributed object technology, data warehousing, workflow systems, document management, groupware systems, ERP and packaged applications, Enterprise application integration (EAI), and the introduction of XML, among other things. The game of introducing each succeeding wave always follows a similar pattern (Moore, 1991, pp. 9–13; Moore, 1995, pp. 13–26). The new innovation first appeals to "innovators"—the technology enthusiasts. Next, it is adopted by visionaries—the "early adopters"—who believe it will produce substantial competitive advantages for them. But then it becomes necessary to persuade "pragmatists" to use the new technology. At that stage of the technology adoption process, the pressure is on information technology vendors to demonstrate the benefits of their new innovation, calculate its costs, and show that the ratio of benefits to costs is favorable enough to make the pragmatists want the innovation. "What will it do for our bottom line?" becomes the critical question in deciding whether to go ahead with an IT innovation.

In this respect, the introduction of the enterprise information portal (EIP) is no different from other waves of IT innovation. The benefits of adopting EIPs are widely claimed, even though the EIP wave has hardly touched the pragmatist shore. How justifiable are these claims of EIP benefits? That is the question I try to answer in this chapter.

EIP benefits

Even though the EIP field is very young, many benefits are already being claimed for EIPs. As we review the main benefits, the relevant question about each claimed benefit is whether the arguments supporting it describe a tight coupling of EIP effects to corporate goals, or whether the connections drawn between EIPs and benefits are still largely speculative and hypothetical.

Competitive advantage

The argument for competitive advantage begins with the idea that valuable information is currently still locked away in disparate, badly integrated corporate data stores. Corporations that can get at it will have a competitive advantage because they have access to timely and accurate information on marketing, performance, and customer relationships as well as in other areas. In addition, having this information will allow them to develop better forecasts, to adapt faster to changes (to be more agile), and to provide better support for decisions than their competition. The key to getting such information, with its attendant competitive advantages, is said to be EIP software.

Why? Because EIP software (according to some of its promoters) combines and integrates internal and external information and standardizes, indexes, analyzes, publishes, and distributes all the information needed in a user's job role. Therefore, the user's job performance is affected and, specifically the efficiency, quality, effectiveness, and net benefit and cost of the user's job performance is upgraded. Insofar as part of the user's job is to cooperate with others in the enterprise, the performance of the tasks the user participates in will be upgraded and so on up the business process hierarchy, until business processes show an increase in efficiency, quality, effectiveness, and net benefit.

While this argument is very plausible, its plausibility comes from its abstractness and its generality. In many corporations information may no longer be locked away. It may be available through relatively new browser interface–based ERP or data warehousing applications. It may be managed and published and distributed by content management applications. It may be analyzed by business intelligence applications. That is, previous corporate investments in new IT systems may already have enhanced the competitiveness of many corporations.

That doesn't mean that an EIP application may not further enhance competitiveness by providing improved access to data stores. But it is to recognize that arguments based on "locked-up" data stores may not carry as much weight now as they did a few years ago at the beginning of the data warehousing boom. It also doesn't mean that the new integration offered by EIPs does not enhance competitiveness. It almost certainly does. But it is important to begin to ask whether the amount of enhanced competitiveness expected is due to the EIP or to DW, content management, or BI components that can exist and be implemented without an EIP application. If it is the latter, an objective analysis of benefits and costs would need to take into account the competitive advantage available from such existing, or, at least separately implementable, applications. Then the marginal or incremental improvement from installing an EIP could be analyzed and forecast, and a better basis would exist for any EIP build or buy decision.

In other words, to establish competitive advantage as a benefit in any concrete instance of corporate decision making about implementing an EIP, an analysis is needed that assesses specific EIP and other IT alternatives comparatively from a benefit/cost viewpoint. This kind of analysis of the benefits of EIPs is not currently being provided. Instead, more general claims about comparative advantage are made. They rely for their plausibility on the fact that an EIP is a composite of a number of applications and that it therefore must bring to the EIP table previously established justifications for data warehouses, content managers, and ERP-based DSS applications. In order to go further, though, and to provide an EIP justification based on competitive advantage, arguments are necessary that will compare software alternatives and trace both EIP and alternative capabilities through the impact they make on various business processes, goals, and objectives, and finally translate any differences in impact on goals and objectives into differences in benefits and costs produced by the alternatives.

Increased ROI

Another frequently mentioned benefit of EIPs is that they increase return on investment (ROI). The argument here is that packaged EIP applications should produce higher ROI than other IT applications for the following reasons. First, packaged applications are less expensive than customized systems. Second, packaged applications contain functionality specific to particular industry vertical markets. Third, packaged applications are easier to maintain. And fourth, they are faster to deploy.

While it is hard to argue the point that packaged applications may produce ROI benefits, they also may not necessarily be associated with EIP solutions. While EIPs may be focused on packaged vertical applications, they also may not. It depends on the particular EIP project being implemented. Second, the adoption of packaged applications is a general trend in IT. There is no exclusivity for EIP applications in participating in this trend. Packaged DSS, or content management, or ERP applications may be offered and implemented outside of an EIP framework. So if a corporation is considering a packaged application implementation, it will need to choose between those within and external to an EIP framework, and it will need to face the question of the expected *marginal improvement* in ROI in case of EIP implementation.

Another problem with the ROI argument rests with the claim that packaged applications are easier to maintain than custom applications. While certainly this is true for each individual packaged application, is a system of packaged applications easier to maintain if the goal is enterprise application integration? Not necessarily, as the history of attempts to integrate SAP and other ERP packaged applications in a broader enterprise framework seems to show. Packaged *applications can too easily become stovepipes* representing differing and incompatible definitions of the same critical concepts and differing business models.

One of the advantages of implementing packaged applications in an EIP framework may prove to be the tighter coupling of applications provided by an EIP solution. But tighter integration is problematic and depends on EIP architecture. Front-end integration involving mere placement of different packaged applications on the portal screen and the portal's ability to aggregate content from different applications is unlikely to offer a great increase in ROI over standalone, non-portal packaged application implementations. So again, we come back to the central problem of demonstrating the marginal improvement in ROI in a specific EIP implementation compared with standalone packaged application alternatives.

Increased employee productivity

This argument refers to productivity in the very narrow sense of improving the cycle time involved in information acquisition. One version of the argument is that if users now spend x amount of time surfing the Web to gain information, they can be expected to spend $x-y$ amount of time getting the same amount of information when they use a portal. If we multiply y times the number of employees in an organization, we have the gross amount of time saved by the portal, which, of course, can easily be converted to a benefit in dollars (Plumtree, 1998; Plumtree, 2001).

This sounds like the simplest and most straightforward argument for realizing a benefit from an EIP. However, even that is not so easy to demonstrate and requires empirical studies to gauge the effects of portal introduction. The portal may speed up cycle time and therefore produce increased efficiency, but whether that really produces a benefit in dollars depends on whether the time freed up is used for a productive purpose in the broad sense of the term. If the portal saves fifteen minutes of surf time per employee per person day, that won't translate into actual savings unless the fifteen minutes gained contributes to quality, effectiveness, and net benefit. And this requires more precise analysis to establish.

Accelerated innovation

An extension of the increased productivity argument can be developed in the area of accelerated innovation as well.

> Innovation is a completed knowledge process life cycle event, beginning with knowledge production and ending in incorporation of knowledge structures within business structures. Innovation acceleration involves continuous decrease in the cycle time of the knowledge process life cycle. (Firestone, 2000, p. 55.)

Certain EIP applications can save time in specific areas of the knowledge life cycle (to be discussed in detail later on), all of which make some contribution to knowledge production and knowledge integration and ultimately to knowledge utilization in business process behavior. Specifically, these EIPs can save time in information acquisition; individual and group learning; knowledge claim formulation, knowledge claim evaluation, broadcasting knowledge claims; searching for and retrieving knowledge; sharing; and teaching. If an average of 20 percent of cycle time is saved across the board in a typical enterprise KLC event as a result of implementing an EIP, this translates into 20 percent more innovations

While an EIP productivity benefit may be produced by 20 percent additional innovations in a fixed time period, it is also possible to estimate a financial benefit in terms of time saved alone, in analogy to the simple calculation for EIPs provided above. But here the benefit is produced in targeted efforts to produce and integrate knowledge with the assistance of the portal, so the time saved by it is more likely to translate into productive and valuable knowledge life cycle activity.

Increased effectiveness

The claim of increased effectiveness is based on the idea that portals not only make available new information to users that was not available before but also provide that information in an integrated and personalized way. Integration and personalization *focus* information on the job role of the user and therefore lead to improved job performance and eventually to a more knowledgeable and effective organization.

Here is another plausible argument requiring further analysis and demonstration. First, we don't know yet whether portals provide enough of an increased focus to increase effectiveness. Second, we don't know whether the increased actual exposure to information provided by portals may have the negative effect of further diffusing employee attention away from job roles. To explore these questions, once again, empirical analysis accompanied by explicit modeling is needed.

Decreased cost of information

The benefit of decreased cost of information is a consequence of both Web-based publishing and the automated character of portals. For companies that still distribute information on paper, portals promise big savings. For companies already involved in Web publishing, portals offer the possibility of saving on Web administration personnel costs.

The savings inherent in delivering information over the Web are not exclusive to the portal alternative. This benefit applies to any Web-based publishing application. The savings from Web administration are an unambiguous benefit of EIPs, but they are clearly only a small part of any justification for EIP applications.

Increased collaboration

One of the most important benefits of EIPs may be increased collaboration within the enterprise. In effect, increased collaboration translates to more sustained common effort to accomplish corporate goals and to greater social integration of corporate environments, especially across departmental and geographic barriers. Insofar as one of the major problems of modern decentralized enterprises is fragmentation and isolation of its components, collaboration through portal structures could provide a powerful antidote.

Having made the positive case, however, it's important to note that collaboration across formal boundaries can also have the effect of lessening integration within an organization's formal structures. While this often is an effect to be welcomed, it is not always and everywhere advantageous. The truth is that increased opportunity for collaboration is not always an unmixed blessing, and careful analysis is also needed here in order to validate this prospective benefit for any concrete business contemplating an EIP.

Universal access to enterprise resources

A particularly attractive appeal of EIPs is their promise to provide universal access to enterprise and extended enterprise (extraprise and interprise) information and knowledge resources. The cost-effectiveness of the Internet as the foundation for such access is the key point. It is finally possible to use both "push" and "pull" technologies to ensure that users have the right information available to them at the right time and at the right price (for the enterprise and the extended enterprise).

The appeal of this argument rests on a few assumptions. The first is that the Internet requires a universal portal if it is to provide this advantage. Clearly this is not the case. A series of Web applications not integrated into a portal could also provide such access. The question is the marginal benefit provided by the portal, not the benefit provided by universal access, which might be delivered without a portal.

The second is that it is also assumed that universal access to information is itself a benefit. But many argue that we currently have an information glut and that mere access to information is not a benefit. Portals can organize this glut in such a way as to bring it under control, but this power of organization is clearly a function of individual portals, with specific architectures, implemented in specific situations, having an impact on specific business processes, tasks, and job roles. It is not a general benefit of all portals. In particular, the best way to alleviate an information glut is to synthesize information and to produce new knowledge. Knowledge production, however, may or may not be effectively supported by a particular EIP implementation. If it is not, the universal access to information provided by an EIP can carry with it costs (side effects) as well as benefits.

A unified, dynamically integrated and maintained view of enterprise data and information

Another attractive benefit claimed for EIPs is that they produce a common view of data and information in the enterprise. The common view is justified by pointing to a number of favorable assumed consequences.

- First, the existence of such an enterprise view may have a positive impact on the education, socialization, and integration of new employees in a corporation.
- Second, widely distributed employees are presented with the same view of information wherever they work for a company in the world. This helps them to identify with the company and to feel themselves a part of it.
- Third, the existence and availability of the common view helps employees share information and cuts down dependency on a few key employees for information.
- Fourth, since the common view contributes to the education of new employees, it also empowers them to more easily deal with and handle the increasing complexity of the products being produced by the most sophisticated companies.
- Fifth, since the common view is dynamically maintained and integrated and also comprehensive, it is an aid to competitive intelligence in the business and helps support more effective selling and customer service.

These consequences of the common view provide some strong benefit claims for proponents of EIPs. But there are still problems with the argument. First, the common view of an enterprise need not be created and maintained by an EIP. In fact at present, commercial EIPs would be hard-pressed to create a truly integrated common view of the enterprise, in contrast to a superficial common view represented by icons on a portal desktop. Other applications such as Web-enabled distributed data warehouses, integrated ERP applications with a common ERP backbone, and document management applications with an object model of content running on an application server, may be much closer to providing a common view than many EIP solutions.

Second, all of the favorable consequences of the common view are plausible in theory, but they are vaguely stated and have not been subject to study and to confirmation. Intuitively, we believe a common view of the enterprise produced by an EIP will deliver these expected benefits. But to what degree in absolute terms and in comparison with competing applications such as DW, content management, and ERP is an unanswered question.

Conclusion

In addition to the arguments provided above questioning the easy assumption of benefits from EIP implementations, there is yet another argument that applies to the claims for competitive advantage, increased ROI, accelerated innovation, and increased effectiveness. It is the argument that all of these claims assume the truth or validity of the information managed by the EIP in question. But, the problem is that EIPs, in general, don't support evaluating or validating information or knowledge claims (Firestone, 1999). Therefore, the information they provide has not necessarily been tested and evaluated against alternative claims in an effort to eliminate error. So EIPs, in general, carry with them a risk of error that threatens these primary four benefits. If a particular EIP solution is to be viewed as providing these benefits, therefore, it must be shown to provide facilities for validating knowledge claims and tracking the history of such efforts at validation.

Finally, how are the various claimed EIP benefits just discussed related to corporate goals, business processes, and IT applications? Most discussions of EIPs and, for that matter, of the benefits of other software alternatives, are not tightly coupled to corporate goals and business processes. In the literature on EIPs, the discussion of benefits thus far has not approached a systematic analysis of corporate goals, objectives, and benefits in the context of IT alternatives, including the EIP.

Instead, the tenor of the discussion is illustrated by the arguments I reviewed. There is a listing of envisioned *outcomes* or *effects* of the introduction of EIP software in an ad hoc manner. And there is an assertion that these outcomes are unequivocal benefits. The approach is basically intuitive rather than analytical, and it does not clarify the relationship of the claimed or envisioned outcomes to corporate goals or business processes. We can and should do better than that in providing justifications for EIP projects.

References

Firestone, J.M. (1999). "Enterprise Information Portals and Enterprise Knowledge Portals," *DKMS Brief*, 8, Executive Information Systems, Inc., Wilmington, DE, March 20, 1999.

Firestone, J.M. (2000). "Accelerated Innovation and KM Impact," *Financial Knowledge Management*, (Q1, 2000), 54–60.

Moore, G. (1991). *Crossing the Chasm* (New York, HarperBusiness).

Moore, G. (1995). *Inside the Tornado* (New York, HarperBusiness).

Plumtree, Inc. (1998) "Corporate Portal," Plumtree Software, San Francisco, CA.

Plumtree, Inc. (2001). "A Framework for Assessing Return on Investment for a Corporate Portal Deployment," San Francisco, CA.

CHAPTER 4

Estimating Benefits of Enterprise Information Portals: Concepts, Methodology, and Tools

Enterprise information portal benefits and corporate goals

How are various claimed EIP benefits related to corporate goals, business processes, and to IT applications? Most discussions of EIP benefits and, for that matter, of benefits of other software alternatives to EIPs, are not tightly coupled to corporate goals and business processes (see Chapter 3). In the EIP literature the discussion of benefits thus far has not approached a systematic analysis of corporate goals, objectives, and benefits in the context of IT alternatives.

Instead, in most analyses there is an ad hoc listing of envisioned *outcomes* or *effects* of the introduction of EIP software and an assertion that these outcomes are unequivocal benefits. The approach is basically intuitive rather than analytical and comprehensive. It doesn't clarify the relationship of the claimed or envisioned outcomes to corporate goals or business processes. And it often doesn't distinguish the outcomes in terms of the degree of benefit they provide.

This chapter presents concepts, methodology, and tools for producing improved EIP benefit estimates. My objective is to provide a framework for thinking about a more comprehensive estimation of EIP benefits—an estimation that is tightly coupled to corporate goals and that distinguishes benefits according to their relative importance. I will not propose a specific methodology for estimation in all situations, because, as we will see, no single methodology is appropriate for every corporate situation. Comprehensive benefit estimation is not practical in many situations. In others, varying degrees of comprehensiveness will be appropriate. Instead of a single methodology, I will define an *abstract pattern* of comprehensive benefit estimation (CBE) that would, if implemented, achieve the goal of tight coupling of benefits, goals, and software alternatives. Then I will point out how in different concrete situations one may tailor the pattern to achieve a feasible estimation procedure.

A framework for EIP benefit estimates

To improve EIP benefit estimates both a broader conceptual perspective and more substantial methods and tools are needed than those provided by ad hoc analytical approaches. The road from IT applications to benefits leads through business processes and corporate goals. So here is an introductory conceptual framework that can lead us down this road. The first part of the framework relates business processes, corporate goals, and IT applications. The second focuses on the relationship between corporate goals and benefits. Once the framework is developed, I will discuss issues related to applying it to estimating EIP benefits tightly coupled to corporate goals.

Corporate goals, business processes, and IT applications

For every multi-person corporate organization, we can distinguish analytical properties, structural properties, and global properties (Lazarsfeld and Menzel, 1961). Analytical properties are derived by aggregating (summing, averaging, or performing other elementary mathematical operations on) data describing the members of the corporation. Structural properties are derived by performing operations on data describing relations of each member of the business to some or all of the others. Lastly, global properties are based on information about the corporation that is not derived from information about its members. Instead, such properties are produced by the intra-corporate interactions comprising the system they characterize and, in that sense, may be said to "emerge" from these interactions (Holland, 1998).

Corporate goals are one category of global properties of corporations. Corporate goal-strivings are predispositions to perform actions calculated to create or maintain certain intrinsically valued states of the world, either internal or external to a corporation. Corporate goals are no more than these valued states—the targets of goal-strivings. I distinguish between corporate goals and corporate objectives by defining objectives as states that are valued instrumentally for the contribution they make toward achieving corporate goals. So there is, in this conception, a cause-and-effect relation between goals and objectives. Objectives cause an agent to move closer to its goal. Goals may or may not reinforce objectives.

This distinction between goals and objectives is conceptually precise, but actual states of the world may be both goals and objectives. This is true because they can be simultaneously valued in themselves, and for their instrumental value.

Corporate goals can be highly abstract, or very concrete. They can also be general in their geographic or temporal focus, or very specific. Of course, highly abstract goals also tend to be very general in scope, while highly concrete goals tend to be very specific. The same variations of abstractness and concreteness and generality and specificity apply to corporate objectives.

Both goals and objectives are often expressed in generalized and vague form in corporate discussions of them. "Our goal is to be the most competitive corporation in our industry." "Our goal is to be an ethical and socially responsible member of the community." "Our goal is bring the vision of the integrated desktop to all consumers." These are three examples of vague statements of goals one might find in marketing literature. But, there are also precise ways to express corporate goals.

Since goals are states of the world, we can also look at them as sets of ordered attribute values describing the corporation or its environment. Imagine a row in a database table or a row vector in an algebraic matrix, recording a set of values for a corporate entity. This row might define the actual state of the corporation at a particular time. Now imagine that this row was made up not of actual values, but of desired values intrinsically valued by a corporation. The row now defines a multi-attribute goal-state of the corporation at the particular time.

The conceptual "distance" between the goal-state and the actual state is *the predecision descriptive instrumental behavior gap.* It is the gap that must be closed for the corporation to get to its goal. Figure 4.1 illustrates the ideas of the multi-attribute goal-states and actual states of a corporation through a geometrical interpretation. The geometric space defined by the component attributes of the goal-states and actual states I will call *corporate reality space.*

The goal-states and actual states are represented by line vectors drawn from the origin to the points in corporate reality space defined by the attribute values of the components of the vectors. The pre-decision descriptive instrumental behavior gap is represented by the distance vector "a." A benefit is provided to a corporation when an instrumental action has the effect of moving it closer to its goal-state on one or more of the component attributes of the goal-state. A cost, in the general sense of the term, is levied to the same corporation if the effect of the action is to move it away from its goal-state on one or more of the component attributes. A net benefit results when the sum of all benefits is greater than the sum of all costs resulting from the action. A net cost results when the sum of all costs is greater than the sum of all benefits. In the geometric interpretation, a net benefit reduces the distance between the actual state and the goal-state. A net cost increases this distance.

These statements raise the issue of measurement of the amount of benefit and cost resulting from a decision. While it is generally true that a reduction in

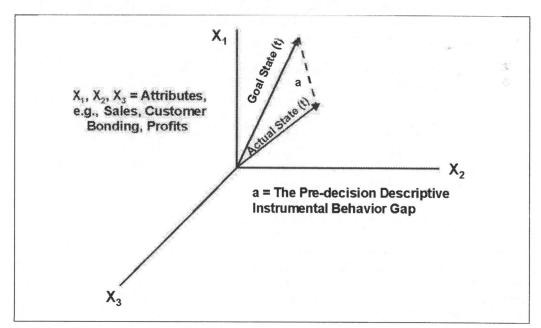

Figure 4.1. Corporate reality space.

the distance "a" can be called a net benefit, the amount of distance reduction is *not* the amount of net benefit. Nor is the amount of increase in "a" the amount of net cost increase. The conceptual distance between the *descriptive* goal and actual states does not, alone, provide enough information to measure *amount* of benefit and cost; because corporate reality space and the component attributes comprising it are purely descriptive and not evaluative in character.

To say that there is a net *benefit* when we close the descriptive gap between the actual and goal-states in corporate reality space is to go beyond the purely descriptive character of reality space and to place a *value interpretation* on such a movement. But this value interpretation is still less than explicit and somewhat ad hoc, because it assumes a correspondence between reality and benefit without clarifying exactly what this correspondence is. To make the correspondence explicit, we need to work with both a descriptive (corporate reality) representation of goal-states and actual states, *and* with a valuational (benefit/cost) representation of these. And we need to define a value interpretation mapping corporate reality space to corporate valuational space. I will return to this subject in the section on corporate goals and EIP benefits, below.

Corporations try to achieve their goals and to produce benefits by performing business processes. Business process *activities* may be viewed as sequentially linked and as governed by validated rule sets of agents (i.e., their knowledge) (Firestone, 1999, 1999a; Knowledge Management Consortium, 1999). A linked sequence of activities performed by one or more agents sharing at least one corporate objective or goal is a *task*. A linked sequence of tasks governed by validated rule sets of the agents performing them and producing results of measurable value to these agents is a *task pattern*. A cluster of task patterns, not necessarily performed sequentially but often performed iteratively and incrementally, is a *task cluster*. Finally, a hierarchical network of interrelated, purposive, activities of intelligent agents that transforms inputs into valued outcomes, a cluster of task clusters, is a *business process*. This activity to business process hierarchy is illustrated in Figure 4.2.

Business processes in corporations may be evaluated in terms of their efficiency, quality, effectiveness, and net benefit or cost.

- *Efficiency* refers to the cycle time of the business process compared with some norm.
- *Quality* refers to how well the activities and tasks constituting a business process are performed relative to some set of quality standards.
- *Effectiveness* refers to whether or not the business process moves the corporation toward or away from its goals and by how much.
- *Net benefit and cost* refer to how much a business process is benefiting or costing a corporation.

Information technology applications, like other corporate activities, help or harm corporations in attaining goals and producing benefits. In order to measure their impact, it is necessary to view them as part of a corporation's business processes and in terms of making an impact on those business processes and, through them, on movement toward or away from corporate goals and/or objectives. This applies to EIPs as well. In attempting to measure, analyze, or forecast their likely benefits, we need to trace the impact or forecasted impact of the introduction and operation of an EIP application on the various business processes it is attempting to support.

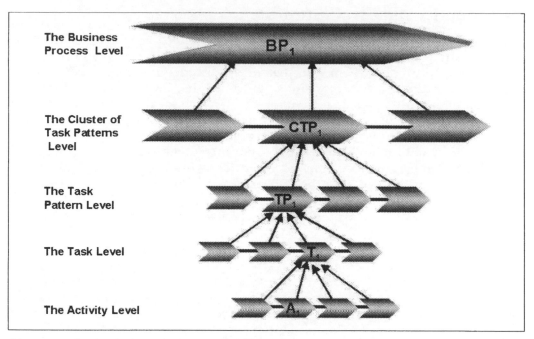

Figure 4.2. The activity to business process hierarchy.

We then need to trace this impact through the business processes to its further impact on corporate goals and benefits (see Figure 4.3). Assessments of this kind are not easy or straightforward. But they are necessary if a claim about the likely benefits of an EIP project is to amount to more than nonsense or hyperbole.

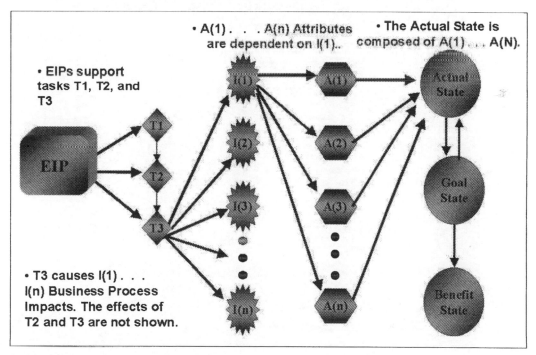

Figure 4.3. Business process impacts on attributes.

EIP benefits and corporate goals

I pointed out earlier that to relate corporate goals to corporate benefits we needed both descriptive and valuational representations of actual and goal-states and of the gap between them, and that we also needed a mapping between the two representations. Such a mapping is called a value interpretation. It is a rule (for example, an if ... then statement) or set of rules that establishes a correspondence between the components of reality space and the components of the valuational space that is the target of the mapping.

From a geometric point of view a value interpretation of corporate reality space is defined by a set of correspondence rules mapping the dimensions (coordinate axes) of reality space onto the dimensions of valuational space. If the valuational space is one whose coordinate axes or attribute components are measured on an absolute benefit measurement scale, then we can call this valuational space *corporate benefit space.*

Both the actual and goal-states will have corresponding vectors in corporate benefit space. Let's call these the *actual benefit vector* and the *goal benefit vector.* The distance between the actual benefit vector of a corporation and the origin of corporate benefit space is the total net benefit enjoyed by a corporation at a point in time. The distance between the goal benefit vector of a corporation and the origin is the total net benefit desired by the corporation. The distance between its actual and goal benefit vectors is the *instrumental behavior benefit gap.* It is this gap, even more than the descriptive instrumental behavior gap, that corporations seek to close.

This framework expresses the relationship between corporate goals and benefits clearly. Corporate goals are expressed by the multi-attribute, descriptive, goal-state vector of corporate reality space. Corporate benefits are expressed by the multi-attribute, valuational goal benefit vector of corporate benefit space. The relationship between the two is precisely defined by the set of correspondence rules defining the mapping between the two spaces. Figure 4.4 illustrates the relationship.

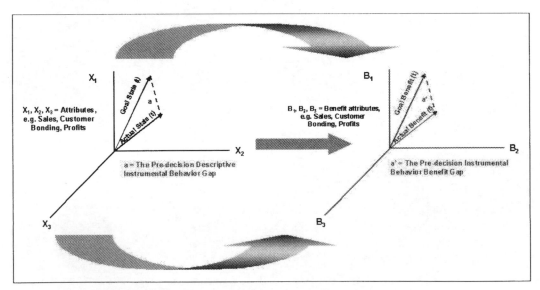

Figure 4.4. The relationship between corporate goals and corporate benefits.

Methodology and tools for estimating the benefits and costs of EIPs

If we look at EIP benefit assessments from the viewpoint of the foregoing conceptual framework, it is clear that a thoroughgoing EIP benefit assessment would

- Explicitly postulate and measure goals and objectives and the progress made toward them.
- Gauge the impact of EIP introduction on business processes and their success in attaining goals and objectives.
- Interpret these descriptive analyses of EIP impact or projected impact on goals in terms of corporate benefit so that descriptions of impact are not confused with measurements of actual benefit.

Following is a list of the steps involved in each of these phases of comprehensive EIP benefit estimation, along with some comments describing a little of the work involved and tools that might be used to accomplish it. The list of steps is an outline of a methodology. By comprehensive I mean that it takes into account both benefits and costs and also provides for measuring those benefits and costs that cannot be expressed well in monetary terms.

In this technique of benefit estimation, attributes expressing value in monetary terms are viewed as descriptive attributes. They become benefit attributes only during the mapping from reality to benefit space and after the transformation that mapping entails. Therefore, measures in benefit space transcend monetary value and incorporate it into the overall framework. In particular, monetary costs and benefits are measured as a by-product of applying the framework and as a step along the road to more comprehensive measurement.

Measuring actual and goal-states

Step one: Perform measurement modeling
(Firestone, 1998; Firestone and Chadwick, 1975)

Conceptualize and select

- Attributes to *describe goals and objectives* in reality space
- Attributes hypothesized to *cause* changes in actual states moving them toward or away from goal-states
- Attributes describing possible unintended *side effects* of actions activating causal attributes
- Other *outcome* attributes important for description

Many of the selected attributes will be abstractions. These are not defined by data attributes but are assumed to be computable from them. They are measurable attributes. Other attributes are directly defined by data and are measured attributes. So we have a mix of measured and measurable attributes in each of the four categories.

Organize attributes into measurement clusters. That is, group the abstract attribute (e.g., customer acquisition, customer retention, customer profitability, revenue growth) that is the target or focus of measurement, with the set of already measured attributes that will provide values to be used to compute, measure, or derive the values of the abstract target attribute. The outcome of this task is a categorization of measured attributes by the measurable attributes that are the primary focus of the measurement modeling effort.

Construct measurement models. These are models made of rules expressing measured attribute values as antecedent conditions and target (measurable) attribute values as consequents, with no temporal priority specified between the antecedent and consequent values. They are not limited to goals and objectives, but include causes, side effects and other outcomes as well. The rules are called semantic rules or rules of correspondence. They frequently create multi-attribute composites as measures of the target attributes. Such composites can often be complex and demanding to construct. Measurement models are essential to modeling and can always be distinguished as logical components in any systems model. You can't formulate a testable model of an aspect of the world without using a measurement model. The only question is whether the measurement model is explicit or implicit.

There are at least four types of ("crisp logic–based") measurement rules that provide the foundation for a composite in measurement models (Firestone and Chadwick, 1975). In addition, there are fuzzy logic–based rules that map crisp values to linguistic variable values through fuzzy membership functions (Firestone, 1998). Among other things, such rules establish priorities among the attributes entering the composite.

The activity of prioritizing attributes for their relative importance to a criterion variable is frequently part of measurement modeling. A measurement model is different from a causal model in that the latter requires temporal asymmetry between antecedent and consequent (Firestone, 1971), whereas measurement models imply that values of the measured and measurable attributes are being viewed in cross-section. I've provided detailed accounts of measurement modeling in other places and won't review them here (Firestone and Chadwick, 1975; Firestone, 1998).

Use ratio scaling methods where possible. Ratio scaling methods should be used in constructing measurement models of abstractions because they allow easy mathematical manipulation and composition of measured attributes into target attributes. That is, they are easy to work with when you want to create an overall measure from a set of component attributes.

Ratio scaling should be used in doing priority assessments among attributes, because the resulting weights are defined on the same scale and facilitate combining the measured attributes into the target attributes. It should also be used along with direct judgmental assessments of quantitative properties of agents and corporations where attributes are not measured and you want to convert them to measured attributes. In that case ratio scaling provides a further basis for combining measured attributes into target attributes.

Ratio scaling techniques are now well known and easy to implement. Saaty's work on the subject is particularly accessible, and his development of the analytical hierarchy process (AHP) over a period of more than thirty years has featured an emphasis on practical ratio scaling methods and their application to a wide variety of subjects (ExpertChoice, 2001). I have also recently treated techniques for ratio scaling in the context of knowledge discovery in databases (Firestone, 1998).

Step one can be greatly facilitated by the proper tools. While a wide variety of tools including a spreadsheet such as Excel with fuzzy logic add-ins or a mathematics package such as MATHEMATICA (2001) or MATLAB (with fuzzy logic add-ons) (2001) can accomplish everything you need to do in this step, the best combination of ease of use and power will be found with an omnibus statistical/ modeling package such as SAS (2001), SPSS (2001), or Statsoft's Statistica (2001) (my personal favorite because of its great spreadsheet module, graphics, and general combination of friendliness and power), supplemented by Inform Software's Fuzzytech (2001). With these two tools you can accomplish all of the measurement modeling and ratio scaling you need to do, and when you're done you can communicate results with external packages and back-end databases.

Step two: Gather data or perform direct assessments to measure attributes that cannot be derived from measured attributes or that have no data

Once the measurement model is constructed, you cannot apply it without having values for its measured variables. You get these by gathering data from documents, surveys, or direct observation. Data from these sources is preferable to data gathered from direct assessments of properties of corporations and agents by "expert raters" because it is thought to have greater reliability and validity. But data gathered from direct judgmental assessments produced by panels of expert raters is certainly better than missing data. And there is a good deal of evidence in both Saaty's work (see ExpertChoice, 2001) and some of my own (Firestone and Brounstein, 1981, pp. 127–151) suggesting that reliability and validity levels in models using direct assessment data are comparable to those achieved by models using document or survey-based data. It is also suggested that they exceed the levels found in models based on opinion and attitude surveys.

Step two uses the same tools as Step one for direct assessments. For more conventional data gathering and data staging you may need data warehousing ETL/ data cleansing tools such as Informatica, Sagent, or Evolutionary Technologies' ETI-Extract, and, of course, a commercial relational database.

Step three: Determine actual states by using measurement models to compute attribute values

Once values are given to the measured attributes, the measurement model is used to compute the values of the target measurable attribute(s) to arrive at a description of the actual state.

Step four: Determine goal-states by specifying goal attribute values

The goal-state could be specified without first determining the actual state. But it is easier to do a compete job of specifying the goal-state once the actual state is measured and available for examination. Then one can begin by using the actual values of the attribute components of the actual state as a baseline for estimating the goal-state values of the same attributes. A variety of methods can be used to perform these estimates, including pair comparison rating methods. The trick is to estimate goal-state values at different points in the future, so there is enough data to measure the logical consistency of the judgmental estimates. Once these values are derived from the estimation procedures, a consistency check can also be made on the fit between the computed future values of the abstract attributes and the judgmental estimates of those abstract values. The judgmental forecasts of measured attribute values may then be adjusted until they are consistent with the forecast values of target attributes.

Step five: Compute the pre-decision instrumental behavior gap

Subtract the goal-state vector from the actual state vector to get the distance or gap vector. Compute the length of this vector, which, in the most commonly used mathematical interpretation, is the Euclidean distance between the goal-state vector and the actual state vectors.

Modeling the impact of EIPs

Step one: Select abstract attributes that are the focus of measurement models as target attributes for impact modeling

Classify these attributes into exogenous attributes, mutually endogenous attributes, and endogenous attributes.

- *Exogenous attributes* are causes of other attributes, but are "not caused" by any other attributes included in the impact model.
- *Mutually endogenous attributes* have effects on other attributes in the model and are affected by these same attributes.
- *Endogenous attributes* are affected by other attributes and only affect other attributes without being affected by them.

- No additional tools are needed for this step.

Step two: Specify impact model

Specify hypotheses expressing the values of

- Mutually endogenous attributes as a function of other mutually endogenous attributes and exogenous attributes, or as a function of exogenous attributes alone
- Mutually endogenous attributes as a function of other mutually endogenous attributes
- Endogenous attributes as a function of mutually endogenous attributes

In these hypotheses, all determining attribute values must temporally precede all determined attribute values.

The result of this step has been variously called a cognitive map, a conceptual graph, a causal model, an impact model, and many other terms. It is composed of nodes and connecting rules. The rules can be expressed in terms of "crisp" logical rules or in terms of fuzzy rules. If the latter is the case, it has been called a "Fuzzy Cognitive Map" (Kosko, 1992)

A variety of modeling tools can be used for this task depending on one's impact modeling orientation. The statistical packages mentioned earlier support *linear structural equation modeling*. In the *system dynamics* area a good choice is High Performance Systems (2001) products. Other leading products are Vensim (2001) and Powersim (2001). For *fuzzy cognitive mapping* you can use Fuzzytech (2001). If you prefer a *complex adaptive system* (CAS) approach, then Santa Fe Institute's agent-based Swarm simulation is the indicated choice.

Step three: Expand the impact model by adding hypotheses comparing the effects of EIP and other software alternatives on mutually endogenous and endogenous variables

It is better if this is done by expressing the software alternatives in terms of component attribute values that describe them and allow (1) direct comparisons of features among alternatives and (2) formulation of hypotheses relating software features to business process attributes. However, you can also add hypotheses specifying the relative magnitude of the impact of EIP software versus alternative software options on each mutually endogenous or endogenous attribute in the model. Ratio scaling techniques can also be used here to measure these relative magnitudes and to check on the consistency of the judgments. No additional software is needed for this step.

Step four: Implement empirical tests and simulations of competing impact models and evaluate software alternatives

The tests will provide forecasts and analyses of the impact of EIP vs. other software introductions in moving the corporation toward its goal-state. If you use a fuzzy systems approach to impact modeling you'll need some neural network estimation software for testing and validation. The statistical packages mentioned above also provide such software, as does Fuzzytech, which specifically supports neuro-fuzzy estimation. But if you're willing to go beyond these packages to vendors more specialized in neural networking, I believe Ward Systems Group (2001) and NeuroDimension (2001) offer excellent and versatile software.

Mapping from reality to benefit space

Step one: Define rules of correspondence between attributes of reality space and attributes of benefit space

There are a number of things to keep in mind when doing this mapping. First, only some of the target attributes of reality space need be directly represented by attributes of benefit space. The determining factor is whether an attribute is intrinsically valued as a benefit. An important implication is that benefit space may be of much lower dimensionality than reality space. Second, an attribute of benefit space may be the result of a composite mapping from multiple attributes of reality space. This is another source of possible lower dimensionality in benefit space. Third, even if an attribute in reality space is represented in benefit space, the mapping is unlikely to be a simple correspondence in values. Mappings can be similarity transformations, linear transformations, nonlinear transformations of various kinds, or fuzzy membership functions of diverse form (Cox, 1994).

A mapping from an attribute in reality space to a corresponding attribute in benefit space is called a principle of correlation (Ellis, 1966, p. 41) (Firestone and Chadwick, 1975). Such a rule should be validated through consistency testing and graphical means (ibid.).

Step two: Establish benefit priority weights among attributes of benefit space

This is done using the same type of ratio scaling techniques used in measuring actual and goal-states.

Step three: Compute the instrumental behavior benefit gap

The same method can be used as in computing the descriptive instrumental behavior gap, but keep two differences in mind. First, the attributes used are mapped transformations of the descriptive attributes called benefit attributes. Second, in computing the Euclidean distance, priority weights determined in Step two are used to weight the attributes of benefit space to arrive at an overall measure of benefit. No additional software is needed for these three steps.

Implementing estimation

The estimation methodology I have described has the advantages of being comprehensive and of tying the analysis of benefits to corporate goals, but the disadvantage of being expensive in effort and money. It is much more likely to be used to evaluate an EIP introduction after the fact than it is to be used to forecast likely impact during the planning stage. Not least because, if begun from scratch, it will take months to implement, an unacceptable time period for an EIP planning study and, at times, even for an EIP implementation.

To make it useful, then, abbreviated versions of the estimation methodology are needed that will represent an improvement over ad hoc benefit analysis but that can still be accomplished in a few weeks of effort. The nature and extent of abbreviation will depend on the corporate environment encountered. Here are three cases. Together they define the limits for abbreviating the methodology. Real-world situations will fit some synthesis of the cases.

Case one: No prior work has been done on development of an enterprise performance management (EPM), balanced scorecard, ERP, or data warehousing system

This situation is hard to imagine in any major corporate environment today. In it, the comprehensive methodology of benefit estimation cannot be applied without going through all of the steps outlined, because little prior work on measurement and impact modeling already exists. In a situation such as this, it won't be possible to accurately estimate the benefits of an EIP alternative relative to another EIP, or to data warehousing, or to a balanced scorecard system with any degree of confidence absent months of effort. On the other hand, this is also the situation where an EIP, or any of the other alternatives, is likely to have its highest ROI. This is because it introduces not only the single point of access to all enterprise resources but also a whole system of measurement and performance analysis that was previously not available. So a decision selecting any data warehousing, EPM, ERP, balanced scorecard, or EIP alternative can be made with reasonable confidence of substantial payback.

Once this point is recognized, the question becomes not so much whether an EIP produces enough benefit that it should be funded but whether one should be funded in preference to one of the other alternative initiatives that can improve delivery of information to end users. If the question is whether an EIP will bring greater benefits than other alternatives, rather than the broader one of providing an estimate of EIP benefits relative to those provided by other alternatives, then there is an inexpensive method of software benefit assessment that can be used to project the impact of various software alternatives relative to one another.

The method is Saaty's analytical hierarchy process. It has been applied by Fatimeh M. Zahedi (1993, Ch. 12) to quantitative evaluation of expert systems and can be adapted to the problem of deciding which of a group of software alternatives will provide the greatest benefit relative to other members of the group.

The nice thing about using the AHP when no prior work has been done is that it needs no measured data to work except data generated by the method from judgmental assessments. It takes judgmental assessments about decision options generated at the lowest, most concrete level of a hierarchy and combines that data with ratio scaled attribute priority data, also generated by judgmental assessments. Let us review the method in detail.

The analytic hierarchy process (AHP) and EIP benefit estimation
It is easy to develop a set of criteria to use in comparing alternative software systems. One of these can be cost. You can rate alternatives according to monetary expense. Find out which is the most expensive, which is the least, and which alternatives are in the middle. You can go on to compare alternatives based on other criteria of evaluation, presumably criteria relevant to nonmonetary costs and to benefits. But when your comparisons are all done,

- How do you assess the degree of nonmonetary cost?
- How do you assess the degree of benefit?
- How do you combine different nonmonetary costs to arrive at summary measures?
- How do you combine monetary and nonmonetary costs?
- How do you combine different benefits to arrive at summary measures?
- How do you compare costs and benefits to arrive at benefit/cost ratios?
- More generally, what is the relationship between specific costs and the overall summative concept of cost?
- What is the analogous relationship on the benefit side?

None of these questions can be answered by an ad hoc comparative approach. If you use one, the process you use to aggregate comparisons on individual criteria into an overall assessment of which EIP or another software alternative system is best for you and your organization will of necessity have to be a subjective, implicit process. The justification for your choice will certainly be incomplete, probably flawed, and subject to obvious criticism from those who quickly perceive other subjective criteria you didn't consider.

A better comparative evaluation is produced if you use a rigorous framework that (1) specifies the meaning of benefit and cost in terms that connect and tightly couple the overall goals of your organization and the characteristics of the EIP and other alternatives within the context of a broad benefit/cost concept and (2) provides a means of quantitatively comparing goals, characteristics, and intermediate criteria comprising the evaluation scheme. In such a framework, the criteria used to directly assess the alternative systems are themselves assessed by other criteria that are more directly related to cost or benefit, while these are assessed relative to still other criteria more directly related to cost or benefit, and so on until one reaches a set of criteria that may themselves be directly evaluated in terms of overall cost or benefit. The last step in this progression produces a simplified mapping from reality to benefit space. The fact that all the assessments in the progression are quantitative in nature means that questions of the sort posed above may all be answered by applying the evaluation framework.

In addition, any criticisms involving formulation of additional evaluation criteria to be applied to the alternatives would have to be related to the benefit/cost framework before their validity could be asserted. If they were so related, they would not change the result of an evaluation unless their quantitative significance were great enough to have a major impact on overall scores. In other words, in contrast to subjective evaluation frameworks, a rigorous evaluation framework of the kind offered here produces cumulative results. Even if mistakes of omission are made, the results of a prior evaluation need not be scrapped but only revised, and the overall result is much less likely to be disturbed.

The AHP fits the specification for a rigorous comparative evaluation and assessment framework just described. The AHP has had more than 30 years of development since its inception in the late 1960s and early 1970s. The primary developer of the AHP is Professor Thomas L. Saaty of the University of Pittsburgh. Saaty began work on certain aspects of the AHP while he was with the U.S. Arms Control and Disarmament Agency (ACDA). He published the first studies applying the AHP during the early 1970s, when he had moved to the University of Pennsylvania (Saaty, 1972, 1974). There, and later at Pittsburgh, Saaty, his colleagues, and students have applied the method to a wide range of practical problems, including planning; prioritizing; optimization; benefit/cost analysis; decision making; and studies of national influence, terrorism, international conflict, transportation, energy policy, and many other areas (Saaty, 1990; Saaty and Xu, 1990; Harker, 1986; Zahedi, 1986). These represent only a few of a voluminous list of references available (see ExpertChoice, 2001).

The AHP was developed by Saaty to provide a rational basis for multi-criteria decision making of the sort involved in evaluating and selecting software alternatives. The AHP has three aspects. First, it focuses on decomposition of the decision problem to identify various components of an attribute hierarchy—goals, objectives, criteria, subcriteria, elements, actors, or characteristics—relevant for decision; and grouping and ordering these components into sets or clusters of attributes comprising the levels of a hierarchy, or into clusters that share levels of a hierarchy.

Second, it focuses on comparative judgments between pairs of attributes within each cluster. These comparative judgments serve as the raw data for computations producing a priority rating of each component attribute of a cluster compared with all other components of that cluster in relation to some criterion attribute specified at the immediate higher level of the hierarchy. The priority ratings produced are defined on a ratio scale. One ratio scale is defined for each criterion attribute. Since the priority ratings are defined on a ratio scale, they can be meaningfully multiplied or divided, thus providing a basis for later benefit/cost computations. The ratings are also tested for logical consistency within the AHP, so the extent of departure from the classic ratio scale model is measured and used to evaluate the validity of AHP evaluations.

Third, the AHP focuses on the synthesis of priorities within the hierarchical framework. This means that "local" priority ratings, those established for a particular component attribute in relation to other components of its cluster and a particular criterion variable, are adjusted or weighted according to priority ratings computed for that component in relation to other criterion variables. It also means they are weighted by the priority ratings computed for the criterion variable itself within its hierarchical level and its cluster. This adjustment process results in a "global" priority rating being determined for each component of each cluster and level of the hierarchy relative to the focal concept or goal of the hierarchy. If the focal concept is a goal attribute such as customer profitability or monetary cost, and the decision alternatives at the bottom of the hierarchy are EIP and other software alternatives, then the analytic hierarchy provides no mapping from reality to benefit space. It provides only a kind of relative impact evaluation of each software alternative on the goal attribute. If the focal concept (or concepts in the case of more than one goal attribute) is a benefit attribute, then the priority weights defined at the goal level of the hierarchy (relative to the benefit level) will provide a simple mapping (a linear composite) from reality space to benefit space, as well as a relative assessment of the impact of the software alternatives on goals and benefits.

Thus, in a benefits hierarchy the adjustment process produces a rating or measure of the "global" or overall contribution to the "benefit" of each member of the hierarchy. The analogous result also holds for a cost hierarchy. So if global ratings of software (or any other decision) alternatives at the lowest level of an attribute hierarchy are developed through the synthesis of priorities, the AHP yields benefit and cost ratings that may then be divided to arrive at meaningful benefit/cost ratios for each EIP or other software alternative being evaluated. As with local priority ratings, consistency tests for "global" priority ratings are also provided by the AHP. If the observed inconsistency is too great, the hierarchy may be revised until consistent ratings are provided by decision makers.

Software for implementing the AHP has been developed by Ernest Forman and Thomas Saaty at Expert Choice, Inc. (2000) The Expert Choice software comes in a number of versions for individuals and teams and enterprises. In all cases it is friendly, and it is much easier to implement the AHP with it then it would be using the computational tools recommended earlier for occasional prioritizations using the AHP method.

Case two: ERP and/or data warehousing systems exist

This situation is more favorable for implementing the comprehensive benefit estimation methodology. Much of the work of specifying attributes in the goal/objective, cause, side effects, and outcome categories will have been done. In addition, data will have been gathered on many of the attributes in the system. Still, comprehensive benefit estimation will remain difficult, because most of the steps in the measurement, impact modeling, and mapping reality to benefit space categories will remain.

The solution is to once again apply the AHP, but to substitute measured attribute values in the hierarchy where they are available, and to use the real data to enrich AHP judgments where necessary.

Case three: A balanced scorecard or enterprise performance management (EPM) system is already available

This is the most favorable situation for implementing comprehensive benefit estimation prior to EIP construction. Such systems contain measured attributes, measurable attributes, goals, objectives, causal and side effect attributes, and outcome attributes. Balanced scorecards also may sometimes include cause-and-effect hypotheses relating measurable attributes to one another.

To implement comprehensive benefit estimation on a balanced scorecard or EPM foundation, supplement the measurement and causal models already present with additional rules and hypotheses, particularly those relating software alternatives to mutually endogenous and endogenous attributes in the model. In addition, the presence of "missing measurements" will also require generating data from direct judgmental assessments. Nevertheless, most of the data gathering, measurement, and causal modeling activities will have already been completed. The main remaining task is the mapping from reality to benefit space. This mapping should follow the pattern for the general method I described earlier.

Summary

This chapter presented concepts, a methodology, and tools for producing improved EIP benefit estimates. It provided a corporate reality/corporate benefit space framework for thinking about a more comprehensive estimation of EIP benefits—an estimation that is tightly coupled to corporate goals and that distinguishes benefits according to their relative importance. No single methodology is appropriate for every corporate situation. Comprehensive benefit estimation is not practical in many situations; in others, varying degrees of comprehensiveness are appropriate.

Instead of a single methodology, the chapter defined an *abstract pattern* of comprehensive benefit estimation (CBE) that would, if implemented, achieve the goal of tight coupling of benefits, goals, and software alternatives. It then showed how the general pattern could be abbreviated and tailored in three different "ideal type" situations to achieve a feasible estimation procedure. Actual situations will mix the characteristics of these ideal types.

References

Cox, E.D. (1994). *The Fuzzy Systems Handbook* (Cambridge, MA: Academic Press).

Ellis, B. (1966). *Basic Concepts of Measurement* (Cambridge, UK: Cambridge University Press).

ExpertChoice, Inc. (2001) http://www.expertchoice.com.

Firestone, J.M. (1971), "Remarks on Concept Formation: Theory Building and Theory Testing," *Philosophy of Science,* 38, 570–604.

Firestone, J.M. (1998) "Knowledge Management Metrics Development: A Technical Approach," *Executive Information Systems White Paper,* Wilmington, DE, June 25, 1998. Available at http://www.dkms.com/White_Papers.htm.

Firestone, J.M. (1999). "Enterprise Knowledge Management Modeling and Distributed Knowledge Management Systems," *Executive Information Systems White Paper,* Wilmington, DE, January 3, 1999. Available at http://www.dkms.com/White_Papers.htm

Firestone, J.M. (1999a). "The Artificial Knowledge Manager Standard: A Strawman," *Executive Information Systems Working Paper for Knowledge Management Consortium, International,* Wilmington, DE January 25, 1999. Available at http://www.dkms.com/White_Papers.htm

Firestone, J.M. (2000). "Accelerated Innovation and KM Impact," *Financial Knowledge Management,* (Q1, 2000), pp. 54–60. Available at http://www.dkms.com/White_Papers.htm.

Firestone, J.M., and Brounstein, S.H. (1981). *Strategic Evaluation and Planning System (STEPS): The Needs Assessment Capability (NAC)—A Description of Products* (Hyattsville, MD: Program Evaluation Staff, Farmers Home Administration, USDA, September, 1981).

Firestone, J.M., and Chadwick, R.W. (1975). "A New Procedure for Constructing Measurement Models of Ratio Scale Concepts," *International Journal of General Systems,* 2, pp. 35–53.

FuzzyTech (2001) at www.fuzzytech.com.

Harker, P.T. (ed.) (1986). "Special Issue on the Analytic Hierarchy Process," *Socio-economic Planning Sciences,* 20, no. 6.

High Performance Systems (2001) at www.hps-inc.com.

Holland, J.H. (1998) *Emergence* (Reading, MA: Addison-Wesley).

Knowledge Management Consortium (1999) "What is Knowledge Management? A Complex Adaptive Systems Approach," *KMCI PowerPoint Presentation, Draft 3.0,* February, 1999.

Kosko, B. (1992). *Neural Networks and Fuzzy Systems* (Englewood Cliffs, NJ: Prentice-Hall).

Lazarsfeld, P.F., and Menzel, H. (1961). "On the Relation Between Individual and Collective Properties," in Etzioni, Amitai (ed.), *Complex Organizations,* New York, NY: Holt, Rinehart and Winston.

Mathematica (2001) at www.wolfram.com.

Matlab (2001) at www.mathworks.com.

NeuroDimension (2001) at www.nd.com.

Plumtree Software, Inc. (2001), "A Framework for Assessing Return on Investment for a Corporate Portal Deployment," Plumtree Software, Inc., San Francisco, CA.

Powersim (2001) at www.powersim.com.

Saaty, T.L. (1972), "An Eigenvalue Allocation Model for Prioritization and Planning," Energy Management Policy Center, Philadelphia, PA: University of Pennsylvania.

Saaty, T. L. (1974) "Measuring the Fuzziness of Sets," *Journal of Cybernetics,* 4, no. 4, pp. 53–61.

Saaty, T.L. (1990). *Decision Making for Leaders* (Pittsburgh, PA: RWS Publications).

Saaty, T.L., and Xu, S. (1990). "Recent Developments in the Analytic Hierarchy Process" in Saaty, T.L. (ed. and author) *The Analytic Hierarchy Process: Panning, Priority Setting, Resource Allocation,* 2nd Edition (Pittsburgh, PA: RWS Publications).

SAS (2001) at www.sas.com.

SPSS (2001) at www.spss.com.

Statistica (2001) at www.statsoft.com.

Vensim (2001) at www.vensim.com.

Ward Systems Group (2001) at www.wardsystems.com.

Zahedi, F. (1986), "The Analytic Hierarchy Process: A Survey of the Method and Its Applications," *Interfaces,* 16, no. 4, pp. 96–108.

Zahedi, F.M. (1993). *Intelligent Systems for Business: Expert Systems with Neural Networks,* Belmont, CA: Wadsworth.

PART THREE

Architecture of Enterprise Information Portals and Enterprise Artificial Systems Integration

In this Part, I present an analysis of the underlying architecture of enterprise information portals, both current and prospective. Chapter 5 begins with an identification of the two "islands" problems of enterprise artificial systems integration (EASI) and of the meaning of EASI itself. It then proceeds to consider thirteen types of EASI as the basis for an analysis of the two islands problems and the architecture of enterprise information portals. The discussion covers Stonebraker's account of enterprise integration, the distinction between natural and artificial system integration, enterprise application integration (EAI), the data federation approach, content integration, artificial information integration, and artificial knowledge integration. The results of this analysis are then used as the basis for proposing the distributed information management system (DIMS) as a solution to the islands of information problem. In laying out the solution, I discuss: the artificial information manager (AIM), connectivity services, application servers, object/data stores, object request brokers (ORBs) and other components, protocols, and standards supporting distributed processing. The consideration of the islands of information problem then ends by relating the DIMS solution to it to data federations and the enterprise information portal.

Chapter 5 next moves on to consider the islands of automation problem. Here three of the thirteen types of EASI, which together offer a solution to the islands of automation problem are discussed: (1) user interface subject matter integration, (2) application integration through workflow, and (3) information integration from application to application through ad hoc navigation while sharing information and maintaining a common view across them.

After completing its analysis of the two islands problems, Chapter 5 applies the results to portal architecture by developing a taxonomy of portal architectural types. First, EIP integration is related to architecture, then passive access to content (PAC), data federation integration (DFI), structured application integration (SAI), distributed content management (DCM) and portal application integration (PAI) approaches to architecture are specified, considered, and evaluated. The chapter then concludes with the recommendation that incremental PAI architecture is the appropriate architectural goal of EIP solutions.

Chapter 6 considers an important aspect of PAI architecture and EASI not covered in Chapter 5. That aspect is the role of intelligent agents in EIPs and in PAI architecture. Chapter 6 discusses definitions, agents in PAI architecture (including their role in in-memory proactive object state management and synchronization across distributed objects; component management; use case and workflow management; and transactional multithreading). Chapter 6 moves on to consider a view of agents as scaled-down business process engines and ends with conclusions on the role of intelligent agents in EIPs and in creating the virtual enterprise.

CHAPTER 5

EIP Architectural Questions and Approaches: EASI and the Two Problems of IT

Introduction

The key to EIP architecture and to the integration problem is provided by a related IT area I call enterprise artificial systems integration (EASI). After all, a central element of the definition of the EIP is its function as an integrator of data, content, applications, and components. Indeed, the nature of the integration problem in EIPs may be summarized by reference to two central problems of IT applications that support information and knowledge management: the "islands of information problem" and the "islands of automation" problem.

The "islands of information" problem is the problem of integrating disparate information sources to produce a coherent view of enterprise data, information, and knowledge. It focuses on integrating middle-tier application servers and back-end data and content stores into what looks like a single pool of data, content, information, and knowledge from the viewpoint of the user.

The "islands of automation" problem is the problem of integrating today's desktop environment of disparate, program-by-program, task-isolated IT applications. It focuses on replacing the Windows desktop's unrelated application icons with a new interface that emphasizes a personalized combination of subject matter (content) categorization/networking, workflow patterns, and the capability to navigate from application to application in an ad hoc manner while sharing information and maintaining a common view across them.

What, then, does EASI have to say about the two problems? I will first try to answer this question generally and then directly address EIP integration and types of portal architecture.

Definition of enterprise artificial systems integration (EASI)

It is necessary to introduce the new concept of enterprise artificial systems integration, because the concept of enterprise application integration (EAI) is too narrow. Two contemporary and representative definitions of EAI are as follows:

- David Linthicum—"Enterprise Application Integration, or EAI, is one of those buzzwords that puts a name on something that's been going on for years: the integration of applications so they can freely share information and processes." (Linthicum, 1999, p. 1.)
- John Mann—"Enterprise Application Integration (EAI) is the process of integrating multiple, independently developed applications that may use incompatible technology and need to remain independently managed. Implementing EAI boils down to moving information between applications. This includes setting the applications up to send, receive, and react to information." (Mann, 1999, p. 49)

And in a nearly identical article Mann adds that there are "a variety of ways to direct the flow of information—one of them being workflow." (Mann, 1999a, p. 1.)

Linthicum's definition states that application integration is the ability to share information and processes freely across applications, while Mann emphasizes the continuing independence of the applications in their management. Neither definition goes very deeply into what is meant by information and processes. Both clearly limit EAI to sharing across applications.

The idea of sharing across applications doesn't facilitate thinking about all of the aspects of enterprise artificial systems that need to be integrated by the enterprise. This is especially true with respect to enterprise information portals, which may integrate, data, content, information, and knowledge as well as applications.

EASI is defined as the process of freely sharing component elements of enterprise artificial systems through a software application.

Types of EASI

I distinguish five main types of EASI relevant to integrating "information islands:"

- Data integration
- Content integration
- Artificial information integration
- Artificial knowledge Integration
- Application integration

Each of these may be further subdivided into physical and logical (or "virtual") types. Altogether, this typology distinguishes ten types of EASI.

I'll clarify what I mean by these categories through a discussion of some work of Michael Stonebraker's on the islands of information problem.

Islands of information and Stonebraker's enterprise integration solutions

In an eloquent article called "United We Stand," (1999), Stonebraker offered a viewpoint on the "islands of information" problem. He defined enterprise integration as the "ability to read from and write to all of the applications and data sources across the enterprise." And he indicated, "Such integration supports unified views of information and lets you update synchronously across systems."

Stonebraker goes on to distinguish four approaches to the "islands of information" problem: (1) application integration, an approach he associates with a number of commercial enterprise application integration packages; (2) data warehousing systems; (3) messaging systems; and (4) data federation systems.

The application integration approach implements integration by attaching a layer of "glue" that provides an interface from an external integration system to each application being integrated. Stonebraker faults commercial EAI systems for (1) their failure to provide a unified view of data across databases; (2) their inability to handle "conceptual mismatches"; and (3) their difficulties in scaling to the enterprise level.

Stonebraker views data warehousing as providing integration of applications at the data level. The integration is *physical* in that data must be extracted, cleansed, transformed, and moved from their original data stores to data warehouses or data marts. He lists the following drawbacks of the data warehousing approach:

- It provides stale data, only periodically refreshed
- Inflexibility in analysis due to unavailability of data not in a data warehouse or data mart
- Copy costs providing a barrier to integration and therefore scalability in certain instances
- Overloaded resources because of the strain on the system caused by retail transactional histories

Messaging systems connect applications by providing an information bus through which updates are published to subscribers. The drawbacks of messaging systems, according to Stonebraker, are (1) subscribers can integrate data only if the data owner has published it onto the information bus, (2) scalability problems, because the bandwidth of the information bus is too narrow to publish all enterprise data, and (3) difficulties in working with dynamic environments.

Data federation performs integration while leaving the source data in place. Multiple physical databases are integrated into a single logical one, and independent enterprise systems produce integrated global behavior through economic forces. Data federation systems retain local control while scaling to hundreds of machines. They also support a global view of enterprise data resources, and dynamic load balancing across system resources, and they adapt and adjust query execution accordingly.

After stating the four approaches Stonebraker (ibid., p. 44) makes three important points:

- "Data federation systems are coming. The only way to integrate real-time data in many independent systems is to federate the systems."
- "Data Transformation is a required feature," since "there are few semantically identical data sets. . . . In a data federation system, conversion is done as the end user accesses data."
- "You can achieve scalability to the enterprise only by logical integration." Messaging and data warehousing systems create physical integration in specific data stores. "Restricting integration to a single physical machine will prohibit enterprise level scalability. Only logical integration over multiple machines offers the possibility of enterprise scalability."

Further, he concludes that an enterprise must decide when to perform application integration and when to perform data integration. In addition, that application integration should be used "when performing update integration for small numbers of existing applications," whereas data integration should be used "when you need unified views or are integrating many systems."

If one does choose the data integration route, then the critical choices are between physical and logical integration, and between aged data and real-time data. Physical integration of aged data leads to data warehouses and data marts, whereas physical integration of real time data leads to the operational data store and messaging systems. Logical integration of either aged or real-time data, on the other hand, leads to data federation systems. Logical integration is necessary if it is impractical to move the data to a single location.

Finally, Stonebraker believes that there are powerful market trends moving away from data warehousing and toward data federation. One such trend is marked by business conditions "demanding real time information, which warehouses can't provide." The second trend is the increasing need of businesses to respond to changing business conditions and external events (especially in e-business). This need creates a corresponding need for IT solutions that can produce dynamic enterprise integration (DEI) (my term, rather than Stonebraker's), rather than static integration. The combination of these trends suggests a move toward data federation and away from data warehousing, because only data federation can produce the necessary access to both integrated real-time data about rapidly changing conditions and integrated aged data providing the historical and baseline information, needed for survival and competitive advantage.

Stonebraker's treatment of enterprise integration was one of those possibly seminal articles providing a philosophy that can quickly grab hold of the IT industry and provide direction for a major cycle of activity. As such, it deserves careful examination from readers and critics alike. The issues he raises need a full airing from as many points of view as possible. The remainder of this chapter will provide this airing and also an alternative point of view—the point of view of distributed information management system-based (DIMS-based) integration.

Natural and artificial systems integration

Enterprise integration is not synonymous with either integrating data or integrating applications, as Stonebraker's IT-centric viewpoint suggests. Enterprise integration refers to integrating a natural system—a social system, to be more precise—and not to integrating only one subsystem of this broader system—its artificial computing system.

When we use the unqualified general term loosely and apply it to artificial systems integration rather than natural systems integration, we gloss over the fact that there is not universal agreement about what we mean in this more specific context. We may all agree that we really do not mean enterprise integration as that term is applied to social systems. We also may agree that we all have in mind integration of certain aspects of the computing system of enterprises. But that is where our agreement ends.

Stonebraker distinguishes between enterprise data integration and enterprise application integration, and also between physical integration and logical integration within the enterprise data integration category. But as I indicated previously, one can also distinguish between enterprise content integration, enterprise artificial information integration, and enterprise artificial knowledge integration, as major categories of approaches to enterprise artificial systems integration. And one can also distinguish between logical and physical subtypes within each of these categories. One's view of what constitutes an adequate enterprise integration solution will depend on which of these types of integration one thinks is essential to the enterprise's ability to compete and adapt.

Stonebraker's view of enterprise artificial systems integration is also too restricted in its development of the application integration category. His discussion of data integration is relatively rich. His discussion of application integration is perfunctory, by comparison. And, considering the relatively short shrift he gives application integration, it is not unfair to say that his discussion is biased toward a data integration approach.

This is certainly the approach that has been most successful in physically integrating data in recent years. But you can't arrive at a fair assessment of its effectiveness for enterprise artificial systems integration through an analysis that either excludes its main competitors or provides them with less than comprehensive consideration. This is especially true now that the focus of software industry integration activity is shifting from physical integration, which favors data-centric approaches, to logical integration, which does not necessarily favor data.

Enterprise application integration (EAI)

Stonebraker criticizes EAI for focusing on synchronized updates across applications and not providing a unified view of data across the enterprise. He also faults it because each application has its own version of some key concept such as "customer" or "order," and he thinks that reconciling such "conceptual mismatches" is much more difficult than integrating the records in an underlying database. Finally, he thinks that the scalability obstacle inherent in integrating 100 different applications by creating 100 specific adapters connecting the applications to the integrative "glue" of an EAI system is insurmountable. These criticisms of EAI are hard to sustain without far more detailed evidence and benchmarking results than Stonebraker presents in his article.

First, certain EAI packages such as Vitria Technology's BusinessWare (Vitria, 2001) and Level8's Geneva Enterprise Integrator (GEI) (Level8, 2001), and Geneva Business Process Automator (GBPA) (Level8, 2001) do provide a unified view of the enterprise. GEI provides a unified view of objects, data, and methods across the enterprise. Vitria and GBPA provide a unified view of business processes and of data and methods as they relate to processes.

Second, certain EAI packages have the capability to handle conceptual mismatches. They do so by using an object model to provide multiple interpretations of the same data. Again, Level8's GEI provides a good example of an existing product that uses a semantic object model to resolve ambiguities across enterprise stovepipes.

Third, Stonebraker's scalability criticism needs to be documented with much more evidence before it can be uncritically accepted. All of the major EAI vendors claim scalability, and many use federation architectures containing distributed application servers to back that claim.

NEON (2001) and Vitria Technology, two of the examples cited by Stonebraker, claim scalability through distributed processing and broadly-based connectivity to varieties of data sources. Level8 GEI, meanwhile, offers as an integrative mechanism a virtual, in-memory, cached, self-reflexive object model, resident in distributed application servers, along with connectivity to data stores and applications of all types.

This is not to say that Stonebraker is necessarily incorrect in all his claims about the application integration approach. But he seems clearly incorrect in claiming that practitioners of the approach don't generally provide a unified view of the enterprise, and it will take a lot more proof than he presents to support his other two criticisms.

The data federation approach

Stonebraker's various comments on the data federation approach also contain some questionable arguments and conclusions. First, "data federation systems are coming." And it is true that federation is the way to go in enterprise artificial systems integration. But federation is not "the only way to integrate real time data in many independent systems," if by this Stonebraker means federating data stores alone. Real time data can also be integrated by federated systems of databases and application servers through an object layer, as has been amply demonstrated by various EAI vendors.

Second, while "data transformation is a required feature," since "there are few semantically identical data sets," it's also true that data transformation is not restricted to data integration approaches. If it is true that "in a data federation system, conversion is done as the end user accesses data," it is also true that in-place, real-time conversion can occur in any of the other major integration approaches, provided only that they employ both federated servers and an object layer for performing integration.

Third, while "you can achieve scalability to the enterprise only by logical integration," I cannot agree with the plain implication of the context of this remark, that a data federation approach is the only appropriate one. Logical integration is also achieved by a federated, object layer approach to integration, and that is the real competitor to Stonebraker's data federation approach, not data warehousing or messaging.

Fourth, the suggestion that application integration should be used "when performing update integration for small numbers of existing applications;" while data integration should be used "when you need unified views or are integrating many systems," is a direct consequence of the view that only logical integration through federated data systems is scalable. But, as I indicated earlier, this view is questionable and is in no way supported by Stonebraker's brief remarks on the subject.

Fifth, in stating that only data federation can produce the necessary access to both integrated real-time data about rapidly changing conditions and integrated aged data providing the historical and baseline information needed for survival and competitive advantage, Stonebraker again draws a conclusion that is dependent on his ill-supported critique of application integration and his refusal to consider other artificial systems integration approaches. He believes that only the federated data approach can produce DEI.

But such a conclusion is unsupported by his arguments against application integration and belied by his failure to consider approaches beyond data and application integration. It is also contradicted by the consideration that DEI must be based on more than data integration alone. To remain competitive, businesses must have more than current and accurate data. They must also have well-confirmed models, validated business rules and procedures, and other classes of useful knowledge, including software applications. An artificial system that provides true dynamic integration must handle changes in all components of knowledge and information, and not simply in the data-based ones. It is for this reason that the data federation approach is by its very nature inadequate. It integrates only islands of data, and it leaves most of the "islands of information" and knowledge of the enterprise still untouched.

Content integration

Stonebraker's treatment of the islands of information problem is also incomplete in that it focuses entirely on integrating islands of structured data rather than unstructured content. Physical integration of unstructured content requires extracting content from fragmented content stores (e.g., Lotus Notes, e-mail, text documents, word processing documents, reports) and through a process that may be called content warehousing, transforming and migrating it to a physical content warehouse.

Current document management systems do not need to transform content to a common format, because they have the capability to read and write to more than 200 document formats. Nevertheless, some transformation is becoming increasingly common in content warehousing as more and more conversion to XML is done. A content management solution that converts all documents to XML format and uses a centralized content store is an enterprise content warehouse (ECW).

Alternatively, content integration can also be accomplished through federated content stores. In these, integration is created by a combination of text mining and analysis capability, semantic networks or "knowledge maps," and connectivity to more than 200 content formats. The semantic network provides a common view of the content in the enterprise. Semantic networks for each member of the federated content store may be compared and transformed in gauging similarity.

Artificial information integration

Artificial information integration, like data integration, can be physical or logical. Since information is composed of both data and conceptual commitments, physical integration requires that both be extracted from their original disparate enterprise stores and, through a process of object warehousing that is very similar to data warehousing, be transformed and migrated to a physical object warehouse. Alternatively, multiple sources of information may be placed in communication through a messaging system in exactly the same way this occurs for data integration.

These physical integration alternatives have the same disadvantages for information integration that Stonebraker identifies for data integration. And again, a better solution for the integration problem is provided by federating information sources, just as it was by federating data and content sources.

An information federation, like data and content federations, does not migrate data or content anywhere; it manipulates data or content in place, according to the business rules specified in the system. It employs multiple distributed application servers along with multiple distributed data stores to maintain a unified view through a common object model. These application servers are called active (or artificial) information managers (AIMs) (Firestone, 1998). They provide process control and distribution services to the information federation to synchronize and adjust it to locally determined changes. Finally, like data and content federations, information federations employ broad ranging connectivity to read from and write to the distributed data and content stores and applications of the enterprise.

An information federation, like a data or content federation, is scalable. It is scalable because its connectivity to application servers allows it to access applications transparently; in addition, new information managers can be added as needed to distribute the processing and query load across broadly distributed resources.

Artificial knowledge integration

The artificial knowledge integration approach is very much like the information integration approach. The difference is in the nature of the information being processed. In the knowledge federation, knowledge production application servers support formal analytical modeling and data mining, apply validation criteria to the knowledge production process, and provide a supportive environment for testing and evaluating knowledge claims in both individual and group settings. Otherwise, the artificial knowledge manager (AKM) (Firestone, 1999) uses the same object model, process distribution and control services, and connectivity features used by AIMs, with one important difference, to be explained in Chapter 10. Knowledge federations share the same capability to provide a unified view, the ability to transform data in place, and scalability as data, content, and information federations. Knowledge federations will be important later on when we discuss enterprise knowledge portals in Chapter 13.

The DIMS solution to the "islands of information" problem

The data, content, information, knowledge, and application integration approaches to enterprise artificial systems integration can all be implemented using distributed information management architecture (DIMA) (See Firestone, 1998, 1998a, 1998b, 1998c on the closely related distributed knowledge management architecture). The key architectural components of the DIMS are:

- The artificial information manager (AIM)
- Application servers
- Stateless application servers
- Application servers that maintain state
- Object/data stores
- Object request brokers (ORBs, e.g., CORBA, COM+) and other components, Web-based protocols, and standards supporting distributed processing

- Intelligent agents (to be discussed in Chapter 6)
- Client application components

The AIM

All the components in the system are integrated by the distributed AIM application server (See Persistence Software, 1998, Rymer, 1998; Template Software, 1998), assisted by the intelligent agents. Here is an account of AIM features.

The AIM provides process control services, an object model of the DIMS, and connectivity to all enterprise information, data stores, and applications. Figure 5.1 illustrates the range of data stores and applications integrated by the AIM, but, of course, provides an incomplete listing of the possibilities. In addition, the AIM provides connectivity to object request brokers (not illustrated in the figure).

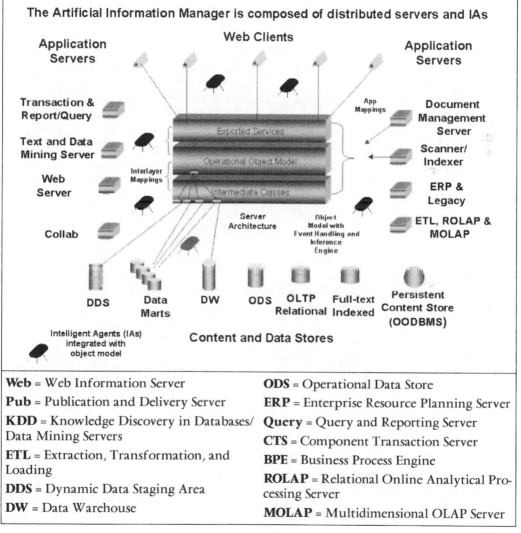

Web = Web Information Server	**ODS** = Operational Data Store
Pub = Publication and Delivery Server	**ERP** = Enterprise Resource Planning Server
KDD = Knowledge Discovery in Databases/ Data Mining Servers	**Query** = Query and Reporting Server
	CTS = Component Transaction Server
ETL = Extraction, Transformation, and Loading	**BPE** = Business Process Engine
DDS = Dynamic Data Staging Area	**ROLAP** = Relational Online Analytical Processing Server
DW = Data Warehouse	**MOLAP** = Multidimensional OLAP Server

Figure 5.1. An AIM and examples of components it integrates.

Process control services

Process Control Services in the AIM include:

- In-memory proactive object state management and synchronization across distributed objects (in business process engines) and through intelligent agents
- Component management and workflow management through distributed business process engines and intelligent agents
- Transactional multithreading
- Business rule management and processing
- Metadata management

I will describe each of these subsequently.

Object state management and synchronization

The DIMS supports a variety of data stores and application servers that allow batch, transaction, and DSS processing to occur in the same system. The result of this diversity of processing activities is to introduce frequent and rapid changes into the DIMS, its data stores, and its application servers. Change in data, methods (including business rules), and behavior is the "law of life" in the DIMS.

The problem of managing, synchronizing and adapting to these changes in the DIMS is the dynamic integration problem (DIP). A primary function of the DIMS, and its AIM integrative component, is to automate dynamic enterprise integration (DEI) as much as is practicable. To perform dynamic enterprise integration, the AIM must

- Look for changes in shared objects and additions to the total pool of objects and relationships
- Alert all system components sharing the objects experiencing such changes
- Make decisions about which changes should be implemented in each affected component throughout the system

The AIM accomplishes these tasks by using its in-memory, shared, active object model with its support for event-driven behavior, a common view of the system's objects, declarative business rules, and caching of data along with use of partial instantiation of objects (see below).

In addition, the AIM relies on a persistent representation of the object model. The objects in the object model are reflexive—aware of their present state and any change of state. The AIM accomplishes proactive monitoring and coordinating of changes in its shared objects through their reflexivity and capacity for event-driven behavior, and through software agents (see Chapter 6). The capacity for event-driven behavior causes the objects to adjust in response to event-induced changes in some shared objects by making corresponding changes in themselves.

Component management and synchronization

Like objects, components can also be shared across applications and physical platforms. And they also change frequently and rapidly and require DEI. Component management is the ability to monitor, coordinate, and synchronize changes in components and is analogous to object state management. It, too, needs to be performed in real time, and it too requires proactive, in-memory operation to be most effective. Component management and synchronization in the AIM requires much the same set of capabilities as object state management and synchronization and can benefit from the use of software agents.

Use case and workflow management and synchronization

The DIMS supports business processes by assisting efforts to gather, organize, create, maintain, and enhance knowledge about them, and also by providing support for planning, implementing, monitoring, and evaluating the course of the business process. Both use cases, and workflows are task sequences within these activities that process, route, and distribute information products, but the connotations of the two terms are somewhat different. The use case concept looks at a task sequence from the point of view of the valued outcome the user will get from that task sequence. Workflow, on the other hand, refers to the automated sequence constructed to implement a use case, a part of a use case, or a set of related use cases. AIM process control services must provide the means to manage both use cases and workflows by

- Facilitating specification of routing and distribution of data, information, and knowledge
- Supporting rapid and easy change in the routing structure, the distribution process, and the business rules governing the workflow
- Providing the capability to either store the product of a workflow task or "push" it to the next step in the workflow
- Providing the capability to distribute the workflow process across multiple computers
- Providing the capability to gather knowledge resources to support the workflow
- Supporting collaborative transactions among workflow participants
- Providing the capability to simulate the workflow
- Providing the capability to customize workflows by integrating custom, legacy, or external data and/or applications

While the AIM in its role as a static business process engine can easily support areas one and two in the foregoing list, AIM agents may also be applied in workflow process control areas 3–8 as outlined in Chapter 6.

In addition to the above, the AIM supports management of workflows composed of tasks performed by multiple application servers of diverse processing type. For example, a collaborative planning workflow application involving a planning business process engine and multiple database servers can be integrated by an AIM. Another example is an integrated database marketing/ Customer relationship management (CRM) workflow involving ETL, Operational data store, DSS database, data mining, business process engine, and Web server components.

Transactional multithreading

Transactional multithreading is the ability to manage each thread within a process as a separate transaction. Each thread can represent an instance of an active object.

Because they support transactional multithreading, AIMs provide for multiple objects, belonging to different classes, to reside in the same process. This form of multitasking allows for concurrent execution of disparate business rules associated with different objects. It provides the AIM with parallelism useful in workflow management as well as in object and component DI.

Business rule and metadata management and processing

Business rule and metadata management and processing are both derivative services of object and component management and synchronization. Business rules are encapsulated in objects and components as methods, while metadata is encapsulated as attributes. So part of what we mean when we refer to object and component state management and synchronization is management and processing of business rules and metadata.

In-memory active object model/persistent object store. The AIM provides an active object model. It is distributed. Much of it is shared across physical platforms. And it can be either persistent or resident in memory. An in-memory active object model/persistent object store is characterized by

- Event-driven behavior
- DIMS-wide model with shared representation
- Declarative business rules
- Caching along with partial instantiation of objects
- A persistent object store for the AIM
- Reflexive objects

Event-driven behavior. Object methods in the active object model are triggered by (1) events, (2) agents, and/or (3) programmed periodic activation. Events include user inputs, changes in object attribute values, changes in attributes themselves, or changes in methods themselves.

Events can trigger agent behavior, which then follows an autonomous course in implementing adjustments. Event-driven behavior is implemented in the DIMS through sequences of rules having antecedents and consequents.

DIMS-wide model with shared representation. Many of the objects in the AIM are shared across distributed physical platforms—either data stores or application servers. In fact, the AIM may be viewed as a special distributed application server or business process engine that maintains state, shares a set of reflexive objects across physical platforms, and manages and integrates multiple processes changing these shared objects. It is this sharing of objects and components across

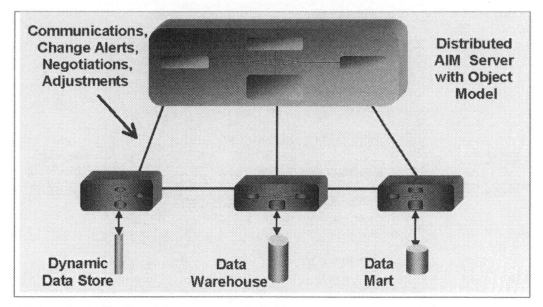

Figure 5.2. A distributed AIM server, shared objects, and dynamic integration

platforms that creates a common view of the AIM and its metadata. Figure 5.2 illustrates the role of shared objects in the AIM and in DEI.

Declarative business rules. Both declarative and procedural business-rule networks are supported as methods in classes and objects of the AIM model. Declarative-rule networks are those whose rules fire in parallel to determine an outcome. Procedural-rule networks are those whose rules fire in sequence. Figure 5.3 illustrates declarative and procedural rule networks.

Event-driven behavior in the AIM is frequently determined by sequences of declarative rules or rule networks constituting procedures (i.e., procedural-rule networks). Agent-driven behavior is triggered by events but then is determined by the agent's autonomous program.

Partial instantiation of objects. The ability to perform partial instantiation of objects is particularly important to the AIM in allowing it to develop rapid query performance. In partial instantiation only those attributes called for in a query and only those records specified are brought into the in-memory object model. In this way, the data entering the AIM from data stores in the DIMS can be "chunked," and the amount of data that the AIM must handle can be minimized. As a result, it is much more likely that the difficult processing involved in any query can be done in the AIM's "virtual database" in-memory. Figure 5.4 illustrates partial instantiation of objects by an AIM.

The persistent object store. The AIM uses either a relational database or an OODBMS to store the active object model in persistent form. In either case the active logical object model must be mapped to the physical data model of the database. The mapping is straightforward in the case of an OODBMS, because the structure of the active object model matches the structure of the database.

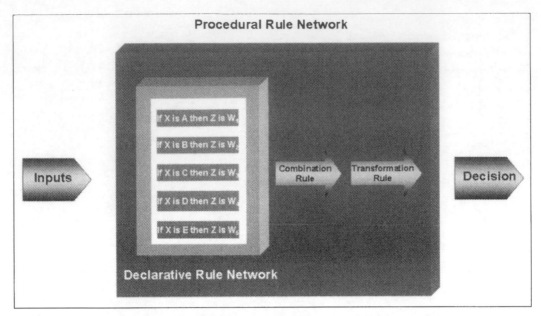

Figure 5.3. Declarative and procedural rule networks.

There is no "impedance mismatch," because there is no need to unwrap the logical objects and map their attributes onto physical table columns. Such unwrapping is necessary with an RDBMS, and if one is used for persistent storage of the object model, a performance penalty is paid.

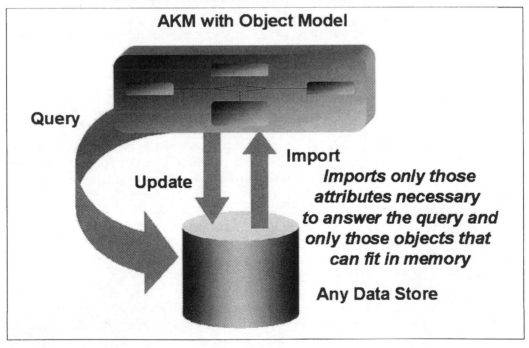

Figure 5.4. The AIM and partial instantiation.

Reflexive objects. AIMs use reflexive objects. Objects are reflexive if they are aware of their present state and any change of state. In this way they are like human agents in natural knowledge management and other business processes. When combined with event-driven behavior, reflexive objects provide the foundation for automatic propagation of events and changes in state among themselves.

Software agents

The role of intelligent software agents in the AIM is discussed in the context of their broader role in EIPs in Chapter 6.

Connectivity services

Connectivity Services have the following:

- Language: APIs: C, C++, XML, Java, CORBA, COM+;
- Databases: relational, ODBC, OODBMS, hierarchical, network, flat file
- Wrapper connectivity for application software: custom-, CORBA-, or COM+-based
- Applications connectivity whether applications are mainframe-, server-, or desktop-based.

Application servers

The development of multi-tier distributed processing systems was characterized by the appearance of application servers. Application servers provide services to other components in a distributed processing system by executing business logic and data logic on data accessed from database servers.

The class of application servers is subdivided by Rymer's (1998, p. 1) distinction between "stateless" and in-memory server environments. Application servers with active in-memory object models he calls business process engines (BPEs), a name similar to Vaskevitch's (1993, Chapter 8) business process automation engines.

Stateless application servers

According to Rymer: "Business state is the information that describes the momentary status of the organization. To create business state, most applications acquire data from a database and then load it into memory for manipulations by the user." (1998, p. 1) This is the "stateless" approach because, in it, a back-end database, rather than internal memory, manages state.

Among stateless application servers Rymer distinguishes:

- Web information servers (they provide access to databases from Web browsers)
- Component servers (they "provide data access and interaction frameworks for software components")
- Transaction processing monitors (they coordinate transactions within a distributed system)

Business process engines: application servers that maintain state

"Business Process Engines manage the most important business state both in a fast in-memory environment and in close coordination with back-end databases." (Rymer 1998, p. 9) Because of their in-memory maintenance of state, BPEs process many user requests without help from a database. In addition, they specialize in complex business-rule processing, because their ability to maintain state is a special advantage in performing such processing.

KM software applications such as KDD/data mining servers, publication and delivery servers, the AIM itself, and many other server types are all BPEs. The job of the DIMS is to integrate the burgeoning list of BPEs into an enterprisewide system.

Therefore, an important aspect of specifying the DIMS is specifying the current universe of application servers and projecting the appearance of new types. The following are some criteria for defining types of business process engines:

- Whether they are distributed across physical components or not
- Whether a BPE application server deals with a single or multiple business processes
- The business process that the BPE supports

Distributed BPEs can be a powerful tool for upgrading performance in DIMSs, as well as for integrating their various components. An AIM is just a BPE that is both distributed and encompasses all of a DIMS's processes. A multi-process BPE can fall short of being an AIM, and can instead be restricted to a cluster of related processes. So, there are at least three types suggested by this criterion: a single process BPE, a BPE cluster, and an AIM.

How well a multi-process BPE performs will correlate with the extent of its distribution and with the complexity of the process it must support. But holding complexity constant, single-process, nondistributed BPEs will generally perform better than multi-process nondistributed BPEs. So, multi-process BPEs will generally be distributed BPEs.

The third criterion for classifying BPEs is the business process supported. For example, here is an incomplete classification of BPE application servers based on knowledge-related, KM, and data warehousing subprocesses.

- Collaborative planning
- Extraction, transformation, and loading (ETL)
- Knowledge discovery in databases (KDD)
- Knowledge base/object/component model maintenance and change management (the AKM)
- Knowledge publication and delivery (KPD)
- Computer-based training (CBT)
- Report production and delivery (RPD);
- ROLAP
- Operational data store (ODS) application server
- Forecasting/simulation server

- ERP servers
- Financial risk management, telecommunications service provisioning, transportation scheduling, stock trading servers
- Workflow servers

Object/data stores

There are few, if any, limits on the types of object/data stores in the AIMS. These data stores incorporate objects, components, or their attributes in a nonvolatile persistent form.

Legacy data, flat files, Relational databases, object relational databases, OODBMSs, multidimensional data stores, and vertical technology databases all fit within the AIMS.

In addition, the AIMS must also integrate image, text, report, video, audio, and file document types. That is, it is the job of the DIMS to develop and maintain connectivity to various data stores, and not simply DBMSs.

Object request brokers (ORBs) and other components, protocols, and standards supporting distributed processing

ORBs provide an intermediate layer between clients and servers in a distributed network. The ORB receives requests from clients and selects servers to satisfy the requests. The ORB can activate appropriate servers. The ORB can translate data between clients and servers. Generally, ORB servers are stateless and therefore are not BPEs (though this is not a necessary consequence of ORB specifications).

The AIM must support common object request broker architecture (CORBA), component object model (COM+), eXtended object-oriented broker architecture (ZOOBA), simple object access protocol (SOAP), Enterprise Java Beans, remote method invocation (RMI), XML, and Web services to fulfill its integrative function. That is, it must be able to act as CORBA, COM+, ZOOBA, etc. servers and clients as required. In this way, the AIM, with its greater integrative functionality, is built "on top of" an ORB or other distributed networking server and architectural standard.

Client-side application components

I discuss the requirements for client-side application components below in the section on solving the islands of automation problem.

Summary

DIM architecture provides a unified view of the enterprise and handles semantic conversions "on the fly" through the AIM's object model. It's also scalable to the enterprise level because of (1) its distributed, federated structure; (2) its partial instantiation capability, allowing it to load parts of objects into memory; (3) its virtual in-memory cached object store; and (4) its broad connectivity to data stores and applications.

The DIMS, federations, and the enterprise information portal

Enterprise information and knowledge portals seem to represent an evolution and convergence of both data warehousing/business intelligence applications and unstructured content management applications. They also represent a very active area of new business activity, growing sales and profits, corporate mergers and acquisitions, and aggressive new application development. The key to the success of EIPs (and EKPs) is their performance and their capability in adjusting to change in the EIP or EKP application. In the end, the success of both is dependent on architecture, and, in particular, on the success of architectures offering logical integration in providing performance and adaptability.

The issue of which type of federated architecture to use will be a critical issue in determining the success and future of EIP/EKP applications. The approach we follow in solving the islands of information problem for portals should not be a data-integration approach or a content-integration approach. I think, instead, it should be at least an information-integration approach (and for reasons to be developed later transcending the problem of integrating islands of information, it should actually be a knowledge integration approach) as embodied in DIM architecture and the DIMS system solution, rather than physical approaches or other types of federations. I will develop this contention in the context of a more concrete discussion of portal architectures later on in this chapter. Now, though, it's time to turn to EASI and the islands of automation problem.

Solving the "islands of automation" problem

The islands of information problem is about the need to integrate data, content, information, and knowledge stores and application servers, both stateless and business process engines (Firestone, 1998c). Solving this problem involves addressing the ten types of integration (data, content, information, knowledge, and application cross-classified by physical and logical) distinguished earlier.

The islands of automation problem is about the need to integrate today's desktop environment of disparate, program-by-program, task-isolated IT applications. It focuses on replacing the Windows desktop's unrelated application icons with a new interface that emphasizes a personalized combination of subject matter (content) categorization, networking, and workflow patterns. So, it emphasizes three different types of EASI: (1) UI subject matter integration, (2) application integration through workflow, and (3) information integration from application to application through ad hoc navigation while sharing information and maintaining a common view across them.

Subject matter integration

When users see their personalized enterprise portal interface, they should see a reflection of the portion of their cognitive map or semantic network (sometimes also referred to as a concept network or a "knowledge map"), relevant to their interpretation of the various roles they play in their enterprise. One aspect of this "cognitive map" is its hierarchical classification of subject matter. Hierarchical classification of subject matter is an essential feature of the first and second gen-

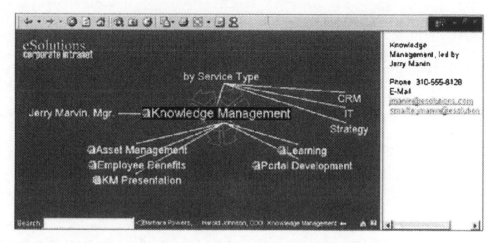

Figure 5.5. TheBrain interface. (Source: TheBrain Technologies Corporation [2002] at http://www.thebrain.com.)

eration of EIP products, modeled as they are on MyYahoo. Hierarchical classification is also the essence of taxonomy development and use and is currently one of the areas of greatest concern in EIP development. In fact, some commentators (Koenig, 2002, p. 21) think that an awareness of the importance of content and its retrievability is the "third stage of knowledge management" (a view that I find somewhat narrow and information technology focused. See Chapters 7–9 on knowledge and knowledge management, including "Second-Generation Knowledge Management").

Current portal products (with the exception of TheBrain EKP) (TheBrain Technologics Corporation, 2002) have not yet incorporated the nonhierarchical network relationships found in the cognitive maps of users. These subject matter relationships are just as important as hierarchical relationships to a user's view of the world and therefore to (1) providing effective access to information related to that view and (2) to the user's decision making. The next step in portal subject matter integration is the development of such network relationships, based on tracking of the nonhierarchical patterns of information and knowledge seeking behavior. Figure 5.5 is an illustration of TheBrain interface (TheBrain Technology Corporation, 2002). This interface suggests the coming of a more flexible, networked portal interface.

Enterprise application integration through workflow

Remember John Mann's (1999a, p. 1) definition of EAI and his emphasis on workflow as one of the ways to control the flow of information in integrating applications? First generation portal UIs, once again, provide subject matter classifications to users. Applications in these portals are integrated only through their middleware and back-end stores. Within the portal itself they still "present" to the user as islands of automation. Integration can be introduced by providing the portals the capability to present and, where possible, implement partially—and even sometimes fully—automated personalized processes or parts of processes to users.

Mann (1999, p. 1) defines workflow as "automated control of process execution." His definition makes clear that workflow is an artificial process, an IT construct.

In another place (Firestone, 1999b), I have distinguished business processes from workflow, by pointing out that use cases (Jacobson, Booch, and Rumbaugh, 1999) and workflows are both task sequences within broader business processes. They process, route, and distribute information products of software applications. The use case concept looks at a task sequence from the viewpoint of the valued outcome the user will get from it (ibid. p. 432). Workflow, on the other hand, refers to the automated system—that is, the new application, constructed to implement a use case, a part of a use case, or a set of related use cases.

So workflows integrate software applications by procedurally linking them in task sequences and by automating or partially automating these sequences through a higher order system. This form of integration is represented in the portal UI, but unlike subject matter integration, it immediately and necessarily reaches beyond the portal UI and directly integrates middle-tier application servers and back-end data, content, information, and knowledge stores in the workflow. Of course, it cannot ensure the integrated behavior of middle-tier and back-end processing. But if the integration of islands of information has been successfully managed, EAI through workflow produces a comprehensive form of integration of both islands of information and islands of automation.

Information integration through ad hoc navigation

While workflow integration is desirable in connecting islands of automation as far as it goes, it does not address the user's need to accomplish work by moving from application to application in an ad hoc manner while sharing information and maintaining a common view. Thus, if a user is working in one application accessed through a portal, EASI requires that the capability must be there to access information supplied by that application and then access related information accessible through another application through minimal interface-based navigation. This form of integration has been implemented by TopTier and acquired by SAP Portals, and will be discussed in greater detail in Chapter 17.

EIP integration and architecture

In addressing the solution to the problem of EIP integration, the question of what is to be integrated (the exact nature of the problem) must be addressed. The answer will drive the architecture selected for the portal. Here are the main approaches to portal architecture, either currently practiced or easily anticipated:

- *The passive access to content (PAC) approach.* Only the portal interface and only subject matter and isolated applications are integrated through content classification and linking into the portal interface).
- *The data federation integration (DFI) approach.* The portal interface and structured data stores are integrated through data federation.
- *The structured application integration (SAI) approach.* The portal interface, both subject matter and workflow of enterprise applications, and structured data stores and applications are integrated.

- *The distributed content management (DCM) approach.* The portal interface, both subject matter and workflow of enterprise applications, and content management content stores and applications are integrated
- *The portal application integration (PAI) approach.* The portal interface, both subject matter and workflow of enterprise applications, and all stores and application servers within and across both structured and content management areas are integrated

The PAC approach

The PAC approach to EIP architecture is currently the most common approach. In it, the Web browser is customized to provide the portal interface. A Web server and an application server(s) then provide: a "business" directory of content and applications accessible through the portal, publishing, subscription, and delivery services; import/export interfaces; and metadata crawlers/filters, search engines, security, and administration facilities. The application servers then connect to various application sources and data and content stores to provide content to users through connections called "gadgets," "widgets," content delivery agents (CDAs), or, most frequently, "portlets." The applications could be decision-processing applications, content-management applications, OLTP applications, and/or collaborative processing applications. The content stores could range from structured data stores to image or video libraries. PAC architecture is illustrated in Figure 5.6.

In the PAC approach, none of the external applications accessed by the portal need be integrated with any others. Portal integration is at the user interface level only, and involves only hierarchical subject matter classification. Perhaps docu-

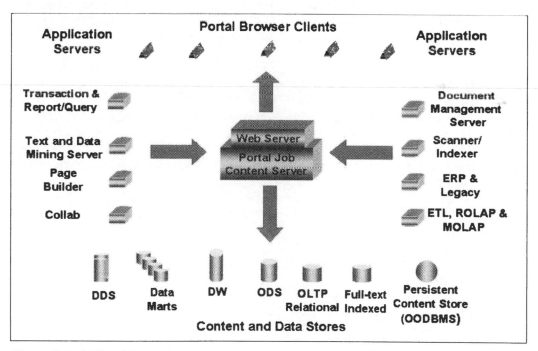

Figure 5.6. PAC architecture.

ment creation using information from different applications is supported, but the ability to access the attributes of objects or tables across different portal applications is not simultaneously available to the end user through the portal interface of those applications. All but a few EIP solutions currently being implemented in the current period of portal implementation are PAC portals.

The DFI approach

This approach builds further on the PAC approach. It begins with portal-based integration and then adds integration of structured data stores through data federation. Data federation performs integration while leaving the source data in place. Multiple physical databases are integrated into a single logical one, and independent enterprise systems produce integrated global behavior through economic forces. Data federation systems retain local control while scaling to hundreds of machines. They also support a global view of enterprise data resources and dynamic load balancing across system resources, and they adapt and adjust query execution accordingly.

Portals based on an enterprise data integration approach are an attractive alternative in the portal space. One of the main proponents of the data federation approach is Cohera Systems, a start-up implementing ideas of Michael Stonebraker. In 1999 Cohera received considerable attention and attracted such portal vendors as Viador and Information Advantage (acquired by Sterling Software which, in turn, was acquired by Computer Associates) as strategic partners. It represents a trend toward integrating the "back end" of enterprise information portals through a data federation architectural approach.

The attempt to integrate portal applications through data-based integration falls short of the integrative goals set by Merrill Lynch (Shilakes and Tylman, 1998) in its attempt to formulate the EIP concept. First, data-based integration does not address the issue of integrating content and document management with structured data management. Second, the logical integration implemented in the data federation approach is exceeded in its scope by the logical integration achievable by a federated, object layer approach to integration. This approach integrates data and methods across the enterprise, rather than data alone, and carries with it a greater capability for intelligent adaptation in the face of changes in objects and data.

To remain competitive, businesses must have more than current and accurate data. They must also have well-confirmed models, validated business rules and procedures, and other classes of useful knowledge, including software applications. A system that provides true dynamic integration must handle changes in all components of knowledge and information, and not simply in the data-based ones. It is for this reason that the data federation approach to portal back-end integration is by its very nature inadequate. It integrates only islands of data while leaving most of the "islands of information" and knowledge of the enterprise still untouched.

The SAI approach

The SAI approach includes portal interface subject matter, workflow, and ad hoc navigation-based integration, but focuses on integrating the structured data and application sources accessed by an EIP. In SAI, an architecture that integrates existing DSS, ERP, and other structured data applications and makes them available through the portal is devised. But there is no integrative layer for content management applications except that related to the basic portal function of accessing individual content sources and applications.

The SAI architecture provides an integrative layer composed of an object model whose component objects encapsulate metadata and methods for monitoring, managing, and synchronizing that metadata across the decision-processing and other structured data applications being integrated by the portal. SAI architecture needs to be distinguished from the metadata "hub and spokes" architecture now frequently implemented in data warehousing systems.

In the hub and spokes architecture, an object model is implemented for a "metadata hub" application server (White, 1999, pp. 6–7). The hub, which can be distributed across multiple servers, maintains a common view of data and metadata in the system, drives the data warehousing process, and integrates metadata across the component applications and data marts found in the data warehousing/DSS portion of the business information supply chain. But the function of this metadata hub is to facilitate technical staff management of the flow of metadata along the supply chain, so that the metadata can be manually synchronized.

In the SAI architecture, in contrast, the object model has methods for performing these functions, but it is also programmed with methods for automatically adjusting and synchronizing the various metadata stores in the system. Within certain limits this "active metadata hub" in the SAI architecture manages the integration of the structured data applications in the EIP without administrative intervention. In fact, SAI architecture is an instance of the pattern of DIM architecture illustrated earlier. It is the first of three such patterns that may become popular in portal architecture.

The "hub and spokes" architecture is available in applications external to EIPs. So, if this type of integration is desired, the PAC architecture can be and is used and connected to a structured data decision processing application that integrates data warehousing and ERP applications. That is, the orientation of the portal to external applications is kept passive, and the integrated structured data application is added to the portal through a "portlet," "gadget," or "widget." But SAI architecture is not already built into decision-processing off-the-shelf software, so if it is a requirement, the DIM pattern it is based on will need to be implemented as part of portal development.

The DCM approach

The DCM approach develops an architecture that integrates the portal interface, workflows, and ad hoc navigation as well as the components of the content management life cycle by using a Distributed Content Manager. This architecture is another instance of the DIM architectural pattern described previously. The DCM provides process control services, an object model of the distributed content management system (the application described by DCM architecture), and connectivity to all file formats used to store content, and to all applications for manipulating content. Figure 5.7 illustrates the range of content stores and applications integrated by the DCM. In addition, the DCM provides connectivity to ORBs and other distributed processing network components and standards (not illustrated in the figure).

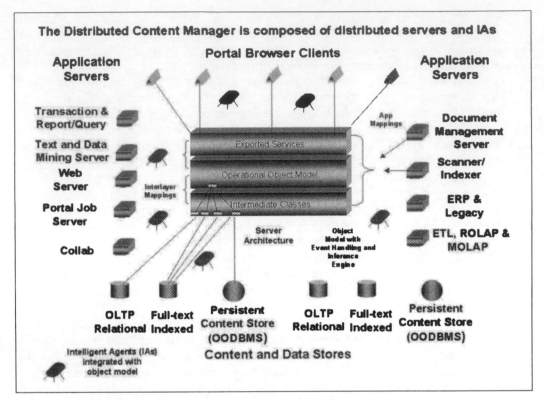

Figure 5.7. DCM architecture.

Process Control Services in the DCM include

- In-memory proactive object state management and synchronization across distributed objects and through intelligent agents
- Component management and workflow management through intelligent agents
- Transactional multithreading
- Business-rule management and processing and
- Metadata management

The DCM's in-memory active object model/persistent object store is characterized by

- Event-driven behavior
- A DCMS-wide model with shared representation across distributed DCM application servers
- Declarative and procedural business rules
- Caching of the object model along with partial instantiation of objects
- A persistent object store for the portions of the DCM object model that cannot be cached
- Reflexive objects (objects aware of their own state)

Connectivity Services include

- *Language APIs*—C, C++, Java, XML, CORBA, COM+, SOAP, Enterprise Java beans, RMI, etc.
- *Content and databases*—text, relational, ODBC, OODBMS, hierarchical, network, flat file, document sources accessible through various open standards
- *"Wrapper" connectivity for application software*—custom-, Web Services-, CORBA-, or COM-based
- *Content applications connectivity*—whether applications are mainframe-, server-, or desktop-based

DCM architecture provides a unified view of content objects in the enterprise and handles semantic conversions "on the fly" through the DCM's object model. It is also scalable to the enterprise level due to (1) its distributed, federated structure, (2) its partial instantiation capability (the ability to load parts of objects into memory) (3) its virtual in-memory cached object store, and (4) its broad connectivity to content stores and applications.

Like SAI architecture, DCM architecture has not been implemented in off-the-shelf content management products. The closest thing to it is probably Documentum's EDMS/Right Sizing Product (Documentum, 1998), and its successors. This product has a lot of the DCM features, but it does not implement the DCM entirely, since the Documentum objects don't contain the inference engine and communication capabilities inherent in DCM objects. So it would not be possible to implement DCM architecture by adding Documentum's product suite to an EIP product, or by using its corporate portal along with the product suite. If DCM integration is desired, it would, again, need to be implemented as part of portal development.

The PAI approach

The Portal application integration approach is an attempt to implement a comprehensive portal architecture that integrates both structured information management and content management aspects of EIPs internally and across application and data types. PAI architecture, another instance of the DKM architectural pattern, is very similar to DCM architecture. But there are differences.

PAI incorporates an integrative layer composed of an AIM, modeling both content and structured aspects of an EIP. Since the AIM integrates both structure and content, the resulting architecture combines the features of PAC, SAI, and DCM architectures and also addresses the interactions of structure and content in a way not addressed by the other architectures. Figure 5.8 illustrates PAI architecture.

The AIM's in-memory active object model/persistent object store is characterized by objects having:

- Structured data attributes as well as content attributes
- methods for manipulating structured data including complex analytical models

- Connectivity services include all of the connectivity available to the DCM
- Structured data applications connectivity whether applications are mainframe-, server-, or desktop-based.

AIM architecture provides a unified view of all objects in the enterprise and handles semantic conversions "on the fly" through the AIM's object model. The object model can also represent subject matter integration of both the hierarchical and networking type. It can also represent workflow models integrating enterprise applications within the portal interface. It is also scalable to the enterprise level due to (1) its distributed, federated structure; (2) its partial instantiation capability (the ability to load parts of objects into memory); (3) its virtual in-memory cached object store; and (4) its broad connectivity to content stores and applications.

Like the SAI and DCM architectures, PAI has, generally, not been implemented in off-the-shelf information management products. PAI integration needs to be implemented as part of portal development projects and it will take substantial effort to accomplish. Yet it needs to be done because it is the only architectural approach that will fulfill the promise of enterprise information portals, solve both the islands problems, and create the desktops without boundaries that are needed to truly make the EIP the work place for tomorrow's knowledge workers.

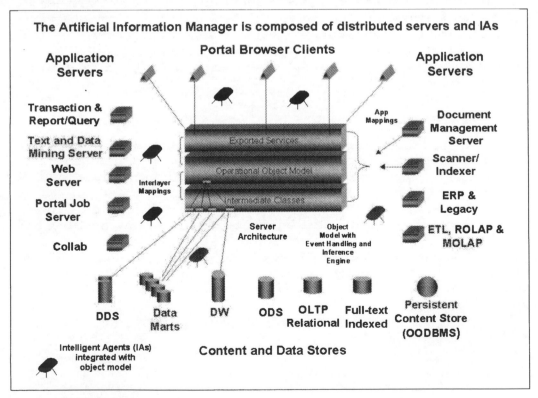

Figure 5.8. PAI architecture.

The incremental PAI approach

Among the five architectural approaches, the ideal is the PAI. It is the form of integration that addresses the thirteen types of EASI and solves both of the island problems. The types of EASI addressed by PAI are as follows:

- Physical data integration
- Logical data integration
- Physical content integration
- Logical content integration
- Physical artificial information integration
- Logical artificial information integration
- Physical artificial knowledge integration
- Logical artificial knowledge integration
- Physical application integration
- Logical application integration
- Subject matter integration of the UI
- Application integration through workflow
- Information integration through ad hoc navigation across applications through the portal UI.

What makes things interesting in the real world of implementing EIPs is that the PAI approach, even though it is the most desirable, is also the most demanding technically. In some respects, the problem is loosely analogous to developing an enterprise data warehouse from a set of data marts. To try to implement a "galactic" data warehouse all at once is not wise if you want to maximize the probability of success. But you also should not construct unrelated individual data marts without constructing an architecture that will relate these through conformed dimensions and metadata as you follow an incremental path to the data warehouse (Kimball, Reeves, Ross, and Thornthwaite, 1998, pp. 153–164).

A similar policy can apply to EIP construction. Each application added to an EIP should not only be provided access to the portal interface but should also be modeled using object modeling techniques in the PAI integrative layer. If the AIM is preplanned and gradually constructed with each incremental addition to an EIP, the basis for a fully integrated portal will develop over time.

Summary

In this chapter, I introduced a framework for viewing enterprise artificial systems integration (EASI), a more comprehensive concept than EAI. After showing that a classification of EASI leads to the idea of DIM architecture as the appropriate construct for enterprise knowledge portals, I raised the specific question of the appropriate architecture for portal integration in the context of a comparative approach and then identified six approaches to EIP architecture. These are as follows:

- The passive access to content (PAC) approach (only the portal interface is integrated)

- The data federation Integration (DFI) approach
- The structured application integration (SAI) approach (the portal interface and structured data stores and applications are integrated)
- The distributed content management (DCM) approach (the portal interface and content management content stores and applications are integrated)
- The portal application integration (PAI) approach (the portal interface and all stores and applications within and across both structured and content management areas are integrated)
- The incremental PAI approach (a portal constructed according to an integrative architectural design using a subset of enterprise applications initially and gradually adding the remaining enterprise applications over time)

Most current portals implement one of the first two architectures. But the incremental PAI approach is the future of EIP development, because it is the only one that solves the twin problems of Enterprise Artificial Systems Integration by providing all 13 types of EASI.

References

Documentum, Inc. (1998). "Delivering True Enterprise Value: Technology and Architecture of the Documentum Enterprise Document Management System (EDMS)," *Documentum White Paper*, Documentum, Inc., Pleasanton, CA.

Firestone, J.M. (1998). "Architectural Evolution in Data Warehousing," *Executive Information Systems White Paper No. 11*. Wilmington, DE. Available at http://www.dkms.com/White_Papers.htm

Firestone, J.M. (1998a). "DKMS Brief No. One: The Corporate Information Factory or The Corporate Knowledge Factory?" *Executive Information Systems, DKMS Brief*. Wilmington, DE, at http://www.dkms.com/White_Papers.htm.

Firestone, J.M. (1998b). "DKMS Brief No. Three: Software Agents in Distributed Knowledge Management Systems, "*Executive Information Systems, DKMS Brief*. Wilmington, DE, at http://www.dkms.com/White_Papers.htm.

Firestone, J.M. (1998c). "DKMS Brief No. Four: Business Process Engines in Distributed Knowledge Management Systems," *Executive Information Systems, DKMS Brief*, Wilmngton, DE, at http://www.dkms.com/White_Papers.htm.

Firestone, J.M. (1999). "The Artificial Knowledge Manager Standard: A Strawman," *Executive Information Systems KMCI Working Paper No. 1*. Wilmington, DE, available at http://www.dkms.com/White_Papers.htm.

Jacobson, I.; Booch, G.; and Rumbaugh, J. (1999). *The Unified Software Development Process* (Reading, MA: Addison-Wesley).

Kimball, R.; Reeves, L.; Ross, M.; and Thornthwaite, W. (1998). *The Data Warehouse Life Cycle Toolkit* (New York: John Wiley & Sons).

Koenig, Michael E.D. (2002). "The third stage of KM emerges," *KMWorld*, 11, No. 3 (March, 2002) 20–21, 28.

Level8 Systems, Inc. (2001), at http://www.level8.com.

Linthicum, D.S. (1999). "EAI without the Hype," *Enterprise Development* (July, 1999), 1–13.

Mann, J.E. (1999). "Workflow and EAI," *EAI Journal*, 1, No. 3 (September–October, 1999), 49–53.

Mann, J.E. (1999). "Workflow and Enterprise Application Integration," at http://www.messageq.com/workflow/approaches_to_EAI_2.html.

New Era of Networks, Inc. (2001), at http://neonsoft.com.

Persistence Software (1998). "The PowerTier Server: A Technical Overview" *Persistence White Paper*, Emeryville, CA: at http://www.persistence.com/products/tech_overview.html.

Rymer, J. (1998). "Business Process Engines, A New Category of Server Software, Will Burst the Barriers in Distributed Application Performance Engines," *Upstream Consulting White Paper*, April 7, 1998, Emeryville, CA, at http://www.persistence.com/products/wp_rymer.htm.

Stonebraker, M. (1999). "United We Stand," *Intelligent Enterprise*, April 20, 1999, 39–45.

Template Software (1998), "Integration Solutions for the Real-Time Enterprise: EIT—Enterprise Integration Template," *Template White Paper*, May 8, 1998, Dulles, VA.

TheBrain Technologies Corporation (2002) at http://www.thebrain.com.

Vaskevitch, D. (1993). *Client/Server Strategies* (San Mateo, CA: IDG Books).

Vitria Technology, Inc. (2001), at http://www.vitria.com.

White, C. "Managing Distributed Warehouse Metadata," *DM Review*, February, 1999, 1–10 (online Web version), at http://www.dmreview.com.

CHAPTER 6

The Role of Intelligent Agents in EIPs

Introduction

In Chapter 5, I discussed the role of DIM architecture in solving the islands of information problem and in contributing to the solution of the islands of auto-mation problem. I also showed that PAI architecture, an instance of DIM archi-tecture, was the portal architecture of choice for delivering the integrative promise of EIPs and EKPs. The central logical component in PAI (and DIM) archi-tecture is the artificial information manager (AIM), or the Artificial knowledge manager (AKM) (not yet described), in the instance of the EKP.

The AIM provides process control/distribution services, an in-memory active object model accompanied by a persistent object store, and connectivity to a vari-ety of data stores and application types. The AIM performs its process control ser-vices through interaction between physically distributed, but logically integrated, intelligent application servers that maintain state (business process engines) and software agents working on behalf of the servers. I will briefly review some fundamentals on software agents, and then extend the concept of the AIM presented in Chapter 5 by explaining how such agents perform process control services by combining their capabilities with those of the servers.

Some definitions

There's a very sizable literature dealing with the definition and conceptualization of software agents. Here I've relied on Kendall, Malkoun, and Jiang, (1998); Green, Hurst, Nangle, Cunningham, Summers, and Evans (1997); and Bradshaw, (1997). A software agent (SA) is a software object that acts on behalf of another software object (its client) and behaves to at least some degree

- Autonomously (without continuous direction),
- Socially (interacts with other agents),
- Proactively (influences its environment), and
- Reactively (is influenced by its environment)

An intelligent software agent is an SA that

- Has an in-memory knowledge base including cognitions, evaluations, goals, and perhaps even affects
- Is rational in the sense that it makes decisions
- Acts to attain its goals
- Learns

A static SA is one that does not move from the platform that creates it. A mobile SA (Orfali, Harkey, and Edwards, 1998, pp. 255–256, 401–405) can move across a network from one physical computer to another. It can do this autonomously, as it perceives the need for such movement. It takes its run-time environment with it wherever it goes. It can stop program execution on one computer, move to another computer, and then begin again at the second computer, interacting with that computer to communicate and/or gather data, information, or knowledge.

Contrast the mobile SA concept with the original client/server model. In the client/server model, a single request is sent over a network and activates a computing procedure at the destination computer. A result is then sent across the network to the client. In contrast, a mobile SA travels to a server and then may perform a variety of transactions with it. Eventually, when its business with the destination computer is done, it either returns to the source computer with the results of its transactions or moves to another destination computer to transact still more business.

The "source computer" of a mobile SA is its home agency (ibid.). The agency consists of a computing environment, an agent scripting capability, and a database. Mobile SAs register with home agencies and also register as visitors with other agencies. Some mobile SAs are broker agents. They recruit other agents to create task forces and delegate work to the agents they recruit. They can also contract with other agents as part of the recruitment process.

Mobile SAs and their agencies require a host environment in order to execute. This is a distributed computing environment overlaying a host distributed computing environment. It provides various essential services to mobile SAs, including the ability to create them and the ability to execute (Green, Hurst, Nangle, Cunningham, Summers, and Evans, 1997, pp. 26–27).

Agents in PAI architecture

EIPs are systems providing support for business processes (see Chapter 4) composed of task clusters. In turn, these are composed of more specific task patterns, and these, in turn, are composed of tasks, or linked sequences of activities. A comprehensive analysis of how agents can participate in EIP process control services would need to go through the details of how each portal uses case (Jacobson, Booch, and Rumbaugh, 1999, p. 432) and the task supporting each task pattern might be performed by agents and the EIP's agent-based infrastructure. That is way beyond the scope of this chapter. I will instead, provide a general characterization of how SAs fit into process control services and leave detailed analyses of how they contribute to individual use cases for the future.

Process control services in the EIP's AIM include

- In-memory proactive object state management and synchronization across distributed objects
- Component management
- Use case and workflow management
- Transactional multithreading

Agents can contribute, as portal architecture evolves into PAI architecture, to all four areas.

Object/component management and agents

In the portal system, business objects will be shared across data warehouse and data mart applications and will be stored in an in-memory object model. The EIP through the AIM must have the ability to monitor and coordinate changes in the shared classes and objects across these applications and across their different physical platforms. This means it has the ability to monitor and coordinate changes in attributes and methods of the shared objects automatically. Let's call this ability dynamic integration (Firestone, 1998). To perform dynamic integration in the EIP system, the AIM must

- Look for changes in shared objects and additions to the total pool of objects and relationships
- Alert all system components sharing the objects of such changes
- Make decisions about which changes should be implemented in each affected component throughout the system.

It is important that changes in shared objects are propagated and new objects are created in real time, so that a single view of the portal system object model is maintained. This is why in-memory, proactive operation is so important.

Like objects, components can also be shared across applications and physical platforms. Component management is the ability to monitor, coordinate, and synchronize changes in components and is analogous to object state management. It, too, needs to be performed in real time, and it too requires proactive, in-memory operation to be most effective.

Agents can play a major role in performing dynamic integration as part of the AIM. The AIM is also composed of distributed object models, made up of reflexive objects (Template Software (now Level8), 1998). A reflexive object is one that is aware of changes in its state. When a change is introduced in one of these objects, it communicates the change (through an alert) to a central object model within the AIM.

The central object model contains a view of all objects and relationships in the portal system. The central object model will respond to this alert by incorporating the changes into the central object model and deleting the old versions of the objects, as long as no other object models share the old object versions. If they do, the server containing the central object model will dispatch Negotiator mobile agents to the various distributed object models incorporating old object versions.

The task of these Negotiator mobile agents is to negotiate with the affected distributed object models about whether the changed objects are acceptable to them. The distributed object models can employ static agents to negotiate for them. If the changed objects are acceptable, the old versions of the objects can be deleted from all object models, and the new objects can be incorporated into all distributed object models. If not, the central object model will maintain both the old and the changed objects to accommodate disagreements among the distributed applications.

Both the mobile and the static agents involved in the mutual coordination process will need some intelligence. That is, they will exhibit cognitions, evaluations, and goals; they will make decisions; and they will have the capacity to learn from previous negotiations with other agents.

Why are Negotiator agents desirable in performing dynamic integration in the EIP system? While dynamic integration can be performed without Negotiator agents, the advantage in using them comes from better system performance.

Without Negotiator agents all of the transactions in negotiations between central and local components of the AIM would flow over the enterprise network and could greatly slow EIP or EKP performance. With them, negotiations actually occur on the target rather than the source platform. Only the agents are sent from one component of the AIM to other components. Or only the results of agent negotiations must be sent from component to component through much abbreviated messaging.

Use case/workflow management and agents

EIPs support business processes by assisting efforts to gather, organize, create, maintain, and enhance knowledge about them, and also by providing support for planning, implementing, monitoring, and evaluating the course of the business process. Both use cases and workflows are task sequences within these activities that process, route, and distribute information products, but the connotations of the two terms are somewhat different. The use case concept looks at a task sequence from the point of view of the valued outcome the user will get from a task sequence. Workflow, on the other hand, refers to the automated system constructed to implement a use case, a part of a use case, or a set of related use cases. Process control services must provide the means to manage such workflows by:

- Facilitating specification of routing and distribution
- Supporting rapid and easy change in the routing structure, the distribution process, and the business rules governing the workflow;
- Providing the capability to either store the product of a workflow task or "push" it to the next step in the workflow
- Providing the capability to distribute the workflow process across multiple computers
- Providing the capability to gather knowledge resources to support the workflow
- Supporting collaborative transactions among workflow participants
- Supporting subject matter integration of the UI

- Providing the capability to model and present individual, personalized workflows at subject matter nodes of the UI
- Providing the capability to define and simulate collaborative workflows
- Providing the capability to customize workflows by integrating custom, legacy, or external data and/or applications

Agents may be applied in all ten of the workflow process control areas.

Area 1: Facilitating specification of routing and distribution information and knowledge retrieval agents resident at each information or knowledge source can model each source in the EIP, and maintain its local object model

Information retrieval agents similar to what I have called knowledge retrieval agents are conceptualized in Green, Hurst, Nangle, Cunningham, Summers, and Evans (1997, pp. 11–12). The agents can alert artificial information servers (AISs) about any changes in the AIM maintaining the enterprise object model. This continuous monitoring provides information to the AISs they can use to specify workflow routing and distribution.

Area 2: Supporting rapid and easy change in the routing structure, the distribution process, and the business rules governing the workflow

The same agents can support rapid and easy changes in process routing and distribution and business rules for workflows. The relevant point here is that Retrieval agents provide object model updating whenever changes occur. This immediate information on change in the EIP is essential for AISs undertaking changes for the system as a whole.

Area 3: Providing the capability to either store the product of a workflow task or "push" it to the next step in the workflow

In deciding whether to store the product of a workflow task or push it to the next step, Negotiator agents of the components performing the steps can exchange information on the depth of their work queues and on their relative abilities to store and process the next step in the workflow. Together they can decide on whether the workflow item in question will be stored or "pushed." In case of disagreement the central AIM component can arbitrate.

Area 4: Providing the capability to distribute the workflow process across multiple computers

Information Retrieval agents based at each component in an EIP can also increase the capability to distribute the workload in a process by continuously monitoring their components and alerting the central AIM component if processing capability is stressed. The central AIS can then assist the "local" agents in negotiations to distribute the work load. Level8's (2001) Geneva Enterprise Integrator (GEI) provides a distributed object model as well as process control and connectivity services useful in developing a distributed AIM.

Area 5: Providing the capability to gather knowledge resources to support the workflow

Information and Knowledge Retrieval agents, next, can also help in providing the capability to gather knowledge resources to support a workflow. Such agents can model each individual information or knowledge resource within the EIP. They can then collaborate with Interface agents, receiving queries from them and transmitting only the results to the interface agents. Various types of knowledge claims may be retrieved by such agents including descriptive, impact-related, predictive, outcome assessment, and benefit/cost assessment knowledge claims.

Area 6: Supporting collaborative transactions among workflow participants

Intelligent Interface agents can support collaborative workflow activity in EIPs in a number of useful ways. For example, in planning, a number of decision makers may have to agree on a hierarchy of goals and objectives and ultimately on a planning option. Interface agents can help planners to be explicit about the goals, objectives, and priorities that constitute their planning hierarchies. Then Negotiating agents for different planners can work together to analyze the similarities and differences in planning hierarchies and to negotiate a common planning hierarchy.

Interface agents and Negotiating agents can also be important in developing concrete planning options incorporating planning hierarchies and action effect scenarios into plans. Planners will differ not only in their planning hierarchies but also in their cognitive maps relating actions and effects. Again, Interface agents can help planners be explicit about their cognitive maps, and Negotiating agents can work together to arrive at a common cognitive map underlying a preferred planning option.

In addition to supporting planning, Interface and Negotiating agents can support collaborative work in knowledge discovery in databases (KDD) activity (Firestone, 1998a). Here, analysts will disagree on both cognitive maps expressed in formal models and on validation criteria used to select among models. Interface agents can help analysts to perform formal modeling, and they can also help them in formulating their validation schema supporting model choice. Negotiating agents can then assist analysts in arriving at common validation schema.

Area 7: Supporting subject matter integration of the UI

Special interface agents called Avatars can, based on a user's own expression of interests and the pattern of selection of subjects over time, categorize subject matter hierarchically and present the hierarchical classification as the basis of the portal interface. The same agents can also capture the nonhierarchical network relationships among concepts in the subject matter hierarchy. This information, *learned over time by the Avatar,* can also be presented as part of the personalized portal UI.

Area 8: Providing the capability to model and present individual, personalized workflows at subject matter nodes of the UI

Avatars can complete the user profiling partly described in Area 7 by modeling the workflows developed by users and attaching them to the subject matter nodes of the user's semantic net or cognitive map. That is, Avatars can create and maintain for users the personalized portal interface they need to perform work using the EIP. In this way they contribute critically to solving the islands of automation problem in EIPs.

Area 9: Providing the capability to simulate collaborative workflow

Agents can also assist in simulating workflow systems in EIPs. Systems can be represented by agents functioning as the nodes of a workflow. Agents can be assigned tasks they perform according to rules programmed in the agents and triggered by events and their parameters. Workflow items can be defined to provide agents something to process. When the simulation is run, various characteristics of the workflow design can be evaluated.

Area 10: Providing the capability to customize workflows by integrating custom, legacy, or external data and/or applications

Agents provide only one way to integrate custom, legacy, or external data and applications into a workflow system. But agent technology can be used to produce a simple information agent by "wrapping" any information source to allow it to conform to the communication conventions of an agent infrastructure (Bradshaw, 1998, p. 31). While this is not so much a contribution to process control in itself, it does support other agents in the EIP infrastructure by facilitating communications between such simple information agents and other more proactive agents, and by providing a capability to script the information agents to perform simple functions such as scheduled reporting and alerting of other agents to important events reflected in the information source.

Transactional multithreading

Transactional multithreading is the ability to manage each thread within a process as a separate transaction. Each thread can represent an instance of an active object. Because they support transactional multithreading, agents provide for multiple objects belonging to different classes to reside in the same process. This form of multitasking allows for concurrent execution of disparate business rules associated with different objects by agents. It provides the agents with parallelism useful in workflow management as well as in object and component dynamic integration in EIPs.

Agents as intelligent scaled-down business process engines

The development of multi-tier distributed processing systems was characterized by the appearance of application servers. Application servers provide services to other components in a distributed processing system by executing business logic and data logic on data accessed from database servers.

The class of application servers is subdivided by Rymer's (1998, p. 1) distinction between "stateless" and in-memory server environments. Application servers with active in-memory object models he calls business process engines (BPEs), a name similar to Vaskevitch's (1993, Ch. 8) business process automation engines.

According to Rymer: (1998, p. 1) "Business state is the information that describes the momentary status of the organization. To create business state, most applications acquire data from a database and then load it into memory for manipulations by the user." This is the "stateless" approach, because in it a back-end database rather than internal memory manages state.

Among stateless application servers Rymer distinguishes:

- Web information servers (they provide access to databases from Web browsers)
- Component servers (they "provide data access and interaction frameworks for software components")
- Transaction processing monitors (they coordinate transactions within a distributed system)

Business process engines are application servers that maintain state. "Business Process Engines manage the most important business state both in a fast in-memory environment and in close coordination with back-end databases." (ibid., p. 9) Because of their in-memory maintenance of state, BPEs process many user requests without help from a database. In addition, they specialize in complex business rule processing, because their ability to maintain state is a special advantage in performing such processing. Software applications such as KDD/data mining servers, publication and delivery servers, the AIS, and many other server types are all BPEs.

One way to view agents in EIPs is as intelligent, scaled-down BPEs. There are a number of reasons for this view. First, intelligent agents, like server-based BPEs, maintain state. They have cognitions, goals, and evaluations. Second, they may share rule-processing capabilities with BPEs. Third, they may provide object models or conceptual maps of the various information and knowledge sources they interact with, and fourth, they may process many queries without help from databases. Finally, some agents may function in EIP systems as lower-capacity BPEs.

Conclusion: agents, EIPs, and the virtual enterprise

When we view agents as scaled-down BPEs, we highlight their integrative function in EIPs and their future role in creating an EIP (or EKP) that is a virtual enterprise. The AIM is made up of artificial information servers and intelligent agents. The role of both is to perform process control services, provide an in-memory active object model/persistent data store, and provide connectivity services. AISs are heavyweight static BPEs that provide extensive memory and processing at a relatively heavy cost. Agents are lightweight, intelligent, efficient, specialized BPEs that provide some memory and a small amount of processing power at almost no cost.

Agents alone cannot yet create the virtual enterprise. For complex processing and an enterprise wide view, AIS servers are indispensable. But agents provide balance to the AIM. They are necessary partners for the AISs in providing the processing power needed for EIPs and the virtual enterprise. When we add agents to AISs to create the AIM (or the AKM), we provide software wiring for the enterprise that connects its central brain components (the AISs) to its sensors (the agents). The result is a flexible and scalable AIM that can integrate the EIP of the virtual enterprise.

References

Bradshaw, J.M. (ed.). *Software Agent,* (Cambridge, MA: AAAI Press/M.I.T. Press).

Firestone, J.M. (1998). "Architectural Evolution in Data Warehousing," *Executive Information Systems, Inc. White Paper,* Wilmington, DE, July 1, 1998. Available at http://www.dkms.com/White_Papers.htm.

Firestone, J.M. (1998a). "Knowledge Management Metrics Development: A Technical Approach," *Executive Information Systems White Paper,* Wilmington, DE, June 25, 1998. Available at http://www.dkms.com/White_Papers.htm.

Green, S.; Hurst, L.; Nangle, B.; Cunningham, P.; Summers, F.; and Evans, R. (1997). "Software Agents: A Review," Trinity College, Dublin, and Broadcom Eirann Research Ltd., May 27, 1997, Available at: http://www.cs.tcd.ie/research_groups/aig/iag/toplevel2.html.

Jacobson, I.; Booch, G.; and Rumbaugh, J. (1999). *The Unified Software Development Process,* (Reading, MA: Addison-Wesley).

Kendall, E.A.; Malkoun, M.T.; and Jiang, C. "A Methodology for Developing Agent Based Systems for Enterprise Integration," Melbourne, Australia: Royal Melbourne Institute of Technology. Available at: http://www.cse.rmit.edu.au/~rdsek/.

Orfali, R.; Harkey, D.; and Edwards, J. (1998). *The Essential Distributed Objects Survival Guide* (New York: John Wiley & Sons).

Rymer, J. (1998). "Business Process Engines, A New Category of Server Software, Will Burst the Barriers in Distributed Application Performance Engines," *Upstream Consulting White Paper,* Emeryville, CA, April 7, 1998. Available at http://www.persistence.com/products/wp_rymer.htm.

Template Software (1998). "Integration Solutions for the Real-Time Enterprise: EIT—Enterprise Integration Template," *Template White Paper,* May 8, 1998, Dulles, VA.

Vaskevitch, D. (1993). *Client/Server Strategies* (San Mateo, CA: IDG Books).

PART FOUR

On Knowledge and Knowledge Management

Parts 1–3 have taken us as far as we can go in analyzing the relationship of enterprise information portals to knowledge management without engaging in an explicit consideration of what we mean by knowledge and knowledge management. It is commonplace, in these days of "industry" discussions about knowledge and knowledge management, to say many things about them while assuming that everyone knows what everyone else means by these words. However, my own experience with the literature, clients, students, and other participants in various Web-based list serves, persuades me that the opposite is true, that everyone uses these words differently; and that there is even more difficulty in finding a common language here than there is in finding it in discussions of EIPs.

Part 4 provides the explicit consideration of knowledge and knowledge management I think is needed to talk intelligently about the relationship of EIPs to knowledge processing and knowledge management. Chapter 7 is a somewhat lengthy consideration of the nature of knowledge. It begins with the problem of definition and contrasts the ideas of definition, specification, and cognitive mapping (or semantic networking). It then surveys alternative definitions of knowledge, including world 2 and world 3 definitions. It discusses the distinctions between world 2 data, information, and knowledge (see Chapter 2 for distinctions among world 3 data, information, and knowledge). It provides a conceptual framework for understanding in broad outline how knowledge is produced and integrated in organizations. This framework views business processes as aggregated from decision cycles of individuals and groups. It views the knowledge processes of knowledge production and integration as responses to problems. These processes are arranged in a problem-solving life cycle called the knowledge life cycle (KLC) that produces and integrates knowledge in an organization for use in business processes and ad hoc activities.

After presenting the framework, Chapter 7 applies it to the analysis of tacit and explicit knowledge, reviews the ideas of Popper and Polanyi and the notion of implicit knowledge, and discusses the relationship of the KLC to individual level knowledge and motivational hierarchies. Chapter 7 also discusses the relationship of the frame-

work to the idea of culture and ends with a critique of the Nonaka/Takeuchi knowledge conversion model and its relationship to the KLC.

Chapter 8 presents a much more detailed conceptual framework of knowledge processing. It specifies information acquisition, individual and group learning knowledge claim formulation and knowledge claim validation, the subprocesses of knowledge production and knowledge broadcasting, searching/retrieving, knowledge sharing, and teaching, and the subprocesses of knowledge integration. All subprocesses are analyzed in sufficient detail to provide an understanding of what types of process activities an EIP would have to support in order to enhance knowledge processing. Chapter 8 ends with a discussion of the relationship of the KLC to accelerating innovation.

After the specification of knowledge and knowledge and knowledge processing, Chapter 9 focuses directly on knowledge management. It presents my approach to KM, the notion of complex adaptive systems (CASs), the idea of the natural knowledge management system (NKMS), the distinction between hierarchical and organic KM, a survey of KM definitions, the difference between Information management and knowledge management, the differences between knowledge processes and information processes, a definition and specification of KM and IM processes, more on how KM and IM differ, how culture relates to KM, and knowledge management impact and innovation. Chapter 9 provides the background needed to move on to analysis of artificial knowledge management systems in Chapter 10.

CHAPTER 7

On Knowledge

Introduction

How are enterprise information portals related to knowledge processing and knowledge management? The answer depends critically on how knowledge, knowledge processing, and knowledge management are defined and specified. This chapter will provide definitions and specifications of knowledge, knowledge processing, and other related concepts including the knowledge life cycle; tacit, explicit, and implicit knowledge; the relationship of knowledge to individual motivational predispositions; the relationship of knowledge and culture; and the relationship of "modes of knowledge conversion" to the knowledge cycle. First, however, a few important words on "definition" itself are in order.

On definition

Many in knowledge management (KM) prefer to avoid defining the meaning of "knowledge.". Their view is that definition is a sterile, time-wasting pastime that contributes little or nothing to the real work of KM. My view is different. It is that definition is an important preliminary step on the road to specifying one's cognitive map of knowledge processing and KM and to ultimately to developing quality models useful for developing KM solutions. I also think that arguments over definition are not fruitless arguments but important exchanges about what is a good starting point for developing a cognitive map of KM.

The purpose of a definition is not to provide necessary and sufficient conditions for its use. Instead, its purpose is to answer a question such as "What do you mean by knowledge management?" with a short, *incomplete* answer that allows the questioner to infer something more of the cognitive map (or conceptual map, or semantic network) of the target of the question and facilitates the beginning of further communication—and perhaps of learning relative to that cognitive map.

Figure 7.1 illustrates the idea of a cognitive map (Axelrod, 1976; Kosko, 1992, pp. 152–158). Nodes represent concepts. Edges are relationships. Single-headed arrows are asymmetric relationships. Double-headed arrows are bi-directional associations. Edges may be weighted between 0 and 1.00, or, alternatively,

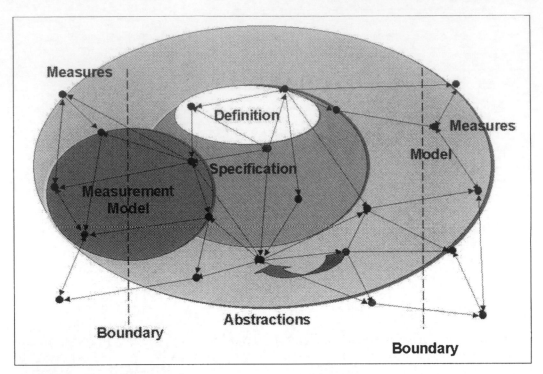

Figure 7.1. A cognitive map.

weighted with words such as "few," "more," "somewhat, and signed (+, -) for increase or decrease in the target node following a change in the source node. Since qualitative concepts can be represented in a cognitive map, it should be clear that the idea can be used to represent fuzzy relationships (Cox, 1994, 1996) as well as logically crisp ones. The cognitive map idea is therefore not limited to mathematical or precise logical relationships but can also accommodate less exacting formulations of relations between concepts.

The white ellipse highlights the area of definition. The darker ellipse containing it does the same for specification and the still darker ellipse the same for a measurement model. The light area represents the full model. The shaded arrow represents a feedback relationship. Measures are experiential concepts. Abstractions are what we measure. The abstraction/measure boundary is crossed by measurement rules. A pattern of measurement rules, abstract relationships, and associations among measures defines a measurement model.

Keeping the complex and comprehensive pattern of the whole cognitive map in mind as well as the small area represented by the definition, I will characterize the definition as the "elevator speech" (the 30-second expression of the idea, Moore, 1991, p. 159–162) representing, however imperfectly, the cognitive map—that is, when communicating with others about any term. You can

- Refuse to explain it
- Define it
- Specify it
- Construct a cognitive map of it

Which would you rather do in response to a basic question from someone either at the beginning of a conversation or at a briefing? Do nothing? Give the "elevator speech?" Give the five-minute overview? Or give the whole briefing?

And if there's disagreement over a specific definition, there are a number of good reasons why that might be the case, other than mere love of philosophical disputation. First, the definition may not provide enough of the definer's cognitive map to evaluate his or her statements using the concept. Second, the definition may not distinguish the concept from other concepts. Third, the definition may redefine the term beyond common usage in a manner that promotes confusion in communication. (This is a frequent occurrence due to the desire of communicators to acquire the "halo effect" of certain terms for their frequently different concepts.) And fourth, those disagreeing may forecast that bad model development will result (wasted time and effort) from the starting place for model construction provided by a particular definition.

So, once again, why bother to define? To save time in responding to a questioner, to create a basis for further communication with others, and finally, to specify a cost-effective starting place for further specification, measurement, and modeling.

Definitions of knowledge

There is no consensus on the nature of knowledge, nor has there ever been in the history of human thought (Jones, 1952). Here's a brief and far from comprehensive survey of definitions offered by writers and researchers in knowledge management.

Knowledge is

- "Justified true belief." This is the venerable definition of many philosophers, especially of empiricists who believe knowledge claims can be justified by facts (Goldman, 1991). It also is the definition adopted by Nonaka and Takeuchi (1995, p. 58).
- "Information in context." This is a definition that may have its roots in Cartesian rationalist epistemology. Its import is that a knowledge claim is valid if it fits without contradiction and adds to the systematic coherence of a larger framework of knowledge (Aune, 1970).
- "Knowledge is understanding based on experience." This is an idea that is central to modern pragmatism and its associated epistemology (James, 1907). It's also a standard definition found in English language dictionaries.
- "Knowledge is experience or information that can be communicated or shared." (Allee, 1997, p. 27)
- "Knowledge, while made up of data and information, can be thought of as much greater understanding of a situation, relationships, causal phenomena, and the theories and rules (both explicit and implicit) that underlie a given domain or problem." (Bennet and Bennet, 2000, p. 19)
- "Knowledge can be thought of as the body of understandings, generalizations, and abstractions that we carry with us on a permanent or semi-permanent basis and apply to interpret and manage the world around us. . . ."

We will consider knowledge to be the collection of mental units of all kinds that provides us with understanding and insights." (Karl Wiig, 1998)

- "The most essential definition of knowledge is that it is composed of and grounded solely in *potential acts* and in those signs that refer to them." (Cavaleri and Reed, 2000, p. 114) This is another definition originating in Pragmatism and, specifically, in the work of Charles S. Peirce. A definition offered in the same spirit is "knowledge is social acts," provided by Ralph Stacey (1996).
- "Knowledge is the capacity for effective action." This definition is the one favored by the organizational learning community (Argyris, 1993, pp. 2-3).

I will discuss these views shortly, but first I want to introduce the framework I prefer for looking at knowledge.

I distinguish three types of "knowledge:"

- *World 1 knowledge*—encoded structures in physical systems (such as genetic encoding in DNA) that allow those objects to adapt to an environment;
- *World 2 knowledge*—validated beliefs (in minds) about the world, the beautiful, and the right;
- *World 3 knowledge*—validated linguistic formulations about the world, the beautiful and the right

All three types of knowledge are about encoded structures in one kind of system or another that arguably help those systems to adapt. The world 1, world 2, and world 3 distinctions were introduced by Karl Popper (1972, 1994; Popper and Eccles, 1977). Popper also defined the distinction between world 2 and world 3 knowledge (1972, pp. 106–122; 1994, Ch. 1) (Popper and Eccles, 1977, pp. 36–50). But he did not define either type of knowledge in precisely the terms I have used. He also never defined world 1 encoding of adaptive information as knowledge, perhaps because he viewed knowledge as the outcome of our intentional attempts to solve problems and our consequent learning. World 1 encoding of information, in contrast, is not intentional and involves a much different time scale than human learning and knowledge seeking.

In many organizations, there is little concern with world 1 knowledge or with the beautiful, and only slightly greater concern with the right, so we are left with world 2 and 3 knowledge of reality as the outcomes of knowledge processes that are of primary concern to knowledge management. Let's consider some of the definitions of knowledge surveyed earlier in light of their internal difficulties and the world 2/world3 distinction.

World 2 definitions

- The definition of knowledge as "justified true belief" has the difficulty that we cannot know for certain that any knowledge belief, no matter how well validated, is true. Yet some knowledge claims, the well-validated ones, are what we mean by knowledge.

- The definition of world 2 knowledge I provided above implies that knowledge is not the same thing as "understanding," whether qualified by experience, greater understanding, or insight. Our ability to understand an invalid network of knowledge claims is as great as our ability to understand valid knowledge claims. So understanding is not a sufficient condition of knowledge.
- Nor is world 2 knowledge the same thing as experience we can share. We can share experiences that communicate unvalidated knowledge claims. On the other hand, some tacit knowledge, as characterized by Polanyi (1958, 1966), is inexpressible. We know it but cannot tell it. So this kind of world 2 knowledge is difficult and, in many instances, impossible to share even through nonverbal communication. So if we accept the idea of personal, tacit knowledge, we must also accept that knowledge is not always experience we can share.

So the above definitions of world 2 knowledge have serious difficulties as accounts of it. In my view, world 2 knowledge is belief that the agent holding it has "justified" it by subjecting it to the agent's validation process. But it need not be true. World 2 knowledge is an immediate precursor of our decisions, and we use it to make them. Such knowledge is "subjective" in the sense that it is agent-specific.

World 2 knowledge exists at levels above the individual. That is, an "agent" holding world 2 knowledge can be a group, a team, an organization, or even a nation. Much research on culture, national character, social movements, political integration, and organizational theory suggests that group cognitive predispositions (including belief and knowledge predispositions) are a useful concept in accounting for group behavior. If we do not recognize their existence, we restrict world 2 knowledge to the level of the individual. Such individual world 2 knowledge is "personal," in the sense that other individuals do not have direct access to one's own knowledge in full detail and therefore cannot "know it" as their own belief. I will return to the idea of group cognitive predispositions later on.

World 3 definitions

Four of the knowledge definitions I surveyed earlier may be viewed as world 3 definitions. These are knowledge as "information in context" and knowledge as "a potential act," "knowledge as social acts," and "knowledge is the capacity for effective action." All four definitions have severe problems. Here they are.

First, the idea that knowledge is information in context doesn't distinguish knowledge from information. Information can have every bit as much context as knowledge. What distinguishes knowledge from information is that *the content of the validation contexts of knowledge.* The history of an organization's tests of knowledge claims and their competitive performance determines the validity of such claims.

Second, world 3 knowledge is also not the same thing as a potential act or as "social acts." *Not every potential or social act is a knowledge claim or even a validated knowledge claim.* Though every potential act may either be or imply a knowledge claim relating the act to its anticipated consequences, unless we already have validated the knowledge claim implied by the potential act, it is just information, no different from any alternative potential knowledge claim act. So the definition of knowledge as a potential act raises the question of how potential acts that are knowledge claims are validated.

Third, The definition of knowledge as "social acts" raises the same concern. Fourth, "knowledge is the capacity for effective action," has the political scientist's problem. That is, knowledge is a *necessary* condition for effective action. But, it is not sufficient. Effective action also requires (a) the *intention* to use one's knowledge, and (b) the *capability or power* to take those effective actions.

Instead of the above, I think that world 3 knowledge consists of validated models, theories, arguments, descriptions, problem statements and the like; it involves linguistic formulations (world 3 information also exists) about these objects in themselves. It is not psychological in nature or even sociological. We talk about the truth or nearness to the truth of such world 3 objects, and of knowledge defined as descriptions, models, theories, or arguments that are closer to the truth than their competitors.

This kind of knowledge is not an *immediate* precursor to decisions. It impacts decisions only through the impact it has on (world 2) beliefs. These beliefs, in turn, immediately impact decisions. This kind of knowledge, further, is "objective."

It is objective in the sense that it is not agent specific and is shared among agents as an object whether or not they believe in it. It is also not "personal," because (1) all agents in the organization have access to it, and (2) it emerges from the interaction of a number of agents. Finally, it is objective because, since it is sharable, we can sensibly talk about its organizational validation. To understand the essence of world 3 knowledge we can do no better than to quote Karl Popper (1972, p. 116) who first formulated this idea of "objective knowledge," on the objective knowledge content in books.

> A man who reads a book with understanding is a rare creature. But even if he were more common, there would always be plenty of misunderstandings and misinterpretations; and it is not the actual and somewhat accidental avoidance of misunderstandings which turns black spots on white paper into a book or an instance of knowledge in the objective sense. Rather, it is something more abstract. It is its possibility or potentiality of being understood, its dispositional character of being understood or interpreted, or misunderstood or misinterpreted, which makes a thing a book. And this potentiality or disposition may exist without ever being actualized or realized.

> To see this more clearly we may imagine that after the human race has perished, some books or libraries may be found by some civilized successors of ours (no matter whether these are terrestrial animals that have become civilized, or some visitors from outer space). These books may be deciphered. They may be those logarithm tables never read before, for argument's sake. This makes it quite clear that neither its composition by thinking animals nor the fact that it has not been actually read or understood is essential for making a thing a book, and that it is sufficient that it might be deciphered.

Thus, I do admit that in order to belong to the third world of objective knowledge, a book should—in principle or virtually—be capable of being grasped (or deciphered or understood, or "known") by somebody. But I do not admit more.

The distinction between world 2 and world 3 knowledge raises the issue of which type of knowledge should be the object of KM? Can world 2 knowledge be managed by organizations? To what extent is world 2 knowledge about an organization determined by organizational interaction, rather than individual predispositions and interactions not manageable by the organization? Where does the distinction between world 2 and world 3 knowledge leave the much better known distinction between tacit and explicit knowledge? Or the less well-known distinction between "implied knowledge" and codified knowledge? These questions will be considered in due course.

World 2 data, information, and knowledge

In Chapter 2, I discussed the distinctions among data, information, knowledge, and wisdom in the context of content management. From the perspective of the world 2/world 3 distinction, we can now see that the earlier discussion was focused on world 3 data, information, and knowledge. Here I will extend the discussion by considering parallel distinctions among world 2 phenomena.

Earlier, I defined world 2 knowledge as validated beliefs (in minds) about the world, the beautiful, and the right. What if the beliefs are unvalidated or invalidated? Then we have information. Are validated beliefs information as well as knowledge? They are nonrandom structures and as such fit Shannon's (1948) definition of information. Therefore, there is no reason to deny knowledge the appellation information, as well.

Where does data come into this picture? World 2 data must consist of beliefs about observational experiences. These beliefs are like other beliefs in that we view them as validated, unvalidated, or invalidated by our experience; further, they fit into and relate to the general structure of the rest of our beliefs So they, like world 2 knowledge and information, are also information.

What about the pyramid? Does the pyramid image (see Figure 2.3) make sense for world 2 data, information, and knowledge? Again, our experience argues against it. Data is not the foundation from which we produce information, from which we produce knowledge, from which we produce wisdom. Instead, we are born with genetically encoded knowledge that enables us to interact with the external world and to learn (Popper, 1972, p. 71–73). This knowledge is more plentiful in quantity than all of the knowledge we will acquire through learning for the rest of our lives. We use it to approach the world with predispositions and beliefs. With these we create and structure experience and from the process of doing this we produce new data, information, and knowledge continuously and in no particular order.

How do we do this? Once again it is through the knowledge life cycle (KLC). The KLC, visualized in Figure 2.4 and in a more detailed fashion in Figure 7.3, produces both world 3 and world 2 data, information, and knowledge. And within its processes, world 2 and world 3 phenomena alternate in influencing the production of the other as the KLC operates through time. This brings us to the subject of knowledge processing.

Business process hierarchies, decision cycles, and knowledge processing

Much of the behavior of organizational systems is produced by business processes performed by individuals, teams, and groups within an organization. Figure 7.2 illustrates the idea that any business process (including knowledge and knowledge management processes) may be viewed as a network of linked activities governed by rule sets or (world 2) knowledge aimed at producing outcomes of value to those performing the activities. A linked sequence of activities performed by one or more agents sharing at least one objective is a *task*. A linked, but not necessarily sequential set of tasks governed by rule sets, producing results of measurable value to the agent or agents performing the tasks, is a *task pattern*. A cluster of task patterns, not necessarily performed sequentially, often performed iteratively, incrementally, and adaptively, is a *task cluster*. Finally, a hierarchical network of interrelated, purposive activities of intelligent agents that transforms inputs into valued outcomes, a cluster of task clusters, is a *business process*.

Any business process, task cluster, task pattern, or task must involve *decision cycles*, themselves composed of tasks and task patterns, through which agents execute their part in a business process or component. These decision cycles are focused on domain-centered tasks and task patterns in the natural knowledge management system (NKMS), because such tasks and task patterns must be executed by agents (individuals, teams, and groups) in order to do work. It is through these domain-centered tasks that decision cycle tasks and task patterns affect the outcomes of task clusters and business processes.

The generic task patterns or *phases* of any decision/execution cycle are: Planning, Acting (including deciding), Monitoring, and Evaluating. *Planning* is a knowledge production and knowledge integration task pattern. It means setting

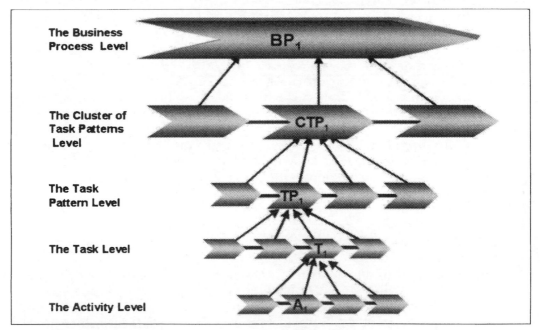

Figure 7.2. The activity to business process hierarchy again.

goals, objectives, and priorities, making forecasts as part of prospective analysis, performing cost/benefit assessments as part of prospective analysis, and revising or reengineering a business process. It involves capturing and using data, information, and knowledge to produce a plan, an instance of world 3 planning knowledge.

Acting means performing the specific domain business process (cluster, pattern, or task) or any of its components. Acting involves *using the planning knowledge, along with other world 3 and world 2 knowledge*, to make and implement decisions.

Monitoring means retrospectively tracking and describing the business process (cluster, pattern, or task) and its outcome. Monitoring involves gathering data and information, modeling processes, and using previous knowledge to produce new descriptive, impact-related, and predictive knowledge about the results of acting. Monitoring is another (world 3) knowledge production and knowledge integration task pattern.

Evaluating means retrospectively assessing the performance of the business process as a value network (Allee, 2000). Evaluating means using the results of monitoring, along with previous knowledge, to assess the results of acting and to produce knowledge about the descriptive gaps between business outcomes and tactical objectives and about the normative (benefits and costs) impact of business outcomes. Evaluating is yet another decision cycle task pattern that produces and integrates world 3 knowledge into business processes.

There is a natural order to the four phases of any decision/execution cycle in a value network. Figure 7.3 illustrates the order of these phases, or task patterns of the decision cycle.

Three of these four phases may require knowledge production and knowledge integration to solve problems that occur in each phase; the fourth, the acting phase, uses the knowledge produced in the other three phases. When problems occur, they are solved through knowledge processing, represented in Figure 7.3 by the double-loop learning (DLL) process. So every decision cycle in every business process may require both knowledge processing (production and

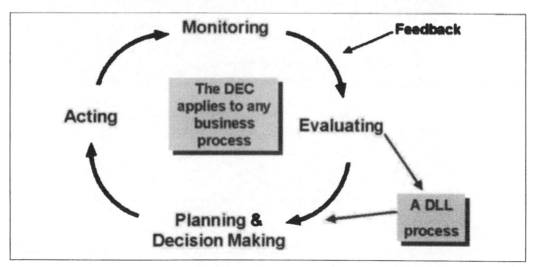

Figure 7.3. The decision execution cycle.

integration) and knowledge use. Knowledge use is not a separate task but rather is part of deciding and acting and involves both world 3 and world 2 knowledge (where the decision maker interprets world 3 knowledge). But planning, monitoring, and evaluating are knowledge production task patterns of different types, each involving sequential patterns of knowledge production and knowledge integration.

A knowledge life cycle (KLC) framework

So decision execution cycles performed by agents in executing tasks and task patterns in business processes are in part sequentially ordered knowledge production and knowledge integration processes. Figure 7.4 provides an overview of a knowledge life cycle (KLC) model begun in collaboration with Mark McElroy, Edward Swanstrom, Douglas Weidner, and Steve Cavaleri (1999), during meetings sponsored by the Knowledge Management Consortium International (KMCI), and further developed more recently by Mark McElroy and myself. Knowledge production and knowledge integration, abstracted from the planning, monitoring, and evaluating phases of decision cycles, are core knowledge processes in the model.

Knowledge production is initiated in response to problems produced by decision cycles in business processes. It produces organizational knowledge (OK). It includes (not shown in the figure) surviving knowledge claims (SKCs), undecided knowledge claims (UKCs), and falsified knowledge claims (FKCs), and information about the status of these. All of the above are codified, explicit, world 3 objects. Organizational knowledge (OK) is composed of all of the foregoing results

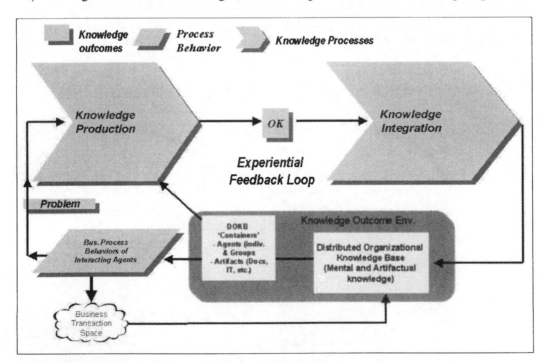

Figure 7.4. The knowledge life cycle (KLC) framework.

of knowledge production. It is part of what is integrated into the enterprise by the knowledge integration process.

The knowledge production process, in combination with previous agent predispositions, also produces *beliefs related to the world 3 knowledge claims.* These are world 2 objects, predisposing various organizational agents to action. In some instances they are predispositions that correspond to organizational knowledge; in other instances they are predispositions that reflect awareness of validated or surviving knowledge claims but contradict them, or supplement them, or bear some other conceptual relationship to them. At the individual level these beliefs are in part tacit, since all of them are not expressible linguistically by the individuals holding them, or implicit, since some that are neither tacit nor explicit may not have been verbally expressed. Where these beliefs have been validated by the individuals or by other intelligent agents holding them, they constitute world 2 knowledge held by those agents. But they are not organizational knowledge. Rather they are outputs of the organizational NKMS to the individual agents.

The knowledge integration process takes organizational knowledge and by integrating it within the organization produces the distributed organizational knowledge base (DOKB). Integrating means communicating organizational knowledge content to the organization's agents with the purpose of making them fully aware of existing organizational knowledge. This also requires making the knowledge available in knowledge stores that agents can use to search for and retrieve knowledge. The result of knowledge integration is that the content of codified organizational knowledge is available in both accessible and distributed knowledge stores and, in addition, is reflected in the predispositions of agents all across the enterprise. The DOKB is the combination of distributed world 3 and world 2 knowledge content.

The DOKB, in its turn, has a major impact on structures incorporating organizational knowledge such as normative business processes, plans, organizational culture, organizational strategy, policies, procedures, and information systems. Coupled with external sources these structures then feed back to impact behavioral business processes through the acting phase of decision cycles, which, in turn, generates new problems to be solved in the planning, monitoring, and evaluating phases—that is, in the next round of knowledge processing. That is why it is called the knowledge life cycle (KLC) framework).

"Drilling down" into knowledge production (Figure 7.5), the KLC view is that information acquisition and individual and group learning, in the service of problem-solving, impact on knowledge claim formulation, which, in turn, produces codified knowledge claims (CKCs). These, in their turn, are tested in the knowledge validation task cluster, a critical examination of knowledge claims including, but not limited to, empirical testing, which then produces organizational knowledge.

The key task cluster that distinguishes knowledge production from information production is knowledge claim evaluation (or validation). It is the subprocess of criticism of competing knowledge claims and of comparative testing and assessment of them that transforms knowledge claims from mere information into tested information, some of which passes organizational tests and therefore becomes, from the organizational point of view, knowledge.

In other words, the difference between information and knowledge is validation. But what is validation? It is testing and evaluation of knowledge claims

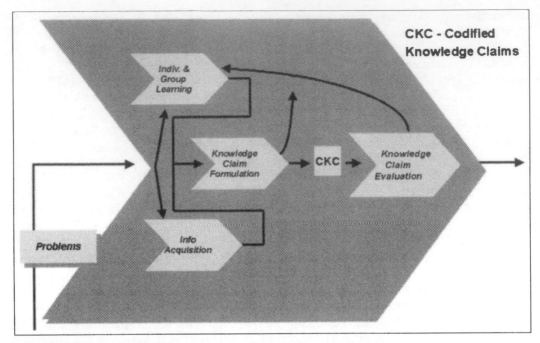

Figure 7.5. Knowledge production.

(world 3), or testing and evaluation of beliefs (world 2). Testing and evaluation of knowledge claims is public and sharable in the sense that the claims themselves are sharable and the tests and their results are sharable. That is why world 3 knowledge is objective. Testing and evaluation of beliefs is private and personal. It is this difference that makes world 2 knowledge subjective.

Validation is not the same thing as justification. Justification is the process of proving that a knowledge claim is true. Validation never proves anything with certainty. It simply provides (1) a record of how well competing knowledge claims stand up to our tests or (2) personal experience of how well competing beliefs stand up to our tests. Justification of knowledge claims and beliefs is impossible, but validation of them is not.

Since validation is just our process of testing and evaluating knowledge claims or beliefs, the practice of it will vary across individuals, groups, communities, teams, and organizations. A particular entity may use validation practices based on explicit rules or specified criteria to compare knowledge claims, but it need not. Agents are free to change their tests or criteria at any time, to invent new ones, or to apply ad hoc tests and criticisms in validation. That is, validation is a free-for-all; it is just the process by which knowledge claims and beliefs run the gauntlet of our skepticism and our criticism.

Looking at knowledge production from the viewpoint of agents at different levels of organizational interaction and keeping the role of knowledge claim validation in mind, it follows that individual and group learning may involve knowledge production from the perspective of the individual or group. From the perspective of the enterprise, however, what the individuals and groups learn is information, not knowledge. Similarly, information acquired may be knowledge from the perspective of the external parties it is acquired from, but not knowledge to the enterprise acquiring it, until it has been validated as such.

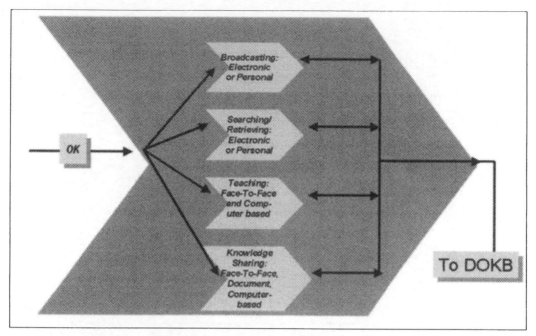

Figure 7.6. Knowledge integration.

Figure 7.5 also illustrates that knowledge validation has a feedback effect on individual and group learning. This occurs because individuals and groups participating in knowledge claim validation are affected by their participation in this process. They both produce world 3 organizational knowledge in the form of codified and validated knowledge claims, and also experience change in their own "justified" beliefs (generate world 2 knowledge) as an outcome of that participation.

Drilling down into knowledge integration (Figure 7.6), organizational knowledge is integrated across the enterprise by the broadcasting, searching/retrieving, teaching, and sharing task clusters. These generally work in parallel rather than sequentially. And not all are necessary to a specific instance of the KLC. All may be based in personal non-electronic or electronic interactions.

An illustration of the distributed organizational knowledge base is provided in Figure 7.7. Here containers of both world 2 and world 3 knowledge are represented. The knowledge of each type is the content of the validated beliefs held by agents and the validated (or surviving) knowledge claims stored in various media and repositories.

Next, the same containers are viewed as business structures influencing behavior rather than as mere containers of knowledge. As such they provide the external background conditions for agent behavior (see Figure 7.8).

The relationship between structures incorporating organizational knowledge and business process behavior is presented in a somewhat different perspective in Figure 7.9. This figure presents the agent, individual, group, team, or organization as a decision maker executing the transactions that are the atomic components of processes. World 2 knowledge is contained in the goal-directed agent and is composed of the memories, values, attitudes, and situational orientations of agents. World 3 knowledge is contained in the cultural conditions that make up part of

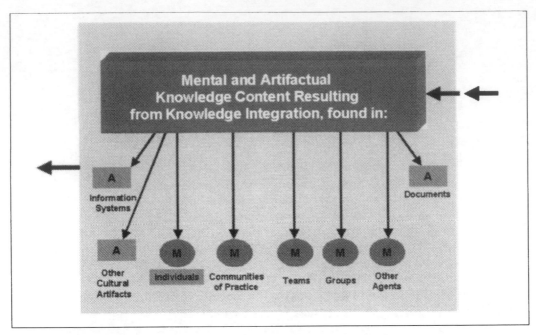

Figure 7.7. The distributed organizational knowledge base.

social ecology. Thus, Figure 7.9 also illustrates the role of world 2 knowledge as an immediate precursor of decisions and transactional behavior in the organizational system, as well as the role of world 3 knowledge as a cultural factor shaping psychological orientations in general and world 2 knowledge in particular.

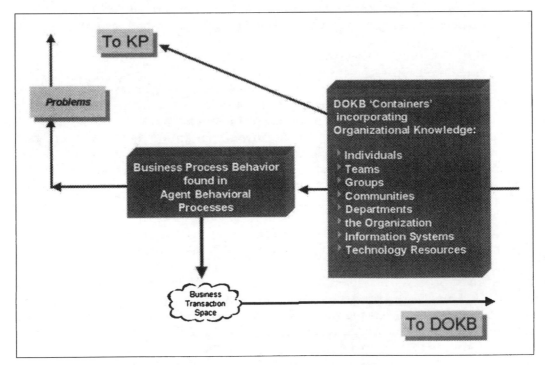

Figure 7.8. Business process behavior and containers of knowledge.

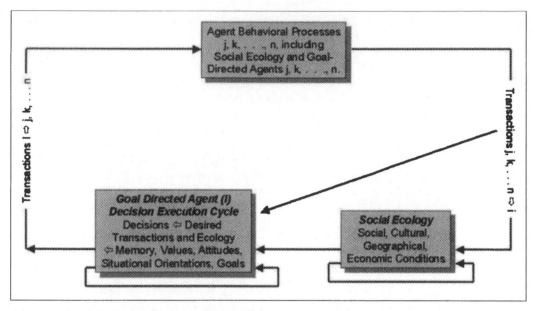

Figure 7.9. The flow of decisions and behavior among agents.

Table 7.1 provides a glossary of the major terms used in the KLC model.

Knowledge production and knowledge integration, their subprocesses, and task clusters, etc., like other value networks, are partly composed of decision cycles through which agents execute their roles in these value networks. This means that planning, acting, monitoring, and evaluating also apply to knowledge processes and to activity in the KLC. That is, higher-level KLC processes are executed by agents performing KLC decision cycles and engaging in planning, monitoring, and evaluating. The knowledge producing and knowledge integrating activities initiated by KLC decision cycles are KM-level knowledge producing and knowledge integrating task clusters, because they address problems in knowledge processing about how to plan, how to monitor, or how to evaluate. These problems are solved by producing and integrating KM-level knowledge.

Tacit knowledge and explicit knowledge

A widely recognized distinction in knowledge management circles is Polanyi's distinction (1958 and 1966) between tacit, personal knowledge and explicit, codified knowledge. By tacit knowledge, Polanyi meant "committed belief"—that is contextual in character and difficult to express. In fact, he characterized some tacit knowledge as inexpressible or "ineffable," and stated that "we can know more than we can tell." He also saw knowledge as inhering in mental models that provide the knower with a *gestalt*. Moreover, the context of the gestalt provides one way in which we can understand the tacit component of knowledge. In a gestalt, we can distinguish the portions we focus attention on from the background context that helps to establish the pattern of the gestalt or that is used as a tool to integrate the focal portions into a more comprehensive whole. The "focal" knowledge in the pattern receives our attention and notice. The "tacit" or background knowledge on the other hand, while much more extensive and absolutely necessary to the pattern, is not noticed and remains unarticulated.

Codified knowledge claims—Information that has been codified but that has not yet been subjected to organizational validation.

Distributed organizational knowledge base—An abstract construct representing the outcome of knowledge integration. The DOKB is found everywhere in the enterprise, not merely in electronic repositories. It is distributed over all of the agents and all of the repositories in the enterprise. It contains both mental (world 2) knowledge and artifactual or cultural (world 3) knowledge.

Experiential feedback loops—Processes by which information concerning the outcomes of organizational learning activities are fed back into the knowledge production phase of an organization's knowledge life cycle as a useful reference for future action.

Individual and group learning (I & G)—A task cluster involving human interaction, information acquisition, individual and group learning, knowledge claim formulation, and validation by which new individual and/or group knowledge is created. This task cluster is recursive in the sense that I & G learning itself proceeds through KLCs at the level of system interaction just below the global level, while I & G learning at this second level is itself a KLC at the level below, and so on until individual learning is reached.

Information about falsified knowledge claims—Information that attests to the existence of falsified knowledge claims and the circumstances under which such knowledge was falsified.

Information about undecided knowledge claims—Information that attest to the existence of undecided knowledge claims and the circumstances under which such knowledge was tested and neither survived nor was falsified.

Information about surviving knowledge claims—Information that attests to the existence of surviving knowledge claims and the circumstances under which such knowledge was tested and evaluated.

Information acquisition—A process by which an organization either deliberately or serendipitously acquires knowledge claims or information produced by others external to the organization.

Falsified knowledge—A collection of codified falsified knowledge claims.

Invalidated knowledge claims—Codified knowledge claims that have not survived an organization's testing and evaluation process. In other words, falsehoods.

Knowledge claim—A codified *expression* that may be held as surviving knowledge at an individual and/or group level, but has not yet been subjected to a validation process at an organizational level. In other words, information. Knowledge claims are components of networks of such claims that, if validated, would become the explicit basis for organizational or agent behavior.

Knowledge claim formulation—A process involving human interaction by which new organizational knowledge claims are formulated. The experience of participating in knowledge claim formulation feeds back to individual and group learning and produces world 2 individual and group level knowledge.

Knowledge integration—The process by which an organization introduces new surviving knowledge claims to its operating environment and retires old ones. Knowledge integration includes all knowledge broadcasting, searching for and retrieving knowledge, teaching, knowledge sharing, and other social activity that communicates either an understanding of previously produced organizational knowledge to knowledge workers, or the knowledge that certain sets of knowledge claims have been tested and that they and information about how they survived tests and evaluation is available in the organizational knowledge base, or some degree of understanding between these alternatives. Knowledge integration processes, therefore, may also include the transmission and integration of information.

Table 7.1. KLC Glossary

> **Knowledge production**—A process by which new individual, group, or organizational knowledge is created. Synonymous with "individual learning," "group learning," or "organizational learning."
>
> **Knowledge (claim) evaluation or validation process**—A process by which knowledge claims are subjected to competitive testing in relation to organizational criteria to determine their value and veracity.
>
> **Organizational knowledge**—A complex network of codified knowledge and knowledge sets held by an organization, consisting of surviving, validated knowledge claims.
>
> **Organizational learning**—A process involving human interaction, knowledge claim formulation, and validation by which new organizational knowledge is created.
>
> **(Business) structures incorporating organizational knowledge**—Outcomes of organizational system interaction. The organization behaves through these structures including business processes, strategic plans, authority structures, information systems, policies and procedures, etc. Knowledge structures exist within these business structures and are the particular configurations of knowledge found in them.
>
> **Unvalidated or undecided knowledge claims**—Codified knowledge claims that have not satisfied an organization's validation criteria but were not falsified either. Knowledge claims requiring further study.
>
> **Validated knowledge claims**—Codified knowledge claims that have survived an organization's tests in the face of its validation criteria. Truth from the viewpoint of the organization.

Table 7.1. KLC Glossary (continued)

The importance of the tacit/explicit distinction for KM is emphasized in Nonaka and Takeuchi's (1995) account of the "Knowledge Creating Company." They assume that knowledge is created through the interaction between tacit and explicit knowledge, and they postulate four modes of knowledge conversion

- From tacit to tacit (called socialization)
- From tacit to explicit (externalization)
- From explicit to explicit (combination)
- From explicit to tacit (internalization)

Since the appearance of Nonaka and Takeuchi's very popular book, the distinction between tacit and explicit knowledge and the idea that knowledge management is about encouraging these four modes of conversion in a kind of spiral model of upward progress has informed the knowledge management programs of many companies.

Polanyi, implicit knowledge, and Popper

In considering Polanyi's distinctions let us begin by noticing that the tacit/explicit distinction is a dichotomy that oversimplifies his more detailed account of knowledge and the gestalt concept. That is, Polanyi indicates that much tacit knowledge can be made explicit, even though there is some that remains ineffable and can never be expressed. Further, he even distinguishes "implicit beliefs," (1958, pp. 286–294), suggesting a third category of knowledge: implicit beliefs, defined as those "held in the form of our conceptual framework, as expressed in our language" (ibid. pp. 286–287).

In short, Polanyi identifies tacit knowledge that can't be expressed, tacit knowledge that can be made explicit, and implicit knowledge as defined just above. So, the Nonaka and Takeuchi interpretation of Polanyi's work is too simple. If we agree that tacit knowledge is sometimes composed of beliefs we cannot express and that explicit knowledge is made of expressed beliefs, then that leaves a third category—those cognitions or beliefs that, while not focal or explicit, are expressible, given the environmental conditions effective in eliciting them. I will call this category implicit knowledge, while recognizing that it contains not only those nonfocal or assumed portions of our conceptual frameworks, but any nonfocal beliefs that can be brought into focus and made explicit. So now we have a three-way distinction relevant to the study of knowledge conversion: explicit, implicit, and tacit.

It is also useful to view this three-way classification from the point of view of Popper's distinction between world 2 and world 3. That is, Popper's objective knowledge (world 3) is obviously all explicit and codified and involves the expression of Polanyi's "focal knowledge." To the extent that we can think of "implicit knowledge" in the world 3 sense, its character is very different from world 2 implicit knowledge. The latter is based on a psychological association with focal knowledge that is part of a gestalt. World 3 implicit knowledge, in contrast, is knowledge that is logically implicit in explicit knowledge, in the sense that it can be derived from such knowledge.

On the other hand, some of Popper's world 2 mental phenomena are obviously personal and "tacit" in the sense that (by definition) they may represent mental objects that cannot be focused in expressible psychological orientations. Other world 2 mental phenomena represent objects that can be focused in such orientations and are therefore *implicit*. Finally, there are still other world 2 phenomena that represent explicit, focal beliefs—situational orientations that express explicit linguistic knowledge in the mind. Such tacit, implicit, and explicit phenomena in the mind are all unobservable abstractions or "hidden variables." They are hypothetical constructs whose characteristics must be inferred using measurement instruments, models, surveys, observation, etc.

Note, also, that all explicit statements are not about world 3 objects and all personal, tacit knowledge is not about world 2. Thus, if I say that I know that the "many-worlds" interpretation of quantum theory is true, this explicit statement is about my *belief* that the many-worlds interpretation is true. It is an explicit statement about a world 2 object. It converts my implicit knowledge (my validated belief) into an explicit knowledge claim about my belief. It is not a direct statement about the (world 3) many-worlds model. It also does not convert my implicit knowledge orientation into explicit linguistic knowledge in the sense that I have fully and faithfully transformed my implicit psychological orientation into an explicit, codified form. That cannot be done because my implicit belief is not a linguistic formulation, and the epistemic gap between internal, nonlinguistic psychological connections and internal or external linguistic formulations is irreducible.

On the other hand, I can also hold subjective knowledge (beliefs) about either subjective states or about world 1 or world 3 objects. My procedural knowledge about how to make lamb stew is about world 1, for example. So subjective knowledge is in no way restricted to knowledge about world 2 objects.

Individual level world 2 knowledge and motivational hierarchies

It is a general characteristic of the various current discussions about the nature of (world 2) knowledge, and the foundations of knowledge management that the relation of such knowledge to psychological motivation is not explicitly considered. One can see this clearly by noting that tacit/implicit and explicit knowledge are all viewed as situationally oriented beliefs. But what are beliefs? They are cognitions, or perhaps at most cognitions combined with evaluations, and both of these represent situationally fixed psychological orientations rather than general psychological predispositions. The knowledge management literature simply does not recognize world 2 *knowledge predispositions* of individuals, even though it is these predispositions that are the product of an agent's knowledge-processing experience and the motivator of its knowledge-processing decisions.

Figure 7.10 illustrates the incentive system of an agent and (see Birch and Veroff, 1966; Atkinson, 1964; Atkinson and Birch, 1978) the complex of motivational predispositions that intervenes between the situational stimuli and the behavior of any agent. Figure 7.10 shows the goal-directed agent depicted in Figure 7.9 in greater detail. It views agent behavior as the product of an interaction of the agent's situation with a hierarchy of motivational predispositions, including value orientations (Kluckhohn and Strodtbeck, 1961; Morris, 1956), and various levels of increasingly focused attitudinal predispositions. These predispositions, combined with the external situation, finally produce a situational orientation, which is the immediate precursor of goal-striving, instrumental behavior, such as business process behavior, and which includes both the tacit and explicit knowledge responsible for decision making and behavior.

The availability and expectancy factors in Figure 7.10 refer to an agent's predispositions to perceive certain classes of behavior alternatives and resources as

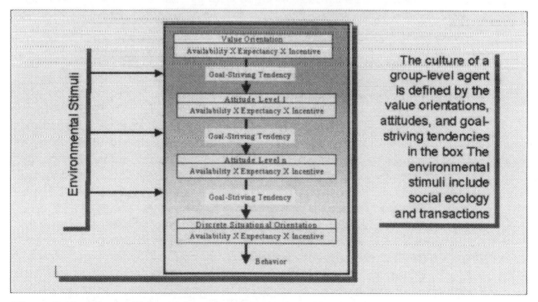

Figure 7.10. The incentive system of an agent.

available for acting (availability), and certain expected consequences as likely to result from implementing the various alternatives (expectancy). The incentive factor refers to the negative or positive attraction, the intensity of affect or emotion, which the perceived consequences of particular alternatives have for the agent. The motive factor is the strength of the goal-striving predispositions resulting from the interaction of the other three factors. The availability and expectancy factors in this framework are cognitive in character and the incentive factor is emotional or affective. Interactions of these factors are knowledge or belief predispositions of agents, and they are an essential part of the world 2 knowledge system of an agent. They play a vital role, not only in decision making but in learning. And they provide a large part of the continuity of individual behavior and knowledge seeking that we observe in the knowledge life cycle and other business process behavior.

Knowledge and culture

What is culture and what is its relationship to knowledge? "Cultural" barriers are often held responsible for failures to share and transfer knowledge in organizations. It is frequently said that knowledge management must undertake the difficult task of changing an organization's culture to achieve the knowledge sharing and transfer necessary to realize the full value of the organization's knowledge resources. But "culture" is one of those terms used loosely, in a multiplicity of ways, to cover a multitude of sins, so when we are told the culture must be changed to solve a problem in KM, we don't always know what that really means.

Alternative definitions of culture

Here are some alternative definitions of culture summarized by John H. Bodley (2000) of the University of Washington from a longer list of 160 definitions compiled in 1952 by the great anthropologists Alfred L. Kroeber and Clyde Kluckhohn (1952).

- *Topical.* Culture consists of everything on a list of topics, or categories, such as social organization, religion, or economy. [I don't think this definition is very relevant for KM.]
- *Historical.* Culture is social heritage, or tradition, that is passed on to future generations. [This may be relevant to KM in that organizations may have traditions that are difficult to change. But to use this concept in KM we need to be very specific about which traditions in an organization impact either KM practices or activities or knowledge processing activities, and we need to realize that "traditions" generally change very slowly and most frequently as a response to behavioral change.]
- *Behavioral.* Culture is shared, learned human behavior, a way of life. [This definition is used successfully in the analysis of cultures at a societal level. To use it at the organizational level, we need to distinguish shared, learned behavior among individuals in an organization that results from general socialization as opposed to shared, learned behavior that results from organizational socialization. This may be difficult to measure. But its measurement may be important because learned behavior

resulting from organizational socialization may be much easier to change than learned behavior resulting from general socialization.]

- *Normative.* Culture is ideals, values, or rules for living. [One could map organizational ideals, values, and "rules for living," But measurement is difficult. If you use behavior to measure these things, you have the problem of explaining KM, knowledge processing, and organizational behavior in terms of such behavior rather than in terms of ideals, values, and rules for living. On the other hand if you don't use behavioral measures, you pretty much have to do analysis of cultural products or surveys to develop measures. In any event, ideals, values, and rules for living are emergent properties of social systems. They, like traditions respond to changes in behavior, but do not change very easily in response to organizational manipulation.]

- *Functional.* Culture is the way humans solve problems of adapting to the environment or living together. [This definition is difficult for KM, because knowledge processing tempered by knowledge management is the way humans solve such problems. So this definition does not explain or predict knowledge processing and knowledge management as much as it equates culture with these things.]

- *Mental.* Culture is a complex of ideas, or learned habits, that inhibit impulses and distinguish people from animals. [This is the "psychologized" version of the normative definition. As stated, it is debatable because certain higher animals (e.g., primates and dolphins) also have learned habits and ideas, so this definition may not distinguish people from animals.

  More important, this definition does not link the ideas or learned habits people have with any shared socialization. That is, ideas or learned habits resulting from individualized experiences are not distinguished from ideas or learned habits resulting from shared societal or organizational experiences. The term "culture" can be coherently applied only to the second class of ideas.

  When this idea is used in KM, it is important to recognize the importance of measuring such "subjective culture" as the result of shared organizational experiences (e.g., in "boot camps," organizational ceremonies, committee meetings, performance reviews). That is, when claiming that culture is a factor accounting for characteristic patterns of knowledge processing, it is necessary to show not only that attitudes, cognitive orientations, and other mental phenomena are affecting knowledge-processing behavior, but also that such phenomena result from some shared experiences the organization is implementing.]

- *Structural.* Culture consists of patterned and interrelated ideas, symbols, or behaviors. [I think this definition covers too much and doesn't distinguish between culture and other aspects of information, knowledge, or KM.]

- *Symbolic.* Culture is based on arbitrarily assigned meanings that are shared by a society. [This is a societal concept. Is it also useful at the organizational level for KM? Perhaps, but this usage seems to me to be marginal.]

The upshot of this brief survey of "culture" is that when someone says that knowledge can't be shared or transferred due to cultural barriers, one really has to ask for clarification to know which sense of culture is intended. Is culture really the barrier to effective KM it is frequently made out to be? The answer may well depend on what the questioner means by "culture."

Culture, or something else?

Indeed it is even possible that when someone talks about cultural barriers they are not talking about culture at all. Thus, when organizational politics is opposed to knowledge sharing and transfer, that is not culture, and while it may be difficult to change, it is easier to change than culture. When the organizational incentive system affecting knowledge worker behavior must be changed to facilitate knowledge sharing and transfer, that is not "culture," and it is certainly easier to change.

In fact, the claim that knowledge sharing and transfer do not occur because of culture sometimes sounds plausible because of the tacit assumption that we must somehow make knowledge workers "altruistic" before they will share and transfer, and that this in turn requires a fundamental change in behavioral culture. But the idea that we must make knowledge workers unusually altruistic to get them to share and transfer knowledge ignores the many examples of social systems and organizations in which collaboration is based on normal motivations including self-interest.

I believe that the problems besetting KM are not, primarily, cultural problems in the historical, behavioral, normative, or mental senses of the term discussed earlier (the only possibilities that apply). Instead, they are problems of structural organization and change that can be managed by political means. Structural changes can align individual motivational and incentive systems, whether of individual or cultural origin, with organizational incentive systems to affect behavioral changes without cultural change. In fact, in social systems, behavioral and structural changes frequently precede and cause cultural changes.

What is culture and how does it fit with other factors influencing behavior?

As you can see from the foregoing brief survey, there is great diversity in definitions of "culture." Is there a definition more or less consistent with previous usage and also useful for KM? I will propose such a definition subsequently and discuss its implications for the role of culture in KM and the relationship of culture to knowledge.

It will help in defining culture if we begin by noting that for every group and for the organization as a whole, we can distinguish analytical properties, structural properties, and global properties. These distinctions were originally introduced by Paul Lazarsfeld in the 1950s (see Lazarsfeld and Menzel, 1961), and later used by Terhune (1972) in a comprehensive review of the National Character literature. Analytical properties are derived by aggregating them from data describing the members of a collective (a group or a system). Examples of analytical attributes include the following:

- GNP
- GNP per capita
- Per capita income
- Average salary
- Total sales
- Sales per sales rep.
- Number of accumulated vacation days
- Number of lost work days due to injury

Structural properties are derived by performing some operation on data describing relations of each member of a collective to some or all of the others. Examples of structural properties are

- Extent of inequality of training
- Extent of inequality of knowledge base distribution
- Extent of inequality of knowledge access resource distribution
- Extent of inequality of knowledge dissemination capability
- Extent of inequality of power
- Intensity of conflict behavior
- Intensity of cooperative behavior
- Ratio of e-messages sent to e-messages received by an agent

Finally, global properties are based on information about the collective that is not derived from information about its members. Instead, such properties are produced by the group or system process they characterize, and, in that sense, they may be said to "emerge" from it or from the series of interactions constituting it. Examples of emergent global attributes include

- Value orientations (reflected in social artifacts) (Kluckhohn and Strodt-beck, 1961)
- Achievement orientation
- Self-realization orientation
- Power orientation
- Mastery over nature
- Lineality (preference for a hierarchical style in social organization)
- Extent of democratic organization of the knowledge life cycle
- Innovation propensity (the predisposition of an organization to innovate)

The classification of social system properties into analytical, structural, and global attributes is exhaustive. To define culture let's first ask whether we should define it as an analytical, structural, or global attribute of some combination? Culture, first, is not an analytical attribute. Culture is not an arithmetical aggregation of survey results or individual man-made characteristics. It is not the percentage of knowledge workers who trust their fellows, believe in systems thinking, believe in critical thinking, or are favorably disposed toward knowledge sharing. Why not? Because (a) culture influences behavior, statistical artifacts don't, and (b) the above attributes are social/psychological, not cultural.

Second, culture also should not be defined as a set of structural attributes derived from relations among individual level attributes. Why not? Because "culture" refers to something comprehensive and regulative that accounts for and determines structure and also because if we define culture as structural in character, we are assuming that we can model the structural relations defining it. Do we want to assume that, or do we want to assume that culture is global in character and emergent, or some combination of the three types of attributes?

Third, the alternative of culture as a combination of attribute types may at first seem attractive, but the following considerations argue against it. (A) The character of analytical attributes as arithmetic aggregations of individual level properties is not changed by defining a construct that includes such attributes with structural and global ones. (B) Analytical attributes still are not reflective of process or system-level attributes that are regulative or comprehensive. At best, they are indicators of conditions caused by structural and global level attributes and are not causal in themselves.

As for culture being a combination of structural and emergent attributes, my objection to this view lies in how I think we want to use the term "culture." If we want to use it as an explainer or predictor of structural patterns, it is ill-advised to confound structure with culture—that is, to confound the "form" of a social system or organization with its predispositions or "spirit." In other words, defining culture as a global attribute rather than as a combination of global and structural attributes appears most consistent with previous usage and with our strategic need to use "culture" as a tool to account for "structure" in our models.

If culture is a global attribute of agents, we still must decide what kind of global attribute it is. The world 1/world 2/world 3 distinction of Popper's is also important here. It suggests that we may distinguish three types of culture. A key characteristic of all three types is that each is man-made (or generalizing this concept, made by an intelligent agent). World 1 artifacts are material products, so *world 1 products are material culture.* World 2 culture I will call subjective culture (Triandis, et al., 1972). And world 3 culture I will call objective culture.

The subjective culture of a group or organizational agent is the agent's characteristic set of emergent pre-dispositions to perceive its environment. It includes group- or organizational-level value orientations and attitudes and the relations among them. It is a configuration of global attributes that emerges from group interactions—that is, from the organization and pattern of transactions among the agents within a group.

The objective culture of a group or organizational agent is the agent's characteristic stock of emergent problems, models, theories, artistic creations, language, programs, stories, etc. reflected in its documents, books, art galleries, information systems, dictionaries, and other containers. It is a configuration of global attributes expressing the content of its information, knowledge, art, and music, apart from the predispositions the group or its agents may have toward this content. The objective culture of an organization is an aspect of the social ecology of its group agents, the cumulated effects of previous group interactions. As such, the perception of it by group agents (part of their subjective culture or psychology depending on the type of agent) influences their behavior.

Subjective culture affects behavior in groups or organizations at two levels:

- It affects agents at the decision-making level of interaction immediately below the level of the cultural group by predisposing these agents toward behavior (see Figure 7.8).

- It affects the behavior of the group itself by predisposing it toward behavior (see Figure 7.9).

The context of objective culture in social ecology and its relationship to interaction within a group or organization is also illustrated in Figure 7.9. The focus of the illustration is the decision-making agent at the bottom left. The agent may be an individual agent or a group level agent, depending on context.

Looking at the right-hand side of Figure 7.9, transaction inputs received from other agents and previous social ecology (the feedback loop on social ecology) determine the current social ecology (including objective culture) affecting an agent's decision. Next, transactions, social ecology, and previous decisions (goal-striving outcome feedback loop) are viewed as "impacting" the goal-directed typical agent, whose internal process then produces decisions which result in transaction outputs from agent (i) directed toward other agents j, k, . . . n. These transaction outputs are inputs into the decision processes of these other agents. The interaction within and among agents j, k, . . . n, finally, produces transactions directed at agent (i) at a later time and thereby closes the loop.

What goes on inside the goal-directed agent (i)? So long as (i) is a group-level agent and its components are also groups, then the interaction process may be viewed in the same way as in Figure 7.9, *but specified at a lower level*. But if one decides to *move from a transactional to a motivational perspective* on a group level agent (i), then the conception is somewhat different.

Figure 7.10 presents a decision-making process in a pre-behavior situation. Here the pre-behavior situation is filtered through the decision-making system of a group-level agent, specifically through value orientations and through attitudes existing at increasingly domain specific levels of abstraction. This interaction between the external world and the agent's predispositonal reality screens produces a discrete situational orientation, a "definition of the situation," which in turn feeds back to the predispositional levels in search of choice guidance. This guidance then determines the final situational orientation, which leads to behavior and to new feedbacks to the situational orientation, and to attitude and value orientation predispositions.

The predispositions in Figure 7.10 represent psychological attributes when the agent involved is an individual, but when the agent is a group, these are the group's characteristic set of emergent pre-dispositions to perceive its environment, including group level value orientations and attitudes and the relations among them. *That is, these predispositions are group subjective culture.* Moreover, as in the case of the individual agent discussed in the previous section, the availability, expectancy, and incentive elements in combination represent *subjective cultural knowledge predispositions*.

Based on this account of culture a number of conclusions are immediately suggested.

- First, there is an organizational objective culture that is part of the social ecology of every group and individual in the organization and therefore is a factor in the decision making of agents at every level of corporate interaction. *This objective culture is composed of knowledge predispositions*, and it is shared. It is not shared in the sense that all agree with what it says or assent to it. Indeed, it may be contradictory in many ways. But it is shared in the sense that all members of the group have access to this objective culture and its world 3 content.

- Second, each group level agent, each team, each community of practice, each formal organizational group, and each informal group all have group subjective cultures, largely composed of knowledge predispositions that predispose their decision making. So the behavior of group agents is influenced both by their internal subjective and objective cultures and by objective organizational culture.
- Third, the most pervasive, but also the weakest subjective cultural predispositions in intensity are those most far removed from situational stimuli. These are the most abstract value orientations and attitudinal predispositions in the hierarchy of Figure 7.10.
- Fourth, although value orientations and high-level attitudes are both the most pervasive and the weakest influences on immediate behavior, they are also the hardest predispositions to change in a short time. This is true because they form and are maintained as a result of reinforcement from behavior patterns in diverse concrete situations experienced by agents in the group or organization. The most abstract patterns of any subjective culture are self-reinforcing through time. To change them one needs to break down the structure of self-reinforcement and the integration of the many subsidiary patterns supporting this structure.

Modes of conversion and the KLC view

The Nonaka and Takeuchi (1995) picture of knowledge dynamics, once again, focuses on the processes of "knowledge conversion" (p. 61), where this means creating and expanding human knowledge "through social interaction between tacit knowledge and explicit knowledge" (ibid.). They also emphasize that knowledge conversion is a "social process," between individuals and is not confined to a single person (ibid.). The framework presented earlier with its emphasis on the knowledge life cycle (KLC); world 2 and world 3 knowledge; tacit, explicit, and implicit individual level knowledge; and world 2 knowledge predispositions as an aspect of motivation and the role of culture is also a social process view of knowledge processing. But it is a good deal more comprehensive, albeit more complex, than the Nonaka/Takeuchi model.

But what difference does it make? Why should one adopt this more comprehensive view at the cost of greater complexity. Generally, my answer is that the KLC view I have presented is much closer to the truth than the Nonaka/Takeuchi model, much more realistic than their model, much richer conceptually, much more consonant with a close reading of Polanyi's (1958, 1966) work, more consistent with the work of other epistemologists of note such as Pierce and Popper, much more fruitful as a conceptual platform for development of metrics, much superior as a conceptual foundation for guiding knowledge processing and knowledge management software applications, and a much better basis for developing KM methodology and KM solutions. I cannot support all of these knowledge claims in this book, but I can perhaps begin to do so by providing the following critique of the Nonaka/Takeuchi model from the viewpoint of the preceding framework.

Specific commentary on the four modes of conversion

Tacit to tacit

Tacit to tacit conversions are *not* instances of knowledge creation *from the organizational point of view.* They involve creation of unexpressed, unarticulated procedural knowledge (world 2 mental process models) in one agent in response to another's sharing of their experience through demonstration or pointing, a process of "ostensive sharing." The knowledge is not organizational, because (1) it is not transferable throughout the organization and (2) it cannot be shown that the knowledge created by the receiver of the demonstration is the same as the knowledge of the demonstrator. Therefore, the knowledge cannot be generally validated from an organizational rather than a personal point of view.

Tacit to explicit

Tacit to explicit conversions also do not create organizational knowledge, primarily because tacit knowledge, as distinct from implicit knowledge, cannot be expressed. If the "conversion" only involves measurement of tacit knowledge, no "creation" is involved, but only an inference of existing subjective knowledge from a measurement. The inferred knowledge can then be considered a knowledge claim formulated in the KLC. Before it becomes organizational knowledge (see the KLC) it needs to be validated.

If the "conversion" involves collaborative organizational development of metaphors, analogies, and models, then this does involve "creation" of knowledge claims that were not implicit in the original tacit knowledge; but this creation is only of a knowledge claim. It still must be validated before it becomes organizational knowledge.

Tacit-to-explicit "conversions" are perceived to be a very important aspect of knowledge production in organizations. They are thought of as one of the primary sources of knowledge creation. The importance of the issue of tacit knowledge in KM relates primarily to this perceived conversion—to the perceived reluctance of employees to share their knowledge and participate in such conversions, and to the perceived inability of the enterprise to "manage" this conversion process.

However, as we have seen, direct tacit-to-explicit conversions are impossible because of the inexpressibility of tacit knowledge, so the above conversion is, in fact, not important for organizational knowledge production. *Instead, the conversion of "implicit knowledge" to explicit knowledge claims is the knowledge creation process of real significance.* But even here, there is no creation of explicit knowledge from implicit knowledge, because the mere conversion of implicit knowledge to the explicit form is knowledge claim formulation absent knowledge claim validation. So the result is mere information, not knowledge.

Explicit to explicit

Explicit to explicit conversion is the combination mode of knowledge creation in which already explicit pieces of knowledge are combined to produce new explicit knowledge. It is doubtful, however, that this form of knowledge creation by human beings exists in just this form. Explicit pieces of knowledge are often combined by individuals to create new knowledge claims. But this combination involves the intervention of individuals who must perform the combination by first understanding one piece of knowledge and then *another and visualizing what a combination of the two in the context of their implicit background knowledge would produce.* The sequence is not from explicit to explicit at all. Instead, it is from explicit to implicit (perhaps with assistance from some tacit knowledge) and then from implicit to explicit.

What if the combination is performed by computer? In that case, the combination is explicit to explicit, but is purely deductive in character. The explicit to explicit conversion is possible only because (1) it is carried out through application of deductive principles alone or (2) it is carried out through such an application in which tacit knowledge was previously built into the programming process through the creative process of formulating rules for combining knowledge through conjecture, inductive inference, abduction, or other methods employing human intuition.

Explicit to tacit

Explicit to tacit conversion is called internalization by Nonaka and Takeuchi. They refer to the process of individuals' learning explicit knowledge and "internalizing" it in their belief systems. But their account of internalization is vague in laying out the actual process. The three-way distinction among tacit, explicit, and implicit world 2 knowledge calls their account into question. That is, it is much more likely that internalization occurs through explicit knowledge receding from the focus of one's gestalts and becoming implicit knowledge than it is that explicit knowledge would be converted to an inexpressible form. In other words, I propose that internalization is an explicit-to-implicit conversion rather than an explicit-to-tacit conversion.

It is through internalization that world 3 objects have an impact on organizational decision making. Knowledge integration is the process that sometimes produces internalization and sets the stage for knowledge use in business processes. But internalization does not itself create organizational knowledge. Instead, it is the process that transfers organizational knowledge to the distributed organizational knowledge base and the structures that contain it.

Does "conversion" produce organizational knowledge or only knowledge claims?

Based on the analysis of the four modes provided above the answer to this question is a clear no. Tacit-to-tacit conversions ("socialization") involve the creation of new tacit knowledge (i.e., encoding of a pattern in the brain), but this result is neither transferable organizationally nor is it possible to determine whether the new encoding is valid relative to the initial tacit knowledge that was shared. Tacit-to-explicit conversions (externalization) are impossible, and implicit-to-explicit conversions only produce knowledge claims, not knowledge. Explicit-to-explicit conversions (combination) also produce knowledge claims, rather than knowledge, because they are actually explicit-to-implicit-to-explicit conversions, at least where humans are involved. And where the conversions are machine generated, then whether "new" explicit knowledge is produced depends on whether one thinks that deduction from axioms creates knowledge that was not logically implicit in the axioms. In any case, this mode does not fit the assumption that all four modes are social in nature. Finally, explicit-to-tacit (internalization) is a questionable mode, probably better characterized as explicit to implicit, but even if this is done, what is actually accomplished? It is the creation of individual level knowledge beliefs and predispositions that are the result of the interaction of world 3 organizational knowledge with the individual agent and its social context. This individual level knowledge is not organizational in character.

An oversimplified classification scheme?

Even with the addition of implicit knowledge to the previous dichotomy, the Nonaka/Takeuchi classification is expanded from four to seven types (tacit to implicit and tacit to explicit are excluded by the definition of tacit). But if one considers that tacit, explicit, implicit world 2 mental objects may also be cross-classified by explicit and implicit world 3 knowledge, we now have twenty-five logically possible conversion types. Some of these types are excluded by definitional considerations. An analysis being performed by Mark W. McElroy and myself indicates that some seventeen types will remain after exclusion of eight types based on definitional considerations. Our analysis, then, suggests that the Nonaka/Takeuchi model identifies only four out of seventeen conversion types actually present in knowledge producing situations. The analysis also shows that none of the seventeen types encompasses knowledge claim validation, the essential final step in knowledge production.

The four modes of conversion and the KLC

Nonaka and Takeuchi's four modes of conversion are all encompassed by the KLC model and are perhaps better interpreted in its terms, in terms of the 3-way distinction among tacit, implicit, and explicit knowledge and in terms of Popper's distinction between world 2 beliefs and world 3 "objective knowledge." The movement in the KLC from individual and group learning to knowledge claim formulation encompasses externalization. World 3 objects (concepts, models, analogies) are created from world 2 beliefs. But externalization does not extend all the way to validation. *Consequently, objective (world 3) knowledge is not produced from externalization.*

Externalization—and therefore knowledge claim formulation—focuses on the major issue in KM related to implicit knowledge: that of sharing it with the enterprise. Enterprises worry about world 2 implicit (though they call it tacit) knowledge, produced in part through work in the enterprise (through internalization), and being lost to it because such individual knowledge has never been converted to world 3 codified knowledge claims. They want to implement processes that will provide knowledge workers with the incentive to routinely produce such conversions, to make their implicit knowledge explicit, and to codify it for the enterprise. From the point of view of the KLC, this is a matter of managing the knowledge claim formulation task cluster so that it provides such incentives.

Explicit-to explicit-conversion, if we view it according to the revised sequence of explicit to implicit to explicit, is located within the knowledge claim formulation and individual and group learning task clusters of the KLC. Combination doesn't involve any validation. It does involve movements back and forth between (world 2) individual and group learning and (world 3) knowledge claim formulation.

Tacit-to-tacit conversion is located solely within the (world 2) individual learning area. No knowledge claims are made or validated. No external information is required. No organizational knowledge is produced. No organizational knowledge is integrated. Nevertheless, increasing the amount and effectiveness of such conversions may improve performance in an enterprise. Therefore, it may be desirable to manage the individual and group learning task cluster in the KLC to support tacit-to-tacit conversions, while recognizing that the knowledge produced is individual-level, inexpressible knowledge that cannot *belong* to the organization.

Finally, internalization is one of the anticipated impacts of knowledge integration on the DOKB. Internalization does not mean replicating world 3 knowledge as world 2 individual beliefs; instead, it means individual learning of the world 3 knowledge, an active process involving interpretation of world 3 knowledge and adaptation of it to the agent's "cognitive map." It also means learning the new adaptation so well so that it leaves the category of focal, explicit knowledge in the mind and becomes implicit, background knowledge.

In sum, the KLC model, incorporates all of the knowledge conversion modes of Nonaka and Takeuchi, while emphasizing Popper's distinction between world 2 and world 3 objects. It also provides a much broader framework than the four modes of knowledge conversion for tracking the interaction of world 2 and world 3 knowledge, a framework that can encompass all of their results and relate them to a much broader range of processes and concepts.

The knowledge conversion model: missing the point

Does the knowledge conversion model and its associated image of the "spiral of organizational knowledge creation" (Nonaka and Takeuchi, 1995, pp. 70–73) miss the point? I believe it does. The point it misses is that knowledge processing and knowledge management are not only concerned with creation of knowledge in individual minds within a social context but are even more concerned with producing objective knowledge through inquiry designed to solve business problems. It is not the conversion of beliefs from tacit to explicit, or from tacit to implicit to explicit, that counts in knowledge creation. Rather it is the movement of knowledge processing from knowledge claim formulation to knowledge claim validation that is primary. And that migration is ignored in the knowledge conversion/spiral model.

But it is not ignored in the KLC view. Rather, knowledge claim validation is at the center of the KLC and highlights its primary purpose of first producing objective knowledge and then integrating it in the organization and its business processes. The KLC is no less concerned with individual-level knowledge, social context, group processes, knowledge sharing, culture, socialization, internalization, and other phenomena highlighted by the knowledge conversion model. But it recognizes that there is a distinction between world 2 and world 3 knowledge production and that both must be fully encompassed by a process model treating both knowledge production and knowledge integration.

References

Allee, V. (1997) *The Knowledge Evolution: Expanding Organizational Intelligence* (Boston: Butterworth-Heinemann).

Allee, V. (2000). "Reconfiguring the Value Network," available at: http://www.vernaallee.com/reconfiguring_val_net.html.

Argyris, C. (1993). *Knowledge for Action* (San Francisco: Jossey-Bass).

Atkinson, J.W. (1964). *An Introduction to Motivation* (New York: Van Nostrand).

Atkinson, J.W., and Birch, D. (1978). *Introduction to Motivation* (2nd edition) (New York: Van Nostrand).

Axelrod, R. (1976). *The Structure of Decision* (Princeton, NJ: Princeton University Press).

Aune, B. (1970). *Rationalism, Empiricism, and Pragmatism* (New York: Random House, 1970).

Barquin, R. (2000). "From Bits and Bytes to Knowledge Management," January–February, 2000, www.e-gov.com; also available at www.barquin.com.

Beller, S. (2001). "The DIKUW Model," *National Health Data Systems*, April, 2001, available at www.nhds.com/toc.htm.

Bellinger, G. (1999). "Data, Information, Knowledge and Wisdom" at http://www.radix.net/~crbnblu/musings/kmgmt/kmgmt.htm.

Bennet, A., and Bennet, D. (2000). "Characterizing the Next Generation Knowledge Organization" *Knowledge and Innovation: Journal of the KMCI*, 1, no. 1, pp. 8–42.

Bodley, J.H. "What is Culture," available at: http://www.wsu.edu:8001/vcwsu/commons/topics/culture/culture-definitions/bodley-text.html.

Cavaleri, S., and Reed, F. (2000). "Designing Knowledge Generating Processes," *Knowledge and Innovation: Journal of the KMCI*, 1, no. 1, pp. 109–131.

Cavaleri, S., and Reed, F. (2001). "Organizational Inquiry: The Search for Effective Knowledge," *Knowledge and Innovation: Journal of the KMCI*, **1, no. 3,** pp. 27–54.

Cox, E. (1994). *The Fuzzy Systems Handbook* (Cambridge, MA: Academic Press).

Cox, E. (1995). *Fuzzy Logic for Business and Industry* (Rockland, MA: Charles River Media).

Goldman, A. (1991). *Empirical Knowledge* (Berkeley, CA: University of California, 1991).

James, W. (1907). *Pragmatism* (New York: Longmans).

Jones, W.T. (1952). *A History of Western Philosophy* (New York: Harcourt, Brace & World).

Kluckhohn, F., and Strodtbeck, F. (1961). *Variations in Value Orientations* (New York: Harper & Row).

Kosko, B. (1992). *Neural Networks and Fuzzy Systems* (Englewood Cliffs, NJ: Prentice Hall).

Kroeber, A., and Kluckhohn, C. (1952). "Culture: A Critical Review of Concepts and Definitions," *Papers of the Peabody Museum of American Archaeology and Ethnology*, 47, (1), (1952).

Lazarsfeld, P., and Menzel, H. (1961). "On the Relation Between Individual and Collective Properties," in Amitai Etzioni (ed.), *Complex Organizations* (New York: Holt, Rinehart & Winston).

Moore, G. (1991). *Crossing the Chasm* (New York: HarperBusiness).

Morris, C. (1956). *Varieties of Human Value* (Chicago, IL: University of Illinois Press).

Nonaka, I., and Takeuchi, H. (1995). *The Knowledge Creating Company* (New York: Oxford University Press).

Polanyi, M. (1958). *Personal Knowledge* (Chicago, IL: University of Chicago Press, 1958).

Polanyi, M. (1966). *The Tacit Dimension* (London: Routledge & Kegan Paul).

Popper, K.R. (1972). *Objective Knowledge* (London: Oxford University Press).

Popper, K.R., and Eccles, J.C. (1977). *The Self and Its Brain* (Berlin: Springer).

Popper, K.R. (1994). *Knowledge and the Body-Mind Problem* (London: Routledge & Kegan Paul).

Shannon, C.E. (1948), "A Mathematical Theory of Communication, *Bell System Technical Journal*, 27, pp. 379–423, 623–656.

Stacey, R.D. (1996). *Complexity and Creativity in Organizations* (San Francisco: Berrett-Koehler).

Swanstrom, E.W.; Firestone, J.M.; McElroy, M.W.; Weidner, D.T.; and Cavaleri, S. (1999). "The Age of The Metaprise," *Knowledge Management Consortium International*, Gaithersburg, MD, available at http://www.km.org/metaprise/MetapriseGrp.htm.

Terhune, K.W. (1970). "From National Character to National Behavior: A Reformulation," *Journal of Conflict Resolution*, 14, pp. 203–263.

Triandis, H.C. et al. (1972). *The Analysis of Subjective Culture* (New York: John Wiley).

Wiig, K. (1998) in Yogesh Malhotra's compilation at www.brint.com.

CHAPTER 8

Knowledge Life Cycle Subprocesses

Introduction

Before discussing knowledge management I want to develop the conceptual framework of knowledge production and knowledge integration in more detail. This is needed for a better understanding of what knowledge processing is and therefore of what knowledge management is trying to impact; in addition, therefore, it will ultimately be important for evaluating the relationship between knowledge management and enterprise information portals.

This development will take the form of a more detailed analysis of each of the subprocesses of knowledge production and knowledge integration; an identification and listing, sometimes with brief comments, of some descriptors and metrics that may be important in each; and a consideration of the meaning of innovation and its relation to the KLC and its subprocesses. The lists are intended as references to expose the concrete detail of objects involved in these subprocesses. Later they will be used in discussing requirements for EIPs that support knowledge processing and knowledge management—that is, enterprise knowledge portals (EKPs) (Firestone, 1999, 2000, 2000a, 2000b, and 2001).

Information acquisition

Information acquisition is a network of task patterns and tasks by which an organization either deliberately or serendipitously acquires knowledge claims or information produced by others external to the organization. That is, it refers *only* to the process of information flow across the boundary of the learning organization, team, group, or individual. It also refers only to the information flow relevant to the process of producing knowledge for solving specific problems generated by business processes.

Information acquisition occurs through interpersonal methods, electronic methods, or combinations of the two. From the viewpoint of the organization, information may be

- Gathered through explicit search activities

- Received as a result of solicited communications (subscriptions, request for alerts, etc.)
- Received as a result of unsolicited communications

Information may be acquired from any of the following external sources:

- Interpersonal peer communications
- Interpersonal expert communications
- E-mail messages
- Web documents
- Web-accessed databases
- Media (CDs, tapes, etc.)
- Printed documents

However information is acquired and from whatever external source, the efficiency and effectiveness of the KLC is related to the cycle time of acquiring information, to the relevance of the information that is acquired, and to the scope of that information. That is,

- The cycle time must be fast enough to provide information to other task clusters in the KLC that require the information.
- The information must be relevant to the problems KLC agents are trying to solve in their decision cycles.
- The information available externally must be broad enough in scope to meet the diversity of problems presented to the decision makers.

In addressing the scope, relevance, and cycle time issues, one needs process and outcome descriptors intended to address these issues. Descriptors of information acquisition are classified into process descriptors and information descriptors in the text that follows. These descriptors are offered for use in analysis and description of the information acquisition subprocess. They may also be used to develop hypotheses about scope, relevance, and cycle time and how they are related.

Process descriptors

Here are some global descriptors of this subprocess that relate directly to accelerating problem solving and innovation.

- Information acquisition cycle time
- Information acquisition velocity
- Information acquisition acceleration
- Intensity of collaborative activity in information acquisition (Collaborative activity may accelerate information acquisition.)

To acquire information through these various methods one must characterize the information acquisition subprocess. The methods can be classified into interpersonal and electronic methods. The following is a list, not necessarily exhaustive, of such methods.

- Methods of interpersonal searching and intelligence gathering:
  - Attending conferences
  - Telephone conversations
  - Meetings
  - Reading books and documents
- Methods of electronic searching and intelligence gathering:
  - KDD/data mining (Fayyad, et al., 1996)
  - Content analysis (see Chapter 2)
  - Cognitive mapping of content (Axelrod, 1976; Kosko, 1992)
  - Text mining (Sullivan, 2001)
  - Web-enabled searching/retrieving
  - Web-enabled application-specific searching/retrieving
  - Web-enabled file sharing
  - Web-enabled communications in communities of practice
  - Portal-enabled searching/accessing/retrieving
  - Agent-based scanning

Information acquisition infrastructure

The infrastructure of information acquisition is also important in describing the process. So here is a classification, again not necessarily exhaustive, of items in an information acquisition infrastructure.

- Internet facilities, both physical and software
- Fax
- Document and book subscriptions
- Intelligence service subscriptions
- Telephone facilities
- Training programs
- Electronic broadcast reception facilities
- Conference programs

Information descriptors

Here I will cover the media in which information is expressed, the type of information expressed, and the characteristics of the information base resulting from information acquisition.

- Media:
  - Hard copy
  - Microfiche
  - Tape
- Removable electronic media
  - Fixed disk

- — Optical
- — Silicon
- Type of information
  - — Structured data
  - — Conceptual models
  - — Data models
  - — Object models
  - — Planning models
  - — Analytical models
  - — Measurement models
  - — Predictive models
  - — Impact models
  - — Assessment models
  - — Electronic repositories
  - — Application software
  - — Validation criteria, perspectives, and frameworks
- Methods
- Methodologies
- Formal languages
- Semi-formal languages
- HTML documents
- XML tags and documents
- SGML tags and documents
- Meta-information
- Planning information
- Descriptive information
- Factual information
- Measurements of abstractions
- Information about impact and cause and effect
- Predictive information
- Assessment information
- Distributed/centralized architecture of acquired information base—the more distributed the better for knowledge claim formulation at a later time, provided connectivity is present to allow free access to the distributed information.
- Degree of integration/coherence of the acquired information base within or between information types or domains—the degree of integration/coherence of the information base is likely to increase the efficiency of KCF later on in the knowledge production process.
- Scope of the acquired information base within and across information types or domains
- Level of measurement of attributes in acquired information base within and across domains
- Types of models used in the acquired information base (conceptual analytic, data models, measurement models, impact models, predictive models, assessment models, object models, structural models)

- Types of formal languages used in the acquired information base (set theory, mathematics, fuzzy logic, etc.)
- Types of semiformal languages used in the acquired information base (object modeling language, information modeling language, etc.)
- Types of methods (features, benefits, specifications)
- Types of methodologies (features, benefits, specifications)
- Software applications (features, benefits, specifications, performance, interface)
- Priority of information components in terms of relevance.

Descriptors of change in processes

Descriptors of change are always important in developing models of impact. Such models are formulated in terms of changes from an existing baseline that appear attributable to some intervention in the subprocess, in this case information acquisition. In saying that one should track and measure changes in these descriptors, I am asserting that these are the ones that are most important either in affecting one another or in affecting downstream problem solving in the KLC value network.

- Change in information acquisition cycle time
- Change in information acquisition velocity
- Change in information acquisition acceleration
- Change in intensity of collaborative activity in information acquisition
- Change in priority of information components in terms of relevance.

Further descriptors can be arrived at by cross-classifying many of the above. Note that if this is done, the few simple change descriptors given suddenly become hundreds of attributes.

Individual and group (I&G) learning

This task cluster or subprocess is recursive in the sense that I&G learning is itself a KLC at the level of system interaction just below the global level, while I&G at the second level is itself a KLC at the level below, and so on until individual learning and knowledge production is reached. KLCs, therefore, occur at the group and individual levels of analysis as well as at the organizational level of analysis. They produce knowledge claims that have been validated from the perspective of the individual or the group, as the case may be, but from the perspective of the organization they are unvalidated information. Figure 8.1 illustrates the nesting of KLCs in an organization.

Process descriptors for individual and group learning are the same as those given for all of the other task clusters of the KLC combined. Outcome descriptors are also those of other task clusters. Specific lists are provided under the other KLC categories.

Knowledge claim formulation

Knowledge claim formulation is a subprocess and task cluster involving human interaction by which new organizational knowledge claims are formulated and

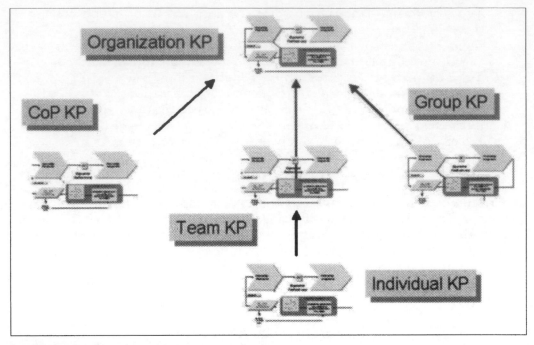

Figure 8.1. Nesting of KLCs in an organization.

codified. From the viewpoint of the organization, knowledge claims may be formulated through

- Deriving them from previously existing mental models
- Gathering data and information and describing the results of that process by asserting a factual claim
- Performing a measurement
- Thinking up a conjecture
- Using intuition
- Developing new models of various kinds—mathematical, statistical, computer, verbal, visual
- Interacting with others in a collaborative environment
- Analyzing textual content
- Text mining
- Data mining
- Using knowledge claim–eliciting collaborative techniques such as Delphi, Knowledge Café (Isaacs, 1999), Nominal Group and Analytical Hierarchy Process Techniques (Saaty, 1990)
- Using knowledge claim–eliciting software applications other than textual content analysis text and data mining
- Reformulating an invalidated model
- Meditation and many other activities

That is, knowledge claim formulation can result from diverse activities. Sometimes these activities are relatively mundane. Often they are creative activities. Always they involve an interaction between world 2 knowledge of those formulating knowledge claims and the world 3 knowledge claims they are producing or have produced in the past. As discussed in Chapter 7 at length, all of the knowledge "conversions" that result in explicit knowledge actually produce new knowledge claims. In other words, knowledge claim formulation activities involve an interaction between the subjective (and sometimes the implicit) and the objective, between individual and group learning and knowledge claim formulation.

In the end, knowledge claim formulation at the organizational level is an emergent process. This does not mean that knowledge claims are not formulated by human agents or that we cannot come to a better understanding of this subprocess. They are, and we can. But they are formulated by human agents interacting in teams, groups, communities of practice, and projects. Viewed at any point in time, the act of formulating a knowledge claim is another decision made by an individual. But viewed from a group perspective, the patterning of knowledge claim formulation is a *cas* phenomenon, and the pattern of knowledge claims produced is an emergent global property of the group or organizational NKMS.

Which activities are most effective for knowledge claim formulation depends on the specific problem situation being addressed by a specific KLC series of events motivated by that problem. There is no general answer to the question of which of the above are most effective in leading to knowledge claims that are likely to be validated. But as more formal approaches to managing the KLC are implemented, it may be possible to develop knowledge on the relative effectiveness of different methods of knowledge claim formulation. Relevant attributes for evaluating success or effectiveness include

- Cycle time,
- Production of knowledge claims that tend to survive validation
- Production of knowledge claims that are relevant to the problems motivating the KLC
- Production of knowledge claims of sufficient scope to handle problems motivating the KLC

Knowledge claims may be formulated from interacting with any of the following internal organizational sources:

- Interpersonal peer communications
- Interpersonal expert communications
- Meetings
- E-mail messages
- Web documents
- Web-accessed databases
- Non–Web-accessed databases
- Web-enabled collaborative applications
- Media (CDs, tapes, etc.)
- Printed documents

Descriptors of knowledge claim formulation are classified into *process* descriptors *and knowledge claim* descriptors. Descriptors were selected because they either relate directly to cycle time, survivability in evaluation and testing (validation), and relevance, or because they may be causally relevant to producing success in these terms.

Process descriptors

My purpose here is to indicate a range of attributes that relate to knowledge claim formulation and that may be useful in its description or measurement. Many of the descriptors are the same as those used for information acquisition but are applied to KCF. The most important descriptors relate to processing throughput, the collaboration/withdrawal bipolarity, and the cooperation/conflict bipolarity. What mix of these attributes is effective for good KCF throughput is not known, but it is likely that future investigation should focus on the question of the mix. Apart from this mix, the question of equality of distribution of access to previous knowledge/information, and social contexts for generating new knowledge claims is also paramount. Without reasonably free access, knowledge claim formulation and therefore knowledge production become restricted to an elite knowledge-producing class in organizations.

- KCF cycle time. In healthy KLCs, it is much easier to generate knowledge claims that are relevant to problems than it is in less healthy KLCs.
- KCF velocity. This may or not be a significant attribute; its significance needs to tested. On the surface, the higher the KCF velocity, the more frequent the innovations, other things being equal.
- KCF acceleration. The higher the better, until the resulting velocity of knowledge claim formulation overloads the capacity of the KLC to test and evaluate knowledge claims (Cavaleri and Reed, 2001).
- Intensity of collaborative activity in KCF. Greater collaboration may be positively related to producing relevant, high-quality knowledge claims.
- Intensity of cooperative behavior in formulating KCs. Intensity is more specific than collaboration. Collaboration can result in cooperative or conflict behavior in developing knowledge claims. Currently we do not know what mix of cooperative and conflict behavior is most effective in accelerating knowledge claim formulation, but the relation of this attribute to KCF acceleration is not likely to be simple.
- Intensity of conflict behavior in formulating KCs. Again, intensity is more specific than collaboration. Similar considerations as those just stated for intensity of cooperative behavior apply here.
- Extent of withdrawal from interaction with other agents as an outcome of collaborative activity. This attribute may be very significant as a partial cause and predictor of the slowing of quality KCF.
- Extent of inequality of access to previous knowledge claims. Lack of equal access may exclude many individuals and groups from effective participation in the KCF subprocess.
- Extent of inequality of access to methods and sources supporting KCF. Same consideration as just above.
- Volume of documents transmitted among all agents making knowledge claim. Again, there is not a simple relationship to KCF effectiveness, but if this volume is too low or too high, KCF effectiveness is likely to be low.
- Ratio of messages received by an Agent to messages sent by that agent related to knowledge claim formulation. This metric may be a measure of the extent to which an agent is participating in the KCF process. If this ratio is too high, it may suggest a lack of participation.

- Use and frequency of use of methods of interpersonal searching, intelligence gathering, and knowledge claim formulation. These methods may be related to an increase in the amount and capability of KCF. Currently, there are no studies that compare the various methods with one another for effectiveness in accelerating KCF.
- Delphi technique
- Knowledge café
- Nominal group technique
- Focus groups
- Joint application design (Wood and Silver, 1989)
- Personal networking
- Project meetings
- Company meetings
- Self-organizing teams
- Communities of practice (Wenger, 1998; Nickols, 2001)
- Credit assignment processes
- Use and frequency of use of methods of electronic searching, intelligence gathering, and knowledge claim formulation. Use of these may also accelerate KCF. Again, there are no studies comparing these to one another nor are there any studies comparing interpersonal and electronic methods for effectiveness.
- KDD/data mining. (KDD is Knowledge discovery in databases.)
- Content analysis. (See Chapter 2 for a definition.)
- Cognitive mapping/semantic networking of content
- Text mining
- Database querying
- Modeling. Modeling activity involves KCF. Types of models include mathematical, statistical, computer, verbal, visual, data, and object.
- Web-enabled searching/retrieving
- Web-enabled application-specific searching/retrieving
- Web-enabled file sharing
- Web-enabled communications in communities of practice
- Web-enabled collaboration
- Project management
- Problem-solving teams
- Portal-enabled searching/accessing/retrieving
- Agent-based scanning. (Refers to scanning of data and content stores by software agents.)
- Web-enabled knowledge claim-eliciting software applications other than textual content analysis and text or data mining. (Refers to applications that lead humans through knowledge claim generation procedures).
- Analytic hierarchy applications (Saaty, 1990)
- Balanced scorecard applications (Kaplan and Norton, 1996)
- Solution specification applications. (Refers to applications that develop a practitioner's framework for problem assessment and specifying a related solution).
- "Thinking outside the box" applications
- Credit assignment applications. These assign credit points to participants who generate knowledge claims.

- Business intelligence and OLAP reporting and analysis (Thomson, 1997)
- Workflow analysis and modeling

KCF infrastructure

- Intranet facilities—both physical and software
- Portal systems
- Databases
- Content and textbases
- Document management systems
- Collaborative systems
- DSS/data warehousing/BI/OLAP
- ERP systems
- Computer hardware
- Network infrastructure
- Fax
- Documents and books
- Telephone facilities
- Training programs
- Electronic broadcast reception facilities
- Conference programs

KCF outcome descriptors

Here I will cover the media in which knowledge claims are expressed, the type of knowledge claims expressed, and the characteristics of the knowledge claim base resulting from KCF.

- Media
  - Hard copy
  - Microfiche
  - Tape
- Removable electronic media
  - Fixed disk
  - Optical
  - Silicon
- Type of knowledge claim. This is a somewhat ad hoc classification of knowledge claim types, similar to the classification of types of information acquired from the world external to the enterprise.
- Structured database knowledge claims
- Descriptive factual statements
- conceptual models
- Data models
- Object models
- Computer models
- Planning models
- Analytical models
- Measurement models

- Predictive models
- Impact models
- Assessment models
- Application software
- Validation criteria, perspectives, and frameworks
- Methods
- Methodologies
- Formal language utility
- Semiformal language utility
- Meta-knowledge claims
- Planning knowledge claims
- Descriptive knowledge claims
- Factual knowledge claims
- Measurements of abstractions
- Knowledge claims about impact and cause and effect
- Predictive knowledge claims
- Assessment knowledge claims
- Distributed/centralized architecture of knowledge claim base. This will affect circulation of and access to knowledge claims. If the connectivity is there, a distributed architecture supports greater circulation and production of knowledge claims; if not, a distributed knowledge claim base may mean isolation
- Degree of integration/coherence of knowledge claim base within or between knowledge claim types or domains. In theory, the more highly integrated the knowledge claim base, the more effective it is in providing a foundation for generating new knowledge claims. But we really know little about how this integration/coherence factor works in real organizations.
- Scope of the knowledge claim base within and across information types or domains. The broader the scope, the more effective the knowledge claim base.
- Degree of relevance of knowledge claims produced to problems motivating the KLC
- Level of measurement of attributes in knowledge claim base within and across domains. This refers to whether the attributes in the knowledge claim base are scaled nominally, ordinally, intervally, logarithmically, or by ratio. No one level of measurement is intrinsically or always preferable to the others. But it is important to know whether the level of measurement employed within and across domains is consistent with the models using the attributes. Models whose level of measurement requirements are not being fulfilled cannot be tested and evaluated against their competitors.
- Types of models used in the knowledge claim base (conceptual analytic models, data models, measurement models, impact models, predictive models, assessment models, object models, structural models)
- Types of formal languages used in the knowledge claim base (set theory, mathematics, fuzzy logic, XML, HTML, SGML, etc.);
- Types of semiformal languages used in the knowledge claim base—unified modeling language (UML), knowledge claim modeling language (KQML)

- Types of methods (features, benefits, specifications)
- Types of methodologies (features, benefits, specifications)
- Software applications (features, benefits, specifications, performance, interface)
- Priority of knowledge components according to relevance

Other outcome descriptors

- Extent of inequality among agents in knowledge claim formulation. The initial working hypothesis is that the greater the inequality, the lower the velocity of KCF in the KLC.
- Types of rewards provided for participation in knowledge claim formulation, Certain types of incentives may be either less or more effective than other types. Present evidence suggests that monetary incentives for increased KCF, when provided in a direct and obvious way are not effective in increasing participation in knowledge production.
- Extent of satisfaction with rewards for knowledge claim formulation.
- Performance metric on establishing organizational knowledge claim base. A summary or composite metric combining a number of the above measures in an as yet undetermined way. Methodology for formulating such composite metrics is developed in Firestone (1998).

Descriptors of growth and change in KCF outcomes

These descriptors are compiled from a number of the ones already mentioned. Many of them would be key variables in modeling efforts directed at explaining changes in KCF.

- Growth/decline of various types of knowledge claims
- Changes in knowledge claim base architecture centralization
- Growth/decline in integration/coherence of knowledge claim base
- Increase/decrease in scope of the knowledge claim base
- Changes in levels of measurement of attributes in knowledge claim base
- Increase/decrease in quantification of attributes in knowledge claim base
- Increase/decrease in logical consistency of attributes in knowledge claim base
- Change in types of models used in knowledge claim base
- Development in formal languages used
- Development in semiformal languages used
- Changes in types of methods (reduction in costs, increase/decrease in capabilities)
- Change in types of methodologies (reduction in costs, increase in scope, increase/decrease in capabilities)
- Increase/decrease in IT-assisted support for decision making provided by software applications
- Change in degree of inequality of knowledge claim formulation
- Change in KCF cycle time
- Change in KCF velocity
- Change in KCF acceleration

- Change in intensity of collaborative activity in KCF
- Change in intensity of cooperative behavior in formulating KCs
- Change in intensity of conflict behavior in formulating KCs
- Change in extent of withdrawal from interaction with other agents as an outcome of collaborative activity
- Change in extent of inequality of access to previous knowledge claims
- Change in extent of inequality of access to methods and sources supporting KCF
- Change in degree of relevance of knowledge claims produced to problems motivating the KLC
- Change in volume of documents transmitted among all agents making knowledge claims
- Change in ratio of messages received by an Agent to messages sent by that Agent related to KCF
- Change in types of rewards provided for participation in knowledge claim formulation
- Change in extent of satisfaction with rewards for knowledge claim formulation
- Change in performance metric on formulation of new knowledge claims

Further descriptors can be arrived at by cross-classifying many of the above. Again, this results in hundreds of attributes.

Knowledge claim validation or evaluation

Knowledge claim validation (or evaluation) is a subprocess or task cluster of knowledge production in which knowledge claims are subjected to competitive testing and evaluation against alternatives with reference to organizationally held criteria, perspectives, and frameworks to determine the value and veracity of knowledge claims. It is the critical task cluster in distinguishing knowledge processing from information processing, because it is the only one that is necessary for producing knowledge; however, it is not necessary for producing information.

The validation and testing process in real organizations is not a cut-and-dried process in which fixed knowledge claim rivals take prescribed tests and are evaluated against static criteria or fixed rules. Instead, knowledge claim validation in organizations is a vortex in which many competing knowledge claims are considered simultaneously against criteria, perspectives, and frameworks that are often being re-weighted, reformulated in various ways, and even introduced into or expelled from the decision cycle of validation.

Surviving, (validated), falsified (invalidated), and undecided (unvalidated) knowledge claims emerge from this vortex of conflict and collaboration in a manner that is not predictable from any simple model. An organization may develop and try to apply fixed formulae to be used by agents for knowledge claim comparison and validation, so that we can sensibly describe a normative knowledge claim validation value network. But the actual knowledge validation subprocess will vary from this normative pattern and will present to the analyst and modeler a *cas* pattern of emergence (Holland, 1998).

Key success criteria in knowledge claim validation are

- Cycle time
- Production of validated knowledge claims that are relevant to the problem motivating the KLC
- Production of validated knowledge claims of sufficient scope to handle problems motivating the KLC

These criteria correspond to those already presented for knowledge claim formulation. Knowledge claims may be validated from interaction with any of the following internal organizational sources:

- Interpersonal peer communications
- Interpersonal expert communications
- Meetings
- E-mail messages
- Web documents
- Web-accessed databases
- Non–Web-accessed databases
- Web-enabled communications in communities of practice
- Web-enabled collaborative applications
- Media (CDs, tapes, etc.)
- Printed documents

Descriptors of knowledge claim validation are classified into process descriptors and knowledge claim descriptors.

Process descriptors

Many of the knowledge claim validation process descriptors are the same as those already presented for knowledge claim formulation. They are listed as follows:

- KCV (or KCE) cycle time
- KCV velocity
- KCV acceleration
- Intensity of collaborative activity in KCV
- Intensity of cooperative behavior in KCVs
- Intensity of conflict behavior in KCVs
- Extent of withdrawal from interaction with other agents as an outcome of collaborative KCV activity
- Extent of inequality of access to previous knowledge claims
- Extent of inequality of access to sources and methods supporting KCV
- Volume of documents transmitted among all agents validating knowledge claims
- Ratio of messages received by an Agent to messages sent by that agent related to KCV
- Use and frequency of use of methods of interpersonal knowledge claim validation
- Delphi technique
- Knowledge café

- Nominal group technique
- Focus groups
- Personal networking
- Project meetings
- Company meetings
- Self-organizing teams
- Communities of practice
- Credit assignment processes
- Use and frequency of use of methods of electronic support for knowledge claim validation
- Text mining
- Database querying
- Modeling
- KCV assessment modeling
- Web-enabled searching/retrieving of knowledge claims
- Web-enabled collaboration
- Problem-solving teams
- Portal-enabled, server-based automated arbitration of agent-mapped knowledge claims (Firestone, 2000a), This method was not included among KCF methods. In it, servers use preestablished rules to arbitrate among knowledge claims and provide machine-mediated evaluation of them as an input to human validation judgments.
- credit assignment for participating in knowledge claim validation (Firestone, 2000)
- Business intelligence and OLAP reporting and analysis

KCV (or KCE) infrastructure

This list is the same as for knowledge claim formulation.

KCV (or KCE) outcome descriptors

This list is also the same as for knowledge claim formulation

Other outcome descriptors

- Type of validation information describing validated knowledge claims
- Extent of logical consistency. This is a traditional validation criterion. It provides that logical arguments in explanation must be consistent, that conclusions must follow from premises, but not that one's entire theoretical network must be formalized.
- Extent of empirical fit. This is the traditional empiricist requirement that deductions from models fit independent descriptions of the facts.
- Extent of simplicity. Another traditional validation criterion, often called "Occam's razor." Simplicity is an intuitively clear criterion, but it is difficult to rigorously formulate (Ackermann, 1960; Goodman, 1958; Rudner, 1961).
- Extent of projectibility. This refers to extending generalized knowledge claims to new cases (forecast validity). It has to do with plausibility of

projections and after the fact measurements of predictive success (Goodman, 1965).

- Extent of commensurability. This refers to the extent to which alternative theories, models, or other knowledge claims may be expressed using a common conceptual framework (Popper, 1970; Kuhn, 1970).
- Extent of continuity. This is the extent to which each alternative theory or model in a comparison is faithful to previous expressions.
- Coherence of measurement modeling. The extent to which measures and descriptors are related through the propositions of a model's semantic network (Firestone, 1971; Firestone and Chadwick, 1975).
- Extent of systematic fruitfulness. The extent of ability to facilitate deduction of new knowledge claims.
- Extent of heuristic quality. The extent of ability to facilitate new conjectural knowledge claims.
- Extent of completeness of the comparison set. The extent to which the set of alternative models includes all reasonable competitive alternatives. This is not a precise criterion, but rather a regulative ideal. There is no way of knowing that a comparison set is in fact complete, just as there is no way of guaranteeing that a knowledge claim is true.
- Cognitive maps of validation information. Like other information, validation information can be modeled in a cognitive map.
- History of knowledge claim validation events
- Relevance priority of validated knowledge claim components
- Types of rewards provided for participation in knowledge claim validation
- Extent of satisfaction with rewards for knowledge claim validation
- Performance metric on establishing organizational validated knowledge claim base

Descriptors of growth and change in validated knowledge claim outcomes

- Growth/decline of various types of validated knowledge claims
- Changes in validated knowledge claim base architecture centralization
- Growth/decline in integration/coherence of validated knowledge claim base
- Increase/decrease in scope of the validated knowledge claim base
- Changes in levels of measurement of attributes in validated knowledge claim base
- Increase/decrease in quantification of attributes in validated knowledge claim base
- Increase/decrease in logical consistency of attributes in validated knowledge claim base
- Change in types of models used in validated knowledge claim base
- Development in formal languages used
- Development in semiformal languages used
- Changes in types of methods (reduction in costs, increase/decrease in capabilities)

- Change in types of methodologies (reduction in costs, increase in scope, increase/decrease in capabilities)
- Increase/decrease in IT-assisted support for decision making provided by software applications
- Increase/decrease in type of validation of various components of the knowledge base
- Logical consistency
- Empirical fit
- Simplicity
- Projectibility
- Commensurability
- Continuity
- Coherent measurement modeling
- Systematic fruitfulness
- Heuristic quality
- Completeness of the comparison set
- Increase/decrease in extent of validation within each type
- Increase/decrease in composite extent of validation of various component.
- Change in degree of inequality of KCV
- Change in KCV cycle time
- Change in KCV velocity
- Change in KCV acceleration
- Change in intensity of collaborative activity in KCV
- Change in intensity of cooperative behavior in KCV
- Change in intensity of conflict behavior in KCV
- Change in extent of withdrawal from interaction with other agents as an outcome of collaborative activity
- Change in extent of inequality of access to previous knowledge claims
- Extent of inequality of access to sources and methods supporting KCV
- Change in volume of documents transmitted among all agents validating knowledge claims
- Change in ratio of messages received by an Agent to messages sent by that Agent related to KCV
- Change in types of rewards provided for participation in knowledge claim validation
- Change in extent of satisfaction with rewards for knowledge claim validation
- Change in performance metric on knowledge claim validation

Further descriptors can be arrived at by cross-classifying many of the above.

Knowledge broadcasting

Broadcasting means that one agent is sending data, information, or knowledge to another agent on the initiative of the first agent. It is one subprocess for transmitting, disseminating, diffusing, and integrating validated knowledge claims throughout an organization. Key success factors are cycle time and relevance of the validated knowledge claims being broadcast.

Process descriptors

Broadcasting process descriptors are analogous to or the same as those already specified for knowledge production subprocesses. This includes interpersonal and electronic support for broadcasting.

- Broadcasting cycle time
- Broadcasting velocity
- Broadcasting acceleration
- Intensity of collaborative activity in broadcasting
- Intensity of cooperative behavior in broadcasting
- Intensity of conflict behavior in broadcasting
- Extent of withdrawal from interaction with other agents as an outcome of collaborative broadcasting activity
- Extent of inequality of access to previous broadcasts
- Volume of documents transmitted to agents in broadcasting
- Ratio of messages received by an Agent to messages sent by that Agent related to broadcasting
- Use and frequency of use of methods of interpersonal broadcasting
- Delphi technique
- Knowledge café
- Nominal group technique
- Focus groups
- Personal networking
- Project meetings
- Company meetings
- Self-organizing teams
- Communities of practice
- Use and frequency of use of methods of electronic support for broadcasting
- Portal-enabled, agent-based broadcasting of alerts
- E-mail alerts and messages
- Telephone alerts
- Fax alerts

Broadcasting infrastructure

Broadcasting infrastructure is also similar to knowledge production infrastructure.

- Intranet facilities, both physical and software
- Collaborative systems
- Computer hardware
- Network infrastructure
- Fax
- Telephone facilities
- Electronic broadcast reception facilities

Broadcasting outcome descriptors

These descriptors focus on questions about the distribution of and support for validated knowledge claims. They also deal with performance of broadcasting itself, and with levels of satisfaction with actual performance.

- Content of validated knowledge claims as outlined earlier
- Extent of distribution of validated knowledge claims
- Extent of acceptance and support for above claims
- Extent of distribution of validated knowledge claims among targets of these claims
- Extent of acceptance and support for above claims
- Degree of knowledge worker satisfaction with broadcasting vehicles and process
- Degree of knowledge manager satisfaction with broadcasting vehicles and process
- Degree of satisfaction with broadcasting vehicles and process by knowledge authority structure
- Degree of satisfaction with broadcasting vehicles and process by organizational authority structure
- Degree of satisfaction with broadcasting vehicles and process by subsystem
- Degree of fulfillment of broadcasting objectives by knowledge assignment
- Degree of fulfillment of broadcasting objectives by knowledge assignment segment
- Degree of fulfillment of broadcasting objectives by knowledge authority structure segment
- Degree of fulfillment of broadcasting objectives by organizational authority segment
- Degree of fulfillment of broadcasting objectives by subsystem segment
- Performance metric on broadcasting the knowledge base

Descriptors of growth and change in broadcasting outcomes

- Change in degree of inequality of access to broadcasting
- Change in broadcasting cycle time
- Change in broadcasting velocity
- Change in broadcasting acceleration
- Change in intensity of collaborative activity in broadcasting
- Change in intensity of cooperative behavior in broadcasting
- Change in intensity of conflict behavior in broadcasting
- Change in extent of withdrawal from interaction with other agents as an outcome of collaborative activity in broadcasting
- Change in extent of inequality of access to previous validated knowledge claims
- Change in volume of documents transmitted among all agents broadcasting knowledge claims

- Change in ratio of messages received by an agent to messages sent by that agent related to broadcasting

Knowledge-related searching and retrieving

Searching/retrieving is the sequence of tasks an agent performs to find and access validated knowledge claims in an organization. Sometimes searching and retrieving is interpersonal (going to a friend) or manual (going to a library). Sometimes it is electronic (as in searching for and retrieving documents or querying structured data to retrieve records that fulfill the query criterion). Success factors are cycle time and relevance of retrieved knowledge to queries. Process and outcome descriptors follow.

Process descriptors

- Searching/retrieving cycle time
- Searching/retrieving velocity
- Searching/retrieving acceleration
- Intensity of collaborative activity in searching/retrieving
- Intensity of cooperative behavior in searching/retrieving
- Intensity of conflict behavior in searching/retrieving
- Extent of withdrawal from interaction with other agents as an outcome of collaborative searching/retrieving activity
- Extent of inequality of access to previous searching/retrieving
- Volume of documents transmitted to agents in searching/ retrieving
- Ratio of messages received by an Agent to messages sent by that agent related to searching/retrieving
- Use and frequency of use of methods of interpersonal searching/retrieving
- Delphi technique
- Knowledge café,
- Nominal group technique
- Focus groups
- Personal networking
- Project meetings
- Company meetings
- Self-organizing teams
- Communities of practice
- Gathering and reading documents
- Use and frequency of use of methods of electronic support for searching/retrieving
- Portal-enabled, agent-based document and document segment searching and retrieving
- E-mail searching
- Database querying and retrieving
- Content analysis and retrieval
- Cognitive mapping of content
- Web-enabled searching and retrieving
- Web-enabled searching and retrieving in communities of practice

- Web-enabled application-specific searching and retrieving
- Web-enabled file sharing and retrieving

Searching/retrieving infrastructure

- Intranet facilities, both physical and software
- Fax
- Document subscriptions
- Telephone facilities
- Electronic broadcast reception facilities

Searching/retrieving outcome descriptors

These are very similar or the same as the descriptors used for broadcasting

- Content of validated knowledge claims as outlined earlier
- Extent of distribution of validated knowledge claims
- Extent of acceptance and support for above claims
- Extent of distribution of validated knowledge claims among targets of these claims
- Extent of acceptance and support for above claims
- Degree of knowledge worker satisfaction with searching/retrieving vehicles and process
- Degree of knowledge manager satisfaction with searching/retrieving vehicles and process
- Degree of satisfaction with searching/retrieving vehicles and process by knowledge authority structure
- Degree of satisfaction with searching/retrieving vehicles and process by organizational authority structure
- Degree of satisfaction with searching/retrieving vehicles and process by subsystem
- Degree of fulfillment of searching/retrieving objectives by knowledge assignment
- Degree of fulfillment of searching/retrieving objectives by knowledge assignment segment
- Degree of fulfillment of searching/retrieving objectives by knowledge authority structure segment
- Degree of fulfillment of searching/retrieving objectives by organizational authority segment
- Degree of fulfillment of searching/retrieving objectives by subsystem segment
- Performance metric on searching/retrieving the knowledge base

Descriptors of growth and change in searching/retrieving

- Change in degree of inequality of searching/retrieving
- Change in searching/retrieving cycle time
- Change in searching/retrieving velocity
- Change in searching/retrieving acceleration
- Change in intensity of collaborative activity in searching/ retrieving

- Change in intensity of cooperative behavior in searching/ retrieving
- Change in intensity of conflict behavior in searching/retrieving
- Change in extent of withdrawal from interaction with other agents as an outcome of collaborative activity in searching/retrieving
- Change in extent of inequality of access to previous validated knowledge claims
- Change in volume of documents transmitted among all agents searching/retrieving knowledge claims
- Change in ratio of messages received by an agent to messages sent by that agent related to searching/retrieving

Teaching

Teaching is a non-peer, often hierarchical interaction in which one agent tries to communicate with another in such a way that the second agent is motivated to understand the conceptual network being communicated by the first person. Success factors are cycle time and success in conveying understanding.

Process descriptors

- Teaching cycle time
- Teaching velocity
- Teaching acceleration
- Intensity of collaborative activity in teaching
- Intensity of cooperative behavior in teaching
- Intensity of conflict behavior in teaching
- Extent of withdrawal from interaction with other agents as an outcome of collaborative teaching activity
- Extent of inequality of access to previous teaching
- Volume of documents transmitted to agents in teaching
- Ratio of messages received by an Agent to messages sent by that Agent related to teaching
- Use and frequency of use of methods of interpersonal teaching
- Lecture classes
- Discussion classes
- Seminars
- Tutorials
- Team teaching
- Self-organizing classes
- Use and frequency of use of methods of electronic support for teaching
- Web-enabled training (e-learning)
- Web-enabled application-specific training

Teaching infrastructure

- Intranet facilities, both physical and software
- E-learning facilities
- classrooms
- Fax
- Document subscriptions

- Books
- Telephone facilities
- Electronic broadcast reception facilities

Teaching outcome descriptors

- Content of validated knowledge claims as outlined earlier
- Extent of distribution of validated knowledge claims
- Extent of acceptance and support for above claims
- Extent of distribution of validated knowledge claims among targets of these claims
- Extent of acceptance and support for above claims
- Production/existence of training vehicles
- Degree of knowledge worker satisfaction with training vehicles and process
- Degree of knowledge manager satisfaction with training vehicles and process
- Degree of satisfaction with training vehicles and process by knowledge authority structure
- Degree of satisfaction with training vehicles and process by organizational authority structure
- Degree of satisfaction with training vehicles and process by subsystem
- Degree of fulfillment of training objectives by knowledge assignment
- Degree of fulfillment of training objectives by knowledge assignment segment
- Degree of fulfillment of training objectives by knowledge authority structure segment
- Degree of fulfillment of training objectives by organizational authority segment
- Degree of fulfillment of training objectives by subsystem segment

Descriptors of growth and change in teaching

- Change in degree of inequality of teaching
- Change in teaching cycle time
- Change in teaching velocity
- Change in teaching acceleration
- Change in intensity of collaborative activity in teaching
- Change in intensity of cooperative behavior in teaching
- Change in intensity of conflict behavior in teaching
- Change in extent of withdrawal from interaction with other agents as an outcome of collaborative activity in teaching
- Change in extent of inequality of access to previously validated knowledge claims
- Change in volume of documents transmitted among all agents teaching knowledge claims
- Change in ratio of messages received by an agent to messages sent by that agent related to teaching
- Performance metric on training personnel to manage and use the knowledge base

Knowledge sharing

Knowledge sharing is the activity of making knowledge available (1) through a knowledge store accessible to individuals and groups in an enterprise or (2) through spoken communication. Some knowledge stores are off-line and store documents or electronic media. Some are contained in online computer databases. Some are contained in virtual databases in computer memory.

When knowledge is shared through the spoken word, knowledge sharing needs to be carefully distinguished from broadcasting and teaching. In broadcasting, knowledge is sent without specific elicitation. In teaching, an agent plays the role of instructor to another in a non-peer interaction. But in face-to-face knowledge sharing, peers communicate organizational knowledge they hold in a conversational context. Cycle time and success in conveying understanding are critical success factors.

Process descriptors

- Sharing cycle time
- Sharing velocity
- Sharing acceleration
- Intensity of collaborative activity in sharing
- Intensity of cooperative behavior in sharing
- Intensity of conflict behavior in sharing
- Extent of withdrawal from interaction with other agents as an outcome of collaborative sharing activity
- Extent of inequality of access to previous sharing
- Volume of documents transmitted to agents in sharing
- Ratio of messages received by an Agent to messages sent by that Agent related to sharing
- Use and frequency of use of methods of interpersonal sharing
- Delphi technique
- Knowledge café
- Nominal group technique
- Focus groups
- Personal networking
- Project meetings
- Company meetings
- Self-organizing teams
- Communities of practice
- Credit assignment processes
- Use and frequency of use of methods of electronic support for sharing
- Web-enabled sharing
- Web-enabled application-specific sharing
- Portal-enabled collaboration
- Portal-enabled agent-based sharing
- Portal-enabled credit assignment applications for sharing

Sharing infrastructure

- Intranet facilities, both physical and software

- Classrooms
- Fax
- Documents
- Telephone facilities
- Electronic broadcast reception facilities

Sharing outcome descriptors

- Content of validated knowledge claims as outlined earlier
- Extent of distribution of validated knowledge claims
- Extent of acceptance and support for above claims
- Extent of distribution of validated knowledge claims among targets of these claims
- Extent of acceptance and support for above claims
- Degree of knowledge worker satisfaction with sharing vehicles and process
- Degree of knowledge manager satisfaction with sharing vehicles and process
- Degree of satisfaction with sharing vehicles and process by knowledge authority structure
- Degree of satisfaction with sharing vehicles and process by organizational authority structure
- Degree of satisfaction with sharing vehicles and process by subsystem
- Degree of fulfillment of sharing objectives by knowledge assignment
- Degree of fulfillment of sharing objectives by knowledge assignment segment
- Degree of fulfillment of sharing objectives by knowledge authority structure segment
- Degree of fulfillment of sharing objectives by organizational authority segment
- Degree of fulfillment of sharing objectives by subsystem segment
- Types of rewards provided for participation in knowledge sharing
- Extent of satisfaction with rewards for knowledge sharing
- Performance metric on sharing the knowledge base

Descriptors of growth and change in sharing

- Change in degree of inequality of sharing
- Change in sharing cycle time
- Change in sharing velocity
- Change in sharing acceleration
- Change in intensity of collaborative activity in sharing
- Change in intensity of cooperative behavior in sharing
- Change in intensity of conflict behavior in sharing
- Change in extent of withdrawal from interaction with other agents as an outcome of collaborative activity in sharing
- Change in extent of inequality of access to previous validated knowledge claims
- Change in volume of documents transmitted among all agents sharing knowledge claims

- Change in ratio of messages received by an agent to messages sent by that agent related to sharing
- Change in types of rewards provided for participation in knowledge sharing
- Change in extent of satisfaction with rewards for knowledge sharing

Accelerated innovation

While "first generation" or "supply-side" knowledge management focused mainly on problems and concerns of managing knowledge storage and distribution, some individuals in knowledge management have recently championed the cause of "demand-side" knowledge processing (McElroy, 1999). They argue that knowledge management is broader than "supply-side" activities, and that, moreover, the KM value proposition is greatly enhanced when we expand its focus to include knowledge production activities—in particular, business innovation.

This new focus of KM, also called the new knowledge management (or TNKM) (McElroy, 2002) is on innovation. It is about managing it and accelerating it, and it is about managing and accelerating innovations in creating business innovations. But what is innovation? There are many ways to define it, and I will not provide a definitional survey here. But my definition is that *innovation is a completed knowledge process life cycle event, beginning with a problem emerging from a business process, moving through knowledge production, and ending in incorporation of knowledge structures (the DOKB) within business structures impacting business process behavior* (see Figure 7.3).

Innovation acceleration is continuous decrease in the cycle time of the knowledge life cycle. This, in turn, means continuous decrease in the cycle time of its subprocesses. But the relationship is not a simple one. We do not know the impact that decreasing cycle time in any or all of the subprocesses has on the others or on the cycle time of the KLC as a whole. So here is something else that must be modeled in detail before we understand how to accelerate innovation. We do know that acceleration involves changing the knowledge subprocesses in the KLC and their interrelations and that this requires knowledge management. I now turn to a more detailed examination of that subject in the following chapters.

References

Ackermann, R.J. (1960). *Simplicity and the Acceptability of Scientific Theories*, Doctoral Dissertation, East Lansing, MI: Michigan State University.

Alexrod, R. (ed.) (1976). *The Structure of Decision* (Princeton, NJ: Princeton University Press).

Cavaleri, S., and Reed, F. (2001). "Organizational Inquiry: The Search for Effective Knowledge," *Knowledge and Innovation: Journal of the KMCI*, 1, no. 3, pp. 27–54.

Fayyad, U.; Piatetsky-Shapiro, G.; Smyth, P.; and Uthurusamy, R. (eds.) (1996). *Advances in Knowledge Discovery and Data Mining* (Cambridge, MA: MIT Press, 1996).

Firestone, J.M. (1971). "Remarks on Concept Formation: Theory Building and Theory Testing," *Philosophy of Science*, 38, 570–604.

Firestone, J.M. (1999). "Enterprise Information Portals and Enterprise Knowledge Portals," *DKMS Brief*, 8, *Executive Information Systems, Inc.*, Wilmington, DE, March 20, 1999. Available at http://www.dkms.com/White_Papers.htm.

Firestone, J.M. (2000). "The Enterprise Knowledge Portal Revisited," *White Paper No. 15, Executive Information Systems, Inc.,* Wilmington, DE, March 15, 2000. Available at http://www.dkms.com/White_Papers.htm.

Firestone, J.M. (2000a). "Enterprise Knowledge Portals: What They Are and What They Do," *Knowledge and Innovation: Journal of the KMCI,* 1, no. 1, pp. 85–108. Available at http://www.dkms.com/White_Papers.htm.

Firestone, J.M. (2000b). "Enterprise Knowledge Portals and e-Business Solutions," *White Paper No. 16, Executive Information Systems, Inc.,* Wilmington, DE, October 1, 2000. Available at http://www.dkms.com/White_Papers.htm.

Firestone, J.M. (2001). "Enterprise Knowledge Portals, Knowledge Processing and Knowledge Management," in Ramon Barquin, Alex Bennet, and Shereen Remez, (eds.) *Building Knowledge Management Environments for Electronic Government,* Vienna, VA: Management Concepts.

Firestone, J.M., and Chadwick, R.W. (1975). "A New Procedure for Constructing Measurement Models of Ratio Scale Concepts," *International journal of General Systems,* **2**, pp. 35–53.

Goodman, N. (1955). *Fact, Fiction, and Forecast* (Cambridge, MA: Harvard University Press).

Goodman, N. (1958). "The Test of Simplicity," *Science,* 128, pp. 1064–1069.

Holland, J.H. (1998). *Emergence* (Reading, MA: Addison-Wesley).

Isaacs, David (1999). "Knowledge Café Presentation," Enterprise Intelligence Conference, Dec. 7, 1999, Lake Buena Vista, FL.

Kaplan, R.S., and Norton, D.P. (1996). *The Balanced Scorecard* (Boston: Harvard Business School Press).

Kosko, B. (1992). *Neural Networks and Fuzzy Systems* (Englewood Cliffs, NJ: Prentice-Hall).

Kuhn, T. (1970). "Logic of Discovery or Psychology of Research," in I. Lakatos and A. Musgrave (eds.), *Criticism and the Growth of Knowledge* (Cambridge, UK: Cambridge University Press).

McElroy, M.W. (2002). *The New Knowledge Management* (Boston: KMCI Press/Butterworth-Heinemann).

McElroy, M. (1999). "The Second Generation of KM," *Knowledge Management Magazine* (October, 1999), pp. 86–88.

Nickols, F. (2001). *Communities of Practice Home Page,* at http://home.att.net/~discon/KM/CoPs.htm.

Popper, K.R. (1970) in I. Lakatos and A. Musgrave (eds.), "Normal Science and Its Dangers," *Criticism and the Growth of Knowledge* (Cambridge, UK: Cambridge University Press).

Rudner, R. (1961). "An Introduction to Simplicity," *Philosophy of Science,* 28, No. 2.

Saaty, T.L. (1990). *The Analytic Hierarchy Process: Planning, Priority Setting, resource Allocation,* 2nd ed. (Pittsburgh, PA: RWS Publications).

Sullivan, D. (2001). *Document Warehousing and Text Mining* (New York: John Wiley & Sons).

Thomson, E. (1997). *OLAP Solutions* (New York: John Wiley & Sons).

Wenger, E. (1998). *Communities of Practice: Learning, Meaning, and Identity* (New York: Cambridge University Press).

CHAPTER 9

On Knowledge Management

Introduction: Approach to KM

Some approaches to knowledge management seem to view any manipulation of knowledge as knowledge management. On this view, knowledge sharing, knowledge production, and knowledge transfer are knowledge management. On this view, knowledge use is knowledge management. On this view, knowledge management is part of every business process. But, is knowledge management really everything and anything having to do with knowledge and knowledge processing?

The obvious answer is no. I sharply distinguish knowledge use and knowledge processing from knowledge management.

- Knowledge use occurs whenever any agent makes a decision. It is part of every business process (see Figures 4.2 and 7.8).
- Knowledge processing is knowledge production and knowledge integration (McElroy, 1999; Firestone, 1999), two distinct knowledge processes constituting the knowledge life cycle (KLC) (see Figure 7.3).
- Knowledge management is knowledge process management—that is, the management of knowledge production, knowledge integration, the KLC, and their immediate outcomes (Firestone, 2000, 2000a; McElroy, 1999). A key aspect of knowledge process management is innovation in knowledge processes to enhance performance of the KLC.

Complex adaptive systems

A complex adaptive system (CAS) is a goal-directed open system attempting to fit itself to its environment. It is "composed of interacting ... adaptive agents described in terms of rules" (Holland, 1995, p. 10) applicable with respect to some specified class of environmental inputs. "These agents adapt by changing their rules as experience accumulates." The interaction of these purposive agents, though directed toward their own goals and purposes, results in emergent, self-organizing behavior at the global system level. This emergent behavior, in a sustainable CAS is itself adaptive.

Emergent behavior is behavior that cannot be modeled based on knowledge of the system's components. It is the ability of *cases* to adapt, along with their emergent behavior that distinguishes them from simple adaptive systems and from Newtonian systems that lack adaptive capacity.

The natural knowledge management system (NKMS)

The NKMS is a *cas*. It is the ongoing, conceptually distinct, persistent, adaptive interaction among intelligent agents (1) whose interaction properties are not determined by design, but instead emerge from the dynamics of the enterprise interaction process itself; and (2) that produces, maintains, and enhances the distributed knowledge base produced by the interaction. An enterprise NKMS includes mechanical and electrical organizational components produced by it, such as computers and computer networks as well as human and organizational agents. An intelligent agent is a purposive, adaptive, self-directed object (see Chapter 6). The notion of a distributed organizational knowledge base was defined in Chapter 7.

Hierarchical vs. organic KM

A central issue in KM is whether it should be hierarchical in nature, focusing on designing and implementing a set of well-articulated rule-governed business processes implementing knowledge production or knowledge integration, handed down by knowledge managers, and implemented in a manner reminiscent of business process reengineering. Alternatively, should KM be organic in the sense that it focuses on implementing policies that support "natural" tendencies of existing knowledge processing patterns occurring in communities of practice and generally outside the formal lines of organizational authority. The hierarchical approach is frequently called "Newtonian," whereas the organic approach is often called the "knowledge ecology" approach.

The organic approach gets a boost from scientific research on complex adaptive systems (*cas*) (Holland, 1995, 1998; Kauffman, 1995). CAS theory supports the idea that there is an NKMS in any organization that is composed of independent, autonomous, individuals, teams, and groups, whose self-organized interaction produces emergent knowledge. This knowledge, in turn, is the chief means organizations use to adapt to their environments and maintain their identity.

Put simply, the objective of KM is to leverage and enhance the natural tendencies toward knowledge production of the NKMS with appropriate policies and above all to do nothing to interfere with these natural tendencies. The motto of organic KM is, "Above all, do no harm!"

CAS theory is very different in character from the essentially Newtonian classical theory of economics based on supply and demand. But it shares with it the idea that the system in question, in this case the NKMS, will naturally, and without interference from management, perform well in producing and integrating knowledge. There is a disposition, then, among those who believe in *cas* theory to be conservative about interfering with existing KM and knowledge processing patterns under the assumption that they are natural. The issue, however, is: are they "natural," or are they simply the result of previous management interventions that distort the natural tendencies of the organizational system to produce and integrate knowledge? If the situation is the latter, then the implication is that KM should not take a hands-off attitude but instead should attempt to intervene to restore the natural, productive tendencies of the NKMS.

So concrete situations in real enterprises may require different postures toward KM interventions. But we lack clear criteria for evaluating when we have an NKMS that requires laissez-faire KM and when we have one that requires a more active KM policy. Without such criteria for making evaluations, the policy posture that follows from a belief in organic KM, is hard to apply and should be approached with caution. The same applies to the reengineering approach. It can easily exacerbate problems in knowledge processing caused by previous ill-advised interventions.

Some definitions of knowledge management

Rather than doing a full survey of the field, (not consistent with my desire to focus on a number of issues in a relatively small space), my purpose here is to raise and address key issues arising from typical attempts to define KM. To fulfill this purpose it is convenient to rely on a range of definitions provided at Yogesh Malhotra's (1998) well-known Web site and a variety of views, beginning with Malhotra's own definition.

Malhotra (1998)

> Knowledge Management caters to the critical issues of organizational adaptation, survival and competence in face of increasingly discontinuous environmental change.... Essentially, it embodies organizational processes that seek synergistic combination of data and information processing capacity of information technologies, and the creative and innovative capacity of human beings.

> Malhotra looks at KM as a synthesis of IT and human innovation!

> While information generated by computer systems is not a very rich carrier of human interpretation for potential action, knowledge resides in the user's subjective context of action based on that information. Hence, it may not be incorrect to suggest that knowledge resides in the user and not in the collection of information, a point made two decades ago by West Churchman, the leading information systems philosopher.

In this definition, it is not clear what management is. Or what knowledge is. It is not clear what information is. If knowledge is personal, does that mean that Malhotra rules out organizational knowledge? And why is information not personal, as well as knowledge? Does Malhotra think there is something about personal information that automatically makes it valid and therefore "knowledge?" Is everything I believe "knowledge" just by virtue of my believing it? If so, this is a highly subjectivist view of knowledge and derivatively of KM.

Sveiby (1998)

> Both among KM-vendors (researchers and consultants) and KM-users (read short descriptions of what companies and other practitioners are doing) there seem to be two tracks of activities—and two levels. Track KM = Management of Information. Researchers and practitioners in this field tend to have their education in computer and/or information science. They are involved in construction of information management systems, AI, reengineering, groupware etc. To them, knowledge = objects that can be identified and handled in information systems. This track is new and is growing very fast at the moment, assisted by new developments in IT.

This definition begs the question of defining KM. It doesn't define "management" or "knowledge." And it doesn't distinguish knowledge from information, or knowledge management from information management.

> Track KM = Management of People. Researchers and practitioners in this field tend to have their education in philosophy, psychology, sociology or business/management. They are primarily involved in assessing, changing and improving human individual skills and/or behaviour. To them Knowledge = Processes, a complex set of dynamic skills, know-how etc., that is constantly changing. They are traditionally involved in learning and in managing these competencies individually—like psychologists—or on an organisational level—like philosophers, sociologists or organisational theorists. This track is very old, and is not growing so fast.

"Knowledge" is clearly not a process. "Learning," "KM," and "knowing" are processes, but knowledge itself, the outcome of processes such as learning and knowing, is not a process.

Sveiby's two alternative "definitions" of KM are presented by him as originating with others, identifying two schools of thought. My remarks just above are not intended to state that either view is subscribed to by him as the correct definition of KM. Rather my remarks should be interpreted as directed at the views stated without the implication that Sveiby subscribes to them. I note, however, that his statement of them declines to offer a critique of either, and that he prefers to remain above the fray.

Ellen Knapp (PWC) (1998)

> We define knowledge management as "the art of transforming information and intellectual assets into enduring value for an organization's clients and its people."

Knapp thinks it is more important to tell us that KM is an "art" than it is to tell us what management is and what exactly it is we are managing. "Intellectual assets" is far too vague a construct to define the scope of KM. "Transforming" is not managing, and things other than knowledge can have "enduring value." In other words, this definition confuses acting on information with managing knowledge and knowledge processing with knowledge management. It is a characteristic error, committed again and again in knowledge management circles

University of Kentucky (1998)

> Knowledge is a vital organization resource. It is the raw material, work-in-process, and finished good of decision making. Distinct types of knowledge used by decision makers include information, procedures, and heuristics, among others. ... A variety of computer-based techniques for managing knowledge (i.e., representing and processing it) have been and will continue to be devised to supplement innate human knowledge management skills. As a field of study, knowledge management is concerned with the invention, improvement, integration, usage, administration, evaluation, and impacts of such techniques.

Rather than being the "finished good of decision making" (a nice turn of phrase), knowledge is more the finished good *for* decision making. In any event, it is hard to see the distinction between information and procedures and heuristics, since these appear to be information also. Also, this definition limits KM to "computer-based techniques," a limitation neither acceptable to the KM community in general, nor justified by the common concept of management, which encompasses far more than computer techniques.

Karl Wiig (1998)

> Knowledge management in organizations must be considered from three perspectives with different horizons and purposes:

> Business Perspective—focusing on why, where, and to what extent the organization must invest in or exploit knowledge. Strategies, products and services, alliances, acquisitions, or divestments should be considered from knowledge-related points of view.

> Management Perspective—focusing on determining, organizing, directing, facilitating, and monitoring knowledge-related practices and activities required to achieve the desired business strategies and objectives.

> Hands-On Operational Perspective—focusing on applying the expertise to conduct explicit knowledge-related work and tasks.

Karl Wiig, one of the more systematic thinkers in the field of knowledge management today, is the closest so far on the management side. The business perspective focuses attention on resource allocation, certainly a managerial activity. The management perspective identifies a number of management activities. The "hands-on" perspective recognizes that knowledge managers must also do knowledge processing. But, as we've seen earlier, Wiig's definition of knowledge as "understandings" and "mental units" is highly debatable and clearly entirely on the world 2 side of things. So his definition of KM doesn't orient us toward managing producing and/or integrating world 3 knowledge, or toward managing how either world 2 or world 3 information is validated and hence becomes "knowledge."

R. Gregory Wenig (1998)

Knowledge Management (for the organization):—consists of activities focused on the organization gaining knowledge from its own experience and from the experience of others, and on the judicious application of that knowledge to fulfill the mission of the organization . . .

Knowledge:—Currently, there is no consensus on what knowledge is. . . . The definition that I have found most useful when building systems is as follows: knowledge is understandings the cognitive system possesses. It is a construct that is not directly observable. It is specific to and not residing outside the cognitive system that created it. Information, NOT knowledge, is communicated among cognitive systems. A cognitive system can be a human, a group, an organization, a computer, or some combination.

Wenig's definition is strong on many of aspects of world 2 knowledge, especially on the distinction between individual knowledge and collective knowledge, and on the idea that it is information and not knowledge that is communicated among cognitive systems. But it is weak on the activities comprising KM and how they are distinguished from knowledge processing activities.

Philip C. Murray (1998)

Our perspective at Knowledge Transfer International is that knowledge is information transformed into capabilities for effective action. In effect, knowledge is action.

For KTI, knowledge management is a strategy that turns an organization's intellectual assets—both recorded information and the talents of its members—into greater productivity, new value, and increased competitiveness. It teaches corporations, from managers to employees, how to produce and optimize skills as a collective entity."

If knowledge were action, we wouldn't need two words. In fact there is a great gap between knowledge and action and even between knowledge and the capability for action. Knowledge is a necessary condition for effective action, but it is not sufficient by itself. Not only knowledge, but also power is required. Also, let us not forget that information combined with capability and intention is also sufficient for action, but not for success. Finally, KM is a process and not a strategy as specified in Murray's view.

Tom Davenport (1998)

Knowledge is defined as "information with value, from the human mind" (adapted from Information Ecology, by Tom Davenport).

KM is defined as "Processes of capturing, distributing, and effectively using knowledge" (Davenport, 1994)

"Information with value" is getting close to knowledge. But what kind of value? Information can have value for producing knowledge and yet not be knowledge itself. Thus, in producing knowledge, I may select among a number of competing models. All may be of value in providing the context for an assessment validating only one of them as knowledge, but that doesn't change the fact that all but one are just information.

This specific definition of KM, further, does not cover the interpersonal and decision-making aspects of KM. Moreover, why are "capturing," "distributing," and "using" knowledge distinctively knowledge management, as opposed to knowledge processing, activities that all knowledge workers as well as knowledge managers engage in? Here is another case of someone confusing knowledge processing with knowledge management.

Most definitions of KM suffer from the lack of careful treatment of both "management" and "knowledge." It's almost as if KM experts think that "knowledge management" is not a form of "management" and therefore does not have to be defined or characterized in a manner consistent with well-established meanings of that term. The above set of definitions are striking in that they tell us so little. Why do KM definitions tell us so little about (1) the activities that are part of KM and (2) the target of those activities?

So the situation with respect to "KM" is very similar to that we have already found with regard to "knowledge." There is no consensus on definition, and attempts to define KM are relatively superficial. It is a case of another key concept in KM being defined so vaguely and ambiguously that research and writing on KM is weighed down with conceptual baggage and difficulties in communication, inhibiting both the search for KM knowledge and effective KM decision making. My own attempt to solve the problem of definition begins with consideration of the differences between information management and knowledge management.

Information management and knowledge management

What's the difference between information management (IM) and knowledge management (KM)? Both concepts refer to managing (handling, directing, governing, controlling, coordinating, planning, organizing) processes and the products of those processes. In addition, since knowledge is a form of information (see Chapter 7), it follows that KM is a form of IM. More specifically, KM is a more robust form of IM that provides management of activities not necessary in specifying the concept of information management.

One difference between basic IM and KM is that basic IM focuses on managing how information is produced and integrated into the enterprise, whereas KM does the same with respect to knowledge. A second difference between basic IM and KM is that basic IM focuses on managing a more narrow set of activities than KM. The two information processes managed by an organization are information production and information integration. The two basic knowledge processes are knowledge production and knowledge integration. Since knowledge processes are more inclusive in the sense that there are classes of activities in knowledge processes not found in basic information processes, let us examine a framework for looking at knowledge processes first. Then we will be able to arrive at how basic information processes are different from augmented information/knowledge processes, by cutting out some of the knowledge activities in knowledge processes. After completing that examination, I will begin to address knowledge management and basic information management in more detail.

Knowledge processes and information processes

Knowledge production (recall Chapters 7 and 8) includes (1) knowledge claim formulation, (2) individual and group learning, and (3) information acquisition. It must also include (4) knowledge claim validation activity. Knowledge integration includes all (a) knowledge broadcasting, (b) searching/retrieving, (c) teaching, and (d) knowledge sharing. The two knowledge processes, once again, may be viewed as part of the KLC, a knowledge "value network" (Allee, 2000). The KLC and the interaction of the two knowledge processes are illustrated in Figure 7.3. The major task clusters within Knowledge Production are illustrated in Figure 7.4. The major task clusters in Knowledge Integration are illustrated in Figure 7.5.

Basic information processes are different from knowledge production and integration processes in that they lack knowledge claim validation and, therefore, any further processing of valid knowledge claims. Information production includes information acquisition, individual and group learning, and even knowledge claim formulation but stops before knowledge validation. So the information "life cycle" or value network is incomplete in comparison with the knowledge life cycle. Similarly information integration includes broadcasting, searching/retrieving, teaching, and sharing, but what is being broadcasted, searched for, retrieved, taught, and shared is information rather than knowledge.

Definition and specification of knowledge management and information management processes

KM is human activity that is part of the interaction constituting the knowledge management process (KMP) of an agent or collective. This definition reduces KM to the definition of the KMP. *The KMP is an ongoing, persistent, purposeful interaction among human-based agents through which the participating agents aim at managing (handling, directing, governing, controlling, coordinating, planning, organizing) other agents, components, and activities participating in the basic knowledge processes (knowledge production and knowledge integration) into a planned, directed, unified whole, producing, maintaining, enhancing, acquiring, and transmitting the enterprise's knowledge base.*

We can distinguish among organizations along two important KM dimensions, thereby providing the basis of a useful classification. The first is the number of levels of knowledge management interaction an organization has implemented. The second is the breadth of knowledge management activities it has implemented at each level.

Levels of knowledge management

By levels of knowledge management interaction, I mean to distinguish multiple levels of KM process activity arranged in a hierarchy. In principle, and, at least with respect to knowledge production, the hierarchy has an infinite number of levels. The hierarchy is generated by considerations similar to those specified by Bertrand Russell (Russell, 1919; Whitehead and Russell, 1913) in his theory of types and by Gregory Bateson (1972) in his theory of learning and communication.

Knowledge processes occur at the same level of agent interaction as other business processes. Let us call this business process level of interaction level zero of enterprise complex adaptive system (*cas*) interaction (Waldrop, 1992).

At this level, preexisting knowledge is used by business processes and by knowledge processes to implement activity. In addition, knowledge processes produce and integrate knowledge about business processes using (1) previously produced knowledge about how to implement these knowledge processes, (2) infrastructure, (3) staff, and (4) technology, whose purpose is to provide the foundation for knowledge production and knowledge integration at level zero. But from where does this infrastructure, staff, knowledge, and technology come. Who manages them, and how are they changed?

They do not come from, by, and through the level zero knowledge processes—these only produce and integrate knowledge about business processes such as the sales, marketing, or manufacturing processes. So, this is where level one of *cas* interaction, the lowest level of knowledge management, comes in.

This level one KM process interaction is responsible for producing and integrating knowledge about level zero knowledge production and integration processes to knowledge workers at level zero. It is this knowledge that is used at both level zero and level one to implement knowledge processes and KM knowledge and information processing. Let's call this level one knowledge the enterprise knowledge management (EKM) model.

The KM process and the EKM model at level one are also responsible for providing the knowledge infrastructure, staff, and technology necessary for implementing knowledge processes at level zero. In turn, knowledge processes at level zero use this infrastructure, staff, and technology to produce and integrate the knowledge used by the business processes. The relationships between level one KM and level zero knowledge and business processes are illustrated in Figure 9.1.

Knowledge about level zero knowledge processes—as well as infrastructure, staff, and technology—change when level one KMP interactions introduce changes. That is, changes occur; they occur when the level one KMP produces and integrates new knowledge about how to implement level zero knowledge processes, and when it adds or subtracts from the existing infrastructure, staff, and technology based on new knowledge it produces. There are two possible sources of these changes.

First, knowledge production at level one can change the EKM model, which, in turn, impacts on (a) knowledge about how to produce or integrate knowledge about (level zero) business processes, (b) knowledge about how to acquire information or integrate knowledge about level one information acquisition or integration processes (c) staffing, (d) infrastructure, and (e) technology. This type of change then, originates in the KM level one process interaction itself.

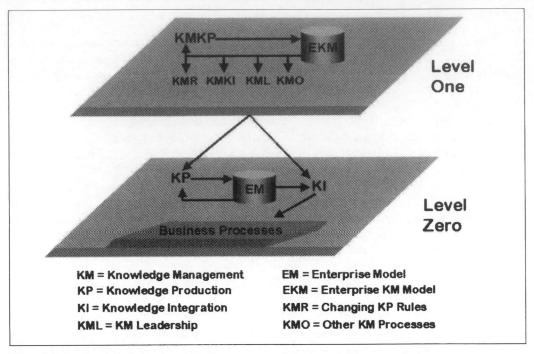

Figure 9.1. Relationships between level one KM and level zero knowledge and business processes.

Second, knowledge expressed in the EKM model about how to produce knowledge at level one may change. This knowledge, however, is used only in arriving at the level one EKM model. It is not explained or accounted for by it. It is determined, instead, by a KM level two process and is accounted for in a level two EKM model produced by this interaction. Figure 9.2 adds the KM level two process to the process relationships previously shown in Figure 9.1.

Instead of labeling the three levels of processes discussed so far as level zero, level one, and level two, it is more descriptive to think of them as the knowledge process level, the KM or meta-knowledge process level, and the meta-KM or metaprise level (Firestone, 1999) of process interaction. There is no end, in principle, to the hierarchy of levels of process interaction and accompanying EKM models. The number of levels we choose to model and to describe, will be determined by how complete an explanation of knowledge management activity we need to accomplish our purposes.

The knowledge process level produces knowledge about business processes and uses knowledge about how to produce (how to innovate) knowledge about business processes. This level cannot change knowledge about how to produce knowledge. It can change knowledge about business processes.

The KM (meta-knowledge) process level produces the knowledge about how to produce knowledge about business processes and uses knowledge about how to produce KM level knowledge about how to produce knowledge about business processes. This level can change knowledge about how to produce knowledge, but it cannot change knowledge about how to produce KM-level knowledge.

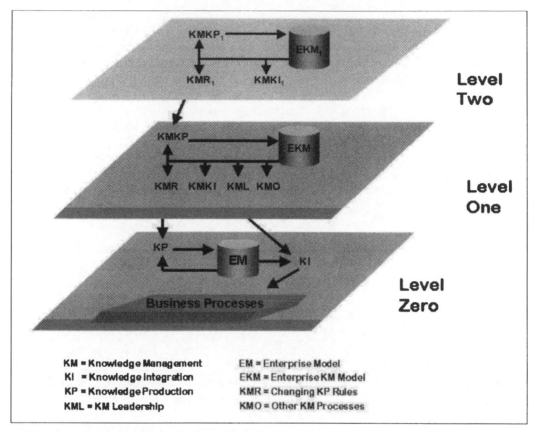

Figure 9.2. Adding KM level two to the relationship.

The meta-KM or first metaprise level produces (a) knowledge about how to produce knowledge about KM knowledge processes, and (b) knowledge about how to produce KM level knowledge about how to produce knowledge about knowledge processes. It uses knowledge about how to produce meta-KM level knowledge about how to produce knowledge about KM knowledge processes. This level can change knowledge about how to produce KM-level knowledge, but cannot change knowledge about how to produce meta-KM level knowledge.

Level three, the meta-meta-KM process or second metaprise level of interaction, produces knowledge about how to produce meta-KM level-produced knowledge about how to produce knowledge about KM knowledge processes, and uses meta-meta KM level-produced knowledge about how to produce knowledge about meta-KM level knowledge processes. This level can change knowledge about how to produce meta-KM level knowledge, but cannot change knowledge about how to produce meta-meta KM level knowledge.

Level two (the first metaprise level) then, seems to be the minimum number of levels needed for a view of KM allowing one to change (accelerate) the rate of change in KM level knowledge. And in some situations, where we need even more leverage over our knowledge about how to arrive at knowledge about KM processes, we may even need to go to levels higher than level 2.

Keeping in mind the foregoing distinctions among enterprises according to the level of knowledge management practiced in them, let us talk about KM, meta-KM, and meta-meta-KM level enterprises and so on. It should be possible to usefully characterize the successful twenty-first century intelligent enterprise, at least on a business domain–specific basis, as a level X metaprise, when we have more empirical evidence on how many KM levels are needed for competitiveness in any business domain.

Thus, the relative effectiveness of enterprises practicing different levels of KM is an empirical question, not something we should assume as given. While it is very likely that effectiveness will increase as enterprises move from the KM level to higher levels, there may be a point at which diminishing returns set in. Or there may even be a point at which movement up the ladder of levels leads to negative returns relative to the investment required to add a KM level or leads to fewer returns than alternative investments in other areas. ROI considerations must apply to enterprise KM enhancements as well as to other enterprise business processes.

Breadth of KM processes

By breadth of knowledge management processes, I mean the extent to which all of the major KM activities are implemented at any specified KM level of the enterprise. So what are these major KM activities? Here is a conceptual framework that begins to specify them.

Consider Figure 4.2, "The activity to business process hierarchy." This hierarchy, ranging from activities to processes, applies to knowledge and KM processes as well as to operational business processes. Enterprise KM activities may be usefully categorized according to a scheme of task clusters which, with some additions and changes, generally follows Mintzberg (1973).

There are three types of KM task clusters: interpersonal behavior, information (and knowledge) processing behavior, and decision making. Each type of task cluster is broken down further into nine more specific types of task pattern activities. Interpersonal KM behavior includes (1) figurehead, (2) leadership, and (3) external relationship-building activity.

Information processing behavior includes (4) KM knowledge production and (5) KM knowledge integration. Decision making includes (6) changing knowledge processing rules, (7) crisis handling, (8) allocating KM resources, and (9) negotiating agreement with representatives of other business processes.

In the following pages I will specify these nine areas of KM activity and also provide lists of descriptors and metrics that maybe useful in analyzing and modeling the areas of KM activity.

Interpersonal behavior

Figurehead or ceremonial representation KM activity. This activity focuses on performing formal KM acts such as signing contracts, attending public functions on behalf of the enterprise's KM process, and representing the KM process to dignitaries visiting the enterprise. Such symbolic representation is an aspect of all managerial activity. Managers have authority. Part of what maintains that authority is the symbolism used and manipulated by them to express the legitimacy of their authority and to claim it.

Figurehead activity in the KM area is similar to that in other areas of executive activity. Methods such as personal networking, meetings, public appearances, Web-enabled representing, and infrastructure such as intranet facilities used for figurehead activity, conference and presentation rooms, fax, telephone facilities, and the like are also similar. What is different is the focus of figurehead activity on conferences, meetings, and events where knowledge processing and knowledge management are the primary topics of interest. Process descriptors include

- Representing cycle time
- Representing velocity
- Representing acceleration
- Intensity of collaborative activity in representing
- Intensity of cooperative behavior in representing
- Intensity of conflict behavior in representing
- Extent of withdrawal from interaction with other agents as an outcome of collaborative representing activity
- Extent of inequality of access to previous representing
- Volume of documents transmitted to agents in representing
- Ratio of messages received by an agent to messages sent by that agent related to representing
- Use and frequency of use of methods of interpersonal representing
  — Personal networking
  — Meetings
  — Public appearances
- Use and frequency of use of methods of electronic support for representing
- Web-enabled representing
- Representing infrastructure
- Intranet facilities, both physical and software
- Conference and presentation rooms
- Fax
- Documents
- Telephone facilities

Representing outcome descriptors include

- Degree of knowledge worker satisfaction with symbolic representation
- Degree of knowledge manager satisfaction with symbolic representation
- Degree of satisfaction with symbolic representation by knowledge authority structure
- Degree of satisfaction with symbolic representation by organizational authority structure
- Degree of satisfaction with symbolic representation by subsystem
- Performance metric on symbolic representation

Descriptors of growth and change in symbolic representation include

- Change in symbolic representation cycle time
- Change in symbolic representation velocity
- Change in symbolic representation acceleration

Leadership. This includes setting policy, hiring, training, motivating, monitoring, and evaluating KM and some knowledge processing staff. It also includes persuading non-KM agents within the enterprise of the validity of KM process activities. That is, KM Leadership activity includes building political support for KM programs, projects, and knowledge processes within the enterprise and influencing the climate and norms within which knowledge processing will occur so that knowledge production will be enabled. Finally, leadership activities cut across all the other nine categories of KM activities. That is, leadership is an aspect of each of the nine classes of KM activities.

That leadership activities are central to KM is axiomatic. Leadership is a key management activity in any business process, and knowledge and KM processes are business processes. Again, what is different here is the focus on leadership of knowledge production and integration activities, on changing knowledge processing rules such as those impacting knowledge claim validation. And in the area of resource allocation, the focus on allocating software applications supporting knowledge production, integration and management is different. I will examine these software applications at some length later on. Process descriptors include

- Leading cycle time
- Leading velocity
- Leading acceleration
- Intensity of collaborative activity in leading
- Intensity of cooperative behavior in leading
- Intensity of conflict behavior in leading
- Extent of withdrawal from interaction with other agents as an outcome of collaborative leading activity
- Extent of inequality of access to leadership
- Volume of documents transmitted to agents in leading
- Ratio of messages received by an Agent to messages sent by that agent related to leading
- Use and frequency of use of interpersonal methods of leading:
  - consensus building
  - Persuading
  - Compelling
  - Incentivizing
  - Informing
  - Obligating
  - Hiring
  - Evaluating
  - Delegating
  - Meeting
  - Memoranda
- Use and frequency of use of methods of electronic support for leading:
  - Web-enabled meeting
  - E-mails
  - Portal-enabled collaboration

Leading infrastructure elements include

- Intranet facilities, both physical and software
- Offices
- Conference rooms
- Fax
- Telephone facilities

Leading outcome descriptors include

- Degree of knowledge worker satisfaction with leading
- Degree of knowledge manager satisfaction with leading
- Degree of satisfaction with leading by knowledge authority structure
- Degree of satisfaction with leading by organizational authority structure
- Degree of satisfaction with leading by subsystem
- Degree of fulfillment of leading objectives by knowledge assignment
- Degree of fulfillment of leading objectives by knowledge assignment segment
- Degree of fulfillment of leading objectives by knowledge authority structure segment
- Degree of fulfillment of leading objectives by organizational authority segment
- Degree of fulfillment of leading objectives by subsystem segment
- Responsibility segmentation
- Depth of authority/assignment structure created
- Scope of authority/assignment structure within and across knowledge management domains
- Growth in scope of authority structure
- Degree of hierarchy in KM leadership process
- Performance metric on leading KM activities

Descriptors of growth and change in leading include

- Change in leading cycle time
- Change in leading velocity
- Change in leading acceleration
- Change in intensity of collaborative activity in leading
- Change in intensity of cooperative behavior in leading
- Change in intensity of conflict behavior in leading
- Change in extent of withdrawal from interaction with other agents as an outcome of collaborative activity in leading
- Change in extent of inequality of access to KM leaders
- Change in ratio of messages received by an agent to messages sent by that agent related to leading
- Change in degree of hierarchy in KM leadership process

Building relationships with individuals and organizations external to the enterprise. This is another political activity designed to build status for KM and to cultivate sources of support for KM external to the enterprise. To build new external relationships requires joining professional associations, serving on committees, attending conferences and presenting visiting colleagues and allies, forming strategic alliances and partnerships, and networking individual contacts. There is no magic here—just the need to design and implement a systematic program to generate alliances and close relationships with individuals. These personal relationships are essential for information acquisition at the KM level. Some information can be acquired only through personal networks. Building external relationships means performing those activities intended to produce friendships, alliances, and "partnerships" with decision makers external to one's own company. These relationships are essential for providing "role models" for knowledge managers. Process descriptors include

- Building ER cycle time
- Building ER velocity
- Building ER acceleration
- Intensity of collaborative activity in building ER
- Intensity of cooperative behavior in building ER
- Intensity of conflict behavior in building ER
- Extent of withdrawal from interaction with other agents as an outcome of collaboration in building ER
- Use and frequency of use of interpersonal methods of building ER
  - Personal networking
  - Public appearances
  - Conferences, tours, meetings
  - Telephone conversations
- Use and frequency of use of methods of electronic support for building ER
  - Web-enabled building ER
  - E-mail communications
  - External-facing portal-enabled collaborative environments

Building ER infrastructure elements include

- Internet facilities, both physical and software
- Conference and presentation rooms
- Fax
- Documents
- Telephone facilities

Outcome descriptors include

- Degree of knowledge worker satisfaction with external relationship building
- Degree of knowledge manager satisfaction with external relationship building
- Degree of satisfaction with external relationship building by knowledge authority structure

- Degree of satisfaction with external relationship building by organizational authority structure
- Degree of satisfaction with external relationship building by subsystem
- Performance metric on external relationship building

Descriptors of growth and change in building external relationships include

- Change in external relationship building cycle time
- Change in external relationship building velocity
- Change in external relationship building acceleration
- Change in intensity of collaborative activity in external relationship building
- Change in intensity of cooperative behavior in external relationship building
- Change in intensity of conflict behavior in external relationship building
- Change in extent of withdrawal from interaction with other agents as an outcome of collaborative activity in external relationship building

Knowledge and information processing

Knowledge production is a KM as well as a knowledge process. KM knowledge production is different in that it is here that the "rules," frameworks, perspectives, and methodologies for knowledge production that are used at the level of knowledge processes are specified. Keep in mind that knowledge production at this level involves planning, descriptive, cause-and-effect, predictive, and assessment knowledge about the two fundamental level zero knowledge processes, as well as these categories of knowledge about level one interpersonal, knowledge integration, and decision-making KM activities. The only knowledge not produced by level one knowledge production is knowledge about how to accomplish knowledge production at level one. Once again, the rules, perspectives, etc. constituting this last type of knowledge are produced at level two. Descriptors and metrics characterizing knowledge production are the same at the KM level as at the knowledge processing level.

KM knowledge integration. KM knowledge integration is affected by KM knowledge production and, in turn, also affects knowledge production activities by stimulating new ones. KM knowledge integration at any KM level also plays the critical role of diffusing "how-to" knowledge to lower KM and knowledge process levels. But the essential character of knowledge integration at the KM level is unchanged from that at the basic KLC level. Descriptors and metrics characterizing knowledge integration are the same at the KM level as at the knowledge processing level.

Decision-making activities

Changing knowledge processing "rules". The task clusters of information acquisition, individual and group learning, knowledge claim formulation, knowledge claim validation, broadcasting, searching/retrieving, teaching, and sharing are all composed of tasks. Knowledge workers execute these tasks, and knowledge managers produce the processing "rules" contributing to the execution of the tasks. Knowledge managers also change the rules once they produce new knowledge about them. Essentially, this involves making the decision to change knowledge processing rules and causing both the new rules and the mandate to use them to be transferred to the lower level. The term "rules" here, should be interpreted liberally, as signifying perspectives, customs, and frameworks, among other things, as well as rules. I am not claiming that *rules* produced by knowledge managers necessarily govern—or should govern—all or even most knowledge production. Process Descriptors include

- Changing knowledge processing rules cycle time
- Changing knowledge processing rules velocity
- Changing knowledge processing rules acceleration
- Intensity of collaborative activity in changing knowledge processing rules
- Intensity of cooperative behavior in changing knowledge processing rules
- Intensity of conflict behavior in changing knowledge processing rules
- Extent of withdrawal from interaction with other agents as an outcome of collaborative changing knowledge processing rules activity
- Extent of inequality of access to previous changing knowledge processing rules
- Volume of documents transmitted to agents in changing knowledge processing rules
- Ratio of messages received by an agent to messages sent by that agent related to changing knowledge processing rules
- Use and frequency of use of interpersonal methods of changing knowledge processing rules: personal networking, meetings, briefings, conferences, telephone conversations
- Use and frequency of use of methods of electronic support for changing knowledge processing rules: Web-enabled changing knowledge processing rules, e-mail communications, portal-enabled collaborative environments

The infrastructure for changing knowledge processing rules includes the following elements:

- Intranet facilities, both physical and software
- Classrooms
- Fax
- Documents
- Telephone facilities
- Electronic broadcast reception facilities

Outcome descriptors include

- Extent of distribution of validated rules knowledge claims
- Extent of acceptance and support for above claims

- Extent of distribution of validated rules knowledge claims among targets of these claims
- Extent of acceptance and support for above claims
- Degree of knowledge worker satisfaction with rule changes
- Degree of knowledge manager satisfaction with rule changes
- Degree of satisfaction with rule changes by knowledge authority structure,
- Degree of satisfaction with rule changes by organizational authority structure,
- Degree of satisfaction with rule changes by subsystem,
- Degree of fulfillment of rule change objectives by knowledge assignment,
- Degree of fulfillment of rule change objectives by knowledge assignment segment,
- Degree of fulfillment of rule change objectives by knowledge authority structure segment,
- Degree of fulfillment of rule change objectives by organizational authority segment,
- Degree of fulfillment of rule change objectives by subsystem segment
- Performance metric on changing knowledge processing rules

Descriptors of growth and change in changing knowledge processing rules include

- Change in degree of inequality of changing knowledge processing rules
- Change in changing knowledge processing rules cycle time
- Change in changing knowledge processing rules velocity
- Change in changing knowledge processing rules acceleration
- Change in intensity of collaborative activity in changing knowledge processing rules
- Change in intensity of cooperative behavior in changing knowledge processing rules
- Change in intensity of conflict behavior in changing knowledge processing rules
- Change in extent of withdrawal from interaction with other agents as an outcome of collaborative activity in changing knowledge processing rules
- Change in extent of inequality of access to previously validated knowledge claims
- Change in volume of documents transmitted among all agents changing knowledge processing rules knowledge claims
- Change in ratio of messages received by an agent to messages sent by that agent related to changing knowledge processing rules

The above descriptors or metrics apply to each of the eight knowledge processing task clusters.

Crisis handling. Crisis handling involves such things as meeting CEO requests for new competitive intelligence in an area of high strategic interest for an enterprise, and directing rapid development of a KM support infrastructure in response to requests from high level executives.

Process descriptors include

- Crisis handling cycle time
- Crisis handling velocity
- Crisis handling acceleration
- Intensity of collaborative activity in crisis handling
- Intensity of cooperative behavior in crisis handling
- Intensity of conflict behavior in crisis handling
- Extent of withdrawal from interaction with other agents as an outcome of collaborative crisis handling activity
- Extent of inequality of access to previous crisis handling
- Volume of documents transmitted to agents in crisis handling
- Ratio of messages received by an agent to messages sent by that agent related to crisis handling
- Use and frequency of use of interpersonal methods of crisis handling: personal networking, meetings, briefings, conferences, telephone conversations
- Use and frequency of use of methods of electronic support for crisis handling: Web-enabled crisis handling, e-mail communications, portal-enabled collaborative environments

Elements of the infrastructure for crisis handling include

- Intranet facilities, both physical and software
- Fax
- Documents
- Telephone facilities
- Electronic broadcast reception facilities

Outcome descriptors include

- Extent of distribution of validated crisis handling knowledge claims
- Extent of acceptance and support for above claims
- Extent of distribution of validated crisis handling knowledge claims among targets of these claims
- Extent of acceptance and support for above claims
- Degree of knowledge worker satisfaction with crisis handling
- Degree of knowledge manager satisfaction with crisis handling
- Degree of satisfaction with crisis handling by knowledge authority structure
- Degree of satisfaction with crisis handling by organizational authority structure
- Degree of satisfaction with crisis handling by subsystem
- Degree of fulfillment of crisis handling objectives by knowledge assignment
- Degree of fulfillment of crisis handling objectives by knowledge assignment segment

- Degree of fulfillment of crisis handling objectives by knowledge authority structure segment
- Degree of fulfillment of crisis handling objectives by organizational authority segment
- Degree of fulfillment of crisis handling objectives by subsystem segment
- Performance metric on crisis handling activities

Descriptors of growth and change in crisis handling include

- Change in degree of inequality of crisis handling
- Change in crisis handling cycle time
- Change in crisis handling velocity
- Change in crisis handling acceleration
- Change in intensity of collaborative activity in crisis handling
- Change in intensity of cooperative behavior in crisis handling
- Change in intensity of conflict behavior in crisis handling
- Change in extent of withdrawal from interaction with other agents as an outcome of collaborative activity in crisis handling
- Change in extent of inequality of access to previously validated knowledge claims
- Change in volume of documents transmitted among all agents crisis handling
- Change in ratio of messages received by an agent to messages sent by that agent related to crisis handling

The above descriptors or metrics apply to each of the eight knowledge processing task clusters.

Allocating resources. This category includes allocating resources for KM support infrastructures, training, professional conferences, salaries for KM staff, funds for new KM programs, etc. Process descriptors include

- Allocating resources cycle time
- Allocating resources velocity
- Allocating resources acceleration
- Intensity of collaborative activity in allocating resources
- Intensity of cooperative behavior in allocating resources
- Intensity of conflict behavior in allocating resources
- Extent of withdrawal from interaction with other agents as an outcome of collaborative activity in allocating resources
- Extent of inequality of access to previously allocated resources
- Volume of documents transmitted to agents in allocating resources
- Ratio of messages received by an agent to messages sent by that agent related to allocating resources
- Use and frequency of use of interpersonal methods of allocating resources: personal networking, meetings, briefings, conferences, telephone conversations
- Use and frequency of use of methods of electronic support for allocating resources: Web-enabled resource allocation, e-mail communications, portal-enabled collaborative environments

The following are elements of the infrastructure for allocating resources:

- Intranet facilities, both physical and software
- Computational facilities
- Fax
- Documents
- Telephone facilities

Outcome descriptors include

- Extent of distribution of validated allocating resources knowledge claims
- Extent of acceptance and support for above claims
- Extent of distribution of validated allocating resources knowledge claims among targets of these claims
- Extent of acceptance and support for above claims
- Degree of knowledge worker satisfaction with allocating resources
- Degree of knowledge manager satisfaction with allocating resources
- Degree of satisfaction with allocating resources by knowledge authority structure
- Degree of satisfaction with allocating resources by organizational authority structure,
- Degree of satisfaction with allocating resources by subsystem
- Degree of fulfillment of allocating resources objectives by knowledge assignment
- Degree of fulfillment of allocating resources objectives by knowledge assignment segment
- Degree of fulfillment of allocating resources objectives by knowledge authority structure segment
- Degree of fulfillment of allocating resources objectives by organizational authority segment
- Degree of fulfillment of allocating resources objectives by subsystem segment
- Performance metric on resource allocation activities

Descriptors of growth and change in allocating resources include

- Change in degree of inequality of allocating resources
- Change in allocating resources cycle time
- Change in allocating resources velocity
- Change in allocating resources acceleration
- Change in intensity of collaborative activity in allocating resources
- Change in intensity of cooperative behavior in allocating resources
- Change in intensity of conflict behavior in allocating resources
- Change in extent of withdrawal from interaction with other agents as an outcome of collaborative activity in allocating resources
- Change in extent of inequality of access to previously validated knowledge claims
- Change in volume of documents transmitted among all agents allocating resources

- Change in ratio of messages received by an agent to messages sent by that agent related to allocating resources

The above descriptors or metrics apply to each of the eight knowledge processing task clusters.

Negotiating agreements. Negotiating agreements with representatives of business processes over levels of effort for KM, the shape of KM programs, the ROI expected of KM activities, etc. Process descriptors include

- Negotiating agreements cycle time
- Negotiating agreements velocity
- Negotiating agreements acceleration
- Intensity of collaborative activity in negotiating agreements
- Intensity of cooperative behavior in negotiating agreements
- Intensity of conflict behavior in negotiating agreements
- Extent of withdrawal from interaction with other agents as an outcome of collaborative activity in negotiating agreements
- Volume of documents transmitted to agents in negotiating agreements
- Ratio of messages received by an agent to messages sent by that agent related to negotiating agreements
- Use and frequency of use of interpersonal methods of negotiating agreements: personal networking, meetings, briefings, conferences, telephone conversations
- Use and frequency of use of methods of electronic support for negotiating agreements: Web-enabled negotiating, e-mail, communications, portal-enabled collaborative environments

Elements of the infrastructure for negotiating agreements include the following:

- Intranet facilities, both physical and software
- Computational facilities
- Fax
- Documents
- Telephone facilities

Outcome descriptors include

- Extent of distribution of validated negotiating agreements knowledge claims
- Extent of acceptance and support for above claims
- Extent of distribution of validated negotiating agreements knowledge claims among targets of these claims
- Extent of acceptance and support for above claims
- Degree of knowledge worker satisfaction with negotiating agreements
- Degree of knowledge manager satisfaction with negotiating agreements
- Degree of satisfaction with negotiating agreements by knowledge authority structure,

- Degree of satisfaction with negotiating agreements by organizational authority structure,
- Degree of satisfaction with negotiating agreements by subsystem,
- Degree of fulfillment of negotiating agreements objectives by knowledge assignment,
- Degree of fulfillment of negotiating agreements objectives by knowledge assignment segment,
- Degree of fulfillment of negotiating agreements objectives by knowledge authority structure segment,
- Degree of fulfillment of negotiating agreements objectives by organizational authority segment,
- Degree of fulfillment of negotiating agreements objectives by subsystem segment
- Performance metric on negotiating activities

The following are descriptors of growth and change in negotiating agreements:

- Change in degree of inequality of negotiating agreements
- Change in negotiating agreements cycle time
- Change in negotiating agreements velocity
- Change in negotiating agreements acceleration
- Change in intensity of collaborative activity in negotiating agreements
- Change in intensity of cooperative behavior in negotiating agreements
- Change in intensity of conflict behavior in negotiating agreements
- Change in extent of withdrawal from interaction with other agents as an outcome of collaborative activity in negotiating agreements
- Change in extent of inequality of access to previously negotiated agreements
- Change in volume of documents transmitted among all agents negotiating agreements
- Change in ratio of messages received by an agent to messages sent by that agent related to allocating resources

The above descriptors or metrics apply to each of the eight knowledge processing task clusters.

The classification

This classification of nine KM categories or task clusters is not complete. There are likely other task clusters and patterns I have overlooked. For now the classification is specific enough to provide the capability to define types of enterprises based on both variation in levels of KM, and in the breadth of KM task clusters and activities that are implemented. This should provide a fairly rich two-dimensional KM-motivated classification of enterprises, which we can then further segment by performance and other characteristics as seems appropriate.

More on how information management differs from knowledge management

IM activities can be defined in analogy to KM activities. There are three categories of IM activities in the information management process (IMP): interpersonal behavior; information processing behavior; and decision making.

Interpersonal IM behavior includes

- Figurehead
- Leadership
- External relationship-building activity

Information processing behavior includes:

- IM information production (no knowledge claim validation)
- IM information integration (only broadcasting, searching/retrieving, teaching, or sharing information, but not knowledge)

Decision making includes

- Changing information process rules
- Crisis handling
- Allocating resources
- Negotiating agreement with representatives of other business processes

The differences between information processes at the IM level and knowledge processes at the KM level, therefore, arise from the absence of knowledge claim validation activity in IM. As a result, broadcasting, searching and retrieving, teaching, and sharing at the IM level are all focused on information and not on knowledge.

How does culture relate to KM?

As I have argued earlier, we can distinguish KM processes, and knowledge processes. And knowledge processes may be viewed in terms of the knowledge life cycle framework. These processes produce knowledge that is used in the other business processes of the enterprise. And these, in turn, produce outcomes. Figure 9.3 illustrates this pattern.

Moreover, KM processes, knowledge processes, and business processes are performed by decision-making, behaving, agents. As we have seen, agents, if they are groups, have an internal culture, both subjective and objective. At the same time, the objective cultural component of social ecology also impacts agent decisions. Finally, knowledge and KM processes are affected by culture through the influence it has on behavior constituting these processes. In turn, these processes are keys to producing culture. So culture is pervasive in KM. But many other factors—social ecology, situational factors, transactional inputs (see Figure 7.8)—also contribute to the complex interactions associated with it. So culture is only a

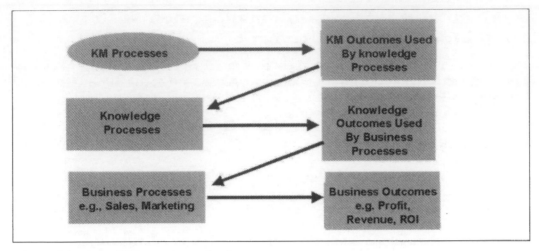

Figure 9.3. From KM processes to business outcomes.

small part of all there is to KM or any other business process, and there remain substantial problems in measuring and analyzing its precise impact.

KM Impact and innovation

Recall the definition of innovation as a completed knowledge process life cycle event, beginning with a problem emerging from a business process, moving through knowledge production, and ending in incorporation of knowledge structures within business structures impacting business process behavior (see Figure 7.3). Keeping this definition in mind, let us now divide KM impact on innovation into three categories: KM impact on knowledge processes, KM impact on knowledge process cycle times, and KM impact on innovation rates and innovation relevance.

Impact on knowledge processes

Figure 9.4 illustrates the relationship between changes in KM task patterns, tasks, and activities and changes in knowledge processes. The main point is that changes in KM cause changes in each of the components of the two knowledge processes. KM impact on knowledge processes is a set of impacts classifiable as impacts in information acquisition, individual and group learning, knowledge claim formulation and knowledge claim validation, broadcasting, searching/retrieving, and teaching and sharing. KM impact on organizational knowledge, the distributed organizational knowledge base, and other outcomes incorporating knowledge structures is indirect. But changes in these products of knowledge processes feed back to impact on future operations of knowledge processes. Though not shown in the figure, they may also feed back to impact the KM process itself, provided a healthy KM process that monitors the results of its interventions in an objective manner is in place.

A more detailed classification of KM impacts can be developed from the cross-classification of KM task patterns and KLC components. There are seventy-two types of KM impact resulting from this cross-classification, and many more

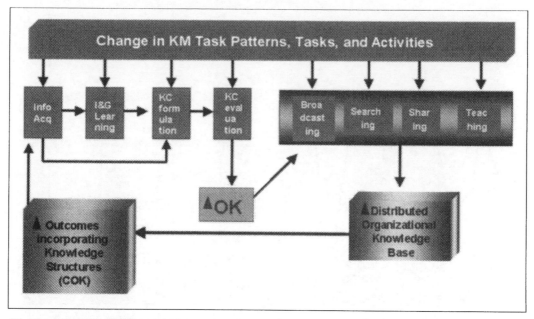

Figure 9.4. The relationship between changes in KM task patterns, tasks, and activities and changes in knowledge processes.

types would result if the KM task patterns were further broken down into tasks. The types of impact can serve as a guide to hypothesis formation and model construction. They provide a framework within which we can seek to formulate and test hypotheses and rules and rule sets in models. The types of KM impact can easily be laid out in a table, but since the cross-classification is straightforward, I will not do that here.

Impact on knowledge process cycle times

If changes in KM have an impact on changes in knowledge process components, it is to be expected that they have this impact indirectly, through changes they induce in the knowledge processing tasks comprising these components, and that these changes, in turn, result in changes in knowledge processing cycle time. Figure 9.5 illustrates this impact of changes in KM on knowledge process cycle times. There is a cycle time for every component of the KLC. The total cycle time in any instance of knowledge processing is the sum of the cycle times involved in that instance of knowledge processing. Note that not every knowledge process component need be present in a given instance of the KLC.

Note also that the impact of KM may be partitioned into separate impacts on each of the cycle times associated with each of the components of the KLC. Moreover, the impacts or changes in individual cycle times are additive in determining the total cycle time changes in the KLC.

Impact on innovation rates and innovation relevance

These impacts are addressed in Figure 9.6. Changes in KM patterns cause changes in the KLC. Two results are changes in component and total cycle times and

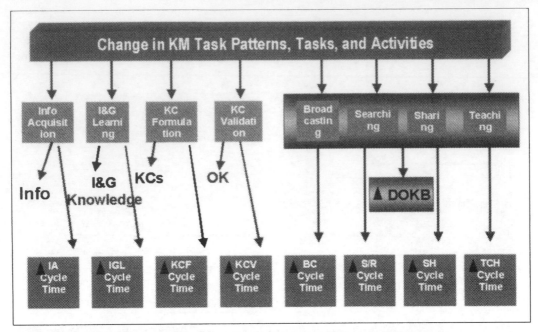

Figure 9.5. The impact of changes in KM on knowledge process cycle times.

changes in the relevance or value of new innovations. Innovations are not automatically valuable, and increases in innovation cycle times are not automatically beneficial. Innovation relevance addresses these questions. The relevance of an innovation is related to the benefits it produces. Benefit/cost analysis of innovations may be addressed through the approach I provided in Chapter 4.

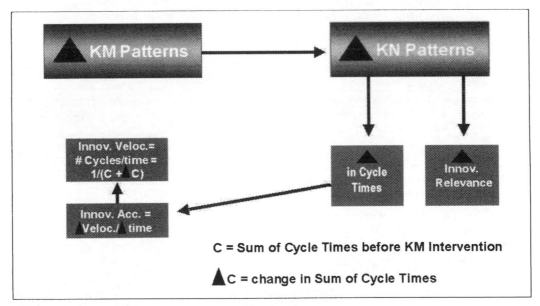

Figure 9.6. KM impact on innovation rates and relevance.

The illustration in Figure 9.6 also addresses what I mean by the following:

- Innovation acceleration—the change in velocity divided by the change in time
- Velocity—the number of innovation cycles per unit time (It will be a small number if time is measured in seconds, minutes, hours, days, or even weeks.)
- Velocity also =1/[the sum of the initial (before KM intervention) component cycle times and the change in the sum of cycle times after KM intervention]

KM interventions and KM metrics

KM process interventions are changes made in the nine task patterns and their relationships and, even more concretely, in tasks comprising the task patterns. These changes impact knowledge process components such as information acquisition, knowledge validation, and knowledge sharing and their relationships and, therefore, also impact the relevance, acceleration, and velocity of innovations. In order to evaluate KM interventions, it is necessary to measure their impact. In turn, this requires metrics for both KM processes and KLC attributes.

There are three categories of knowledge process and product metrics necessary for measuring KM impact and evaluating any KM intervention: (1) internal metrics measuring changes in the task clusters, patterns, tasks, and activities of the KM process and the products of the KM process; (2) knowledge life cycle metrics needed for measuring the impact of changes in KM on KLC process components, relationships, innovation velocity (IV), innovation acceleration (IA), and innovation relevance (IR); and (3) metrics for measuring the impact of changes in IV, IA, and IR on the enterprise.

Still more specifically, to validate any KM intervention, one needs to analyze the impact attributable to it of changes in KM patterns on changes in metrics. This includes metrics related to information acquisition, individual and group learning, knowledge claim formulation, knowledge validation; broadcasting, searching, teaching, and sharing; innovation velocity; innovation acceleration; innovation relevance; and indicators external to the knowledge life cycle such as return on capital employed (ROCE), ROI, operating margin, and numerous balanced scorecard-type measures of organizational performance. This is the validation context of all KM interventions or KM techniques designed to accelerate innovation or to otherwise improve the quality of the KLC. Here are some examples of the three types of metrics needed to evaluate KM interventions.

KM process internal and related product metrics

KM process metrics include change in

- KM knowledge production cycle times
- KM knowledge integration cycle times
- Frequency of change in knowledge production rules
- Intensity of collaboration among KM agents, teams, and groups

- Cycle time in responding to requests for competitive intelligence
- KM product metrics include change in breadth of distribution of KM knowledge within the KM community of practice and increase/decrease in extent of validation of various components of the KM organizational enterprise knowledge model

Knowledge life cycle metrics

KLC process metrics include change in

- KLC component cycle times
- Innovation velocity
- Innovation acceleration
- Intensity of collaborative activity in knowledge production

Some KLC product metrics include change in

- Extent of innovation relevance
- Average level of measurement of attributes in knowledge base within and across domains
- Validation profile of various components of the knowledge base

KM-related enterprise metrics

Some enterprise process metrics include change in

- Manufacturing production cycle times
- Customer service cycle time
- Intensity of collaboration in enterprise business processes

Some enterprise product metrics include change in ROI; profitability, market share, customer retention, and employee retention.

KM impact and sustainable innovation

Sustainable innovation refers to the capability of a knowledge processing system to sustain its rate or velocity of innovation, its acceleration of innovation, and their relevance. The velocity, acceleration, and relevance descriptors already mentioned can track the results of sustainability and describe whether an enterprise is sustaining and accelerating innovation, or dying. Therefore measuring and modeling the impact of KM on sustainability in innovation is closely related to measuring and modeling its impact in accelerating innovation. It requires the same type of analysis and modeling, and the preceding discussions of KLC and KM components are relevant for modeling both impacts on the KLC.

In modeling sustainable innovation, the key is to analyze the impact of KM interventions not only on the velocity, acceleration, and relevance descriptors mentioned above, but also on descriptors whose change has an impact on the primary descriptors at a later time. That is, it is necessary to look for side effects on descriptors whose change will undermine the capabilities of the KLC to maintain the needed levels of velocity, acceleration, and relevance. I believe that many of the descriptors listed for the various KLC components are such side-effect descriptors and can be used to arrive at both acceleration and sustainability models.

Some examples of KM interventions

The key to KM impact on innovation is KM intervention. We must begin to measure and evaluate the impact of KM interventions on the KLC and on innovation if we want to be effective in either accelerating or sustaining innovation. It may be helpful to provide some examples of what we mean by the kind of KM interventions that will need to be evaluated.

- *Allocate KM resources to support involvement in external initiatives.* This may include involvement in outside consortia, think tanks, research initiatives, industry conferences, outside training programs, and industry intelligence subscription services. Impacts on information acquisition, individual and group learning, and knowledge claim formulation are likely.
- *Allocate KM resources to establish and support communities of practice.* This may include implementing Web-based collaborative processing IT applications. The effects may include decentralizing innovation, encouraging cross-disciplinary collaboration, decreasing cycle time in individual and group learning, knowledge claim formulation, and knowledge claim validation.
- *Change knowledge processing rules by introducing a formal knowledge production methodology.* This type of intervention can impact individual and group learning, knowledge claim formulation, and knowledge validation, including establishing new knowledge validation criteria, perspectives, or frameworks. Further impact on innovation acceleration, velocity, and relevance may result and must be carefully evaluated.
- *Implement training programs for KM.* Impact can include rapid increase in awareness of the components of both knowledge processing and knowledge management. In turn, this can lead to acceleration in the various components of knowledge production especially, and to implementation of new IT infrastructure to support knowledge processing in the enterprise.
- *Allocate KM resources to implement an enterprise knowledge portal.* Implementing an EKP can have a comprehensive impact on all components of knowledge processing. EKPs can accelerate information acquisition, individual and group learning, and knowledge claim formulation and can support all of the knowledge integration subprocesses as well. Impact, however, will depend on the specific changes introduced by the EKP. A comprehensive EKP can support communities of practice, introduce a formal knowledge production methodology, and support a variety of information acquisition, knowledge validation, and knowledge integration activities, as well as a variety of KM activities. I will examine the relationship of the EKP to various aspects of knowledge processing and KM later on.

Conclusion

The last three chapters have presented a conceptual framework of basic KM-related concepts, a business process decision model, a knowledge life cycle model, a KM framework, and a detailed listing of descriptors and metrical concepts associated with the main categories of the conceptual framework. Previous work performed on the KLC framework (Firestone, 1999; McElroy, 1999) and on a general conceptualization of KM provide a place to start, but without a detailed framework, such as that provided here, further progress in applying the KLC and KM frameworks would be difficult at best. With it all kinds of applications are within reach. The framework, for example, could be used

- To set up system dynamics or *cas* (swarm) simulations of KM impact on the knowledge life cycle and the organizational system
- As a guide to developing measurement models and measures of KM impact on the KLC
- Along with indicators external to the KLC, to measure the impact of KM on business processes and their outcomes. Examples of such indicators include change in: manufacturing production cycle times; customer service cycle time; intensity of collaboration in enterprise business processes; and changes in ROI, profitability, market share, customer retention, and employee retention.
- As a guide to analysis of any of the processes and task clusters in the KLC or KM components of the framework.

In short, the framework opens the way to further development of knowledge management as a discipline. It provides a map that students of KM can use to conceptualize problems and "puzzles" that, if solved, can produce progress in the discipline.

References

Allee, V. (2000). "Reconfiguring the Value Network," available at http://www.vernaallee.com/reconfiguring_val_net.html.

Bateson, G. (1972). "The Logical Categories of Learning and Communication," in G. Bateson, *Steps to an Ecology of Mind* (New York: Chandler Publishing Co.).

Davenport, T. (1998), quoted in Y. Malhotra, "Compilation of definitions of knowledge management" at www.brint.com.

Davenport, T. (1994), quoted in Y. Malhotra, "Compilation of definitions of knowledge management" at www.brint.com.

Firestone, J.M. (1999). "The Metaprise, the AKMS, and the Enterprise Knowledge Portal," *Working Paper No. 3, Executive Information Systems, Inc.,* Wilmington, DE, May 5, 1999, Available at: http://www.dkms.com/White_Papers.htm.

Firestone, J.M. (2000). "Accelerated Innovation and KM Impact," *Financial Knowledge Management,* 1, no. 1, pp. 54–60, also available at http://www.dkms.com.

Firestone, J.M. (2000a). "Knowledge Management: A Framework for Analysis and Measurement," *White Paper No. 17, Executive Information Systems, Inc.,* Wilmington, DE, October 1, 2000, Available at http://www.dkms.com/White_Papers.htm.

Holland, J.H. (1995). *Hidden Order* (Reading, MA: Addison-Wesley).

Holland, J.H. (1998). *Emergence* (Reading, MA: Addison-Wesley, 1998).

Kauffman, S. (1995). *At Home in the Universe* (New York: Oxford University Press).

Knapp, E. (1998), quoted in Y. Malhotra, "Compilation of definitions of knowledge management" at www.brint.com.

Malhotra, Y. "Compilation of definitions of knowledge management" at www.brint.com.

McElroy, M. (1999). "The Second Generation of KM," *Knowledge Management Magazine* (October, 1999), pp. 86–88.

Mintzberg, H. (1973). "A New Look at the Chief Executive's Job," *Organizational Dynamics, AMACOM,* Winter, 1973.

Murray, P. (1998), quoted in Y. Malhotra, "Compilation of definitions of knowledge management" at www.brint.com.

Russell, B. (1919). *Introduction to Mathematical Philosophy* (London: Allen and Unwin).

Sveiby, K. (1998), quoted in Y. Malhotra, "Compilation of definitions of knowledge management" at www.brint.com.

University of Kentucky, quoted in Y. Malhotra, "Compilation of definitions of knowledge management" at www.brint.com.

Waldrop, M. (1992). *Complexity* (New York: Simon & Schuster).

Wenig, R. G. (1998), quoted in Y. Malhotra, "Compilation of definitions of knowledge management" at www.brint.com.

Whitehead, A.N., and Russell, B. (1913). *Principia Mathematica* (London: Cambridge University Press, 1913).

Wiig, K. (1998), quoted in Y. Malhotra, "Compilation of definitions of knowledge management" at www.brint.com.

PART FIVE

Artificial Knowledge Management Systems and the Role of XML

Part 5 is composed of transitional chapters providing additional background needed for understanding the later EIP segmentation framework and the enterprise knowledge portal. In Chapter 10, I consider the question of how information technology applications may support knowledge processing and knowledge management and, more specifically, the nature of the functional requirements of such technology applications. I begin by specifying the connection between the natural knowledge management system, and a generalized IT construct called the artificial knowledge management system. I show that the AKMS (in theory) partially supports the NKMS by partially supporting processes and tasks in the NKMS through use cases that specify the functional requirements of the DKMS, a realization of the AKMS using present technology. The chapter also discusses AKMS/DKMS architecture including the artificial knowledge manager and its relationship to knowledge claim objects (KCOs) and intelligent agents.

Chapter 11 describes the role of XML in EIPs. XML is the other major trend in IT over the last few years. In this chapter I discuss XML in PAI architecture for EIPs; XML for messaging and connectivity in portal systems; XML on the client side; XML in databases and content stores; XML and agents; and, finally, new developments in XML-related standards, including XML resource description framework (RDF), XML topic maps (XTM), and meaning definition language (MDL).

CHAPTER 10

Knowledge Management and the AKMS/DKMS

Introduction

In the last three chapters I have presented a conceptual framework for viewing knowledge, knowledge processing, and knowledge management. My purpose in doing this has been to prepare the way to providing a detailed and careful answer to the question of whether enterprise information portals (EIPs) are, in fact the "killer app" of knowledge management. And, more generally, my intention is to answer the question of the relationship between EIPs and knowledge management (including knowledge and knowledge processing). I will not be able to provide my final answer to these questions for a number of chapters, until after I have discussed EIP segmentation in much greater detail. But in this chapter I take a critical step toward the answer. That step is to begin with the knowledge processing/KM conceptual framework already developed and explore the question of how information technology applications may support it and, more specifically, the nature of the functional requirements of such technology applications.

The NKMS and the AKMS

In certain circles knowledge management is considered a branch of information technology, as if human beings performed no knowledge management before the invention of the computer. But my view is that knowledge processing and knowledge management are part of a natural knowledge management system (NKMS) present in all of our organizations and social systems (Firestone, 1999, p. 1). The properties of an NKMS are not determined by design. Instead, they emerge from the dynamics of enterprise interaction.

In contrast, an enterprise artificial knowledge management system is an organizationwide conceptually distinct, integrated component produced by its NKMS whose (ibid., p. 1)

- Components are computers, software, networks, electronic components, and so on
- Components and interaction properties are determined by *design*

- Overall purpose is to support the knowledge and KM processes of the NKMS

The AKMS is part of the NKMS. Its purpose is to support its key processes.

A key aspect in defining the AKMS is that both its components and interactions must be *designed*. The idea of *being fully designed* as opposed to being partly designed or not designed is essential in distinguishing the artificial from the natural. Thus, in an enterprise or any other organization, even though we may try to design its processes, our capacity to design is limited by the fact that it is a Complex adaptive system (*cas*) (Holland, 1995). On the other hand, with an AKMS we design both its components and their interactions. The connection between the design and the final result is determinate and not emergent (Holland, 1998). When we interact with the AKMS, we can precisely predict what its response will be.

The AKMS is designed to manage the integration of computer hardware, software, and networking objects and components into a functioning whole, supporting enterprise knowledge production, integration, and management processes. In addition, it supports knowledge use in business processes as well.

Knowledge and knowledge management processes, use cases, and the AKMS

Knowledge management and knowledge processes can be supported, but not automatically performed, by information systems. The relationship between these natural knowledge and KM processes and the artificial processes implemented in information systems depends on the connection between the NKMS and the AKMS. That connection is defined by the functions performed by the artificial system for the natural processes. In turn, these functions are defined by the use cases performed by the artificial system. One or more use cases constitutes an IT application. Use cases were defined by Ivar Jacobson (Jacobson, et al., 1995, p. 343) as: "a behaviourally related sequence of transactions performed by an actor in a dialogue with the system to provide some measurable value to the actor." This definition emphasizes that the use case is a dialog or interaction between the user and the system.

In the unified modeling language (UML) (Jacobson, Booch, and Rumbaugh, 1999) a use case is defined as "a set of sequences of actions a system performs that yield an observable result of value to a particular actor." Both definitions emphasize important aspects of the use case concept, but the first definition, highlighting a use case as something a human uses to get a result of value from a computer, is the focus of our interest here, because it expresses the idea that the NKMS *uses* the AKMS.

The relationship of business processes to use cases is illustrated in Figure 10.1. Figure 10.1 shows that when an IT application is viewed functionally, it may be viewed as performing a set of use cases supporting various tasks within enterprise business processes. But IT applications do not completely automate business processes. They support and enable them by automating only some the tasks in a process and by partially automating others.

An application that supports the knowledge and KM processes is an AKMS. It is an AKMS because among the processes it supports will be knowledge production, including its knowledge validation subprocess or task cluster. It is an AKMS

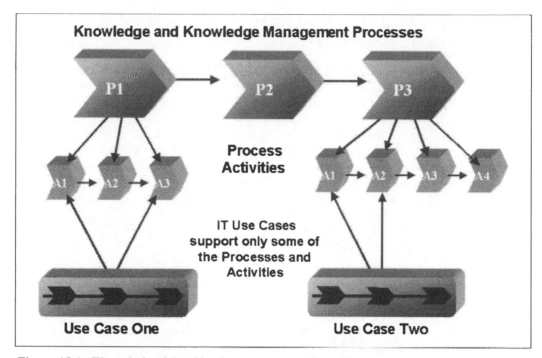

Figure 10.1. The relationship of business processes to use cases.

also because it supports the various activities in the knowledge management process. Again, the AKMS is related to the NKMS and to formal KM activities by the ways in which human agents in the NKMS use it. A view of the business process/ NKMS/use case/AKMS relationship is provided in Figure 10.2.

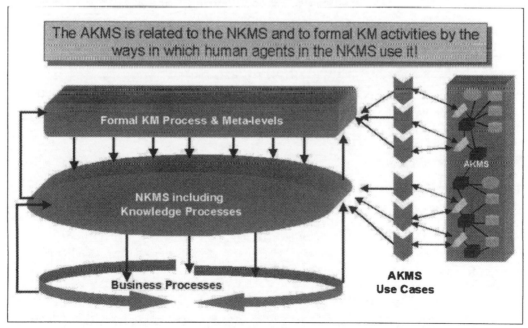

Figure 10.2. A view of the business process/NKMS/use case/AKMS relationship.

The AKMS and the distributed knowledge management system (DKMS)

I developed the idea of the AKMS from the DKMS (Firestone, 1999a) not so much in terms of formal definition, but in terms of the basic architectural concept I will write about later. In any event, the DKMS is a specific type of AKMS that relies on application servers and business process engines based on current distributed object technology for its processing power. The AKMS, on the other hand, is the more general concept and would apply not only to instances of the DKMS but, more generally, to systems barely envisioned today, based entirely on intelligent agents with complex adaptive system learning capabilities. The DKMS is a form of the AKMS that applies current or near future technology. So for all intents and purposes, DKMS and AKMS may be used interchangeably for the time being. The DKMS is designed to manage the integration of distributed computer hardware, software, and networking objects and components into a functioning whole, supporting enterprise knowledge production, integration, and knowledge management processes. In other words, the DKMS supports producing, integrating, and acquiring the enterprise's knowledge/information base.

The DKMS concept was developed initially in my "Object-oriented Data Warehousing," and "Distributed Knowledge Management System" White Papers (1997, 1997a). It was developed further in a series of White Papers and briefs, all available at dkms.com. The concept evolved out of trends in data warehousing (see Chapter 2), including

- Increasing complexity in data storage architecture in data warehousing systems
- Increasing complexity in application servers and functions
- A need to integrate data mining, sophisticated models, and ERP functionality
- A need to cope with rapid changes occurring in data warehousing systems.

The need for the DKMS concept was further reinforced by the appearance of content management, portal, and e-business applications. These accentuate the need for an enterprise application systems integration (EASI) approach to decision support.

DKMS use cases

The DKMS may be understood from two points of view. Use cases provide an external functional point of view; architecture and object models provide an internal point of view. Chapter 5 has already provided an overview of the architecture of the DIMS, which is very similar to the DKMS. Here I will concentrate first on the use-case point of view and later, on details of AKMS/DKMS architecture not covered in the account of the development of DIMS architecture in Chapter 5.

An example of a simplified use case provided by Jacobson, Booch, and Rumbaugh in *The Unified Software Development Process* (1999, p. 42) is: "the withdraw money use case". It is as follows:

- The bank customer identifies himself or herself.
- The bank customer chooses from which account to withdraw money and specifies how much to withdraw.
- The system deducts the amount from the account and dispenses the money

Note that the use case describes a course of events specifying the actions of the agent and the response of the system; it says nothing about the form, structure, or content of the system itself. This is a requirement for all use cases, whether they are simplified, low level, or high level. Use cases focus on the system from a functional, input/output point of view, not from the point of view of system structure and process.

Use cases may be described at various levels of abstractness or concreteness (Jacobson, Ericsson, and Jacobson, 1995). To develop an overall understanding of the DKMS we must focus on "high-level use cases." These are use cases that describe the DKMS functionality at a very abstract level.

An example of a high-level DKMS use case is provided by the "perform knowledge discovery in databases (KDD) use case." Here is a listing of the tasks constituting the use case. The full use case describing the course of events is given in "Knowledge Management Metrics Development: A Technical Approach" (Firestone, 1998).

- Retrieve and display strategic goals and objectives, tactical goals and objectives, and plans for knowledge discovery from results of previous use cases.
- Select entity objects representing business domains to be mined for new knowledge.
- Sample data.
- Explore data and clean for modeling.
- Recode and transform data.
- Reduce data.
- Select variables for modeling.
- Transform variables.
- Perform measurement modeling.
- Select modeling techniques.
- Estimate models.
- Validate models.
- Repeat process on same or new data.

Each of the tasks in "perform KDD" is itself a use case. In fact, the paper cited shows that "perform measurement modeling" itself includes five use cases and these contain still more specific tasks. High-level use cases, in other words, are complex and sometimes include more concrete use cases. But they are not generally "decomposable" in a direct hierarchical manner, and the most one can say is that high-level use cases in abstract use-case models are "traceable" to more concrete use cases in concrete use-case models (Jacobson, Ericsson, and Jacobson, 1995, pp. 320–324). We can classify use cases in the DKMS by whether they support knowledge production (KP), knowledge integration (KI), or knowledge management (KM) and still more specifically by whether they support the various subprocesses and activities in the KP, KI, or KM processes. Here is a listing of DKMS use cases classified in this way.

Knowledge production use cases

Information acquisition

- Performing cataloging and tracking of previously acquired enterprise data, information, and knowledge bases related to business processes
- Perform cataloging and tracking of external data, information and knowledge bases related to enterprise business processes
- Order data, information, or external claimed knowledge and have it shipped from external source
- Purchase data, information, or external knowledge claims
- Extract, reformat, scrub, transform, stage, and load, data, information, and knowledge claims acquired from external sources

Knowledge claim formulation

- Prepare data, information, and knowledge for analysis and analytical modeling
- Perform analysis and modeling (individually and collaboratively) including revising, reformulating, and formulating models and knowledge discovery in databases (KDD) with respect to:
  - Planning and planning models
  - Descriptions and descriptive models
  - Measurement modeling and measurement
  - Cause/effect analyzing and modeling
  - Predictive and time-series forecasting and modeling
  - Assessment and assessment modeling
- Update all data, information, and knowledge stores to maintain consistency with changes introduced into the DKMS

Knowledge claim validation

- Test competing knowledge models and claims using appropriate analytical techniques, data, and validation criteria
- Assess test results and compare (rate) competing knowledge models and claims
- Store the outcomes of information acquisition, individual and group learning, knowledge claim formulation, and other knowledge claim validation activities into a data, information, or knowledge store accessible through electronic queries
- Load data, information, or knowledge and updates into enterprise stores and provide access to enterprise query and reporting tools

Knowledge integration use cases

Storing the outcomes of knowledge integration activities into an accessible data, information, or knowledge store

Searching/retrieving previously produced data, information, and knowledge

- Receiving transmitted data, information, or knowledge through e-mail, automated alerts, and data, information and knowledge base updates
- Retrieving through computer-based querying data, information and knowledge of the following types: planning, descriptive, cause-effect, predictive and time-series forecasting, and assessment
- Search/retrieve from enterprise stores through computer-based querying, data, information, and knowledge of the following types: planning, descriptive, cause-effect, predictive and time-series forecasting, assessment
- Use e-mail to request assistance from personal networks

Broadcasting

- Publish and disseminate data, information, and knowledge using the enterprise intranet
- Present knowledge using the DKMS

Sharing

- Use e-mail to request assistance from personal networks
- Share data, information, and knowledge through collaboration spaces (AKMS support for communities of practice and teams)

Teaching

- Present e-learning or CBT modules to knowledge workers

Knowledge management use cases

Leadership

- Identify knowledge management responsibilities based on segmentation or decomposition of the KM process
- Retrieve available qualification information on knowledge management candidates for appointment
- Evaluate available candidates according to rules relating qualifications to predicted performance
- Communicate appointments to knowledge management constituency
- Plan and schedule motivational events

Building external relationships

- Communicate with external individuals through e-mail and online conferencing technology

KM knowledge production

- All knowledge production and knowledge integration use cases specified for knowledge processing
- Specify (either alone or in concert with a work group) and compare alternative KM options (infrastructure, training, professional conferences, compensation, etc.) in terms of anticipated costs and benefits

KM knowledge integration

- Querying and reporting using data, information, and knowledge about KM staff plans, KM staff performance description, KM staff performance cause/effect analysis, and KM staff performance prediction and forecasting
- Querying and reporting using data, information, and knowledge about assessing KM staff performance in terms of costs and benefits

Crisis handling

- Search/retrieve from enterprise stores through querying and reporting, data, information, and knowledge of the following types about crisis potential: planning, descriptive, cause-effect, predictive and time-series forecasting, and assessment

Changing knowledge-processing rules

- Search/retrieve from enterprise stores through computer-based querying, data, information, and knowledge of the following types about knowledge process rules: planning, descriptive, cause-effect, predictive and time-series forecasting, assessment
- Communicate rule-changing directives through e-mail

Allocating resources

- Select training program(s)
- Purchase training vehicles and materials (seminars, CBT products, manuals, etc.)

This listing of use cases is neither definitive nor complete. It falls far short of a use-case model for the DKMS. My purpose in presenting it is not to produce such a model, but to provide a more concrete idea of the nature of the DKMS by listing the kinds of use cases that such a system must support. If you study the list of use cases at length, you can begin to understand how comprehensive the capability of the DKMS/AKMS must be. And it is that realization that is essential for the coming discussion of enterprise knowledge portals.

MS/DKMS architecture

If use cases specify the functional or activity aspect of the DKMS, the objects and components of the DKMS that support these use cases, along with their interrelationships, provide its structure. We can begin to understand DKMS structure by visualizing a basic, abstract architecture (see Figure 10.3).

Figure 10.3 shows clients, application servers, communication buses, and data stores integrated through a single logical component called an artificial knowledge manager (AKM). The AKM performs its central integrative functions by providing process control and distribution services, an active, in-memory object model supplemented by a persistent object store, and connectivity services to provide for passing data, information, and knowledge from one component to another. I will specify the AKM in much more detail subsequently. For now, a more concrete visual picture showing the variety of component types in the AKMS is given in Figure 10.4.

An important difference between Figures 10.3 and 10.4 is that the communications bus aspect of the AKMS is implicit in Figure 10.4, where I have assumed that the AKM incorporates it. Figure 10.4 makes clear the diversity of component types in the AKMS. It is because of this diversity and its rapid rate of growth in the last few years that the AKM is necessary.

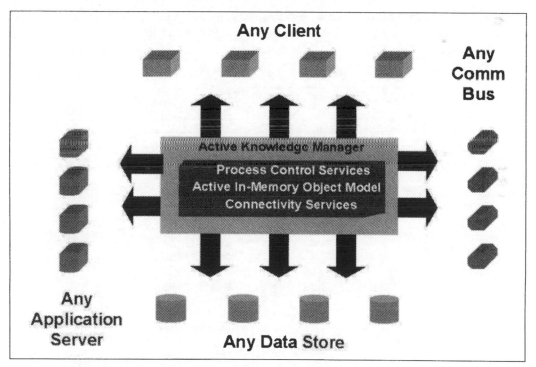

Figure 10.3. An abstract architecture for the AKMS/DKMS.

Change in the AKMS can be introduced through so many sources that if the AKMS is to adapt to change, it needs an integrative component such as the AKM to play the major role in its integration and adaptation. The key architectural components of the AKMS/DKMS, are

- The artificial knowledge manager (AKM) including interacting artificial knowledge servers (AKSs) and intelligent software agents (IAs)
- Stateless application servers
- Application servers that maintain state
- Knowledge claim objects
- Object/data stores
- Object request brokers (e.g., CORBA, DCOM) and other components, protocols, and standards supporting distributed processing
- Client application components

This list of components is similar to the components of the DIMS described in Chapter 5. To develop an AKMS, *one begins with an architecture similar to the DIMS and PAI architectures discussed in Chapter 5* and then adds knowledge claim objects to the AIM object model. Also added are knowledge production applications supporting knowledge discovery in database/data mining applications and various analytical applications designed to support analytical modeling for impact analysis, forecasting, planning, measurement modeling, computer simulation, and

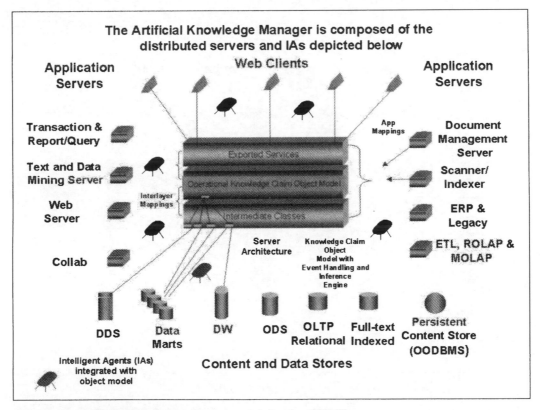

Figure 10.4. The variety of component types in the AKMS.

other supports for knowledge claim formulation. Here, again, is the list of application servers particularly relevant for knowledge processing and KM provided in Chapter 5:

- Collaborative planning
- Extraction
- Transformation, and loading (ETL)
- Knowledge discovery in databases (KDD)
- Knowledge base/object/component model maintenance and change management (The AKM)
- Knowledge publication and delivery (KPD)
- Computer-based training (CBT)
- Report production and delivery (RPD)
- ROLAP
- Operational data store (ODS) application server
- Forecasting/simulation server
- ERP servers
- Financial risk management
- Telecommunications service provisioning
- Transportation scheduling
- Stock trading servers
- Workflow servers.

The critical differences between the DIMS and the AKMS are the presence of *knowledge claim objects* in the AKMS/DKMS and their absence in the DIMS. In addition, the object model in the DKMS also includes validation rules, encapsulated in some of the knowledge claim objects used by the DKMS and knowledge workers to evaluate other knowledge claim objects.

The AKM and knowledge claim objects

An important class of objects in the artificial knowledge manager (both the AKSs and the IAs) is the knowledge claim object (KCO). A KCO is distinguished from an ordinary business object by the presence of:

- Knowledge claims (attribute values, rules, and rule networks) in the object
- Validity metadata about knowledge claims, either encapsulated in the object or recorded in an entity object related to it

Such metadata may be expressed in many different forms and compares the KCO to alternative, competing KCOs, or it may compare competing knowledge claims recorded in the same KCO.

The "metadata" may be qualitative or quantitative, or it may be in the form of textual content. In relatively infrequent but important special cases, the metadata may involve quantitative ratings of a knowledge claim compared with its competitors. When the KCO is accessed by a user, data, metadata, and methods (knowledge claims expressed as rules) are all available, so the user can evaluate the KCO as a basis for decision against competing KCOs. This capability is not available in artificial information managers (AIMs), which express knowledge claims as data or business objects only.

The AKM, KCOs, and intelligent agents

The addition of KCOs to the AKM is very significant to its IA component. The IA role in KCO management and synchronization is similar, though on a smaller scale than the role of the AKS in managing KCOs. The IAs support comparison of conflicting KCOs and the process of validating them against one another. They support tracking the history of validation in the enterprise. In addition, they support a process of local-regional-global knowledge production and integration, based on their distribution throughout the DKMS and on their capacity for learning and negotiation.

Thus, the servers and agents of the DKMS constitute an adaptive system in which knowledge claims formulated at various levels of DKMS architecture can interact in a collaborative learning process influenced by group and organizational level validation rules. The learning process is one in which local knowledge claims aggregated by client-based avatar agents and application server–based agents are submitted to the distributed artificial knowledge server (AKS) for adjudication and evaluation resulting in negative or positive reinforcement of knowledge claims.

IAs in the AKM are characterized by a complex adaptive systems (*cas*) learning capability (Waldrop, 1992, pp. 186–189). This capability begins with the cognitive map of each IA in the system. Next, reinforcement learning through neuro-fuzzy technology (Kosko, 1992; Von Altrock, 1997) modifies connection strength or removes connections. Creative learning through genetic algorithms (Holland, 1992) and input from human agents adds connections that are then subject to further reinforcement learning. So, IAs interact with the local environment in the DKMS system and with external components to automatically formulate local knowledge.

These knowledge claims are then submitted to the next higher level in the system hierarchy, which tests and validates them against previous knowledge and claims submitted by other IAs. This process produces partially automated organizational knowledge production and partially automated adaptation to local and global environments. I say "partially" because the DKMS is in constant interaction with human agents.

Conclusion

In this chapter I have considered the question of how information technology applications may support knowledge processing and knowledge management and, more specifically, the nature of the functional requirements of such technology applications. The method of analysis I chose was to specify the connection between the natural knowledge management system, and a generalized IT construct called the artificial knowledge management system. I showed that the AKMS (in theory) partially supports the NKMS by partially supporting processes and tasks in the NKMS through use cases that specify the functional requirements of the DKMS, a realization of the AKMS using present technology.

The analysis showed the comprehensive nature of the DKMS in supporting a wide range of use cases that in turn support the knowledge processes in the KLC and various activities within the metaprise framework. Many of the use cases as well as much of the functionality in the DKMS are the same as in the DIMS covered in Chapters 5 and 6. But the additional capability of the DKMS is derived from a variety of specialized servers and from the differences between the AKM and the AIM in supporting knowledge claim objects (KCOs) and in providing a *cas* learning capability for IAs.

After the previous discussions of DIMS, SAI, DCM, PAI, and AKMS/DKMS architectures, one can better understand how comprehensive the combination of the physically distributed AKS and the completely distributed network of IAs that is the AKM is in providing process control services, an active object model, comprehensive connectivity, and support for knowledge processing and KM in the enterprise. The AKM does not do everything, but it does provide both the "glue" and the processing capability to support integrated KCO-based processing and distributed partially automated knowledge production through the various subprocesses of knowledge processing, knowledge integration, and knowledge management in the enterprise.

References

Firestone, J.M. (1997). "Object-oriented Data Warehousing," *Executive Information Systems White Paper No. 5*, Wilmington, DE. Available at http://www.dkms.com/White_Papers.htm.

Firestone, J.M. (1997a). "Distributed Knowledge Management Systems: The Next Wave in DSS," *Executive Information Systems White Paper No. 6*, Wilmington, DE. Available at http://www.dkms.com/White_Papers.htm.

Firestone, J.M. (1998). "Knowledge Management Metrics Development: A Technical Approach," *Executive Information Systems White Paper No. 10*, Wilmington, DE. Available at http://www.dkms.com/White_Papers.htm.

Firestone, J.M. (1999). "Enterprise Knowledge Management Modeling and Distributed Knowledge Management Systems," *Executive Information Systems White Paper No. 11*, Wilmington, DE. Available at http://www.dkms.com/White_Papers.htm.

Firestone, J.M. (1999a). "The Artificial Knowledge Manager Standard: A Strawman," *Executive Information Systems KMCI Working Paper No. 1*. Wilmington, DE Available at http://www.dkms.com/White_Papers.htm.

Holland, J.H. (1992). *Adaptation in Natural and Artificial Systems* (Cambridge, MA: MIT Press).

Holland, J.H. (1995). *Hidden Order* (Reading, MA: Addison-Wesley).

Holland, J.H. (1998). *Emergence* (Reading, MA: Addison-Wesley, 1998).

Jacobson, I.; Booch, G.; and Rumbaugh, J. (1999). *The Unified Software Development Process*, (Reading, MA: Addison-Wesley).

Jacobson, I.; Ericsson, M.; and Jacobson, A. (1995). *The Object Advantage* (Reading, MA: Addison-Wesley).

Kosko, B. (1992). *Neural Networks and Fuzzy Systems* (Englewood Cliffs, NJ: Prentice-Hall).

Von Altrock, C. (1997). *Fuzzy Logic and NeuroFuzzy Applications in Business and Finance* (Upper Saddle River, NJ: Prentice Hall).

Waldrop, M. (1992), *Complexity* (New York: Touchstone).

CHAPTER 11

The Role of XML in Enterprise Information Portals

"XML's flexibility is a double-edged sword. It allows data to be described in a host of ways, but in so doing it gives rise to a bevy of potentially incompatible data conventions. One can think of XML as analogous to the Latin alphabet. Communication and translation among European languages is much easier than it might otherwise be because most of them are based on Latin characters, but this does not mean that English speakers can automatically interpret Rumanian. Similarly, XML data formats are not necessarily compatible simply because they are stored in XML. In fact, even in an XML-friendly world, the process of data transformation and exchange will remain problematic and complex. Metadata still needs to be mapped, some schemas will still require information that other schemas do not provide, and expensive data transformation tools will still be required to ensure that what starts out in one format is still valid when it gets to another. XML certainly advances this process, but complete automation and data transparency will remain a distant goal for the foreseeable future." Plumtree (2000, p. 4)

Introduction

The developments of EIP PAI architecture and AKMS architecture, discussed in Chapters 5 and 10, did not consider the role of the eXtensible Markup Language (XML) in such architectures. The development and spread of XML, however, is the other major trend in information technology during the past few years (Finkelstein and Aiken, 1999, pp. 310–311). XML, like the HyperText Markup Language (HTML), is a subset of the older Standardized General Markup Language (SGML). It differs from HTML in that the XML "tags" used to mark up the text of a document provide instructions about how a software application should *structure the content* of a document, whereas the tags used to markup an HTML document provide instructions about how an application should display the document.

XML is an open standard for expressing structured content (and for structuring unstructured content) that has been promulgated by the World Wide Web

Consortium (W3C) (2001). It is not an application. It is a standard method for defining "tags" that may be used to describe documents (Ceponkus and Hood-bhoy, 1999, p. 26). Moreover, it is not a fixed collection of tags, but a standard for constructing meta-languages. Therefore, one of the ways it may be used is to define other markup languages such as Chemical Markup Language (CML), Math Markup Language (MathML), Speech Markup Language (SpeechML), Bean Markup Language (BML), DARPA Agent Markup Language (DAML), Resource Directory Description Language (RDDL), Meaning Definition Language (MDL), Ontology Markup Language (OML), Conceptual Knowledge Markup Language (CKML), and Synchronized Multimedia Integration Language (SMIL).

XML is also an information exchange format (Ceponkus and Hoodbhoy, 1999, p. 12). Why have I called it an information exchange format and not simply a data exchange format? Because XML, with its tagged instructions for applications and its document type definitions (DTDs) provides *context* to either the encoded data or the encoded content in XML documents or messages. In Chapter 2, I defined information as data plus conceptual commitments and interpretations, or as such commitments and interpretations alone. Information is frequently data extracted, filtered, or formatted in some way. An XML message or document is a perfect example of formatted raw content or data—that is, of information.

Since XML documents provide no display instructions, to use XML in Web applications another means of expression is needed to express these display instructions. The W3C has approved another standard for that. It is called XML Stylesheet Language (W3C, 2001a) or XSL. XSL is a specialized XML language. Unlike XML, it has a fixed set of tags. They are used to produce stylesheets or presentation templates.

An XSL stylesheet provides syntax for manipulating XML content. It also provides definitions of a vocabulary for describing formatting information. With XSL, one XML document can be transformed into another XML-based format. XML documents can be displayed in browsers. Searches in XML documents can be performed. Information can be deleted from or added to XML documents. XML documents can be sorted, and if-then conditionals (rules) can be applied in order to format documents. In addition to XSL, Cascading Style Sheets Level 2 (CSS2) and Document Style and Semantic Specification Language (DSSSL) are other stylesheet syntaxes for displaying XML information. But both have disadvantages compared with XSL.

The reason why XML is such a powerful trend is because it is increasingly accepted as a standard of exchange among differing nonstandard formats. XML is thought by many to provide the ultimate answer to the "islands of information" problem. The software industry is going through the process of creating interfaces between every other common format and XML. Thus, application servers and related development environments with the capability to handle XML formatted information *and to map dialects of XML to one another* are, taken together, increasingly in a position to connect and integrate all of the data and content in the enterprise by expressing everything in terms of XML and by structuring unstructured content by modeling it using XML tagging, document type definition (DTD) specifications, and, in the end, object modeling.

Portal product manufacturers have also been active in jumping on the XML bandwagon. Sequoia Software (2000) (recently purchased by Citrix) (2001) has been a pioneer in this area, as has DataChannel (as this is written, just purchased by

Netegrity, 2002) with its EIP product (DataChannel, 2001). Plumtree (2001) is also very much immersed in XML technology and has the capability to convert content into XML format. Other portal vendors —for example, Computer Associates (Jasmine *ii*), 2001; KnowledgeTrack, 2001, now Enfish, 2001; Hummingbird, 2001; and SAP Portals, 2001, among others—have jumped on the bandwagon as well. XML processing capability is rapidly becoming a requirement for all portal development product suites.

Later in my survey and classification of portal vendors, I will review the XML capabilities of each vendor discussed. In the remainder of this chapter, I will analyze the impact of XML on PAI architecture and portal systems as a whole. Specifically, I will discuss (1) XML in PAI architecture for EIPs, (2) XML for messaging and connectivity in portal systems, (3) XML in clients, (4) XML in databases, (5) XML and agents, and (6) XML analytical developments, including the resource description framework (RDF), XML topic maps (XTM), and the Meaning Definition Language (MDL).

XML in PAI architecture for EIPs

Look again at the PAI architecture shown in Figure 5.7. Now look at Figure 11.1, which shows PAI architecture with XML messaging added. In addition, the OODBMS is now an XML OODBMS such as eXcelon (2001, 2001a) or an XML specialized DBMS such as Software AG's Tamino (2001, 2001a), or Ipedo's (2001, 2001a) XML Database. In this architecture, XML provides universal connectivity: from

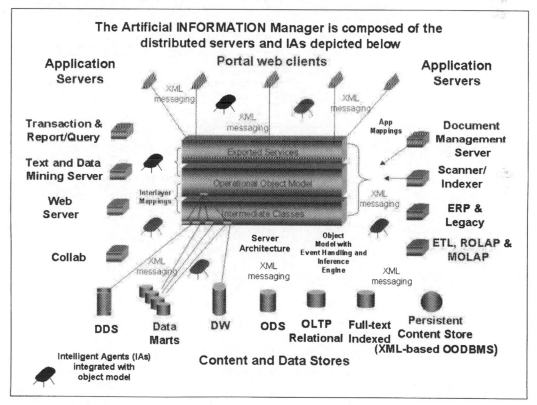

Figure 11.1. PAI architecture with XML.

the front end of clients and client-based agents, to Web servers, page builders, and the AIM, from the AIM to middle-tier application servers (including portal job servers) and IAs, and from the AIM to data and content stores. XML provides a universal exchange format for all communications in the system. This facilitates bringing information into and out of the AIM'S component/object model and reduces the tasks of object, component, workflow, and agent synchronization and integration by removing much, but not all, of the work of interface modeling from the mix.

XML for messaging and connectivity in portal systems

I will divide this part of the discussion into 4 categories: (1) front-end communications with the Web server, (2) Web server communications with the AIM and AIM communications with (3) middle-tier application servers, and (4) data and content stores.

From the front-end to the Web server and back

Suppose a user makes a request of the portal system using a browser that supports XML. The XML request, using HTTP for communications, goes to the portal Web server and is then passed on to the AIM itself. When the XML reply to a request is delivered to the Web server by the AIM, the Web server sends back a raw XML stream to the client's browser. At that point the raw XML is processed.

One type of processing is conversion from raw XML to HTML. It occurs when an eXtensible Stylesheet Language (XSL) application converts the XML to HTML for display in the browser. The XSL application is placed on the browser when the interaction with the Web server begins, at which time both raw XML and the stylesheet application are sent to the client. In subsequent interactions only raw XML need be sent to the client.

Apart from the XSL application, further applications manipulating the XML sent to the client are made possible by the richness of the structured XML content and data. Because such content is available to the portal client, it makes sense to distribute more computing tasks to client systems. Thus, the advent of XML results in a retreat from the thin client idea and a movement back toward the notion of powerful work stations sharing the computing load of the enterprise (Ceponkus and Hoodbhoy, 1999, pp. 20, 41).

From the Web server to the AIM and back

After processing by the Web server, requests are passed to the AIM in XML, using either HTTP or TCP/IP. Using an XML connector/proxy facility (Level 8 Systems, 2001), the AIM maps the incoming XML data stream to its own object model. When the AIM distributes the requests it has received to other application servers or to database servers and results are returned to it, if these are in XML it passes them back to the Web server. If they are not in XML, the AIM with its object model, its mapping to XML intermediate classes, and its export services, is used to convert them.

From the AIM to the portal job server and back

Some requests, after processing by the AIM, are passed to the portal job server, essentially a content manager. This server performs content analysis and management tasks (see Chapter 2) on data and content sources of various kinds. When these tasks are completed, the portal job server delivers XML content back to the AIM.

From the AIM to the middle tier and back

In addition to the portal job server, the middle tier is composed of a variety of application servers, both stateful and stateless. In Chapters 5 and 10, I provided examples of many of these servers. In the XML-based EIP with PAI architecture, such application servers "speak" XML. The AIM maps their object models to its own and sends XML messages to—and receives them from—the application servers and passes them on either to the portal job server, other application servers, or to the portal Web server. In fact, the AIM, in addition to its object model with intermediate and operational objects provides:

- In-memory proactive object state management and synchronization across distributed objects (in business process engines) and through intelligent agents
- Component management and workflow management through distributed business process engines and intelligent agents
- Transactional multithreading
- Business rule management and processing
- Metadata management.

Therefore, the AIM replaces the "stovepipe" form of PAC integration through "gadgets," "wizards," "portlets," etc. with the much more comprehensive form of application integration provided by business process and workflow automation achieved through using the process control and distribution services described at length in Chapters 5, 6, and 10. The XML-based connectivity of this type of portal further facilitates implementing the object model necessary to support these process control and distribution services. Figure 11.1 illustrates the relationship of the AIM to other application servers.

From the AIM to data and content stores and back

The AIM issues XML queries or content-oriented searches of data and contact stores in response to user queries and searches coming from the portal Web server. The content-oriented searches are routed through the portal job server and rely on its content management capability and XML transformation capability. The queries of structured data are sent by the AIM to the various databases and legacy applications. In the XML-based EIP with PAI architecture, all data stores produce XML data in response to queries, either because the data stores are "wrapped" so that legacy data is converted to XML "on the fly," or because the data stores being queried are already in XML.

XML in clients

When XML is transmitted to clients from the portal Web server, it is formatted using XSL to produce HTML for the browser. In addition, since the XML data is available to client-side applications through the XML document object model (DOM) and client-based XML parsers, it may also be processed by client-side applications of any complexity. This opens the way for knowledge workers to use the processing power of "fat clients" for a variety of analytical purposes involving processing of XML data. By distributing analytical tasks across the enterprise, some of the processing load is taken from the application servers, improving the load balancing in the enterprise system.

With client processing based on XML, all locally resident client data may be exchanged among different client applications. Workflow and business process automation applications can integrate client-side applications, while subject matter integration in the portal interface can be provided by a cognitive map-style interface.

XML in databases and content stores

PAI XML-based architecture may also use XML in databases and content stores. Major relational database vendors (e.g., Sybase, 2001; Oracle, 2001; IBM, 2001; Informix, purchased by IBM, 2001; and Microsoft, 2001) already make provision for parsing and mapping XML data to database tables and storing it there.

More generally however, XML may be stored in file systems, flat files, relational databases, object-oriented database systems, and native XML format. Performance in PAI architecture is improved if XML is stored either in object, or in native XML form. Flat files and file systems of various kinds cannot scale to the performance required in enterprise systems. The relational solution has the difficulty of requiring a mapping of the hierarchical structure of XML data to a nonhierarchical format of flat relational tables. That format is not particularly responsive to changes in the system of XML tags that occur frequently in XML systems when new types of documents are added to the system.

That leaves OODBMSs and databases that store XML in native format as the XML heirs apparent in PAI architecture. At this writing, it is not clear which alternative is best for PAI architecture. OODBMSs have the advantage that persistence of XML data in object form removes the "impedance mismatch" between object-based application servers and XML storage in objects (eXcelon, 2001a). On the other hand, OODBMSs are viewed by some as not scaling well to large numbers of users (Software AG, 2001a). In addition, both OODBMSs and RDBMSs involve expansion of native XML data because of their decomposition of XML-encoded documents into data and metadata formats of other types. XML native format has the disadvantage that it must be mapped to object-based application servers through a data mapping process. Later on, I will discuss some developments in XML research that address the problem of data mapping,

The competition between the OODBMS and native approaches to XML databases is represented by products that are already in the market. eXcelon (2001), the leader in OODBMS XML databases, claims outstanding scalability and performance. eXcelon's XML database and development environment maps XML to objects and provides application access through use of the DOM. In the native

XML area, there are four current products of note: Software AG's Tamino (2001), Ipedo (2001), FourThought's 4Suite (2001), and IxiaSoft's TextML Server, (2001, 2001a). The first three products are accompanied by suites of development tools and application servers for integrating XML-based enterprise or e-business systems. TextML however, is a back-end database server engine clearly aimed at the OEM component market.

XML and agents

I examined the role of agents in PAI architecture in Chapter 6. There I characterized agents as scaled-down business process engines with the intent and ability to learn, and I also indicated that they are an essential component of the AIM, along with artificial information servers. XML and XML processing capability enhance the ability of agents to provide content, data, and application integration, just as they enhance the ability of server-based business process engines to provide such integration. Therefore, all of the advantages I described earlier provided to server-based business process engines by XML are also provided to intelligent agents.

When the enterprise is converted to XML data streams and XML messaging, agents, along with other application servers, may all speak dialects or at least extensions of the XML standard. The effect of this is to *decrease the load on agents in translating among diverse communication languages and ontologies.* In fact, agents can speak one dialect of XML to each other such as DARPA Agent Markup Language (DAML) (2001), plus (+) Ontology Interchange Language (OIL) (On-to-Knowledge, 2001)—that is, DAML+OIL (DARPA, 2001)—or Robotics Markup Language (RoboML) (Makatchev and Tso 2001), while specialized agents resident on servers can carry the burden of translating from the variety of XML dialects to the agent language.

XML resource description framework (RDF), XML topic maps (XTM), and Meaning Definition Language (MDL)

The framework for producing XML applications is currently developing rapidly and in a manner significant for implementing PAI architecture in the future. These developments are in the following three areas:

- Resource description framework
- XML topic maps
- Meaning Definition Language

Resource description framework

The resource description framework (RDF) is composed of two parts. The first is a model for describing metadata. This model transcends XML. The second component is a specification for s syntax in XML for expressing metadata so that it may be transported over the Web.

The RDF model is that of a *triple* (an ordered association of three elements) relating

- A document identifier or indicator (identifying a resource, the subject of the metadata)
- The name of the document (or property)
- A value paired with the name

This model is very simple and basic. However, it provides a framework for making descriptive statements about resources—that is, metadata statements about subjects in the form of documents. It also provides a framework for making descriptive statements about these metadata statements, since metadata statements can also be described by a resource, a property, and a value paired with the property. This second class of metadata statements is meta-metadata.

The second component of the RDF framework is an XML syntax for using RDF to express metadata. I will not describe this syntax here, but a careful treatment of both RDF and the XML syntax for it can be found in Ahmed, et al. (2001, Chapters. 4–6, 11).

The development of the RDF and XML syntax for it greatly increases the capability to manipulate XML in PAI architecture. XML data streams using syntax expressing the RDF can be mapped to object models in application servers instantiating the RDF, and these, in turn, can be mapped to the AIM and used by it, in turn, to transmit XML metadata wherever it must be used by an application server or business process engine. Thus the RDF facilitates the interchange of XML data by providing a metadata framework that may be shared across applications.

RDF, however, is only a limited answer to the problem of interpreting XML data streams in terms of object models or other semantic networks. For one thing, RDF doesn't represent the context of relationships between resources. For another, it lacks the conceptual richness needed for providing an interpretation of data streams that is useful for expressing knowledge in semantic networks.

XML topic maps

XML metadata expressing the RDF represents an improvement for expressing and manipulating relationships among objects over previous XML instantiations. But XML topic maps (XTMs) (Ahmed, et al., 2001, Chapters 7 and 11 provide a useful account; see also TopicMaps.org, 2001) are another important development that promises to add even more capability to XML expressions of metadata, because topic maps, unlike RDF metadata, provide the capability to represent not only things, properties, and associations but also the context of relationships.

Topic maps, like the RDF, were specified apart from XML, so that XTMs are only one way of expressing them. A topic map (or topic graph), like the cognitive maps discussed in Chapters 4 and 7, is made up of nodes and edges. The nodes are information objects, things called *topics*, representing subjects of interest. The edges represent relationships among those subjects and are called *associations*. Associations are nondirectional in topic maps—that is, they do not describe the direction of relationships.

The subjects are of two kinds. Some are directly addressable by the computer, and these are called *resources*. Subjects that are not so addressable are called nonaddressable subjects and include all other "things."

When nonaddressable subjects are expressed as nodes in topic maps—that is, as topics—they are said to be "reified," or "made real" from the standpoint of the computer. That is, the topic reifies the subject. This usage seems a bit unfortunate in the sense that it is the nonaddressable subjects that are actually "real," whereas the topics representing them in topic maps are actually artificial representations of these "real things." In addition, the term "reification" has a long history of use in social theory and philosophy where it refers to a kind of fallacy in which someone mistakes a conceptual abstraction for a phenomenon that actually exists; here, the abstract topic identified in the computer may indeed represent, though not in full detail, a real-world thing or object.

Another important aspect of topic maps is that topics have characteristics. There are three types of characteristics that may be assigned to topics: names, occurrences, and roles. An occurrence is a resource that is relevant to a particular subject that has been reified by a topic. A role is the nature of a topic's involvement in an association.

The scope of a topic tells one the context in which a characteristic assignment is valid. It provides the context for assigning a name or occurrence to a topic and for relating topics through associations. "Every characteristic has a scope, which may be specified either explicitly, as a set of topics, or implicitly, in which case it is known as the *unconstrained scope*. Assignments made in the unconstrained scope are always valid" (Topic Map Authoring Group, 2001, p. 18).

A subject indicator is a resource that provides an unambiguous indication of the identity of a subject. A single subject may be indicated in multiple and distinctly different ways. When that happens, topics that reify the same subject cannot be merged in a single topic map. But another topic may be used to establish the identity of the subject with both subject indicators. In this way, topic maps may be used to synthesize ontologies with incommensurable topics that reify the same subject (Ahmed et al., 2001, pp. 409–441).

From this brief explanation of the topic map model, one can see that it is much richer in its linguistic potential than is the RDF. In fact, it suggests that it is much closer to a general framework for modeling the cognitive map concept presented in Figure 7.1 in my earlier discussion of the nature of knowledge. Both the RDF and topic map communities have recognized that it may be possible to combine both RDF and topic maps (XTM). This will be increasingly practical in the near future when RDF is enriched with a DAML+OIL version of RDF (Ahmed, et al., 2001, p. 413). In addition, developments in the next few years promise the beginning of partly automated construction of topic maps with human input, using domain-specific knowledge bases produced by projects such as the OpenCYC Upper Ontology project (ibid. p. 411; Cycorp, 2001; OpenCyc.Org, 2001).

XML topic maps will, in the future, be essential parts of PAI architecture. When combined with DAML+OIL versions of RDF, they can provide the capability for both client-based and server-based agents to model cognitive maps in all parts of PAI architecture. Client-based agents will be more easily able to maintain cognitive maps of knowledge workers and to "map" topic maps communicated from application servers to the AIM's object model. In general, the combination of RDF and XTM will increase the ability to communicate complex models of all kinds across the PAI EIP system, whether that portal network is limited to the enterprise or transcends it.

Meaning Definition Language

Meaning Definition Language (MDL) is an XML language mapping XML language expressions to Unified Modeling Language or DAML+OIL (2001) class models. The MDL draft specification was written at Charteris (2001) by Robert Worden (2001, 2001a). Look again at Figure 7.1. If the class model represents the abstract concepts of a cognitive map or semantic network and the measures and their relations are expressed in one or more XML language expressions, then the MDL expressions are analogous to the relations defining a measurement model relating XML data to an underlying conceptual model.

MDL focuses on XML expressions that approximate non-XML data structures, rather than focusing on expressions of unstructured content. The MDL approach is more general than RDF or XML Topic Maps in that it uses an explicit linguistic transformation to map XML to an underlying semantic model expressed in UML or DAML+OIL. Worden (2001, p. 289) views MDL as "the bridge between XML structure and meaning." The basic idea here is that structure-based approaches to interfacing with XML, such as DOM and XSLT, may be replaced by "meaning"-based approaches that insulate users from XML structure and allow them to relate to XML expressions through a class model that is more intuitive and makes access to XML coding details unnecessary. This attempt to replace structure with meaning parallels previous evolution in the database and other computing fields where the introduction of new languages led first to a focus on applications based on mastery of the structure and details of the new language, and later to attempts to provide access to that language that insulates the user from its technical details.

MDL is a language template. While the same MDL transformation does not apply in translating different XML languages to the same underlying class model or ontology, the same MDL template is used to construct specific MDL transformations translating the different XML languages to the same ontology or class model. In such a situation, the class model or ontology links the different XML languages and allows them to communicate.

MDL fits into PAI architecture by providing the mapping between XML data streams and the class/object models of application servers and the AIM. MDL promises to be a great standard linking XML data to the conceptual bus that is the class/object model. It fits well into the general pattern of the AIM in providing a unified view of the enterprise for communication to the portal interface.

Conclusion

The central concern of PAI architecture is to use the distributed AIM to integrate all data, content, and applications in enterprise systems or in systems transcending the enterprise. The appearance of XML makes the task of developing connectors and proxies and communicating among application servers to support integration much easier as the XML standard spreads. But, as expressed in the Plumtree (2000) quotation at the beginning of this chapter, XML is not the answer to all communication. In fact, XML is subject to its own tower of Babel syndrome as the field develops and XML languages proliferate.

As this movement escalates, the utility of XML as an integrative mechanism is threatened. In response, XML developers are formulating integrative ontology-based approaches for handling XML metadata that can transcend the particularities of different XML languages. I have reviewed three of these here: the RDF, XTM, and MDL approaches supplemented by DAML+OIL ontology. The coming combination of these three approaches promises to provide an increased capability to support the continuous mapping of XML data streams to object models that is at the heart of the AIM's integration of the portal system in PAI architecture, through its network of servers and intelligent agents.

References

Ahmed, K.; Ayers, D.; Birbeck, M.; Cousins, J.; Dodds, D.; Lubell, J.; Nic, M.; Rivers-Moore, D.; Watt, A.; Worden, R.; and Wrightson, A. (2001). *Professional XML Metadata* (Birmingham, UK: Wrox Press).

Ceponkus, A., and Hoodbhoy, F. (1999). *Applied XML* (New York: John Wiley & Sons).

Charteris, Inc. (2001), www.charteris.com.

Citrix, Inc. (2001), www.citrix.com/products/.

Computer Associates, Inc. (2001).

Cycorp, Inc. (2001), www.cyc.com/products.html.

DataChannel, Inc. (2001), www.datachannel.com.

Defense Advanced Research Projects Agency (2001). "DARPA Agent Markup Language Details," at http://www.daml.org/2001/08/intelink-panel-mdean/Overview.html.

Defense Advanced Research Projects Agency (2001). "DAML+OIL," at http://www.daml.org/2001/03/daml+oil-index.

eXcelon Corporation (2001), http://www.cxccloncorp.com/.

eXcelon Corporation (2001a). "Extensible Information Server White Paper," *eXcelon Corporation White Paper,* Burlington, MA.

Finkelstein, C., and Aiken, P. (1999). *Building Corporate Portals with XML* (New York: McGraw-Hill).

Fourthought, Inc. (2001), http://4Suite.org/index.html.

Hummingbird, Inc. (2001), www.hummingbird.com.

IBM (2001), http://www-4.ibm.com/software/data/eip/.

Ipedo, Inc. (2001), www.ipedo.com.

Ipedo, Inc. (2001a). "Ipedo XML Database," Product Brochure, Redwood City, CA.

IxiaSoft, Inc. (2001), www.ixiasoft.com.

Ixiasoft, Inc. (2000). 'White Paper," *Ixiasoft White Paper,*

KnowledgeTrack, Inc. (2001), http://www.knowledgetrack.com/products/eip_techinfo_faqs.htm.

Level8 Systems, Inc. (2001). Geneva EI Version 3.0: "Using the XML Connector/Proxy," *Geneva Enterprise Integrator Instruction Manual Series,* Cary, NC: Level8 Systems.

Makatchev, M., and Tso, S.K. (2000). "Human-Robot Interface Using Agents Communicating in an XML-Based Markup Language," *Proceedings of the 2000 IEEE International Workshop on Robot and Human Interactive Communication,* Osaka, Japan, September 27 n29, 2000, pp. 270–275.

Microsoft, Inc. (2001), http://msdn.microsoft.com/library/default.asp?url=/library/en-us/dnexxml/html/xml07162001.asp.

Netegrity, Inc. (2002), www.netegrity.com.

On-To-Knowledge Project (2001), www.ontoknowledge.org/oil.

OpenCyc.Org (2001), http://www.opencyc.org/.

Oracle, Inc. (2001), http://www.oracle.com/xml/.

Plumtree, Software, Inc. (2000). "XML and Corporate Portals," *Plumtree Software White Paper,* San Francisco, CA

Plumtree, Inc. (2001), www.plumtree.com.

Robotic Markup Language Project (2001), www.roboml.org/

Sequoia Software Corporation (2000). "Automating Business Processes with an XML Portal Server," *Sequoia Software White Paper,* Columbia, MD.

Software AG (2001), www.tamino.com.

Software AG (2001). "Tamino Technical Description" at www.softwareag.com/tamino/technical/description.htm.

Sybase, Inc. (2001), www.my.sybase.com/detail?id=1013017.

TopicMaps.Org (2001), http://www.topicmaps.org/xtm/index.html.

TopicMaps.Org Authoring Group (2001). "XML Topic Maps (XTM) 1.0," *TopicMaps.Org Specification,* vol. 116, August 6, 2001.

Worden, R. (2001). "Meaning Definition Language," in Ahmed, et al., (2001), *Professional XML Metadata* (Birmingham, UK: Wrox Press).

Worden, R. (2001a). "A Meaning Definition Language," Draft 2.02, *Charteris, plc., Working Paper.*

World Wide Web Consortium, Inc. (2001), www.w3.org.

World Wide Web Consortium, Inc. (2001a). "XSLT 2.0 Requirements Working Draft," at www.w3.org/TR/xslt20req.

PART SIX

EIP Frameworks, Portal Product Case Studies, and Applications to E-Business

In Part Six, I present a comprehensive framework for segmenting portal products, specify a particular type of EIP of great importance to knowledge processing and knowledge management—the enterprise knowledge portal (EKP)—in more detail, and apply both frameworks to an analysis of portal product case studies and to an analysis of the role of the portal in e-business. In other words, in this part, I answer questions about where the product EIP space is now, where many of its products fit into a forward-looking segmentation, what precisely, they contribute to knowledge processing and knowledge management, and what applications portal technology has in e-business.

Chapter 12 presents the forward-looking conceptual framework for segmenting portals and offers a simplified segmentation that may be serviceable for the current crop of portal products. The chapter begins with a discussion of the first EIP product segmentation, then presents a forward-looking EIP segmentation framework including function, type of architecture and integration, portal scope, and data and content sources dimensions. Chapter 12 ends with consideration of the special importance of knowledge processing and knowledge management portals along with a simplified forward-looking segmentation.

Chapter 13 develops the EKP concept as a standard for evaluating the gap between actual portal products and solutions and this standard. It covers: a story contrasting Windows desktops, EIPs, and EKPs, formal definition and specification of the EKP, EKP architecture and components, the adaptive, problem-solving essence of the EKP, the EKP, the AKMS/DKMS, and EKP functional requirements, EKPs knowledge sharing and corporate culture, e-business knowledge portals, whether there are any EKPs, and types of knowledge portals.

Chapters 14–17 provide twenty-three portal product case studies. The twenty-three products were selected based on the prominence of the vendors, the innovations offered by them, the availability of products across both UNIX and NT platforms, and the ready availability of information about the product. I resisted the temptation to review more portal products than the twenty-three initially selected, because (1) the *portal space is shrinking anyway and most of the likely survivors for the short term are probably covered here and (2) I had to stop somewhere to keep the length of this work within reasonable bounds.*

Each product included as a case study is described and analyzed in terms of its features, architecture, vision and direction, and touchpoints with knowledge processing and knowledge management. Chapter 14 reviews two decision processing portals. Chapter 15 reviews nine content-management portals. Chapter 16 reviews four collaborative portals. And Chapter 17 reviews eight decision processing/content-management portals. Each chapter presents conclusions emerging from the analysis, and Chapter 17 presents conclusions applying to all four chapters.

Chapter 18 looks at e-business from the viewpoint of the EKP. It covers EIP technology and e-business applications, the DKMS, the knowledge portal, and e-business applications, the KLC framework and e-business, the EKP and ECRM, the EKP and ESCM, the EKP and EERP, the EKP and e-commerce, the DKMS, EKP applications, and the future of e-business.

CHAPTER 12

A Forward Looking EIP Segmentation Framework

Introduction: The first EIP product segmentation

In Chapter 1, I pointed out that three types of EIPs (and three types of enterprise portals) were distinguished in the early stages of development of the EIP marketplace: decision processing, collaborative processing, and knowledge portals. But this is a very abstract segmentation and it uses only broad functions to differentiate portal products. Another more recent segmentation of *enterprise portals* is offered by Clive Finkelstein (2001, p. 7). This, too, uses only broad functions to distinguish three major types of portals: collaborative processing, business intelligence, and integration portals. Finkelstein's definitions of these types are preceded by his definition of enterprise portal as: (ibid. p. 1)

> A single gateway (via a corporate intranet or internet) to relevant workflows, application systems, and databases—integrated using the Extensible Markup Language (XML) and tailored to the specific job responsibilities of each individual.

This definition, like the original of Shilakes and Tylman (1998), has the advantage of comprehensiveness, but its specificity in terms of XML limits it to a particular language type for messaging and exchange and excludes all enterprise portals that accomplish integration through means other than XML. In this respect I don't think it is an improvement over the Merrill Lynch definition. His definitions of the three types of enterprise portals follow.

- Collaborative processing portals are defined as those focused "on unstructured knowledge resources" (ibid.) that provide access to collaborative applications such as Lotus Notes and Microsoft Exchange.
- Business intelligence portals "focus on structured knowledge resources with access to data warehouses and information system databases" (ibid.).
- "Integration portals focus on easy integration between structured and unstructured knowledge resources existing in information systems, data

warehouses, ERP environments and others—either within an enterprise via the corporate intranet or between enterprises via an extranet or the internet." (ibid.)

This classification is very similar to White's (1999) classification reviewed in Chapter 1, with the addition of the integration portal category. This addition is a useful enhancement, but (1) the knowledge portal is absent from the classification, (2) no distinction is made between a collaborative portal and a content-management portal, and (3) the segmentation scheme provides no product or solution segments as yet unoccupied by products. So, the segmentation identifies no categories that may be occupied in the future. It is not a forward-looking conceptual framework.

As the portal marketplace grows and develops, it is inevitable that a more detailed, specific, and useful segmentation will be developed than either Finkelstein's or the one I extracted from the early literature in Chapter 1. As portal vendors compete, they will seek advantage by specializing, by finding a product niche that fulfills a particular market need. This increasing specialization will define a hierarchical classification segmenting the portal product space that will transcend the first elementary tripartite segmentations of this product space.

Here then, is a detailed hierarchical classification for segmenting the EIP product space. The classification is not complete. It is more detailed in some segments than in others. It clearly needs to undergo further development. But it is still far more detailed than other alternatives yet offered, and I believe it provides a much better feel for the dimensions of variations among portal systems than other alternatives. This classification is a forecast of the evolution of the product space. It is an attempt to define the ecological niches that EIP vendors will seek and occupy as their competition grows more intense, and to provide a kind of cognitive map of the EIP space.

A forward-looking EIP product segmentation framework

The current segmentations of the EIP space into decision processing, collaborative processing, and knowledge portals, or into the first two and integration portals, is based primarily on distinctions about portal function. Even in terms of functional distinctions the classification is much too narrow. It doesn't begin to exhaust the different primary functions portals may fulfill. In addition, however, there are at least three other useful dimensions for distinguishing portals: type of architecture and integration approach, portal scope, and data and content sources. Table 12.1 presents a much expanded categorization scheme for enterprise information portals.

Not many of the types of portals implied by this categorization scheme can be found yet in the marketplace. But I think the categorization is useful as a tool for anticipating future developments. Let us discuss some of the specifics of the product segmentation framework to get a feel for the widely varying product differences we may see in the EIP space.

Highest Level	Second Level	Third Level	Fourth Level
Most basic segmentation	Types of functions, architecture, portal scope, data and content sources supported	Segmentation of types of functions, architecture, portal scope and data and content sources supported	Lowest level segmentation of types of functions, architecture, portal scope, and data and content sources supported
Function Classes of use cases or requirements supported	Structured data management (type of function or use case supported)	Online transaction processing (OLTP)	Packaged applications (e.g., financial management)
			Enterprise resource planning (ERP)
			Operational data store (ODS)
			Legacy applications
			Data management (extraction, transformation, and loading processes)
		Decision support processing (DSS)	Querying and reporting/DW/data mart
			Knowledge discovery in databases (KDD)/data mining
			Packaged analytical applications (e.g., Balanced Scorecard)
			Analytical modeling and simulation (e.g., system dynamics, CAS simulation, analytic hierarchy modeling, economic modeling)
		Batch	Data management and processing
			Computer simulation
			Statistical estimation

Table 12.1. A Forward-Looking EIP Segmentation Framework

Highest Level	Second Level	Third Level	Fourth Level
Function *(continued)*	Unstructured content management	Searching	Query-based searching
			Agent-based searching
		Scanning	Agent-based scanning/"crawling"
		Retrieving	Query-based retrieval
			Continuous retrieval and updating
		Filtering and classifying	Manual classification
			Automated classification
			Bayesian adaptive classification
			Fuzzy-based classification
		Text mining and structuring content	Semantic network and hierarchy development
			Text abstracting
			Full-text indexing
			Concept network creation in response to querying
			Concept tagging and metadata with XML
			Non-XML concept tagging
	Collaborative processing	Prioritization (support for arriving at priorities through group decision making)	
		Planning (support for group planning)	

Table 12.1. A Forward-Looking EIP Segmentation Framework (continued)

Highest Level	Second Level	Third Level	Fourth Level
Function *(continued)*	Collaborative processing *(continued)*	Project management (facilities for collaborative project management)	
		Distributed expert collaboration support	
		Training	
		Problem solving (support for group collaboration in problem solving)	
		Knowledge claim production (collaborative, as opposed to individual)	(See Knowledge processing below)
		Workflow	
	Knowledge processing	Knowledge production	Information acquisition (the subprocess of acquiring information from external sources)
			Individual and group learning (the sub-processes of nested knowledge life cycles within groups reaching down to the level of the individual)
			Knowledge claim formulation (the sub-process resulting in new knowledge claims)
			Knowledge claim validation or evaluation (the subprocess of testing and evaluating knowledge claims)

Table 12.1. A Forward-Looking EIP Segmentation Framework (continued)

Highest Level	Second Level	Third Level	Fourth Level
Function *(continued)*	Knowledge processing *(continued)*	Knowledge integration (the subprocesses that communicate validated knowledge claims or related data and information to knowledge workers)	Broadcasting: electronic or personal (This means pushing validated knowledge claims, or related data and information to knowledge workers.)
			Searching/retrieving: electronic or personal (This refers to knowledge workers pulling validated knowledge claims, or related data and information organizational stores.)
			Teaching: face-to-face and computer-based
			Knowledge sharing: face-to-face, documents, and computer-based
	Publication and distribution of content	Posting	
		Broadcasting	
	Information management	(See Third-level knowledge management activities for analogs to IM activities)	(See Fourth-level knowledge management activities for analogues to IM activities)
	Knowledge management	Interpersonal behavior-focused KM activities	Leadership (hiring, training, motivating, monitoring, evaluating, etc.)
			Building relationships with individuals and organizations external to the enterprise

Table 12.1. A Forward-Looking EIP Segmentation Framework (continued)

Highest Level	Second Level	Third Level	Fourth Level
Function *(continued)*	Knowledge management *(continued)*	Knowledge and information processing KM activities	Knowledge production (a KM as well as a knowledge process)
			Knowledge integration (another KM and knowledge process)
		Decision-making KM activities	Changing knowledge process rules at lower KM and knowledge process levels
			Crisis handling
			Allocating knowledge and KM resources
			Negotiating agreements with representatives of other business processes
Type of architecture/integration	Portal–interface-based integration	Incremental portal-based integration	
		"Big-bang" portal-based integration	
	Data federation-based integration (DFI)	Incremental DFI	
		"Big bang" DFI	
	Workflow-based integration (WFI)	Incremental WFI	
		"Big-bang" WFI	
	Object/component-based integration	Structured application integration (SAI)	Incremental SAI
			"Big-bang" SAI
		Distributed content management (DCM)	Incremental DCM
			"Big-bang" DCM
		Portal application integration (PAI)	Incremental PAI
			"Big-bang" PAI

Table 12.1. A Forward-Looking EIP Segmentation Framework (continued)

Highest Level	Second Level	Third Level	Fourth Level
Portal scope	Galactic (enterprise-wide) information/ knowledge portal		
	Department oriented	Departmental EIP	Departmental types
	Business process-oriented	Business process EIP	Business process types
		Business multi-process EIP	Various business multi-process combinations
		Galactic business-process EIP	
Data and content sources *(continued)*	Databases	Hierarchical	
		Network	
		Relational	
		OODBMS	
		Flat file	
		Inverted file	
		Multidimensional	
		Fractal	
		XML	
		Other	
	BI reports		
	Programs		
	Documents	Text	
		Word processing	
		e-mail	
		SGML	
		HTML	
		XML	
		Other	
	Data feeds		
	Images	TIFF	
		GIF	

Table 12.1. A Forward-Looking EIP Segmentation Framework (continued)

Highest Level	Second Level	Third Level	Fourth Level
Data and content sources (*continued*)	Images (*continued*)	JPEG	
		WMF	
		PPT	
		Other	
	Other files		

Table 12.1. A Forward-Looking EIP Segmentation Framework (continued)

Function

I have divided the "function" category into structured data management, unstructured content management, collaborative processing, knowledge processing, publication and distribution of content, information management, and knowledge management. *Structured data management* is broken down further into portals focused on OLTP, DSS, and batch applications, and OLTP and DSS applications are further categorized.

OLTP is broken down into portals focused on packaged applications, operational data stores, Enterprise resource planning applications, and legacy applications. DSS applications are categorized as querying and reporting/DW/data mart, data mining, and packaged analytical applications. Of course, any mix of OLTP, DSS and batch processing and any mix of the subcategories is also possible.

The decision-processing portal concept that has received so much attention in the portal literature covers only one of the three main categories within the structured data management category, and it also provides no hint of the possible hybrid combinations of structured data management processing inherent in the broader category scheme. In brief, it does not begin to describe the variation inherent in structured data management. In contrast, while the segmentation provided in Table 12.1 can certainly be improved upon, it considerably broadens one's perspective in viewing the EIP landscape.

Unstructured content management of documents is another major dimension of emphasis in enterprise information portals. Content-management activities include searching, scanning, retrieving, classifying, filtering, text mining, and structuring content. All of these activities may be further categorized by sub-activities, many of which make explicit the role of intelligent agents, content analysis, and AI technologies in content management. EIPs will differ in the technologies they use to implement these activities and sub-activities, and some of these differences are reflected in the names I have given to the subcategories. Marginal differentiation of EIP tools is occurring around technological competition within these subcategories, with vendors claiming that one or another AI feature provides them a decisive advantage in content-management performance.

A key fault-line has developed around the issue of how automated updating of taxonomic content in EIPs should be done. Some vendors (such as Plumtree, Inc., 2001) insist that the role of humans in updating taxonomies is essential. Others (such as Autonomy, Inc., 2001) incline toward the position that effective automated updating of taxonomies is both possible and to be preferred. Whichever position wins in the long run, and many products provide some mix of human and automated taxonomic updating, the difference in the degree to which EIP products provide for manual or automated updating is an important difference from a marketing and functionality standpoint.

Another important issue in unstructured content management is the extent to which products support text mining and conversion to XML for the purpose of transforming unstructured to structured content. While present trends will make this a staple of portal functionality eventually, in the short run products are distinguishing themselves from one another based on this functionality.

As I mentioned in Chapters 1 and 2, the idea of a *collaborative processing* portal has received considerable attention. But treatments of the idea in the EIP space have not been very explicit about the varying functions that might be contained in such EIPs, and they normally distinguish very generalized functions, such as the ability to work collectively on documents, chat rooms, expertise location and tracking, conferencing, and other generalized capabilities. Table 12.1 distinguishes: more specific capabilities, including prioritization, planning, project management, distributing expertise, training, problem solving, knowledge claim production, and workflow as categories of collaborative processing functionality.

Each of these areas represents nontrivial functions, currently realized in complex applications, that to some extent represent distinct functional sub-spaces and that could each be wrapped into portals either separately or in combination with one of the other categories.

The abstract idea of a collaborative processing portal does not begin to do this area justice in providing for an adequate segmentation. Products such as Instinctive's eRoom (2001) or Intraspect (2001), that focus on collaboration in general or collaboration in support of project management, are very different from products intended to support strategic planning implementations such as Engenia's Unity (2000). (Engenia, 2001, recently retired the Unity product and now markets an agent platform focused on business processing applications.)

These are very different from products that provide for group collaboration on analytical modeling and/or data mining, or that provide for a team approach to prioritized decision making, such as Expert Choice (2001). These, in turn, are very different from products such as Sopheon's Organik (Orbital Software, 2001) that allow knowledge workers to access the expertise of "gurus" in specialized fields. In brief, the label "collaborative processing portal," is not very illuminating for segmenting the EIP product space. Only a segmentation that breaks down collaboration into types can begin to get at the range of variation and differentiation that could occur in this part of the EIP product space.

Knowledge portals are another major portal category that has received attention but not a great deal of clarification. Table 12.1 indicates that a portal with a knowledge process focus supports enterprise knowledge production and knowledge integration activities (see Chapter 7). In turn, the knowledge production process can be subdivided into individual and group learning; information acquisition, knowledge claim formulation, and knowledge validation (see Figure 7.4), whereas knowledge integration can be subdivided into broadcasting, searching/retrieving, teaching, and knowledge sharing (see Figure 7.5). In their turn, each of these subcategories may be readily subdivided, even though I do not go that far in Table 12.1. For example, in a previous paper I explored the various tasks involved in knowledge claim formulation and even more specifically in the knowledge claim formulation task called "perform measurement modeling" (Firestone, 1998). In the area of information acquisition many applications already exist that encompass a number of distinct use cases, and so on through the various subcategories of Table 12.1.

Thus, the twin knowledge processes, knowledge production and knowledge integration, encompass a wide range of tasks and activities. For a portal to merit the name "knowledge portal," it would have to support a similarly wide range of component applications. But even if a particular portal did have such a wide range of applications, the complexity inherent in the knowledge production and knowledge integration categories would leave room for substantial variations in types of knowledge portals, based on which of the many knowledge production and knowledge integration functions were supported.

Publication and distribution of content includes posting and broadcasting activities. I have not further subdivided these categories, because subcategorizations are common and easy to come by. But clearly, the many different types of posting and broadcasting applications in use today also support the general point I am making here: that wide variations in portal types within the posting and broadcasting segments may exist.

Information management is a category that parallels knowledge management in its diversity and complexity. Its subdivisions, in my view, are analogous to the subdivisions of the KM category, the difference being that it is knowledge that is being managed rather than just information. The differences between data, information, and knowledge were specified in Chapter 2. Knowledge is a subset of information that has been subjected to, and passed tests of, validation. So, as I argued in Chapter 9, knowledge management is a type of information management with the difference that it is more exacting in nature. Both knowledge and information management are characterized by wide variation in practices and, therefore, types of knowledge or information management. So, once again, we have a situation in which detailed segmentation is possible and probably significant.

This is clearer from the range of KM activities specified in Chapter 9 and in Table 12.1. Once again, I subdivide these into interpersonal behavior-focused KM activities, knowledge and information processing KM activities, and decision-making activities. Interpersonal activities break down into (1) leadership (e.g., hiring, training, motivating, monitoring, evaluating) and (2) building relationships with individuals and organizations external to the enterprise. Knowledge and information processing KM activities include (3) knowledge production (a KM as well as a knowledge process) and (4) knowledge integration (another KM and knowledge process). Though not shown in the table, KM knowledge production and KM knowledge integration may be subcategorized in the same manner as the knowledge-production and knowledge-integration knowledge processes. Finally, decision making is divided into (5) changing knowledge process rules at lower KM and knowledge process levels, (6) crisis handling, (7) allocating knowledge and KM resources, and (8) negotiating agreements with representatives of other business processes.

These diverse KM and information management activities need to be supported by an equally diverse set of IT applications. The applications, in turn, would all have their place in a comprehensive enterprise knowledge portal. Moreover, instances of information or knowledge portals will vary according to the specific KM and information management activities they support. Here then, is another basis for EIP segmentation according to function.

Type of architecture and integration

Portal integration may be based on (1) the portal interface, (2) workflow applications mediated through the portal, (3) data federations, and (4) object-component–based integration. In *portal interface–based integration*, the browser serves as a single point of access to a variety of applications and data stores, but there is no integration among the applications themselves. Each application is accessed in isolation from other applications, and each application runs without interaction with other applications. In Chapter 5, I characterized the architecture associated with portal interface–based integration as passive-access-to-content (PAC) architecture.

Even within PAC architecture differences can be found in the type of interface offered for accessing content, data, and applications. Until recently, all vendors favored a hierarchical interface, either of the Yahoo type or using a Windows folder metaphor. Now, however, TheBrain Technologies Corporation has released an interface that emphasizes networking relationships or associations among "ideas" (where an idea is any information object or topic accessible through TheBrain's connectivity module). Of course, some of these associations are hierarchical. So hierarchy, too, is encompassed by this type of network-based subject matter integration as well as by peer relationships.

In *workflow-based integration*, a workflow application structures patterns of systematic, serial use of structured data and content resources. This is task-based integration. It doesn't necessarily require tight integration of structured and content resources (though component applications in workflow may well require such integration). It provides for phased access to structured and content resources rather than for ad hoc and perhaps simultaneous access to heterogeneous applications and stores. In Chapter 5, I treated workflow–based integration in the context of DCM, SAI, and PAI architecture and also as one of the thirteen types of EASI.

In *integration based on data federation* the source data remains in place. Multiple physical databases are integrated into a single logical one. Independent enterprise systems produce integrated global behavior through economic forces. Data federation systems retain local control while scaling to hundreds of machines. They also support a global view of enterprise data resources and dynamic load balancing across system resources, and they adapt and adjust query execution accordingly. Data federation integration (DFI) architecture is the type associated with this form of integration. It was also treated in Chapter 5.

Object/component-based integration is the most comprehensive form of portal integration. It is integration through information rather than data federation. Like a data federation, an information federation doesn't migrate data anywhere; it manipulates data or unstructured content in place according to the business rules specified in the system and encapsulated in its integrative object layer. (This kind of integrative layer is at the bottom of the information integration through ad hoc navigation form of EASI discussed in Chapters 5 and 17.)

An information federation employs multiple distributed application servers along with multiple distributed data stores to maintain a unified view through a common object model. As indicated in Chapter 5, these application servers are called artificial information managers (AIMs). They provide process control and distribution services to the information federation to synchronize and adjust it to locally determined changes. Like data federations, information federations employ broad-ranging connectivity to read from and write to the distributed data stores and applications of the enterprise. Finally, information federations may focus on structured data and related applications (I've called this type of architectural approach to integration SAI in Chapter 5), unstructured content and related applications (DCM), or both (PAI or incremental PAI).

An information federation, like a data federation, is scalable (see Chapter 5). It is scalable because: its connectivity to application servers allows it to access applications transparently and also because new information managers can be added as needed to distribute the processing and query load across broadly distributed resources.

Enterprise information portals may exhibit any of the types of integration just discussed. Most portal products and solutions currently are examples of portal interface–based integration; but as the EIP field develops, more and more portals will be integrated on the basis of workflow, data federation, or object-based federations of structured data and applications, unstructured content and applications, or both. Type of integration is therefore a significant dimension of portal segmentation.

Portal scope

Enterprise information portals can be "galactic" in scope, issue specific, or department specific. A *galactic EIP* is a subject-oriented application providing a Web browser as a single point of access to an integrated collection of data/content stores and applications providing support for all enterprise business processes and departments and for all roles within the enterprise. Obviously, a galactic EIP requires nothing less than the integration of all enterprise data and applications in a single portal construct. The effort involved to implement one would be much greater than the effort required to construct a "galactic data warehouse." From experience in data warehousing, we know that such "big bang" projects are accompanied by a high failure rate. It is likely that an even higher failure rate would accompany attempts to apply the "big bang" galactic orientation to portals.

A *business process–oriented EIP* is a subject-oriented application providing a Web browser as a single point of access to an integrated collection of data/content stores and applications providing support for one or more business processes, and their interactions with one another and the external world. If an EIP supports all business processes, it begins to approach a galactic EIP in scope. Business process–oriented EIPs will vary according to the number and types of business processes they support.

- A *business process EIP* is focused on a single business process.
- A *business multi-process EIP* supports more than one but less than all business processes.
- A *galactic business process EIP* supports all business processes.

A *department-oriented EIP* is a subject-oriented application providing a Web browser as a single point of access to an integrated collection of data/content stores and applications providing support for one or more departments, and their interactions with one another and with the external world. If an EIP supports all departments, it begins to approach a galactic EIP in scope. Department-oriented EIPs will vary according to the number and types of departments they support. A *departmental EIP* is focused on a single department. A *multi-departmental EIP* supports more than one but less than all departments. A *galactic departmental EIP* supports all departments.

The probability of initial success of an EIP project is inversely related to the scope of its focus. The probability is highest if an EIP project implements a business process EIP or a departmental EIP, and least probable if it implements a galactic EIP of some type. On the surface this suggests that attempts to implement EIPs should focus on business-process or departmental EIPs and worry about a full enterprise information system down the road. The history of data warehousing however, suggests that this is an unwise course, and specifically that a concentration on the specific and the local will defeat the very purpose of EIPs by creating a new layer of partial, badly integrated EIP applications, which themselves have to be integrated.

The solution to this new "stovepipe" problem also comes from the history of data warehousing. Specifically, data warehousing now applies the motto, "think globally, act locally." That is, translated into EIP terms, pursue EIP development by implementing an enterprise-scalable architecture along with business-process or departmental EIP applications. Then, over time, more and more business processes or departments may be added to a developing EIP and progress toward a galactic EIP if either a process or departmental type is possible.

Data and content sources

Portals can vary in their ability to access types of databases, business intelligence reports, programs, documents, data feeds, images, other files, and any one of these categories. Currently, portals can access most document formats as well as the major database formats. But not all provide support for XML. The ability to manage content in e-mail messages is becoming available. The ability to manage content within images and video streams is not currently provided in most portal products.

Portal variations

Again, the lesson to be learned from the preceding categorization is that portal variation can produce a rich universe of portal types. We do not yet have a clear idea of how the portal product space will be segmented. But the segmentation framework clearly demonstrates that a division into decision-processing portals, collaborative portals, and knowledge or integration portals is too broad and does not tell us very much about what products to expect.

Subsequently, I will provide a different portal segmentation based on the foregoing framework of categories along with some reasons for clustering categories into types. Before I do that, however, I want to consider the special importance of knowledge-processing and knowledge management portals in any portal product segmentation.

The special importance of knowledge-processing and knowledge-management portals

In Chapter 2 and again in Chapter 10, I pointed out that the future evolution of EIPs to enterprise knowledge portals (EKPs) is a likely event. Once again, an EKP is a type of EIP. It is an EIP that

- Is goal-directed toward knowledge production, knowledge integration, and knowledge management focused on enterprise business processes (e.g., sales, marketing, and risk management) (Firestone, 1999)
- Focuses on, provides, produces, and manages information about the validity of the information it supplies.

Knowledge portals have special importance because they promise to either accentuate a number of the benefits of EIPs mentioned in Chapter Four or to provide unique benefits beyond those provided by EIPs.

In the area of *competitive advantage*, EKPs can accentuate the benefit provided by EIPs by making possible the production and integration of knowledge (i.e., validated information). Real competitive advantage comes from knowledge and not from unvalidated or invalidated information, however plentiful or accessibly packaged. In the area of *increased ROI* resulting from integration applications in EKPs, a similar point applies. If a packaged application makes knowledge accessible rather than just information, the result of using it as a basis for decisions and actions will be to produce higher ROI than otherwise.

Claims for *increased employee productivity* in consequence of implementing an EIP are based on the idea that EIPs save time by making information more easily accessible. But saved time is another benefit that is accentuated by EKPs, because rather than only seeking information through EIPs, employees are, even more, seeking the most valuable information—knowledge—to use as a basis for decision. EKPs are focused in part, on knowledge integration and therefore will make knowledge more accessible to employees in less time than EIPs.

A unique benefit of EKPs, not provided by EIPs, is a way of *decreasing information overload*. By providing access to even more information, EIPs have a contradictory effect in relation to information overload. On the one hand, in making more information quickly and easily accessible they exacerbate the problem of information overload. On the other, by organizing accessibility to different types of enterprise information through a portal, they introduce a force for order and organization, which can decrease information overload.

But EKPs go still further. By prioritizing information according to the extent of its validity, they distinguish the relatively small amount of information that is really essential from the surrounding sea of suppositions, assumptions, speculations, and knowledge claims that are also information. This prioritization is the real cure for information overload.

Conclusion: A forward-looking EIP segmentation

The segmentation framework provides the foundation for product segmentation, but it is not itself a segmentation. To arrive at that, we need *product profiles* based on the framework. Even more specifically, we need to identify the relatively few such profiles that are largely descriptive of the present state of the portal space as well as another set of profiles describing the segments we believe will become inhabited during the next few years.

The three portal segments identified in the first wave of portal literature are decision-processing portals, collaborative portals, and knowledge portals. But, in spite of claims to the contrary by companies such as IntegrationWare (now Practicity, 2001) and FutureNext—Zyga (2001) during earlier days of portal development, and IBM/Lotus (2001), Comintell (2001), and Hyperwave (2002), more recently, knowledge portals are not represented yet in portal products.

Instead, a category of content-management portals represented by Plumtree and its direct competitors represents the third current portal segment defined by actual products. A fourth current segment combines decision processing (DP) and content-management (CM) capabilities without integrating them. Table 12.2 describes decision-processing, collaborative, content-management, and DP/CM portals in detail in terms of the segmentation framework (refer to Table 12.1 for translation of row abbreviations.). It goes on to specify four projected portal types: advanced collaborative portals, structured information management portals, structured knowledge-processing portals, and comprehensive knowledge-processing portals.

Profile Name (Abbreviations)	Dec Proc Portal	Cntnt MGMT Portal	Basic Collab Portal	DP/CM Portal	Adv. Collab	Strct IM Portal	Strct Kn Portal	Comp Kn Portal
	Current Segments				Future Segments			
Profiles	I	II	III	IV	V	VI	VII	VIII
F/SDM/OLTP/Packaged (function/structured data management/onlIne transaction processing/ packaged application)				X	X	X	X	X
F/SDM/OLTP/ERP (function/structured data management/online transaction processing/ enterprise resource planning application)				X	X	X	X	X
F/SDM/OLTP/ODS (function/structured data management/online transaction processing/ operational data store)				X	X	X	X	X
F/SDM/OLTP/Legacy				X	X	X	X	X
F/SDM/OLTP/Data management	X			X	X	X	X	X
F/SDM/DSS/Querying and reporting	X			X	X	X	X	X
F/SDM/DSS/KDD/Data mining				X	X	X	X	X
F/SDM/DSS/PackagedAN-Apps				X	X	X	X	X
F/SDM/DSS/Analyti-calMod&SIM				X	X	X	X	X
F/SDM/Batch/Data Management and Processing				X	X	X	X	X
F/SDM/Batch/Computer Sim				X	X	X	X	X
F/SDM/Batch/Stat Estimation				X	X	X	X	X

Table 12.2. Current and Projected Profiles of Portal Product Segments

Profile Name (Abbreviations)	Dec Proc Portal	Cntnt MGMT Portal	Basic Collab Portal	DP/CM Portal	Adv. Collab	Strct IM Portal	Strct Kn Portal	Comp Kn Portal
Profiles	Current Segments				Future Segments			
	I	II	III	IV	V	VI	VII	VIII
F/UCM/Searching/Query based	X	X	X	X	X	X	X	X
F/UCM/Searching/Agent based	X	X		X	X	X	X	X
F/UCM/Scanning/Agent based		X		X	X			X
F/UCMRetrieving/Query based		X	X	X	X			X
F/UCM/Retrieving/Continuous		X		X	X			X
F/UCM/Filtering&Class/Manual		X		X	X			X
F/UCM/Filtering&Class/Auto		X		X	X			X
F/UCM/Filtering&Class/Bayesian				X	X			X
F/UCM/Filtering&Class/Fuzzy				X	X			X
F/UCM/TextMining/Semantic Net				X	X			X
F/UCM/TextMining/Text Abstract				X	X			X
F/UCM/TextMining/FlltxtIndexing				X	X			X
F/UCM/TextMining/ConceptNet				X	X			X
F/UCM/TxtMinng/ConcptXMLTag				X	X			X
F/UCM/TxtMng/CncptNn-XMLTag				X	X			X
F/CollabProc/Prioritization					X		X	X
F/CollabProc/Planning			X		X		X	X
F/CollabProc/Project Management			X		X		X	X
F/CollabProc/Dist. Expertise			X		X			X
F/CollabProc/Training								
F/CollabProc/Problem solving			X				X	X
F/CollabProc/Knowledge Producing							X	X

Table 12.2. Current and Projected Profiles of Portal Product Segments (continued)

Profile Name (Abbreviations)	Dec Proc Portal	Cntnt MGMT Portal	Basic Collab Portal	DP/CM Portal	Adv. Collab	Strct IM Portal	Strct Kn Portal	Comp Kn Portal
	Current Segments				Future Segments			
Profiles	I	II	III	IV	V	VI	VII	VIII
F/CollabProc/Workflow		X	X		X	X	X	X
F/KnProc/KnPrd/Learning I&G					X		X	X
F/KnProc/KnPrd/Info Acquisition					X		X	X
F/KnProc/KnPrd/KnClaimForm					X		X	X
F/KnProc/KnPrd/KnValidation							X	X
F/KnProc/KnInt/Broadcasting							X	X
F/KnProc/KnInt/Searchng/Retrvng							X	X
F/KnProc/KnInt/Teaching							X	X
F/KnProc/KnInt/Kn Sharing							X	X
F/Pub&DistrbCntnt/Posting	X	X	X	X	X	X	X	X
F/Pub&DistrbCntnt/Broadcasting	X	X	X	X	X	X	X	X
F/IM/Interpers/Leadership					X	X	X	X
F/IM/Interpers/BldngExternal					X	X	X	X
F/IM/InfoProc/InfoProd					X	X	X	X
F/IM/InfoProc/InfoInt	X	X	X	X	X	X	X	X
F/IM/DM/ChngngInfoProcRules					X	X	X	X
F/IM/DM/Crisis handling					X	X	X	X
F/IM/DM/Allocating resources					X	X	X	X
F/IM/DM/Negotiating agreements					X	X	X	X
F/KM/Interpers/Leadership							X	X
F/KM/Interpers/BldgngExternal							X	X
F/KM/Kn&InfoProc/KnowldgProd							X	X

Table 12.2. Current and Projected Profiles of Portal Product Segments (continued)

Profile Name (Abbreviations)	Dec Proc Portal	Cntnt MGMT Portal	Basic Collab Portal	DP/CM Portal	Adv. Collab	Strct IM Portal	Strct Kn Portal	Comp Kn Portal
	Current Segments				Future Segments			
Profiles	I	II	III	IV	V	VI	VII	VIII
F/KM/Kn&InfoProc/KnowldgInt							X	X
F/KM/DM/ChngngKn-ProcRules							X	X
F/KM/DM/Crisis handling							X	X
F/KM/DM/Allocating resources							X	X
F/KM/DM/Negotiating agreements							X	X
AI/PIIntegration/Incremental	X	X						
AI/PIIntegration/BgBang								
AI/DataFIntegration/Incremental				X				
AI/DataFIntegration/BgBang								
AI/WorkFIntegration/Incremental			X		X			
AI/WorkFIntegration/BgBang								
AI/ObjInt/SAI/Incremental						X	X	
AI/ObjInt/SAI/BgBang								
AI/ObjInt/DCM/Incremental				X				
AI/ObjInt/DCM/BgBang								
AI/ObjInt/PAI/Incremental					X			X
AI/ObjInt/PAI/BgBang								
PS/Departmnt/Deprtmntal/Combs				X	X	X	X	X
PS/Departmnt/Deprtmntal								
PS/BusProc/BP/Types	X	X	X	X	X	X	X	X
PS/BusProc/BPmult/Combs	X	X	X	X	X	X	X	X
PS/BusProc/GalacticB-PEIP								
DCS/DBs/Network					X	X	X	X

Table 12.2. Current and Projected Profiles of Portal Product Segments (continued)

Profile Name (Abbreviations)	Dec Proc Portal	Cntnt MGMT Portal	Basic Collab Portal	DP/CM Portal	Adv. Collab	Strct IM Portal	Strct Kn Portal	Comp Kn Portal
	Current Segments				Future Segments			
Profiles	I	II	III	IV	V	VI	VII	VIII
DCS/DBs/Relational	X	X		X	X	X	X	X
DCS/DBs/OODBMS	X	X		X	X	X	X	X
DCS/DBs/Flat file	X	X		X	X	X	X	X
DCS/DBs/Inverted file					X	X	X	X
DCS/DBs/Multidimensional	X	X		X	X	X	X	X
DCS/DBs/Fractal					X	X	X	X
DCS/DBs/XML				X	X	X	X	X
DCS/DBs/Other								
DCS/BIReports	X	X		X	X	X	X	X
DCS/Programs							X	X
DCS/Docs/Text	X	X		X	X	X	X	X
DCS/Docs/Word Processing	X	X		X	X	X	X	X
DCS/Docs/e-mail				X	X		X	X
DCS/Docs/SGML							X	X
DCS/Docs/HTML	X	X		X	X	X	X	X
DCS/Docs/XML		X		X	X	X	X	X
DCS/Docs/Other								
DCS/Service Feeds	X	X		X	X	X	X	X
DCS/Images/TIFF								
DCS/Images/GIF								
DCS/Images/JPEG								
DCS/Images/WMF								
DCS/Images/PPT								
DCS/Images/Other								
DCS/Other Files								

Table 12.2. Current and Projected Profiles of Portal Product Segments (continued)

The four new portal segments shown in Figure 12.1 are my projections of where I think the market will evolve over the next couple of years. Here are some trends in portal evolution.

First, decision-processing portals and content-management portals are merging into a combined DP/CM portal. Products in this segment combine a full complement of decision-processing and content-management capabilities and also offer much tighter integration through data federation–based integration in the DP area and object-based integration in the content-management area.

Second, advanced collaborative portals are being developed combining comprehensive structured and unstructured data-management capabilities, collaboration capabilities, information-management capabilities, with some knowledge-production capabilities and portal application integration (PAI) architecture. This trend is accelerated by e-business applications of portals that are strongly oriented toward collaborative commerce.

Third, structured data-based information-management (IM) portals will combine comprehensive structured data-management capability with comprehensive structured data and information store connectivity, comprehensive information-management capability, and SAI-based integration.

Fourth, structured knowledge processing portals will combine comprehensive structured data-management capability with comprehensive information-management, knowledge processing, knowledge-management, and SAI-based integration.

Fifth, comprehensive knowledge portals will combine all of the earlier types into a portal supporting structured and unstructured data and content, knowledge management, and collaboration.

The portal segments just distinguished, suggest a loose progression from the four current portal types through the various future segments to the most advanced comprehensive knowledge portal segment. But there is nothing inevitable about such a progression, and all kinds of marketplace factors may cause one of the other future portal types to be the marketplace winner, or, even more likely, may lead to the dominance of types of portals I have not projected here. Hopefully, future marketplace or technical developments will not invalidate the segmentation framework underlying my forecast during the next two or three years. So the usefulness of the framework may remain intact even if the specific development forecast I have offered goes awry. In the meantime, and in closing, in Chapter 19, I will venture some guesses about likely pathways of development for current EIP products. Before getting there, however, I will discuss enterprise knowledge portals and their architecture (Chapter 13), segmenting EIPs and product case studies (Chapters 14–17), and portal technology, e-business, knowledge processing and knowledge management (Chapter 18).

References

Autonomy, Inc. (2001), at http://www.autonomy.com.

Engenia, Inc. (2001), at http://www.engenia.com.

eRoom, Technology, Inc. (2001), at http://www.eroom.com.

ExpertChoice, Inc. (2001), at http://www.expertchoice.com.

Finkelstein, C. (2001). "Enterprise Portals" *Business Intelligence Advisory Service Executive Report*, 1, no. 2.

Firestone, J.M. (1998). "Knowledge Management Metrics Development: A Technical Approach," *Executive Information Systems White Paper No. 10*, Wilmington, DE. Available at http://www.dkms.com/White_Papers.htm.

Firestone, J.M. (1999). "Enterprise information Portals and Enterprise Knowledge Portals," *DKMS Brief*, 8, Executive Information Systems, Inc., Wilmington, DE, March 20, 1999. Available at http://www.dkms.com/White_Papers.htm.

Intraspect, Inc. (2001), at http://www.intraspect.com.

Orbital Software, Inc. (2001), at http://www.orbitalsw.com.

Plumtree Software, Inc. (2001), at http://www.plumtree.com

Shilakes, C.C., and Tylman, J. (1998). *Enterprise Information Portals* (New York: Merrill Lynch).

White, C. (1999). "The Enterprise Information Portal Marketplace," *Decision Processing Brief DP-99-01,* Database Associates International, Inc. Morgan Hill, CA.

CHAPTER 13

The Enterprise Knowledge Portal and Its Architecture

Introduction: Enter the enterprise knowledge portal

On March 20, 1999, I introduced the *concept* of the "Enterprise Knowledge Portal" (in "Enterprise Information Portals and Enterprise Knowledge Portals," (1999) to the IT world by defining it and distinguishing it from the Enterprise Information Portal (EIP). The *term* had been used earlier (March 5, 1999) by Hummingbird Communications (1999), in a press release announcing their impending acquisition of the PC DOCS/Fulcrum group and also in an article in DataPro Industry News by Karen Shegda and Allan Tiedrich (1999) entitled "Knowledge Management—Access + Collaboration + Retrieval + Analysis." But these authors declined to define or characterize the EKP except to say that it would integrate structured and unstructured content and provide a single point of access to all relevant enterprise information, essentially the same characterization being provided for the EIP. On March 25, IDC published its "Sourcebook for Knowledge Superconductivity" (1999). In this report Gerry Murray, then IDC's Director of Knowledge Management Technologies distinguishes four types of corporate portals, including EKPs, and offers some definitions (which I discussed previously in Chapter 1).

The introduction of the EKP concept was immediately followed by remarkably little activity on EKPs. Google (2000) searches on "enterprise information portal" (1,015 hits), "enterprise information portals" (943 hits), "enterprise knowledge portal" (56 hits) and "enterprise knowledge portals," (66 hits) tell the story of EKP vs. EIP during 1999 and the first two months of 2000. (The figures (Google, 2001) as of 09/09/2001, are EIP—15,300, EIPs—8,000, EKP—489, and EKPs—401.) Other than URLs reflecting writings by Gerry Murray or myself and third-party links to what we had written, there are few evidences of EKP activity on the Web, and only six vendors that billed themselves as having EKP products. Hummingbird promised an EKP in March 1999 but by March 2000 had released an EIP instead; to this day Hummingbird has never produced an EKP. During its first two years, the EKP space gave every evidence of being swallowed up by its EIP parent.

In spite of the initial failure of the EKP to grab mind-share in the portal space, the future is bright for it because a number of the claims of primary benefits of EIPs, (e.g., increased ROI, competitive advantage, increased effectiveness, and accelerated innovation) assume that information delivered by EIPs is correct information. But the risk associated with EIPs is that if the information is not correct, these four benefits are lost. An overriding justification for implementing an EKP rather than an EIP is to *secure* these four benefits and to minimize decision-making risk by increasing the *quality and validity* of information supplied by the portal. To see this clearly, we need to examine the idea of the EKP more carefully. Let's begin to develop the EKP concept in more detail with a story illustrating differences among Windows desktops, EIPs, and EKPs and then continue with a more formal attempt to specify the EKP concept.

A story about desktops, EIPs, and EKPs

The following three scenarios may provide a practical understanding of how a knowledge worker works with a Windows desktop (John); how a knowledge worker's production is increased using an information portal (Jennifer); and how a knowledge worker's production is dramatically increased with a knowledge portal (Jackie).

John and the Windows 98 desktop

John comes into work at 8:30 AM and boots up his PC. He signs on and then finds himself in his Windows 98 desktop. He then needs to remember

- Where he left his work the day before
- What subject he was working on
- How it relates to other subjects he's interested in
- What task he was engaged in relating to that subject
- What application on his desktop he was using or should be using to accomplish that task

He must then

- Open the appropriate application
- Select the file he was working with
- Proceed to complete his task

During this process, the only help John gets from his computer is provided by the application he uses to complete his task. He receives no computer support at all in getting to that application. He gets there on his own based on his own knowledge of where he needs to go. Once he completes the immediate task in that application, he must then decide on what the next step in his workflow process will be, navigate his way to that application, open it, execute it, complete it, and move on to the next task and so on until the process is completed.

In short, John works his way through a process of interrelated tasks, which his computer does not recognize as related. The applications used to implement the various tasks represent "islands of automation." From the viewpoint of his computer they are entirely isolated and unrelated. In using the applications, he may want to access heterogeneous data, information, and knowledge stores. These stores represent "islands of information." From the viewpoint of his computer, they are also entirely isolated and unrelated.

Jennifer and her brand spanking new EIP

When Jennifer arrives at 8:30 AM, she boots up into an enterprise information portal. The portal greets her with a personalized classification of information by subject. She clicks on a subject. The portal responds with another classification, breaking down further the subject matter category she selected. Eventually she works her way to the bottom of this hierarchical classification. At the bottom is a list of subjects or applications. If she opens a subject category, she gets a page of information on the subject she selected. She can then access this information for various purposes.

If the information does not answer her questions, Jennifer can query data or document stores in the portal system to search for more information. If the EIP is properly integrated, she can access a variety of data, information, and content stores in the enterprise. The location of these stores is transparent to her. She sees no "islands of information," but experiences a unified view of all of the information sources in the enterprise. However, most current portal systems are not properly integrated. As a result, she is likely not to experience the unified view but to experience only partial access to data or to text or document content.

But whether Jennifer experiences a partial or a unified view of all information in the enterprise and whether or not she can access transparently whatever she sees in the portal interface, the portal still provides her *no information about the validity of the information she is accessing.* She cannot tell if an answer to a query or search request of hers is likely to be the correct answer. She cannot tell about the degree of its validity. She cannot tell how the information has been tested or whether it has proved out in the past. She cannot tell whether the information can help her make a decision. In short, she is flying blind, with plenty of environmental input but precious little radar; with lots of information, but not a clear idea of what is relevant.

If she opens an application rather than a subject category, Jennifer can use the application to perform a task. If the portal system is properly integrated, she can use more than one application to perform the task. But most current EIPs, while able to provide access to more than one application simultaneously, cannot integrate applications into an automated workflow or task sequence, so Jennifer has to figure out the workflow or to remember or reinvent a workflow she previously used. Her computer still presents "islands of automation" to her instead of a synthesized higher-order application that she can use, reuse, or enhance to make herself more productive.

Jackie and her enterprise knowledge portal

At 8:30 AM, Jackie boots up into the enterprise knowledge portal. Like Jennifer, she sees a personalized classification of her subject matter, and when she selects a category, she drills down into a hierarchy of subcategories of subjects and classifications. A nice thing for Jackie, though, is her ability, at any level of this classification, to see a conceptual network of the nonhierarchical, associative, and causal relationships that any subject matter or application concept has to any other subject matter or application concept.

If she drills into "sales performance," for example, she can immediately expose relationships to sales performance metrics, to profit metrics, to sales forecasting, to sales growth, and to numerous other concepts related to sales performance.

Seeing the conceptual network, a model of the relationships existing in her own mind and in the minds of others in her company, Jackie can quickly hyperlink from her entry into this conceptual network to any node that she thinks is relevant to the work she wants to do. She does not need to think about the relationships that let her link to the desired node. The EKP, through an intelligent agent—an avatar representing her preferences and previously recorded behavior—has tracked and maintained her previously created relationships in the form of her personalized conceptual network. It is there, ready for her to access and to enhance whenever she wants to continue work where she previously left off.

Next, Jackie works with her conceptual network by selecting a subject matter or application node of the network. If she accesses a subject matter node, she gets a page of information. But along with the information, she also gets information about how valid that information is and about the previous usage and testing that has validated it. She has not only information but also the means to determine its value and its relevance. She is flying with radar, and she can tell which portal inputs are important to her and which she can screen out or relegate to the outer reaches of her conceptual network.

If the information does not answer her questions, Jackie can query data and content stores with no "islands of information" limitations. She can transparently query and search any kind of data, information, or content in the enterprise. The portal provides her with a unified view of information and with a way of transparently accessing, combining, and then evaluating it all.

When she wants to move beyond mere subject matter to applications work that uses or transforms data, information, or knowledge, she can drill into a subject-matter node of the conceptual network until she accesses a part of the network forming a workflow. At that point the portal will provide her with the options of automatically executing, guiding her through manual execution of the steps of the collaborative or individual workflow she selected, or modifying the workflow. The workflow will utilize applications at each step and integrate them serially within its framework.

In this way, the EKP provides Jackie with access to a sequence of applications supporting the steps in a workflow. Her computer, through the portal, no longer presents "islands of automation" to her. Instead, it presents a synthesized higher-order application that Jackie herself, through her avatar, created in previous uses of the portal.

In addition to providing integrated individual and collaborative workflows, the EKP also transcends EIPs by providing Jackie with formal knowledge production tools and related workflows. So when she wants to innovate or manufacture new knowledge through the portal in response to a problem, she can use old knowledge stored in the portal knowledge base, along with the diverse information and data stores and the formal knowledge production tools, both individual and collaborative, available to the portal to execute new and old knowledge production workflows. The result is new knowledge, enhanced validated information that Jackie can later access from the portal system's knowledge base.

What is the EKP?

The story of John, Jack, and Jennifer provides a feel for the difference the EKP makes to people performing work, but it doesn't provide a precise treatment of the nature of EKPs and how they differ from EIPs. It is best to begin this more comprehensive analysis by recalling some of the definitions of business and enterprise information portals surveyed in Chapter 1. According to Wayne Eckerson (1999), a Business portal is an application that "provides business users one-stop shopping for any information object they need inside or outside the corporation." It also provides shared services such as "security, metadata repository, personalization, search, publish/subscribe," etc., as well as a common look and feel to the portal gateway.

According to Merrill Lynch's Shilakes and Tylman (1998): "Enterprise Information Portals are applications that enable companies to unlock internally and externally stored information, and *provide users a single gateway to personalized information* needed to make informed business decisions. . . . an amalgamation of software applications that consolidate, manage, analyze and distribute information across and outside of an enterprise (including Business Intelligence, Content Management, Data Warehouse & Mart and Data Management applications)."

What characterizes EIPs is that they

- Use "push" and "pull" technologies to transmit information through a standardized web interface
- Provide "interactivity"—the ability to "question and share information on" user desktops
- Exhibit a trend toward verticalization in applications, including packaged applications with targeted content toward industries or corporate functions
- Integrate disparate applications and data/content stores into a single system
- Access both external and internal sources
- Support bi-directional information exchange from sources
- Use data and information acquired for further processing

An EKP is an enhanced enterprise information portal (EIP). It is an EIP that

- Is goal directed toward knowledge production, knowledge integration, and knowledge management
- Focuses upon, provides, produces, and manages information about the validity of the information it supplies
- Provides information about your business and meta-information and about the degree to which you can rely on that information
- Distinguishes knowledge from mere information
- Provides a facility for producing knowledge from information
- Orients one toward producing and integrating knowledge rather than information

The following sections specify these.

An EKP is an EIP

An EKP shares the characteristics of other EIPs. It is a particularly comprehensive version of an EIP, however, incorporating a personalized browser-based interface, structured data management, unstructured content management, and collaborative as well as knowledge production, knowledge integration, and knowledge management functionality. It also requires an integrative architecture incorporating knowledge claim objects (KCOs) encapsulating knowledge claim data, metadata describing the validity characteristics of these knowledge claim objects, and methods producing the behavior of the objects. EKP architecture is described in greater detail subsequently.

Knowledge processing means knowledge production and knowledge integration

This should be clear from the previous knowledge processing/knowledge management framework, presented in Chapters 7–9. The point is that to be an EKP, an EIP application must implement use cases (see Chapter 10) that support knowledge production and knowledge integration. That means the use cases must support information acquisition, individual and group learning, knowledge claim formulation, knowledge claim validation, broadcasting, searching/retrieving, sharing, and teaching. In each of these areas it must also support planning, monitoring, and evaluating phases of decision cycles. This again underlines how comprehensive EKPs are compared to EIPs.

The knowledge management process

Another distinguishing characteristic of the EKP is that it must support the knowledge management process (KMP) as defined earlier. This means that the EKP must implement use cases that support the nine task patterns, tasks, and activities of the KMP as well as the phases of decision cycles encompassed by the KMP. There is no similar requirement for EIPs.

An EKP provides, produces, and manages information about the validity of information it supplies

Knowledge is validated information. EKPs distinguish knowledge from mere information by providing information about the results of tests of the validity of any piece of information. That means that EKPs *must track and store such meta-information while EIPs in general need not.*

This requirement is one that distinguishes EKPs from other EIPs. It is a requirement that greatly expands the diversity and volume of metadata found in EKPs as compared with EIPs, since the validity meta-information provided by the metadata and its context must record the full history of the discussions and interactions that transform information into knowledge.

An EKP provides business information along with meta-information about the degree to which you can rely on it

Validity information about a knowledge claim is meta-information about that claim. This validity base includes meta-information comparing the knowledge claim against competing knowledge claims. This meta-information tells you the degree to which you can rely on the target knowledge claim compared to its competitors. It tells you the relative strength of the knowledge claim compared to its competitors. Thus, EKPs record the history of the competitive struggle among ideas (knowledge claims) put forward to solve problems within the enterprise. EIPs need record no such history.

An EKP distinguishes knowledge from information

By providing validity information (meta-information) about knowledge claims, EKPs provide information on the relative strength of such knowledge claims. The stronger the claim, the closer it approaches organizational knowledge and the stronger the support it provides for decisions. The weaker the claim, the more closely it approaches false organizational information and the weaker the support it provides for decisions.

An EKP provides a facility for producing knowledge from information

By providing services for knowledge claim formulation and validation and tracking and storing the results of validation activities in knowledge claim objects, EKPs provide a facility that supports producing knowledge from knowledge claims—or, put another way, supports producing better or worse validated knowledge claims from unvalidated ones. Since knowledge claims are information and knowledge is validated knowledge claims, it follows that EKPs provide a facility for producing knowledge from information.

An EKP orients one toward producing and integrating knowledge rather than only information

Because the EKP supports the full set of knowledge life cycle activities including, and most critically, individual and group learning and knowledge validation, it orients one toward knowledge production. Because new knowledge results from use of the EKP, enterprise information integration processes will be oriented toward integrating knowledge and validity information as well as business information.

EKP architecture and components

The specification of the EKP just completed may provide a more detailed concept of it than the John, Jennifer, and Jackie story, but to really understand the construct it is necessary to describe both its architecture and its functional requirements. Here is an overview of its functioning and a more specific account of its architecture.

The EKP provides a

- Knowledge worker–centric, knowledge workflow–oriented, single point of access to enterprise data and content stores and to applications supporting knowledge production, knowledge integration, and knowledge management
- Personalized desktop browser–based portal that with the assistance of an integrative, logically centralized, but physically distributed *artificial knowledge manager (AKM)*, composed of distributed *artificial knowledge servers (AKSS)* and *intelligent mobile agents*, is connected to all enterprise mission-critical application sources and data and content stores
- Secure, seamless, single-logon capability for all network, application, and service resources

The distributed AKM balances processing loads across the enterprise and provides for dynamic integration of the portal system in the face of change. The EKP system is managed, in part, by the AKM's ubiquitous intelligent agents serving all application servers, data and content stores, and clients in the enterprise. The EKP system provides a new work environment for enterprise knowledge workers, one that is aligned with and supports and partially automates their individual and collaborative workflow in creating, distributing, and using data, information, and knowledge, and in making and implementing decisions and actions.

More specifically, the EKP in operation provides: a wide range of functionality (including structured data management, unstructured content management, collaborative processing, information processing, information management, knowledge processing, and knowledge management); a wide range of data and content stores as sources of previously developed information and knowledge, and an integrative object/component-based portal architecture. Here is an introduction to knowledge portal architecture and components.

Figure 13.1 presents an overview. Note the complexity of the EKP system with respect to diversity of data and information stores and application servers, the presence of structured data and unstructured content sources, the publication and agent capabilities, the Web server and portal capabilities, the text- and data-mining capabilities, the collaborative capabilities, and the dynamic integrative capabilities provided by the AKM with its agents and logically centralized but physically distributed AKS servers and intelligent agents.

Note also that this view of the EKP does not emphasize its front-end aspects or format. In the EKP the action is in the middleware and in how it functions to support knowledge production, knowledge integration, and knowledge management. In fact, the EKP is very similar to the DKMS illustrated in Chapter 10, but it also includes a portal front-end and, as illustrated in figure 13.1, XML capabilities.

Though Figure 13.1 illustrates the diversity of components that may enter an EKP, it does not specify its necessary generic components. These are as follows:

- Browser and e-mail clients
- The avatar, a client-based intelligent agent
- The portal application server(s)
- The access management system
- Knowledge claim objects (KCOs)

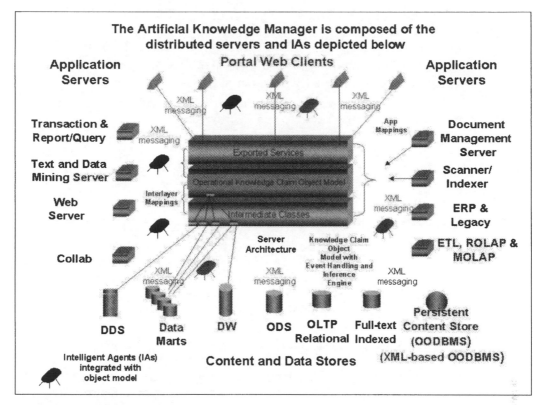

Figure 13.1. EKP architecture.

- The enterprise artificial knowledge server(s) (AKSs),
- Complex adaptive system (CAS) intelligent agent platform
- The formal knowledge production application server(s) and its associated clients supporting analytical and statistical modeling, KDD and data mining, text mining, simulation, impact analysis, and forecasting,
- The collaborative processing application server
- A persistent storage component

Among these components, the avatar, knowledge claim objects, the AKS, the CAS agent platform, and the collaborative processing application server are all unusual and deserve further analysis in specifying EKP architecture.

The avatar

The purpose of the avatar, a client-based CAS agent, is to create a highly automated, enterprise knowledge-enabled, self-learning/adaptive portal interface that is personally and dynamically tailored to each user. The types of automation involved here include

- Assimilation of the user's local environment, personal preferences, and cognitive patterns
- Learning from, interacting with, and utilizing enterprise knowledge communicated by the artificial knowledge servers

- Providing the user autonomous negotiating capabilities with the rest of the EKP system
- Supporting performing personal and collaborative workflows, by
  — Providing workflow memory, accessible from the portal interface adapting in accordance with anticipated needs of the user
  — Providing access to user cognitive maps and producing knowledge claims and submitting these to the EKP system

The knowledge claims of the avatar represent local knowledge in contrast to the rules that have been validated by the EKP system's network of artificial knowledge servers.

Knowledge claim objects

An important class of object in the EKP system is the knowledge claim object (KCO). As I stated previously during the discussion in Chapter 10 on the AKMS and the AKM, a KCO is distinguished from an ordinary business object by the presence of validity metadata encapsulated in the object. Such metadata compares the KCO to alternative, competing KCOs and may be expressed in many different forms.

Again, the "metadata" may be qualitative or quantitative, or it may be in the form of textual content. In relatively infrequent but important special cases, the metadata may involve quantitative ratings of a knowledge claim compared with its competitors. When the KCO is accessed by a user, data, metadata, and methods are all available, so the user can evaluate the KCO as a basis for decision against competing KCOs. This capability is not available in EIPs, which express knowledge claims as data or business objects only.

The artificial knowledge server

The distributed AKS provides process control services; an object model of the EKP system; and connectivity to all enterprise information, data stores, and applications. Process control services include

- In-memory proactive object state management and synchronization across distributed objects
- Component management and workflow management
- Transactional multithreading
- Business rule management and processing
- KCO management and processing
- Metadata management

The in-memory active object model/persistent object store is characterized by

- Event-driven behavior
- An EKP-wide model with shared representation
- Declarative and procedural business rules
- Caching along with partial instantiation of objects

- A Persistent object store for the AKS
- Reflexive objects and KCOs

Connectivity Services required by the EKP include

- Language APIs: C, C++, Java, HTML, XML, CORBA, and DCOM
- Databases: relational, ODBC, OODBMS, hierarchical, network, flat file, XML
- Wrapper connectivity for application software: custom, CORBA, or COM-based
- Applications connectivity including all the applications in the enterprise, whether these are mainframe-, server,- or desktop-based

CAS agents

The second type of component comprising the EKP's AKM is the intelligent agent (IA). The avatar, already reviewed, is one type of EKP intelligent agent. In general, EKP IAs are lightweight, intelligent, efficient, specialized business process engines (BPEs) that provide some memory and a small amount of processing power at almost no cost. They also provide bi-directional communication, an inference engine, an ability to model semantic networks, and an ability to learn through reinforcement of semantic network connections and creation of new nodes. It is this last ability to learn that makes them intelligent.

Intelligent agents alone cannot yet create the virtual enterprise. For complex processing and an enterprisewide view, the AKS is also indispensable. But IAs provide distributed load balancing to processing in the AKM. They are necessary partners in providing the processing power needed for implementing the EKP. When we add agents to the AKS to create the AKM, we provide software wiring for the enterprise that connects its central brain components (the AKSs) to its sensors (the agents). The result is a flexible and scalable AKM that can integrate the various components of the EKP into a virtual enterprise.

Collaborative processing application server

The eight categories of collaboration are as follows:

- Prioritization,
- Planning,
- Project management
- Distributing expertise
- Training
- Problem solving
- Knowledge production
- Workflow

Each of these areas represents nontrivial functions that are currently realized in complex applications, that to some extent represent distinct functional subspaces, and that could each be wrapped into a collaborative or knowledge portal either separately or in combination with one of the other categories.

Products such as Intraspect (2001) or eRoom (2001), which focus on collaboration in general or collaboration in support of project management, are very different from products that intend to support strategic planning implementations such as Engenia's Unity (2000). And these are very different from products that provide for group collaboration on analytical modeling and/or data mining, or that provide for a team approach to prioritized decision making, such as Expert Choice (2001). And these, in turn, are very different from products such as Orbital Software's Organik Knowledgeware (2001) that allow knowledge workers to access the expertise of "Gurus" in specialized fields.

In short, the term "collaborative application server" covers a variety of applications. In the context of the EKP, collaborative processing requirements should encompass all categories specified above, because all are related to knowledge outcomes or knowledge processes. EKPs then, are particularly comprehensive in their collaborative processing functionality.

The essence of the EKP

Every individual, team, or group within the enterprise encounters problems in the course of the workday. Every problem has alternative solutions, and every alternative solution is subject to criticism and to replacement if it performs less effectively than its competitors. The best problem solution is the competitive alternative that best survives criticism. And it is that alternative that is the enterprise's best knowledge at any given moment.

The set of problem-solving interactions in an enterprise constitutes a continuous, dynamic "swirl" from which knowledge is produced and integrated with the business processes of the enterprise. The essence of the EKP is its support for facilitating this knowledge "swirl" and its management. The EKP supports every phase of the KLC and every KM activity. It supports business processes with new knowledge production and integration. It supports collaboration focused on knowledge production by providing the history of knowledge-validating activities in the enterprise to each participant in the collaboration. It also supports knowledge production through automated arbitration between local knowledge claims and regional and global knowledge claims. But most of all, by supporting every phase of the KLC and by subjecting knowledge claims to competition more efficiently than ever before, it subjects them to evolutionary forces and thus supports the acceleration of innovation and the growth of knowledge in the EKP-supported enterprise.

The EKP, the AKMS/DKMS, and EKP functional requirements

By now the description of the architecture of the EKP has perhaps suggested similarities between it, DIMS architecture, and PAI architecture in EIPs, both covered in Chapter 5 (with the role of IAs described in Chapter 6), and especially DKM architecture in the DKMS/AKMS construct described in Chapter 10. Indeed, a comparison of the two will indicate that EKP architecture is a specific realization of the DKMS/AKMS architectural pattern and that the EKP is therefore an instance of the DKMS/AKMS, which anticipates it. The EKP is more specific in its emphasis on the portal interface and in its identification of the avatar as a specific type of IA of great importance in the EKP. Otherwise, the constructs are identical.

Given the identification of the DKMS and the EKP, my previous analysis of use cases necessary for the DKMS (Chapter 10) is also important for the EKP. As with the DKMS, one can classify use cases in the EKP by whether they support knowledge production (KP), knowledge integration (KI), or knowledge management (KM) and still more specifically by whether they support the various sub-processes and activities in the KP, KI, or KM processes. A tentative listing and classification of KP, KI, and KM use cases, and therefore of the functional requirements of the EKP, is presented in Chapter 10. Use that listing to arrive at a still more concrete understanding of what the EKP must do.

EKPs, knowledge sharing, and corporate culture

Many people believe that though knowledge production and knowledge sharing incentive systems are necessary to achieve the benefits of knowledge management, they may face cultural resistance in organizations considering EKPs. EKPs may or may not face such resistance, but if they do, it may not be necessary to overcome it by *inducing* knowledge workers to share information or knowledge through the EKP system by means of a credit-assignment system or some other incentive system application built into the EKP. Specifically, the collaborative knowledge processing and knowledge management capabilities of the EKP will integrate all organizational content, including memoranda, e-mails, reports, and any other written documentation of a collaborative decision making or problem solving process into the distributed organizational knowledge base.

Knowledge workers cannot really avoid generating content when working with others in the enterprise. This content will naturally incorporate knowledge claims that may be modeled as knowledge claim objects. It will also incorporate counterclaims and arguments supporting competing knowledge claims. The EKP will be able to track the give-and-take involving such claims, whether or not individuals choose to explicitly use the portal system to "publish" their content or to distribute it to others. Through this continuous capturing of explicit knowledge claims, the portal system will acquire information and knowledge that can be retrieved by other interested parties or pushed to them based on portal personalization activity. So the portal system will be able to implement knowledge distribution even where individuals are reluctant to share. In addition, it is able to implement credit assignments to knowledge workers based on their unobtrusive contributions to the enterprise's information and knowledge bases, if such assignments are considered useful.

E-business knowledge portals

Portal technology is currently in full migration to the field of e-business. EIP technology is equally applicable to trading communities and trans-enterprise and externally-facing enterprise applications of all types. Eventually, when true EKP products and solutions are implemented, they too will be used in e-business. They will be used especially in trading communities and in communities of practice in medicine, pharmacology, architecture, engineering, and science, more generally, and in other areas in which the distinction between true and false information is central. E-business knowledge portals will be discussed along with other e-business portals in Chapter 18.

Are there any enterprise knowledge portals?

There are some vendors who claim or who have claimed that they manufacture EKP products. Based on the account I have presented of knowledge, knowledge processing, knowledge management, and now the EKP, this claim is simply unjustified. There are no EKPs, in the sense specified here, yet.

In support of this conclusion, I will briefly review the products of a number of claimants to the EKP crown in the following text. During the portal case studies in the next four chapters, I will provide abundant further support for the conclusion.

IBM/Lotus

The IBM WebSphere Portal product platform (2001), also referred to as an "enterprise knowledge portal" by IBM, combines solutions (template libraries, plus methodologies, plus services), a "knowledge portal" that organizes and manages personal and community assets, a "discovery engine" containing an expertise locator (manages demographic and affinity information), and a content catalog ("connects people and content in context to discover meaning, value and relationships"). That is, it has substantial content management, text-mining, collaborative, and enterprise application integration capabilities. But it lacks the kind of broad-ranging formal knowledge production; structured data management; collaborative, enterprise data, and application integration; comprehensive knowledge validation; workflow; knowledge claim object; knowledge processing; and knowledge management processing specified earlier for knowledge portals supporting knowledge processing and KM.

As I indicate in Chapter 16, it has recently begun to approach the middleware foundation and broad integrative capability necessary for an EKP. But it still lacks the automated synchronization, change management, knowledge production, and cumulative knowledge validation capability of one. In particular, it lacks the IA and inference engine capability necessary for the EKP, and it also does not provide a validation framework for people, intelligent agents, and artificial knowledge servers.

Hyperwave

Hyperwave (2002) sells an information portal and an information server, not an EKP, but it claims (2002) that its eKnowledge Infrastructure provides an "eKnowledge Portal." The Hyperwave products support collaboration, document and content management, personalization, and workflow. In the latest version (to be reviewed in Chapter 17) they provide structured data management capability as well. They do not, however, provide formal knowledge production, knowledge validation processing, knowledge claim object, artificial knowledge server, or IA capability. They are therefore not ideal for deploying EKPs without addition of considerable functionality important for knowledge processing and knowledge management. Hyperwave's products allow a sophisticated information portal solution combining content management and collaboration, but no more. Later

(Chapter 17) I will support this conclusion with a more detailed analysis of the Hyperwave portal.

Practicity (formerly IntegrationWare)

Until recently, Practicity (2000) marketed a product called IntraBlocks. The company characterized IntraBlocks as an EKP combining a "knowledge warehouse with advanced middleware, collaboration, and web presentation capability." IntraBlocks was constructed around "knowledge objects," apparently business objects by another name, not to be confused with the knowledge claim objects defined earlier, and a knowledge object server providing "the ability to apply categorization, clustering, searching, notification agents, security, and auditing to Knowledge Objects." The middleware server provided a solid basis for content management, limited structured data manipulation capability, and substantial collaboration features. It also provided the basis to "plug in" new knowledge objects to extend the capability of IntraBlocks. A relational database is used in IntraBlocks to provide persistent storage for knowledge objects.

IntraBlocks was one of the most advanced of the first-generation portals. Diverse functionality was provided in its eleven knowledge objects. Before the company decided to target the vertical area of professional services portals, it was likely that IntegrationWare would be among the first knowledge portals. But as of this date, Practicity (recently acquired by TrueSource, Inc. (TrueSource, 2002)) is perhaps most advanced in the area of collaborative processing. It does not offer the full range of structured data management, unstructured content management, collaborative processing, knowledge management, enterprise application integration, and formal and informal knowledge production/validation capability necessary for an EKP. In particular, it does not distinguish, track, or model validation information through knowledge claim objects or through artificial knowledge server or agent-based middleware.

Comintell

Comintell (2002) is a European vendor promoting an EKP product called Comintell Connect. Combined with Comintell's ComCoder context management, its WhoWhatWhere expertise locator, and its FlowBoard graphic visualization of products, Comintell offers significant across-the-board capabilities in content management, personalization, delivery of information in context, collaboration, and workflow. But these capabilities do not make an EKP. Comintell's collaboration capabilities are not broad enough in scope, its product does not include knowledge claim objects, nor the artificial knowledge servers and IAs necessary to process them, to track validity information, and to partially automate knowledge production.

Unisys

The Unisys (2001) EKP provides online cataloging, indexing, and document management along with a single point of access for performing most daily computing functions. Most recently, it has added the XML processing capabilities of the Netegrity Interactive Server. Given Unisys's description of this portal it is difficult to understand why it is called an EKP. The product is positioned entirely in the

	Enterprise Knowledge Portals	Extraprise Knowledge Portals	Interprise Knowledge Portals
Structured Knowledge Processing Portals			
Comprehensive Knowledge Processing Portals			

Table 13.1. Six Knowledge Portal Types

context of the Microsoft BackOffice and Office 2000 suite of products. It apparently has no formal knowledge production, structured data management, text mining, collaborative, knowledge validation, or enterprise application integration capabilities. It has none of the distinguishing characteristics of an EKP.

This brief evaluation of the IBM/Lotus, Hyperwave, Practicity, Comintell, and Unisys products does not describe these portals in sufficient detail to classify them, but I think it does show that they are not EKPs. Nor have any other vendors approached the EKP segment yet. EKP applications remain to be implemented, and the reward will be great for the first successful developer of a bonafide EKP solution that will support knowledge production, knowledge integration, and knowledge management.

Types of knowledge portals

Since there are no knowledge portals at present, it may seem premature to segment this category. But I think it is useful to specify a few types that seem likely to be the first in the knowledge portal segment. First, the distinction between extraprise and interprise information portals, discussed briefly in Chapter 1, suggests a parallel distinction between two types of e-business knowledge portals: extraprise knowledge portals (ExKPs) and interprise knowledge portals (IIPs). Since enterprise knowledge portals constitute a separate category, the result is a three-fold typology.

Further, in Chapter 12 I mentioned a distinction between structured knowledge-processing portals and comprehensive knowledge-processing portals. That distinction is based on the idea that some portals might develop a capability for knowledge processing and knowledge management using SAI-based integration with its restriction to structured data and information–management capability, while others would develop a comprehensive knowledge and knowledge management–processing capability based on PAI and the full-blown EKP architecture described earlier in this chapter. Cross-classifying the two categorizations provides the six-fold typology provided in Table 13.1.

Conclusion

The enterprise knowledge portal is an application on the verge of development. The technology it requires is in existence now. The cost of its development is low as software applications go, since its implementation is largely a matter of systems integration, with the exception of its IA component that exceeds current IA capabilities. On the other hand, the benefits associated with the EKP are great. They are nothing less than realization of the promise of the EIP to achieve increased ROI, competitive advantage, increased effectiveness, and acceleration of innovation.

As I indicated previously, EIPs are risky because (neglecting data quality applications, which involve relatively superficial quality issues) they fail to evaluate the information they produce and deliver for quality and validity. Nothing, including EKPs, can ensure certainty about information, models or knowledge claims. But EKP applications incorporate a systematic approach to knowledge claim testing and evaluation (knowledge claim validation) that eliminates errors and produces quality assured information. In the category of portal technology they, not EIPs, are the best we can do. They, not EIPs, represent the future of portal technology.

References

Comintell, Inc. (2002), http://www.comintell.com.

Eckerson, W. (1999). "Business Portals: Drivers, Definitions, and Rules," *The Data Warehousing Institute,* Gaithersburg, MD.

Engenia, Inc. (2000), http://www.engenia.com.

eRoom Technology, Inc. (2001), http://www.eroom.com.

ExpertChoice (2001), http://www.expertchoice.com.

Firestone, J.M. (1999). "Enterprise Information Portals and Enterprise Knowledge Portals," *DKMS Brief*, 8, Executive Information Systems, Inc., Wilmington, DE, March 20, 1999, http://www.dkms.com/White_Papers.htm.

Firestone, J.M. (1999a). "Defining Enterprise Information Portals," *Executive Information Systems White Paper No. 13*, Executive Information Systems, Inc., http://www.dkms.com/White_Papers.htm.

Google (2000). "Search Results on Enterprise Information Portals, Enterprise Information Portal, Enterprise Knowledge Portals, and Enterprise Knowledge Portal, http://www.google.com.

Google (2001). "Search Results on Enterprise Information Portals, Enterprise Information Portal, Enterprise Knowledge Portals, and Enterprise Knowledge Portal, http://www.google.com.

Hummingbird Communications, Inc. (2001). Press release on pending acquisition, March 5, 1999, available at: http://www.hummingbird.com/press/1999/pcdocs.html.

Hyperwave, Inc. (2002), www.hyperwave.com.

IBM, Inc. (2001), www.lotus.com/products/kstation.nsf.

IDC, Inc. (1999). "Enterprise Knowledge Portals to Become the Shared Desktop of the Future," *IDC Press Release,* March 25, 1999, http://www.idc.com/Data/Software/content/SW032699PR.htm.

Intraspect, Inc. (2001), http://www.intraspect.com.

Orbital Software, Inc. (2001), http://www.orbitalsw.com.

Practicity, Inc. (2000), http://www.practicity.com.

Shegda, K., and Tiedrich, A. (1999). "Knowledge Management = Access + Collaboration + Retrieval + Analysis," *DataPro Industry News.* http://gartner5.gartnerweb.com/public/static/datapro/industry/indnews28.html.

Shilakes, C., and Tylman, J. (1998). *Enterprise Information Portals* (New York: Merrill Lynch).

TrueSource, Inc. (2002), www.truesourceinc.com.

Unisys, Inc. (2001), www.unisys.com.

CHAPTER 14

Decision Processing Portal Products

Introduction

Decision-processing portals were among the first to be released. In the beginning, the Viador, Brio, and Information Advantage "My Eureka" portal products were models of this type of portal. They provided little content management and collaborative capability, focused mainly on structured data processing and analysis, and had a strong orientation toward business intelligence (BI) and reporting applications. But now Viador, Brio, and Computer Associates (acquirers of the Information Advantage technology) have added significant content-management capability to their products, and a few new entrants in the portal field are concentrating on decision-processing portals alone. So now there are a few simple decision-processing portals available. Two of these will be reviewed here. They are Business Objects InfoView and Cognos UpFront.

Business Objects InfoView

InfoView (Business Objects, 2002) fits the concept of a basic decision-processing portal very closely. It is primarily focused on providing a secure, personalized gateway to business intelligence data, information, and reports. It can handle documents but has only limited content-management and collaboration capabilities. Business Objects is one of the leading software vendors in the area of DSS-related computing including OLAP, querying and reporting, analysis and data mining, and data warehousing. InfoView is essentially a product that allows Business Objects to deliver its suite of DSS data warehousing–related services to knowledge workers through a portal environment. These services revolve around the management, analysis, and display of structured data in the form of reports.

Business Objects's InfoView can function either as a standalone portal or as a business intelligence content provider for other portal products. That means that InfoView can work as the BI component of portal solutions that rely on other portal tools to provide the primary display and content-management functions for a portal solution. InfoView provides its own repository for storing e-business intelligence content and reports.

This repository can store all types of documents for later display. Content checked into the repository may be categorized by attribute values expressed in metadata. Some of these attributes, such as document name, author, title, and date created may be used to do quick keyword searches for documents. Other attributes and their values (e.g., department, document type, and position) may be used to categorize content in a less specific, role-based manner, so that the types defined by combinations of attribute values are associated with roles and, ultimately, with knowledge workers.

InfoView provides a feature called "My InfoView" that allows personalization of portal interfaces. Up to four frames may be displayed in My InfoView. The frames may display specific reports, categorizations of content, and dynamic Web pages delivering applications.

Security in InfoView is provided at the document level for unstructured content. For structured data, however, data-level security is provided such that particular attributes may be selected for BI and report-based delivery to particular roles, positions, or individuals. This last is accomplished through profile-based administration, which uses the metadata I mentioned above to define document and report profiles and to associate them with groups of knowledge workers.

InfoView allows any report or document to be shared among knowledge workers. Further, InfoView lets users provide notes and messages along with BI content. People can add notes and comments to reports and analyses, and discussion can be carried on about any document in the InfoView repository. Infoview also allows notification when new content is created. So participants in a document focused on collaboration may be alerted when a new contribution to their collaboration is produced.

InfoView also provides publication capability. Knowledge workers can schedule and distribute content throughout the enterprise or to customers, suppliers, and partners using the portal. Knowledge workers can also publish Business Objects's WebIntelligence™ reports and BI information to InfoView Mobile, from which they can be provided to personal digital assistants (PDAs) of customers and others anywhere in the world through downloading. These reports can the be viewed in an offline mode—for example, by sales managers traveling on a train or plane and looking for updates on activity of major customers or perhaps on sales revenue by territory.

Taken as a whole, Infoview provides a fine example of a decision-processing portal. Since it can deliver Business Objects DSS tools to a portal interface, it can also be viewed as a portal product that when coupled with its companion Business Objects tools is capable of providing the front-end to a portal systems architecture of the data federation integration (DFI) type. I say this because:

- DSS applications are accessed through the portal interface according to the pattern of passive access to content (PAC) architecture.
- The Business Objects WebIntelligence™ tool "provides access to data via the patented Business Objects semantic layer" (Business Objects, 2002a), a layer that interfaces data sources to BI query tools while providing a unified logical view of those sources.
- The BI WebIntelligence tool does not provide the rule-driven object and component synchronization necessary for SAI architecture.
- Infoview does not track the history of testing and evaluation of knowledge claims that is required in knowledge portals.

In fact, Infoview provides only partial support for knowledge processing and knowledge management. The greatest part of this support is in the area of knowledge processing of structured information. Support for generating unstructured knowledge claims is minimal. Further, this conclusion also applies at both the organizational knowledge-processing and individual and group learning levels. Further, as indicated in (4) above, there is also little support for knowledge claim validation.

Cognos UpFront

Cognos and Business Objects are direct competitors. So it is not surprising that Cognos offers a decision-processing portal focused on an end-to-end total BI solution. The portal system with Cognos UpFront as its portal gateway and single point of access to both BI and non-BI content includes ad hoc query, analysis, merged report, visualization, score-carding, and key performance indicator (KPI) capability (Cognos, 2002). The steps in the end-to-end solution include: data mart creation, metadata delivery, building BI content with data mining, OLAP, and other proven BI servers as well as deploying such BI capability and access to it across and beyond the enterprise.

Navigation in Cognos UpFront is provided by "an intuitive user interface" employing hierarchical news indexes displayed in shared and personal news boxes (Cognos, 2002a). The shared news boxes can be assigned to individuals based on their roles using metadata about BI content. The user interface supporting navigation is composed of customizable HTML and XML templates. The portal configuration can be highly personalized (Cognos, 2002b). The basic portal look-and-feel may be personalized in terms of content, colors, placement of windows and content panes, etc. Customization possibilities also include more advanced options such as time zones and language.

UpFront provides "zero-footprint" Web deployment (Cognos, 2002c) and also claims impressive enterprise scalability through a distributed but logically integrated network of servers. The servers also supply enterprisewide security for the portal system and a single, consolidated view of the BI content of the enterprise. Upfront also supplies centralized administration of the scalability, security, access, and integration aspects of the portal.

Cognos UpFront does not provide much support for collaboration (Cognos, 2002d). Reports or analyses may be shared easily, and users can publish OLAP reports, visualizations, cubes, ad hoc queries, and any URL that can be accessed from a browser, from any Cognos client. But project management functions, collaborative data analysis, prioritization, problem solving, and other team and community functions are not strongly supported without integration of external applications.

While Cognos is primarily focused on BI, it does provide an open XML API for integrating other applications (Cognos 2002e). Cognos has strategic alliances with: Corechange (Cognos 2001) to deliver wireless portal access, Bowstreet (Cognos, 2001a) to deliver its process-oriented eCRM, eSCM, syndicated store fronts, and Web business portal applications, and Plumtree (Cognos, 2001b) to integrate Cognos's end-to-end BI solution into the Plumtree portal content-management environment.

Cognos UpFront is a capable, portal-based interface to an end-to-end BI solution provided by Cognos. It does not, however, provide more than basic capability in managing content. It does not support collaboration, document and content management, communities of practice, enterprise application integration, workflow, expertise location, or advanced collaborative processing. It also does not support knowledge claim validation, provides minimal support for individual and group learning, for knowledge processing of unstructured information, and for the various knowledge-management activities such as leadership, knowledge processing, crisis handling, and resource allocation. Instead, it is a portal product focused on managing structured data for classical decision support. It does that well, and also provides a means to integrate other applications through its XML interface.

Conclusion

Decision-processing portals constitute a category whose members are vanishing rapidly. While this was a popular starting place for companies entering the portal space, many of the original entrants have moved on to other categories. Moreover, the Cognos and Business Object offerings are clearly defensive offerings designed to meet customer requests for a portal interface to the excellent BI products of these two companies. The need for these interfaces is not entirely clear, because their BI functionality can be accessed through the "portlet," "gadget," or "widget" capabilities of other portals. Therefore, it's unlikely that these products will prove viable without further evolution through development of strategic alliances with other vendors. Indeed, as I write this, Business Objects and Knowledge Management Software have announced an alliance (KMWorld, 2002) to allow Business Objects to offer access to both structured and unstructured information through its portal, suggesting that it will soon join earlier migrants from the decision-processing portal category to the decision-processing/content-management category.

References

Business Objects (2002). "Business Objects Infoview," at www.businessobjects.com/infoview.html.

Business Objects (2002a). "Web Intelligence: An Integrated Web Solution," at www.businessobjects.com/web01.htm.

Cognos (2002). 'Upfront," at www.cognos.com/products/upfront/index.html.

Cognos (2002a). "Navigation," at www.cognos.com/products/upfront/Cognosup_fabs_navigation.html.

Cognos (2002b). "Personalization," at www.cognos.com/products/upfront/Cognosup_fabs_personalization.html.

Cognos (2002c). "Enterprise Ready," at www.cognos.com/products/upfront/Cognosup_fabs_enterprise.html.

Cognos (2002d). "Collaboration," at www.cognos.com/products/upfront/Cognosup_fabs_collaboration.html.

Cognos (2002e). "Open, Customizable, Portal Environment," at www.cognos.com/products/upfront/Cognosup_fabs_open.html.

Cognos (2001). "Corechange and Cognos® team up to offer business intelligence over any wired or wireless device," at www.cognos.com/cognoscorechange_2001_01_23-cognos.pdf.

Cognos (2001a). "Bowstreet and Cognos® team up to offer portal-based data analysis and reporting," at www.cognos.com/ cognos071601_bowstreet_and_cognos.html.

Cognos (2001b). "The Plumtree Portal Network: Cognos," at www.cognos.com/ cognos datasheet.pdf.

KMWorld. "Blending KM and BI" *KMWorld*, 11, no. 2 (2002), p. 1.

CHAPTER 15

Content Management Portal Products

Introduction

Most of the portal products released either before or just after the first wave of enthusiasm after the Merrill Lynch Report on EIPs were actually what I have called content-management portals in Chapters 1 and 12. In Chapter 2, I defined content analysis and content management in the following way.

- *Content Analysis* is the transformation of unstructured content into data, information, or knowledge by describing it in terms of attributes of media objects, attribute structures, and rules relating attributes.
- *Content Management* is the process of organizing, directing, and integrating content analysis and distribution efforts aimed at producing or distributing data, information, or knowledge.

Content-management systems acquire, process, filter, analyze, and distribute previously "unstructured" internal and external media objects contained in diverse paper and electronic formats. They also archive and often restructure these media objects so they can more easily be retrieved and manipulated. And they store the resulting data, information, or knowledge in a corporate repository (either centralized or distributed). I will now review the following portal products that both embody this idea of content management and generally fit the profile of content management portals as specified in Table 12.2: Plumtree, Autonomy, Oracle, Enfish Enterprise, Netegrity, Citrix, Verity, Sun ONE, and CoreChange.

Plumtree

To the extent it may be said that a single company originated the enterprise portal space, Plumtree Software is that company. Its first portal release in 1998 preceded the Merrill Lynch report defining the EIP space and brought to the marketplace a Yahoo-like hierarchical navigation-enabled interface to content and data stores for both private and public enterprises. Since then, Plumtree has implemented a vision of a framework platform that integrates a wide variety of content, structured data, and applications at the level of the portal interface (portal interface integration). In the course of pursuing its vision, it has introduced, or popularized the following innovations in portal technology:

- Personalization
- Portal plug-ins or "gadgets" (called by others, "widgets," "portlets," "content delivery agents," etc.)
- Content and application syndication
- Parallel processing for portal information and application delivery
- Multi-tier portal architecture for load balancing and scalability

Let us now review each of these Plumtree innovations.

Plumtree innovations and architecture

The "second generation" of the Plumtree (1999) portal offered users the opportunity to personalize their portal pages. The personalization capability focused attention on the use of portals to support job roles of individuals, and personalization has now become a major requirement in portal installations as well as a major oft-cited benefit of portals.

Plumtree "gadgets" further contributed to the emerging picture of the portal as a generalized framework for supporting work. Gadgets are Janus-faced software plug-in components or modules that interface with various content sources and applications through appropriate connector code; they also communicate with Plumtree Portal Servers using XML or HTML over HTTP. In effect, they are object "wrappers" for information and/or applications. With the introduction of gadgets, it became feasible to develop portal frameworks incrementally and to think seriously about continuously enhancing the functionality of one's portal over time. This innovation, then, gave rise to the image of the ever-evolving portal system, a never-finished, almost organic application, growing and changing in response to changing user needs and understanding.

While most portal vendors have followed Plumtree's lead in offering gadget equivalents, no one is as active as Plumtree in encouraging and supporting third-party development of gadgets. Hundreds of gadgets have been developed for the Plumtree framework at this writing, thus creating the capability for third parties to develop portal solutions considerably beyond the content-management category of the basic Plumtree portal framework and its most frequently integrated gadgets.

Content and application syndication involves publishing gadgets on a schedule to secure Web sites that are, in turn, subscribed to by users. Each syndication site has is own security profile and is keyed to a single subscribing Web site or device. Its content and applications are periodically syndicated to its subscribers in a format and configuration appropriate for their portal configurations. Syndication provides Plumtree with the capability to quickly distribute portal framework configurations to new portal users and to different types of portal display devices including telephones and mobile portal devices. In more general terms, syndication allows Plumtree gadgets to be widely distributed very quickly throughout an enterprise.

Plumtree (2000) promotes its introduction of the massively parallel portal engine (MPPE) very heavily. Plumtree (2001, p. 6) calls attention to two scalability problems. The first is caused by the fact that in most portal architectures plug-in modules execute serially on the portal server when they are being embedded in the Web page and do not take advantage of distributed computing resources in the portal systems architecture. It also claims (p. 6), second, that serial architecture in which gadgets are executed on the Web server also has a serious fault-tolerance problem, because an application that develops a problem interacting with a back-end data or content source can freeze the portal server and prevent end users from accessing the portal at all.

Plumtree goes on to point out that MPPE solves these problems by implementing "HTTP as a high speed, server-to-server communication system," (2001, p. 7), and by employing "connection pooling to support many simultaneous connections between the Plumtree web server and other servers." These changes make it possible to move gadget services off the portal (Web) servers and on to physically distributed gadget servers, which may even be the application servers in the system themselves. And this move allows the Web servers to make requests of the gadget servers in parallel and the gadget servers to compute results in parallel. When the gadget servers return the results to the Web server, these are then assembled by the Web servers and sent as HTML and XML to browsers. MPPE also automatically balances processing loads among gadget servers.

Plumtree's claims for MPPE have been minimized by its competition, mainly through circulating the view that loads on portal servers can be handled adequately by distributing processing across more portal servers, making MPPE an unnecessary feature. This argument may be credible at present when portal implementations tend to focus on static content and when applications integrated into portals are limited in scope and integrated only at the portal-interface level. But this is not the future of the portal. In that future, much greater emphasis will be placed on integrating applications both into the portal interface and into process implementations integrating different applications. This emphasis will place a very heavy processing load on even distributed portal servers, and the MPPE will then be a welcome addition to the processing capabilities of the portal system viewed as a whole.

Even before its addition of the MPPE to its product, Plumtree was involved in a long-term process of developing multi-tier portal architecture to provide load balancing and scalability in portal systems. The Plumtree design includes Web (portal) servers in the first tier. These control a network of job-processing servers and gadget servers in the second tier. The job-processing servers handle polling of data and content sources, publishing new content, and synchronizing the Plumtree User Directory with external directories. The gadget servers access a wide variety of content sources and applications, "wrap" the applications, and deliver their functionality to the Web servers. In the third tier are the application servers themselves, and the final tier is made up of data and unstructured content sources. An illustration of the architecture of a Plumtree portal system is provided in Figure 15.1.

The integration in the Plumtree architecture is focused on the front end of the portal system. It is integration among the Web servers, the job-processing servers, and the gadget servers. But it does not address the problems of integration among the gadgets or the application servers themselves. Therefore, it is not integration aimed at the "islands of information" problem, but only integration applying to the portal interface and specifically to the problem of assembling

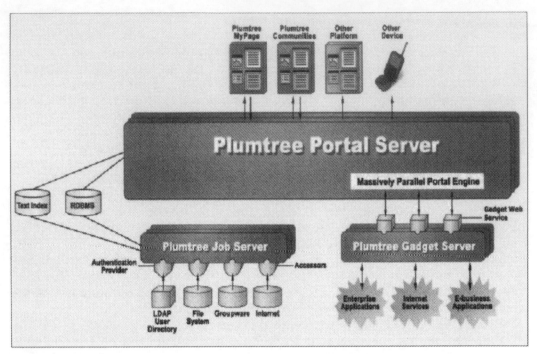

Figure 15.1. Plumtree corporate portal architecture. (Source: Plumtree Software, Inc. [2002] at www.plumtree.com.)

content and applications for delivery to the pages comprising the portal presentation layer. That is, it is one of the prime examples of PAC architecture.

More Plumtree features

Plumtree provides the full-range of features required for a content-management portal. A list of features is provided in (Plumtree, 2000, pp. 32–37), which includes full-text network searching; up to six MyPages for personalization (ibid. p. 31); an embedded search engine (Verity's), providing Boolean, proximity, fuzzy, linguistic stemming and advanced metadata searching; crawlers that scan repositories looking for new documents to index; automated filtering, routing, and classification; workflow-enabled content approval, single sign-on (SSO); lightweight directory access protocol (LDAP) integration for authentication, synchronization, and personalization; XML messaging and rendering; role-based distributed administration and content management; and the ability to assign new users and targeted communities default profiles (invitations) and, therefore, role-based portal installations.

Plumtree is not a collaborative portal, but in addition to the above features it also delivers (Plumtree, 2002) a gadget for threaded discussions, an OurPage for communities, creation and distribution of task lists, and a document-sharing facility with check-in and check-out. While this is far from the full set of features specified for collaborative portals in Table 12.2, it provides a foundation for augmenting it with other gadgets to approach the collaborative portal type more closely.

Vision and direction of Plumtree

The strategic direction of Plumtree seems increasingly clear. It is to clearly define a sophisticated, flexible, highly scalable and *open* front-end portal system platform component with excellent search, navigation, and security and access capabilities. Plumtree's product is increasingly a framework in which desired functionality of all types—with the exception of content-management functionality related to information acquisition and including EAI functionality—is provided by third parties. Plumtree therefore emphasizes the MPPE engine for scaling gadget integration and processing; syndication, its methodology for arriving at portal solutions and developing and maintaining taxonomies; and its rapidly growing network of strategic allies and gadget providers. It does not emphasize technological innovations in other areas.

Plumtree's strategy is a generic one that characterizes a class of content-management portal vendors. In it, the company relies on other vendors and on trends in the marketplace to fill out its offerings and give strength to its solutions. It is an appropriate strategy for a small startup whose resources are limited compared with many of the more recent entrants into the portal space.

"Touch points" with knowledge processing and knowledge management

Plumtree's Corporate Portal supports information acquisition well with its integration of Verity's search-and-retrieval technology. However, its direct support for other areas of knowledge processing and knowledge management is less impressive. Or perhaps I should say that such support is indirect through the openness of the Plumtree architecture and is dependent on gadgets supporting individual and group learning, knowledge claim formulation, and knowledge claim validation that may be integrated into Plumtree solutions.

Therefore, when you begin with the Plumtree platform, you begin with little native knowledge-processing and knowledge-management capability other than information acquisition and content-management capability. To move beyond that point to knowledge-processing and knowledge-management functionality, much must be added in the areas of analytical, collaborative, and problem-solving gadgets as well as gadgets not yet available that support knowledge claim validation.

Autonomy

The name Autonomy is synonymous with an automated approach to content categorization, updating, aggregation, navigation, management, and delivery. Autonomy's (2002) offering in the portal space is called "Portal-in-a-Box."™ In the content-management portal category, its approach to category formulation, based on automated analysis of text and continuous human work input, is in sharp contrast to Plumtree's human judgment stakeholder-based approach to defining roles and categories.

1. In effect, Plumtree and most other portal vendors are claiming that the category scheme that should serve as the basis for content classification

and hierarchical navigation can be developed only through knowledge production, where the knowledge involved (i.e., the category scheme to be used for the portal) is formulated and validated by humans. On the other hand, Autonomy is claiming that automated computer processing of continuous human work inputs (documents, e-mails, etc.) can produce a valid categorization scheme and can do so much more effectively and efficiently than a manual, human judgment–based administrative process.

2. On the surface, Plumtree's claim is accepted by many as having greater plausibility, whereas Autonomy's is viewed skeptically. But that segment of the portal market that is interested in avoiding heavy administrative costs in portal maintenance welcomes the Autonomy portal "solution." Other companies are very interested in Autonomy's concept extraction and search technology and frequently incorporate it in portal systems using other portal front ends (as I will indicate later in this survey). In short, they try to implement a portal solution that combines the strengths of the manual and automated approaches.

Autonomy features

1. Autonomy's portal offering is very feature-rich. It provides automated content aggregation and management, "intelligent" navigation and presentation, personalization, information delivery, interface management, internationalization and globalization, and extensibility.

2. By "automated content aggregation and management," Autonomy is referring to its automated scanning, concept extraction, and categorization of documents and content (optional functionality). According to Autonomy (2002a), the portal can assimilate content from any information source (optional functionality), structured or unstructured, can be integrated with any existing infrastructure and system, and can provide "support for existing security models and systems in major repositories."

3. To accomplish all this, it employs (Autonomy, 2002a) Web spiders for retrieval of content; an import module; a content retrieval and hyperlink query engine; an aggregator that extracts key concepts from documents, eliminates duplicates, and performs other essential tasks' and an auto-indexer with a polling mechanism, content filtering, batch processing, and support for multiple job processing. The hyperlink query engine has a number of notable characteristics including natural language, Boolean, proximity, agent, wildcard, fuzzy (Cox, 1995) and concept querying.

4. "Intelligent" navigation and presentation includes (Autonomy, 2002a) hierarchical directories whose categories are populated automatically, and (Autonomy, 2002b) 7,500 predefined Web or news channels (easy to navigate directories) supplying changing content that is populated automatically with new documents. It also includes automatic hyperlinking (creating hypertext links to content), automatic summarizing of concepts and context, and retrieval using natural language, conceptual or key word search, a "more like this" feature, and a refinement by example feature.

5. Personalization (Autonomy, 2002a) includes automatic user profiling based on analysis of browsing and content consumption of knowledge workers. This eliminates the need to survey users or have them fill in forms, or to infringe on their privacy. Personalization features also include personalized splash pages and agents that monitor knowledge workers' input to a list of content sources feeding their portal pages. The agents automatically create "personalized reports" of developments relevant to a knowledge worker's interests and role, and they alert knowledge workers by e-mail to new content matching their interests (optional functionality). Personalization also encompasses creating "virtual communities" by first matching users' interest profiles and then supplying the necessary information to them to let them find one another.

6. Information delivery refers to automatic delivery of personalized information. Autonomy provides for such delivery using any of the various types of delivery mechanisms available to the portal. Interface Management includes user access through single sign-on (SSO) "against LDAP compliant, Notes, NT, Novell, UNIX, Exchange or built-in user directories" (Autonomy, 2001). It also includes the ability to broadly customize the portal interface to create a consistent look-and-feel. Internationalization/Globalization refers to Autonomy's capability to process and cross-link to and from content in more than twenty languages.

7. Extensibility refers to Autonomy's capability to add products to the portal. These products and features include

   - Support for wireless protocols
   - Automatic alerting to new content relevant for users
   - Autonomy automatic categorizer
   - Automatic XML tagging with the Autonomy XML engine (AXE)
   - Navigator (category management and retrieval system)
   - Visualizer (a Java applet for graphical navigation through the portal)
   - Active Service (a plug-in module providing automatic hypertext links from the content of the current user task to related information. Autonomy uses ActiveKnowledge™ or Kenjin™ as the plug-in)
   - Automatic targeted advertising (refers to automatically personalizing advertising or announcements to user profiles)
   - Distributed search (distributed across all content sources, uses all Autonomy navigation and personalization features and provides for load balancing)
   - Integration with other Autonomy products and partners' solutions (occurs through Autonomy content infrastructure (ACI) application compliance) (Autonomy, 2001a, 2001b).

Autonomy in perspective

The features of Autonomy are impressive and powerful and its approach to portal content management is a credible alternative to the Plumtree approach. Yet in evaluating Autonomy against other EIP products there are at least three main issues to keep in mind.

First, the issue of human as opposed to automated construction of the portal category scheme remains a significant one. In deriving a portal navigational category scheme automatically, Autonomy both produces a knowledge claim (again a category scheme derived from automated content analysis is a knowledge claim), and also *validates* that claim according to the rules programmed into the software. Autonomy makes clear that these rules are derived from Bayesian statistics and information theory and that the categorizations are produced through Bayesian adaptive modeling ("adaptive probabilistic concept modeling" (APCM)). However, there is no widespread acceptance among scientific investigators (or any other kind for that matter) that the theory of category scheme production through utilizing APCM is at all valid. The idea, that is, on which the use of Autonomy as a portal is based, is only an unsubstantiated theory about how one arrives at useful portal categories and how one validates those categories. Even the basic assumption that category systems and other knowledge claims can be validated by recourse to automated application of rules is currently controversial. Thus, it is indeed amazing that Autonomy has had such a friendly reception without having to demonstrate or validate the effectiveness of its theory of category discovery.

In saying the above, I am not claiming that Autonomy does not produce categorizations of use in portal navigation. That is not the issue. Rather, the issue is whether its categorizations are useful in the sense that they produce navigational schemes that really work for people in their job roles better than the alternative schemes that result from human-based categorizations. This issue is not being raised in a rhetorical fashion. On the contrary, it cuts both ways. The portals that use human judgment–based categorizations have also not proved their validity in comparison with the Autonomy approach. Perhaps buyers considering and selecting portal tools should keep in mind that neither approach is well-validated.

Second, in addition to the big issue of whether Autonomy categorizations really work, there is an issue regarding the portal's extensibility. Though Autonomy's product is highly extensible with respect to content, it is not as extensible as other portal products in the area of "gadgets," "widgets," "portlets," "plug-ins," etc. While other portal products can easily "wrap" applications and access them from the portal interface, Autonomy does not offer "plug-ins" except for those produced by itself or by OEMs who have created applications compliant with Autonomy's content infrastructure. Therefore, Autonomy cannot fulfill the vision of the portal as the hub of all enterprise data, information, knowledge, and applications. Even if its machine-based categorizations do turn out to be useful, its portal product can still not fulfill the role of a generalized front end to the portal system, or of a foundation for incremental development toward a portal solution that will synthesize the capabilities of decision processing, content management, and collaborative portals and develop past them toward the comprehensive knowledge-processing portal.

Autonomy's current inability to plug in structured data applications has an implication, further, with respect to scalability. Autonomy is highly scalable with respect to its content-management functions and the plug-ins it supports. But there is no scalability issue with "gadgets" in general, since Autonomy does not provide the capability to plug in arbitrary gadgets. So the scalability issue for Autonomy is different from the scalability issue for other portals employing a more open model of application integration.

Third, it is an implication of the second issue that Autonomy provides another example of PAC portal architecture, since if there is only limited capability to interface additional applications to the infrastructure it follows that their integration is beyond the capability of the portal. In short, Autonomy does not begin to solve the islands of information problem.

Vision and direction of Autonomy

Although Autonomy has released a portal product, the vision of the company seems more oriented toward supporting other portal vendors with Autonomy technology than toward developing its portal product as a dominant portal vendor. Many other vendors have incorporated Autonomy search, categorization, and navigation technology. And in the context of developing portal solutions Autonomy is sometimes added to portal systems already using manual categorization capabilities and Verity technology in order to provide "concept-based" searching and retrieving. Since to compete as a first-line portal vendor it will be necessary for Autonomy to develop a more open infrastructure for integrating third-party gadgets and also third-party EAI tools, it seems likely that the company will choose instead to continue to focus on development of its core technology and, increasingly, to develop its business as a support for other portal vendors.

"Touch points" with knowledge processing and knowledge management

Autonomy's search, retrieval, navigation, concept extraction, and automated taxonomy capabilities strongly support automated information acquisition. But it is striking that even though Autonomy is one of the portal products most closely identified with knowledge processing and knowledge management, it does not seem to touch the value networks of knowledge processing and knowledge management at many other "touch points." It provides some support for knowledge claim formulation, but not much for individual and group learning. It attempts to provide automatic validation of taxonomic knowledge through application of Bayesian decision algorithms, but it does not provide support for developing alternative validation rules. Nor does it provide support for human inputs into the validation process, or for the human conflict and collaboration processes that underlie it. In short, it does not provide support for the full spectrum of problem-solving steps, and it does not provide support for the various activities and transactions in the value network of knowledge management.

Oracle9*i*AS portal

Oracle is a relative latecomer to the portal marketplace. The product strategy it selected was not to produce a "me too" product, but rather to introduce a kind of "do-it-yourself" portal framework for building e-business portal applications from previously existing and newly created components that are, nevertheless, very closely identified with its own database and application server platform. Thus, Oracle9*i* Application Server Portal (Oracle9*i*AS Portal) (Oracle, 2002) enforces the application logic, generates the user interface (dialogs, wizards, etc.) and manages all user operations and user-entered data). It is implemented as an integrated service within Oracle9*i* Application Server, along with Oracle9*i*AS single sign on services (user authentication, user management, and single sign on (SSO)), and

Oracle HTTP Server (middle-tier Web communication services). The integrated portal service provides tools for building portal pages out of *portlets*. A portlet is defined as a

- "Reusable information component" that "summarizes, promotes, or provides "basic access to an information source within a defined area of a Web page" (Oracle, 2001, p. 5)
- "Standardized and secure object" composed of PL/SQL procedures or a Java or other servlet that (a) executes on a server and (b) produces a live area of HTML or XML/XSL within a Web page when the procedure or servlet is called and the page is assembled (ibid.)

Any Oracle9*i*AS Portal implementation is nothing but a collection of portlets for accessing information and bringing it into a user's personalized portal. So building a portal implementation is a process of selecting, constructing, adding, and organizing portlets within portal pages. These pages are divided into regions, and one or more portlets may be added to each region.

To add portlets, however, an entity that "owns" the portlet(s)—that is, a portlet provider—must first be created and then registered in Oracle Portal. "A portlet provider is a Java class, or PL/SQL package that exposes a data source or application to Oracle Portal through one or more portlets." (Oracle, 2002a). It (1) "provides a communication link between the portal services and portlets," (2) "implements session startup and provider login," (3) "acts as a proxy to all portlet calls," and (4) "manages the portlet repository list." (ibid.) In other words, a portlet provider is a component that packages portlets and mediates between them and portal services.

An example of a portlet provider is a business intelligence application that incorporates a number of reporting and analytical portlets. A second example is a collection of portlets all accessing related content delivery services. Yet another example is the basic Oracle Portal product itself. All Oracle Portal product features are exposed as portlets, including Oracle Portal security, administration, application building, and self-service publishing.

Variety of Oracle portlets and variations in Oracle portal functionality

Since Oracle Portal is a framework for portlets, almost all of its functionality is provided by them, and individual Oracle Portals may vary widely depending on the portlets incorporated in each. This means that personalization within a single company can, theoretically, result in widely varying portal visualizations across individuals and groups. It also means that Oracle Portal visualizations may vary greatly from company to company in the access they provide to functionality.

Oracle has created a library of portlets it calls the Portlet Repository (Oracle, 2002a). The repository is refreshed periodically, and its list of portlets is updated with newly added or deleted ones. All Oracle Portal authorized users have access to the repository, which contains three classes of portlets.

- Bundled portlets—These are (Oracle, 2002a) portlets that are delivered with Oracle Portal as a foundation. They include development tools for creating new portlets; new portal pages; content areas and applications; administrative portlets for managing users, their accounts, and their profiles; global settings and defaults; monitoring portal activity; managing metadata; creating role-based portal configurations; database administration; and establishing community groups, and end-user portlets such as those for searching, saving search criteria, storing/retrieving frequently accessed URLs, accessing external applications, and publishing content.

- Partner portlets—These are portlets created by Oracle Partners (ibid.). The list here is long (See the various partner pages at Oracle's (2002) Web site), and includes: business intelligence (Business Objects Documents), search (Alta Vista, Autonomy, Inktomi, Northern Light, Open Text, Verity, YellowBrix), document management and "knowledge management" (Northern Light Federated Search, Open Text collaboration, project collaboration, news channels, PiroNet Probase, Verity Knowledge Organizer/Taxonomy selector, WebPE Property Management, Technical Skills Inventory), and collaboration (eCal ASP Event Server, Calendar, Open Text Livelink Discussions, Tasks and Inbox, SiteScape Collaboration Summary and Calendar, Webex Communications My Meetings, Zaplel Portal Appmail service for Process Collaboration).
- Custom portlets—These are portlets (Oracle, 2002a) that are created to fulfill specific needs not addressed by the other two classes of portlets. There are two ways to create custom portlets. First, Oracle Portal's Publishing Services (e.g., components, dynamic pages, and content areas) can be used to build new portlets by capturing, manipulating, and displaying portlet data or by publishing content area objects such as folders and categories to the portal. Oracle calls these "Built-in Portlets." Second, you can program new portlets using published APIs and the Oracle Portal Development Kit (PDK).
- The PDK supports two types of programmatic portlets. There are database portlets and Web portlets. Database portlets are produced by writing stored procedures executable in the Oracle Database in PL/SQL or Java. Web portlets are produced by using any Web development environment. They are executed on application servers and are called using HTTP.

Oracle's portal architecture

Oracle9*i*AS Portal systems use a three-tier architecture (Oracle, 2001, p. 51). The first tier is the Web browser. The middle tier contains application servers, including the Oracle9*i* Application Server, which hosts portal services, single sign-on, and HTTP services. Other application servers may be third-party servers that communicate with the portal over HTTP. The back end of this architecture is the Oracle database, which runs the stored procedures necessary to generate the portal. Oracle describes (ibid. pp. 52–53) the pattern of operation of the portal architecture as follows.

- User types in URL, browser issues HTTP request to specified server.
- When Oracle HTTP Server receives a request, it translates it and issues a call to Oracle9*i*AS Portal procedures stored within the Oracle database serving the portal.

- The database then (ibid.) "retrieves page definition metadata and user defined customizations. If required, a call is issued to one or more providers that passes user identity information. This information is used by the provider to establish any session information it needs for this user, including the issuing of a cookie, if necessary."
- Logic in parallel page engine accepts and inspects page definition. It then issues portlet show requests, in parallel, to portlet providers. The calls may be database procedure calls to a local or remote Oracle9iAS Portal node or HTTP requests containing callouts to provider methods.
- Providers return portlet output to parallel page engine. Parallel page engine accepts portlet output and composes a single page merging results. Page content is sent to the browser.
- If user clicks links within the portlet, browser sends cookies set in the previous request.
- If URL requires authorization (a non-partner application or an application in a different domain), provider may re-direct the request to the Login Server for authentication.

This account of Oracle's architecture makes clear the similarity between the architecture of Oracle9iAS Portal systems and that of the Plumtree portal in at least three respects. First, there is the similarity of gadgets to portlets. Both products rely on "plug-ins" for functionality. Second, Plumtree's MPPE works in a manner similar to Oracle's parallel page engine in that it issues calls and receives results of portlet processing on other application servers and back-end databases in parallel. However, Oracle's parallel-page engine appears not to balance processing loads among application servers executing portlet functionality as does the MPPE. Third, both products, in spite of their evident scalability, are still instances of passive access to content (PAC) architecture (See Chapter 5). That is, they both provide integration of portal information and applications in the portal interface but do not address the islands of information problem at the business process automation or workflow levels.

Oracle's vision and direction

In some ways the approach to the market taken by Oracle is quite similar to Plumtree's. There is the same concern to provide basic functionality to users that is readily customizable, while also taking care to provide an architecture that third parties can supply gadgets—or in this case, portlets—for, so that the vision of the EIP as a single point of access to all information and applications in the enterprise or in the e-business system may be realized. There is also the same concern to supply a secure and highly scalable and distributed portal platform that can handle the growing processing load accompanying the growing number and sophistication of gadgets or portlets integrated into the portal.

But Oracle's orientation is somewhat different from Plumtree's in a very important respect. While Plumtree is primarily a portal vendor and develops its portal product to allow as many third parties as possible to relate to it, Oracle orients its portal platform strongly toward its own application server and database platforms. So, in the end, it is closed to other database vendors and to corporations that have committed to other databases.

"Touch points" with knowledge processing and knowledge management

Considering the generic nature of the Oracle9iAS Portal, it is not surprising that little specific support for knowledge processing and knowledge management is provided by this product. Except for information acquisition, supported by the search, navigation, and categorization capabilities, there is little support for the other areas important to knowledge processing and knowledge management. Individual and group learning is not supported. Knowledge claim formulation and validation are not explicitly supported, and the various knowledge management activities remain unsupported. All support for knowledge processing and KM must be provided through the integration of appropriate "portlets." This does not mean that good KM solutions cannot be provided using this product. But users should be clear that the addition of knowledge processing and KM capabilities is a do-it-yourself integration into the portal framework activity. A specific knowledge processing or KM solution is not offered by Oracle.

Enfish Enterprise Portal (KnowledgeTrack) product

KnowledgeTrack, Inc. recently merged with Enfish, Inc. (Enfish, 2002). KnowledgeTrack's KnowledgeCenter, now called Enfish Enterprise Portal, was one of the first EIP products to enter the market. Enfish Enterprise now promotes its portal as a solution for supporting knowledge workers in performance of their job roles, and emphasizes its integration of personal desktop resources with enterprise and Internet resources and its support for collaboration. It attempts to differentiate itself from other portal products by emphasizing (Enfish, 2001d) its

- Powerful desktop component that makes available personal knowledge to the enterprise
- Integration of personal content, communities, and enterprise data
- Emphasis on the full-range of data and content sources for the portal rather than just legacy data
- Emphasis on personalization, e-communities, and collaboration
- Automatic delivery of relevant information to users in context.

"Enfish Enterprise *automatically* organizes and cross-references users' email, contacts, appointments, documents, favorite Web sites and enterprise data, regardless of the disparity of the data sources." (Enfish, 2001, p. 1). In doing this, Enfish claims that it is the first portal product that integrates the knowledge worker's personal computer with the enterprise portal. Enfish Enterprise places corporate, community, and Internet content in a common context and environment with knowledge workers' content. It enables the personalized and collaborative use of knowledge among employees, customers, and vendors. Here are Enfish Enterprise features (2002a) in more detail.

Personal information sources supported include: personal file and documents, e-mail messages, contacts, and Web sites. Workgroup information sources include shared documents on network drives, indexed workgroup community information (shared group calendar, discussions, projects, and tasks), and personal content on computers other than one's own without the need to go through servers. Enterprise information sources include the EIP itself, ERP, CRM, SCM, sales force automation (SFA), Web pages, data warehouses, newsgroups, Groupware databases such as Lotus Notes and Microsoft Exchange, and other enterprise applications and files (graphics, etc.) integrated into the portal. Enfish Enterprise indexes and manages information from all of the above sources.

Enfish Enterprise can index and manage virtually any type of data. Information about such data ("metadata" or "meta-information") is stored as XML schema. Document- and index-level security mechanisms restrict access to Enfish stores. Knowledge workers can find information through both full-text and metadata searches against Enfish Enterprise data and content sources

Community and collaborative features include self-publication of documents, shared information organized by topic, management of threaded discussions including filtering discussion content using criteria, creating new discussion threads, and directing user attention to the appropriate place when they join a discussion, setup of group tasks and meetings, synchronization of personal calendars and community calendars, and the ability to visit a "meeting room," and to participate in a virtual meeting. Technology features include integration with Web application servers to achieve scalability; role-based security and access; tight adherence to Web standards: compatibility with both UNIX and NT operating systems; and integration with almost any data and application source using Enfish Enterprise infomediary technology.

The Enfish Enterprise Infomediary (Enfish, 2002b) is the mechanism used by Enfish to integrate any source providing content, data, or documents with the portal. These sources include structured data, unstructured content, Web, and third-party application sources, and virtually anything that can provide information to the portal. The infomediary manages a collection of "Infoports" (Enfish's name for "gadgets" or "portlets"). It also provides the programmatic framework to create an infoport, and provides user interfaces for entering queries and HTML templates for specific infoports. The extensibility of Enfish Enterprise is based on the Infomediary's capability to integrate diverse and distributed content, data, and application sources through infoports.

Examples of Infoports used by Enfish Enterprise include

- Microsoft Index Server InfoPort—provides index and search capabilities
- Structured Data InfoPort—provides connectivity to any ODBC compliant data source.
- Enterworks InfoPort—provides access to more than seventy-five relational, hierarchical, flat-file, and network databases
- MoreOver.com InfoPort—delivers industry-specific news to the portal

Enfish Enterprise strongly supports portal interface personalization by letting users determine the content they want and the communities they will join. Users can control the type of content they want monitored, the news they will subscribe to, and the information sources they will access on a routine basis. In addition the taxonomy guiding their navigation of portal resources is automatically specified by Enfish Enterprise based on their usage patterns. Enfish Enterprise, like Autonomy, is a portal product that relies on automated content management rather than manual administration to maintain its taxonomy.

Enfish Enterprise architecture

The basis of Enfish Enterprise architecture is its portal server software. This server runs on both NT and UNIX platforms and on a variety of Web application server platforms. Like Plumtree, Oracle, Viador, and other portal servers, Enfish Enterprise supports distributed processing. Its integration with application servers allows it to take "advantage of application partitioning, multiple CPU systems, application server clusters, and multithreaded operating systems to maintain high availability through fault tolerance and load balancing (Enfish, 2002c). The combination of Web application server, portal server, and Infoports provides Enfish Enterprise with the basic capability described earlier to manage access and manipulation of a wide range of data and content sources. Enfish Enterprise, however, lacks a parallel page-processing engine to help its performance. Moreover, in Enfish Enterprise, we see another example of portal interface integration and PAC architecture. The islands of information that are plugged into the portal are integrated only within the portal interface through its taxonomy and by the humans using the portal system to access and manage content and to collaborate in problem solving. But the portal itself does not integrate back-end applications.

Enfish Enterprise vision and direction and "touch points" with knowledge processing and knowledge management

The merger with Enfish changed the vision of KnowledgeTrack from one oriented primarily toward enterprise content management and collaboration to one of a product that *claims* to synthesize personal knowledge processing, knowledge management, and desktop computing capability with enterprise-level collaborative knowledge processing and enterprise portal capability. It is the first portal product generally supporting the orientation expressed in Chapters 5, 6, and 13, in which the portal system includes individual-level knowledge producers whose emerging intellectual assets must then be integrated with enterprise-level content.

Enfish will not be alone for long in implementing the orientation of supporting individual/collective integration in an EIP or EKP. It is, after all, the interaction of the individual, community, and corporate levels that produces new knowledge in organizations, or, to place this in terms of the terminology of earlier chapters, the KLCs within organizations are nested and multi-level in character and feed one another in a complex interaction. New knowledge claims emerge from this "swirl." So it is important that EIP products support such interactions, and to do this, the knowledge products of the different levels must be placed in the context of one another. Again, Enfish is the first, but not the last, portal company to support this interaction.

Is Enfish Enterprise a content-management, collaborative, or knowledge portal? Though it exhibits certain characteristics in common with knowledge portals, it seems to be a content-management portal with collaborative characteristics, rather than a knowledge portal. Enfish would probably characterize its product as highly collaborative, but if we match the list of collaborative capabilities in Table 12.2 with Enfish Enterprise features, it is clear that only some collaborative characteristics are realized in this portal. In particular, prioritization, workflow, expertise location, project management, and other collaborative capabilities listed in Chapter 12 are not supported in the basic portal.

Moreover, Enfish does not support knowledge claim validation by tracking the history of knowledge claim testing and evaluation. In Enfish Enterprise, one can't distinguish between knowledge and information and track the meta-information that supports the distinction without considerable additional development and systems integration. Nor does Enfish support knowledge claim formulation with applications that support analysis of structured and unstructured data. Such applications may be added as InfoPorts, but this doesn't distinguish Enfish Enterprise from numerous other portals.

Finally, Enfish Enterprise does not support the various KM activities distinguished in Chapter 9. There are no leadership, crisis-handling, resource-allocation, bargaining and negotiation, or rule-changing applications included in Enfish Enterprise. So for this reason as well, one could not characterize it as an enterprise knowledge portal.

In sum, Enfish Enterprise, in common with other EIPs, supports information acquisition, integration of other applications, automated categorization, some collaboration, and multi-level integration of information across organizational levels of interaction. It also supports knowledge claim formulation and validation insofar as its good support for publishing and interaction through the portal supports these activities. But it does not support many of the collaborative activities identified in Chapter 12, or processes that track the formulation and testing of knowledge claims, or processes supporting analytical knowledge production activities, or those supporting KM activities. So its touch points with the knowledge and KM value networks are relatively sparse. To fulfill its vision, Enfish will have to increase the density of its touch points with these value networks.

Netegrity Interaction Server

Netegrity, Inc. recently acquired DataChannel, Inc., one of the early entrants into the portal marketplace, and one of its leading players in the area of XML-related functionality. Its initial market differentiator from other portal products was its ability to process XML and to use it to distribute and manage content. During the past two-and-a-half years however, DataChannel developed and Netegrity acquired a content-management portal platform that is one of the more advanced in the portal space, extensive enterprise application integration (EAI) capability, and a portal architecture that is scalable and extensible.

The Netegrity Interaction Server 5.1 is a portal server built on a (DataChannel, 2001, p. 2):

> . . . framework of modular components built with Java 2 Platform Enterprise Edition (J2EE) technologies. It is deployed on J2EE-compliant application servers, leveraging their strengths in performance and scalability, through segmenting and distributing functionality among clustered machines . . .

> DataChannel Server takes full advantage of the J2EE platform and technologies. It uses beans for system components, Java Naming and Directory Interface (JNDI) to address user and group management, Java Database Connectivity (JDBC) to interact with the server database, Java Message Service (JMS) to enable inter-object communication, Java Server Pages (JSP) for

user interface creation, and the Java Servlet API to integrate the system with a Web server.

Netegrity Interaction Server runs on Web application servers such as BEA Web Logic, IBM WebSphere, Iona iPortal Application Server, and Sun ONE Application Server. The portal interface is a canvas on which workspaces, which may be role, individual, or group-based, are placed. Portlets and content are then published to the workspaces. Netegrity Interaction Server (2001a, pp. 2-4) has the following features. In the area of integrated content management it has

- "Drag-and-drop content management," using a taxonomy-tree metaphor to create taxonomies
- End-user publishing
- Integrated search and indexing (through Convera [2002] search engine) supporting semantic networking and natural-language processing
- Version control
- Workflow creation and management
- Virtual taxonomy creation and management through use of topics expressed in XML representing virtual folders to which content can be assigned (Virtual folder/topics may be used to create any number of virtual taxonomies.)
- Event subscription and notification
- Scheduled availability of content or users
- Document life cycle management
- The ability to easily integrate Documentum, Interwoven, or other content-management applications as portlets

In the area of comprehensive application integration, the features of Netegrity include

- Application portlets integrating enterprise applications such as Seibel, SAP, Lotus, and PeopleSoft
- An EAI Adapter providing access to more than seventy-five enterprise applications
- Support (a "Web Services Wizard") for Web Services, Web Parts and Web Services Definition Language (WSDL) that can integrate "next-generation Web applications and external content"
- The ability to wire portlets together to create inter-portlet integration
- EAI framework administrative tools, and
- A shared object repository database (SORD) (DataChannel, 2001b) for caching data from enterprise applications, a local repository for data published to the EAI platform, maintaining transactional integrity between portal and EAI layers, filtering data, and other features

In the area of rapid deployment features of DataChannel it offers

- Simplified installation
- Predeveloped enterprise application, collaboration tools, and Internet content source portlets

- Workspace templates for creating role-based workspaces
- Portlet generation wizards for creating EAI, Web Services, and application portlets
- Workspace Publisher with a drag-and-drop interface
- Bulk publishing for populating new taxonomies and placing multiple documents in the content repository at once

In the area of enterprise-class scalability and administration features of Netegrity Interaction Server include

- J2EE architecture
- Advanced clustering for distributing server loads
- Parallel-page composition engine
- Functional segmentation separating front-end and out-of-band functions
- Administrative delegating to others of specific areas of portal pages
- Delegated administration among organizational groups
- LDAP integration

In the area of development tools provided by Netegrity are

- Standards-based design incorporating JSP, JMS, and LDAP
- Portlet wiring tools for creating new portal process applications by linking existing portlets together
- Software development kit for adding portlets to Netegrity Interaction Server

In the area of portlets currently available for Netegrity, there are applications in

- Content management
- Document management
- Business intelligence
- E-mail
- Calendaring
- Groupware
- Collaboration
- Search
- News
- Stock
- Weather
- Productivity tools
- EAI tools

In the area of security and access provided by Netegrity (2001), features include single sign-on (SSO) and authentication capability provided by integration with Netegrity's (2002a) SiteMinder™ 4.5.

Netegrity architecture

Netegrity architecture is different from the now familiar pattern of PAC architecture already seen with Plumtree, Oracle, Enfish Enterprise and other portal products reviewed thus far. Figure 15.2 illustrates the architecture with Netegrity's (2002, p. 2) own image.

Given that Netegrity's is a very comprehensive portal architecture, in many ways similar to Plumtree's and Oracle's, the most important difference in Netegrity architecture from other content management portals is in its EAI and Web Services framework and connectivity. Both make it easy to interface the kind of AIM or AKM business process engine discussed in Chapters 5, 6, 10, and 13. Netegrity is a very short step away from having an AIM server (though not its intelligent agents) integrated within its portal system; thus, with the EAI and Web services frameworks it has taken a step beyond PAC architecture, though without reaching either DCM or PAI.

The architectural picture in Figure 15.2 does not make explicit the parallel-page composition engine, an important feature similar to capabilities found in Plumtree and Oracle. It also does not make explicit a very important innovative feature—"portlet wiring." Portlet wiring (DataChannel, 2001c) is among the first attempts to build support into a portal product for integrating portlets and solving the new version of the "islands of information" problem manifest in PAC portal architecture. Portlet wiring is supported by the workspace publisher and by the EAI framework. It involves inter-object communication across portlet boundaries.

An instance of portlet wiring defines a part of a business process. For example, the sale of a commodity may require changes in sales order applications, billing and accounting applications, inventory applications, etc. If all of these are port-

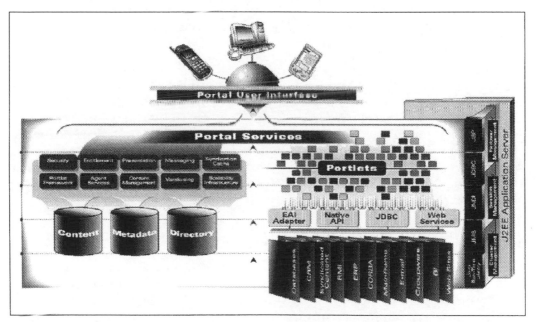

Figure 15.2. Netegrity architecture. (Source: Netegrity, Inc. [2002] at www.netegrity.com.)

lets, portlet wiring would involve linking the sale event to corresponding events represented in other applications. All the related portlets could be represented in the same workspace, and an entry in one of the applications would result in appropriate changes to all of the others with no need for further manual entry.

Netegrity vision and direction

Of all the content management portal vendors, Netegrity is one of a few that is most focused on integrating applications, data, and content across the enterprise. Its comprehensive focus on portal product development using Web standards such as XML, WSDL, and universal description, discovery, and integration (UDDI), its focus on Web Services, EAI, workflow management, and portal wiring indicates its awareness and determination to end the "islands of information" problem by integrating portlets around chunks of automation in business processes.

Projecting the use of Netegrity portlet wiring in enterprises, the result of using it would be the gradual creation of libraries of "processlets." These "processlets" might be created by many ad hoc creative efforts, or there might be planning processes applied to creating them. If ad hoc creation prevails, the inevitable outcome would be a tangle of processlets, largely unconnected to one another and perhaps introducing actual conflict in computational results, provided that different "processlets" are in logical conflict.

To prevent such a chaotic outcome, it will be necessary to develop a unified view of enterprise processlets and a rules-based inference engine for synchronizing processlets. This again brings one back to the need for an AIM, a construct that Netegrity, pushed by its portlet wiring innovation, is likely to evolve towards over time.

"Touch points" with knowledge processing and knowledge management

Netegrity Interaction Server 5.1 provides a platform oriented toward content management and EAI. It provides no support for any knowledge or knowledge-management activities beyond the support it provides for information acquisition. Unquestionably, the ability to integrate other applications into the Netegrity platform indicates that touch points with knowledge and knowledge-management value networks could certainly be developed. But as with the other portals reviewed earlier, creating such touch points is a matter of enhancement of the basic Netegrity capability, not a matter of activating capabilities already supplied with the portal.

Citrix (formerly Sequoia) XML Portal Server (XPS)

In the Spring of 2001, Sequoia Software, a pioneer in developing a content-management portal product employing XML to ease communication and content management, was acquired by Citrix Systems, Inc. (Citrix, 2001), a rapidly growing application server vendor. Sequoia had developed and marketed a portal product called XML Portal Server (XPS) (Sequoia, 2000). XPS, now called Citrix XPS, remains one of the leading portal products applying XML to content management and distribution and to portal processing.

In common with other portal products reviewed earlier, XPS emphasizes content aggregation and delivery, personalization (individual and role-based), searching, indexing, spidering, taxonomy creation and categorization, easy integration of software applications, and portal interface–based integration. In addition, it provides authentication and security, and content and metadata management. There are a number of more distinctive features to be highlighted however.

First, XPS (Sequoia, 2000, p. 7) calls its gadgets content delivery agents (CDAs). They should not be mistaken for software agents in the sense defined in Chapter 6. CDAs integrate both applications that have a Web interface and those, including legacy applications, that do not. Where there is a Web interface, CDAs provide a direct connection between the application and the user's desktop. Where there is no Web interface, CDAs connect content and applications through the Citrix XML Foundation Server (XFS) (Citrix, 2002), formerly called the Sequoia XML Application Server (XAS) (Sequoia, 2000, p. 4). Citrix CDAs connect a wide variety of applications to the portal. Some of these are: Exchange, Lotus, Siebel, SAP, Baan, Peoplesoft, Cognos, Actuate, Documentum, Filenet, PCDOCS, among many others. Most recently, Citrix has used CDAs to integrate the Business Objects Web Intelligence™ and Infoview™ applications I have reviewed earlier.

Though CDAs are like other portlets in that they provide a window to content, data, and applications, they are also different. The difference arises where the sources they communicate with can receive and interpret XML packets. Where this is the case, communication between the CDS and the source, through the CDAs and the XFS can be bi-directional, and this in turn opens the way for a higher level of interaction and collaboration among knowledge workers using the portal.

The second important feature of XPS is its use of two servers (Citrix, 2001a). It employs a portal or content delivery server (CDS) to perform content delivery services, and the XFS to perform middle-tier business integration and automation services. The CDS mediates between the portal desktop and both the XFS and the Web. It handles requests from Web servers or wireless access protocol (WAP) gateways. It also mediates between the portal desktops and those CDAs interfacing with the XFS. The CDS does the page rendering for the portal. In particular, it is through the CDS that CDAs are associated with particular portal pages and regions on a portal page.

The XFS is an application server with load balancing and distribution, fault tolerance, security, communications, data integration, and workflow/business process automation capabilities. The XFS mediates between non-Web application servers and CDAs. It also receives messages coming into the portal and mediates between CDAs and integration agents (IAs in Citrix terminology) that connect the data tier to the portal. The XFS is, in effect, an XML-based enterprise application integration (EAI) server bundled into the XPS. It will be described in more detail in the following section on architecture.

Third, XPS implements a messaging architecture based on XML and Microsoft Message Queuing (MSMQ). In this architecture, business objects, data, and XML metadata are encapsulated in XML envelopes by the XFS. XPS implements a rules engine that can interrogate these envelopes and also support workflow applications.

Fourth, XPS provides Smart Spiders™ that not only crawl and index metadata describing Web-based content, but in addition, spider and encapsulate as XML objects enterprise content and structured data sources in a wide variety of file formats.

Fifth, XPS also includes some collaborative capability. It includes message boards, real-time chat rooms, and voting capabilities. It also provides end-user publishing capabilities including versioning and check-in/check-out capabilities along with a repository with a WebDAV interface that supports Microsoft Office and other applications.

Citrix architecture

Comparing Citrix XPS architecture (see Citrix, 2001a, p. 3) with Netegrity Interaction Server architecture represented in Figure 15.2, the most obvious difference is the absence of a business process automation/workflow/integration server in Netegrity's product, and the presence of an EAI adapter implying the integration of a third-party EAI engine with Netegrity's product. This difference between the two architectural diagrams raises two questions: (1) can third-party EAI products be integrated with Citrix XPS? (2) whether they can or not, how adequate are the EAI capabilities of XFS compared to such third-party EAI products? In addition, a third question is suggested by the "portlet wiring" feature of Netegrity. How does the XFS EAI capability compare to Netegrity's capability in creating new "composite" CDAs or "portlets"?

The answer to the first question is inherent in the nature of XPS "integration agents." These are comparable to Netegrity "Adapters." They are created using XFS and are designed with standard XML interfaces. In other words, any EAI product can plug into the portal if it has an XML interface.

Second, though XFS has workflow, business process automation, and integration capabilities, it is not yet comparable in its development facilities, rules engine, object-modeling facilities, or template resources for rapid development with full-blown EAI products such as Vitria (2001), TIBCO (2001), or Level8 (2001). Even though Citrix XPS with XFS provides greater EAI capability than other portal products, the capability it offers is not comparable to the best EAI products. More important, it is not adequate to provide the object, component, workflow, business rule, and metadata management; distributed memory caching of objects; and synchronization services needed by AIM and AKM servers. Nor does it provide the fully articulated, reflexive object model and partial instantiation features of some EAI products.

Third, however, it is also clear that the integrative capability provided by XFS is much more flexible and comprehensive than that provided by the "portlet wiring" capability of Netegrity Interaction Server. You can do much more with XFS's workflow capability in creating new CDAs than you can with "portlet wiring." On the other hand, Netegrity's portlet wiring feature is one that can be used by power users whereas XFS's workflow feature is one that is better implemented by programmers.

Vision and direction of Citrix XPS

Before the acquisition of XPS by Citrix, the vision and direction of Sequoia was to combine the portal and EAI visions to create an application portal product that would not only deliver information and applications to the portal interface but also integrate them into new composite CDAs. The ultimate objective was to allow the construction of multipurpose portals that would transcend content management and create multipurpose portal solutions. In terms I have used in Chapters 5 and 12, Sequoia was committed to move away from PAC architecture and toward at least DCM architecture and perhaps beyond to PAI architecture.

The vision and direction of Citrix XPS, however, is not so clear. There is a strong emphasis on wireless applications and on e-business. In addition, the complete integration of Citrix's NFuse™ portal product with XPS is emphasized. But whether development efforts being planned by Sequoia to extend the integration and business process automation capabilities of XPS will be supported and implemented by Citrix is still to be determined. If this occurs, XPS will continue in its progression toward PAI architecture and in creating a technological foundation for advanced application portals. If not, XFS will gradually atrophy, CDS will be combined with Nfuse,™ and Citrix will integrate third-party EAI capabilities into solutions that require a closer approach to PAI architecture.

"Touch points" with knowledge processing and knowledge management

Citrix XPS, like Plumtree, Oracle, Netegrity and other platforms previously discussed, provides information acquisition and management capabilities. This product doesn't touch individual and group learning, knowledge claim formulation, knowledge claim validation, or most KM activities.

Verity Portal One™

Verity Portal One is a relatively late entry into the portal space. In late 1998 and 1999 Verity's involvement was through third parties such as Plumtree, Hummingbird, and others to which Verity supplied its search, spidering, and categorization technology. Verity's own "portal play" was released in June 2000 (Verity, 2000). It emphasizes content management features very heavily. And while its search, retrieval and categorization technologies work with structured, semi-structured and unstructured data or content, it does not easily integrate BI applications or offer the wide range of "portlets" or "gadgets" characteristic of other portal products.

Where Verity Portal One (Verity, 2002) does excel is in

- Personalization
- Search
- Navigation
- Intelligent classification of information
- Security
- Scalability
- Reliability

I discuss these in more detail subsequently.

Knowledge workers can personalize Verity Portal One by choosing the data, information, knowledge, applications, and categories they need to support their decisions and do their jobs. They can also customize both the layout and content the portal delivers to them. "Connectors," Verity's (2002) version of portlets, are made available to users by administrators, who also determine the scope of who they apply to and, in particular whether or not they are role-based.

Portal One's search features (Verity, 2000) are perhaps the most comprehensive available. They include: Boolean, fuzzy, proximity, zone-restricted, density, typo, frequency, field and concept. In addition, Verity Query Language (VQL) implements a decision algorithm for estimating the conditional probability that a document fulfills a query. The algorithm may implement criteria of relevance to users such as number of times a search term appears in a document, density of a search term, its proximity to other terms, metadata criteria, and others. VQL supports concept extraction through clustering of documents according to similarity, query by example (searching for documents similar to examples), and automated document summarization. It also supports fuzzy search.

Verity search technology is based on a full-text index of each document recorded in a "Verity collection" (Verity, 2000, p. 6). Each collection contains a word list of the contents of a document along with metadata about the document. Collections are nonintrusive—that is, the original documents remain in their location and with their original names. The collections, or indexes against which searches are executed, are separate from the original documents. Both structured and unstructured content are indexed in collections. The collections are then queried with VQL. Verity can search against and view some 250 file formats including PDF files, without opening the applications that were the original sources of the documents.

Navigation in Verity One uses hierarchical taxonomies (which it mistakenly refers to as "knowledge trees") assigned to individuals and roles. Earlier, I pointed out that portal products frequently differ in their approach to taxonomy construction and maintenance, with Plumtree providing a good example of the manual approach to taxonomy and Autonomy providing the most visible example of the automated approach. Verity combines both approaches in Verity Portal One, and so takes advantage of both the greater face validity of manual classifications and the utility and convenience of automated classification in suggesting and refining categories and classification rules. Verity's taxonomies and rules are developed using the following combinations of methods.

Verity Intelligent Classifier (Verity 2000a) provides (1) a graphical user interface for constructing manual taxonomies, (2) the capability to extract a taxonomy from URL paths or file paths, (3) the capability to fetch categories from metadata fields of a collection; and (4) the capability to generate a hierarchy from document clusters created by using Verity's clustering algorithm. All methods may be used in constructing a taxonomy.

Once a taxonomy is generated, classification rules are needed to apply it. When using Verity Portal One, you can (1) manually construct classification rules; (2) use Verity Intelligent Classifier to automatically generate classification rules from exemplary documents associated with categories of the taxonomy; and (3) refine classification rules interactively by providing feedback in response to results testing previously built rules. (Verity, 2000b, p. 9) You can also use any combination of these methods in developing a model for applying a taxonomy.

Because of the way it indexes content in collections, Verity Portal One also is able to provide unified access to multiple information sources. All sources aggregated into collections are searched and queried by Portal One as if they were in a single content warehouse, with all data and content "normalized" into the same format. Categories and classification rules can be developed and applied consistently across all Verity collections and derivatively on the information sources and applications on which the collections are based. It no longer matters whether the original sources were unstructured, semi-structured, or structured.

Portal One provides four levels of security:

- Access and submission rights (Access rights to content and application connectors may be granted or restricted on a per-user basis.)
- Collection-level security (Administrators may specify or restrict permissions to search against collections).
- Document and results-level security (This refers to authentication checks against the repository in which the document resides.)
- Category/results filtering (Here administrators can control whether a restricted document will appear in someone's search results.)

Scalability and reliability of Verity Portal One are a consequence of its architecture.

Portal One architecture

Verity's Portal One architecture is illustrated in Verity (2001). In this parallel, multi-tiered architecture, the portal server is connected to a layer of multiple "K2 brokers" and these brokers in turn distribute the search and query load across the multiple K2 servers operating in parallel. Verity claims that this architecture is linearly scalable (ibid. pp. 3, 6), and that one needs only to add knowledge brokers and K2 servers to maintain performance as the number of users increases. In addition, the architecture is fault tolerant, since if one of the servers or brokers goes offline, the system can keep functioning with the remaining brokers and servers.

While Verity's search and query architecture is impressive, its architecture for expanding portal functionality exhibits no special features. Connectors may be added to Verity Portal One solutions, but there are no special capabilities for facilitating their incorporation into the portal. In addition, Portal has no EAI capabilities, or, apparently, parallel-page engine capabilities for processing connector applications in parallel.

Vision and direction of Verity Portal One

Verity Portal One is an adaptation of the company's technology to produce a standalone portal offering. The search, taxonomy construction, categorization, navigation and other content management aspects of the portal are excellent. But the Verity vision doesn't extend to EAI or to a comprehensive architecture for integrating other applications into Portal One. Until it does, Verity will remain a portal solution focused on content and its management. It will not support BI and it will not provide substantial support for collaboration.

"Touch points" with knowledge processing and knowledge management

Verity claims that its taxonomies are "knowledge trees," and this raises the question of the relationship of Portal One to knowledge processing and knowledge management. Verity, along with other portals, supports information acquisition. In addition, in the area of taxonomy generation, Verity supports knowledge claim formulation with its facilities for both manual and automated taxonomy generation. However, Verity supplies no structure for either knowledge claim validation or for any of the activities of KM. In the end, Verity Portal One remains a content-management application. Its main competitor is Autonomy, and for the most part it is a collaborator rather than a competitor of other portal vendors.

Sun ONE Portal Server

Sun ONE Portal Server Enterprise Edition (whose name was recently changed from Sun iPlanet Portal Server Enterprise Edition), with some important unique aspects, presents the now familiar pattern described earlier in connection with products from Oracle and Netegrity. That is, the pattern of a portal server hosted by an applications server, relying on a wide range of open computing standards including Java, XML, HTTP and many others, and offering strong EAI capabilities. According to Sun Microsystems (2001):

> The iPlanet Portal Server: Enterprise Edition is a next generation portal platform, with enhanced scalability and a J2EE™ compliant application platform that features rich integration capabilities. Its robust design enables iPlanet Portal Server: Enterprise Edition to handle millions of users and transactions. Because it is based on the iPlanet Application Server, Enterprise Edition, iPlanet Portal Server: Enterprise Edition leverages an extensive list of features including:
>
> • Load balancing
> • Session failover
> • Transactional capability
> • Databased connection pooling.

In addition, Sun ONE Portal Server (Sun Microsytems, Inc. 2002) also offers the following portal services.

Membership management services

These include "community building" and policy management infrastructure.

Using Sun ONE Portal Server, an administrator "builds communities" by creating users, groups, roles, and domains. Sun ONE Portal Server supports multiple domains and delegated administrators for each domain. It also supports defining roles and groups for those domains in a hierarchical structure.

Sun ONE Portal Server also features an integrated Policy Manager. "The Policy Manager is a centralized location where an administrator (or delegated administrator) associates access rules with restricted objects and users, groups, roles, and domains." (Sun Microsystems, 2002). Thus, the Policy Manager enforces authorization to access a variety of object types associated with a user's role, group, domain, and user name.

Presentation services

These include support for a client platform with access to the Internet and a browser, channels, aggregation, personalization, security services, single sign-on, and integrated services.

A channel is the way a content provider delivers information to a client. A content provider interface (CPI) allows custom content providers to be integrated with the portal. "Channels" are Sun ONE's name for portlets or gadgets; the ability to integrate them into the portal makes Sun ONE functionality extensible. The channels on a user's desktop can represent a range of content providers, including

- Third-party brokered or syndicated content (e.g., news or stock quotes)
- Sun ONE Portal Server content
- URL scrapings
- Third-party applications content (e.g., Actuate or Epiphany applications)
- Direct access to intranet applications

Personalization services include the ability for administrators to stop channels from being deselected by users; the ability for users to choose optional channels; the ability to configure default views based on role, group, or domain; and user control over the portal display. Security services include the Sun ONE Portal Server authentication subsystem. Authentication methods include

- LDAP
- RADIUS
- NIS
- UNIX® (login and password)
- Secure ComputingSafeWord digital token
- Security Dynamics SecurID digital token
- Cryptocard, Inc. digital token
- S/Key one-time password (implemented on the Sun ONE Portal Server platform)
- JavaCard™ technology/Smartcard
- X509 Digital Certificates
- Microsoft Windows/ NT domain
- API to other customer authentication mechanisms

In single-sign on, if a user connects to an application or system, the Sun ONE Portal Server caches the username and password and automatically sends this information to other systems as the user accesses them. Single sign-on, further, leverages the session API of the Portal Server Platform. Through it, a custom internal application can participate in the portal server's authentication framework. The application can query the Sun ONE Portal Server Platform to derive the username, authorization level, and profile contents.

Integrated services are provided through the portal server's CPI. It allows deployment of applications in the portal interface. Examples include the following:

- Syndicated content

- HTML front ends to internal applications
- E-mail and/or calendar HTML front ends
- Document access through the Portal Netfile Application (Applet)
- External applications that can be integrated with the Sun ONE Portal Server
- Internal HTML front ends and Web sites for Web-based application access
- X11 and Microsoft Windows applications
- Mainframe and AS/400 applications.
- Content Management

Sun ONE Portal Server offers content-management solutions through Open Market Content Server Enterprise Edition (CSEE). Sun and Open Market (Open Market and Sun MicroSystems, 2002) are strategic allies, and both Sun ONE Portal Server and CSEE may be run on the Sun ONE application server platform. CSEE services are supplied to the portal through a channel.

Knowledge management

Sun ONE Portal Server Personalized Knowledge Pack™ (Sun Microsystems, 2002a) organizes documents automatically, allows users to subscribe to content, provides the capability to search by category, and enables users to collaborate on content. Personalized Knowledge Pack simplifies searches by providing the ability to construct category trees. Using these trees, automated searches may be carried out on general topics, not just specific words or phrases. PKP supports collaboration by enabling knowledge workers to comment on and discuss documents. They can also rate a document's importance and search based on document ratings. PKP is tightly integrated into Sun ONE Portal Server, in contrast to channels providing pluggable content.

Collaboration

The Instant Collaboration Pack (ICP) (Sun Microsystems, 2002b), a channel extension of Sun ONE Portal Server, provides reasonably extensive collaboration services. More specifically, the ICP provides instant messaging and chat for one-on-one communication and group collaboration, expertise location, virtual teams, file sharing, conferencing, polling, and team chats for project-based collaboration, Also available are news channels to access published information on a subscription basis, and integration with Sun ONE Portal Server to incorporate community management, single sign-on, and secure remote access capabilities.

Development and enhancement capabilities

Sun ONE emphasizes an "open tools" strategy for application development for the Sun ONE Application Server platform (Sun Microsystems, 2002c). Development can be performed with a number of toolkit options, as follows:

- Sun ONE Application Builder offers wizard-based development along with tight integration with the Sun ONE Application Server.

- An Integrated Development Environment (IDE), Forte for Java, Enterprise Edition, is supported. Forte features enterprise-class team development capabilities, including distributed debugging for large-scale application requirements and extensive EAI template support.
- Third party products, including WebGain Visual Cafe, IBM VisualAge, Macromedia DreamWeaver, and Inprise JBuilder plug into the Sun ONE Application Server architecture and may also be used for new application development and enhancement.

Architecture of Sun ONE Portal Server

Earlier I pointed out that Sun ONE exhibits the now familiar pattern of a portal server hosted by an applications server, relying on a wide range of open computing standards including Java, XML, HTTP and many others, but in Sun ONE's case offering strong EAI capabilities. The specific architecture of Sun ONE portal systems is illustrated in Figure 15.3.

The biggest difference between a Sun ONE platform and portal solution and the Oracle, Enfish Enterprise, Citrix, and even Netegrity solutions is the additional capability provided by Sun ONE Application Server in the area of additional EAI features of Sun ONE Portal Systems. Specifically, the Sun ONE Application Server solution provides the ability to automate business processes and business logic across both J2EE application servers and enterprise legacy systems. Sun ONE Process Manager is a Web-based solution for designing, deploying, and managing business processes on the Sun ONE Application Server. Integration with multiple back-end information systems is provided by the Unified Integration Framework, along with Enterprise Connectors that extend the application and data assets for ERP environments into dynamic Web services.

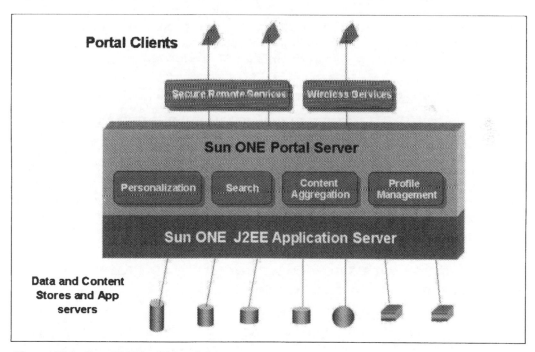

Figure 15.3. Sun ONE portal architecture.

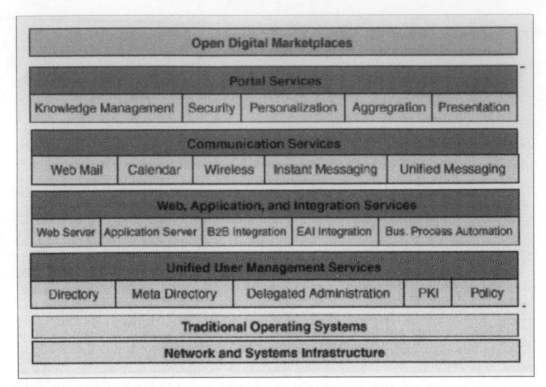

Figure 15.4. Sun ONE Web services and E-commerce infrastructure offerings. (Source: Sun Microsystems, Inc. [2001a].)

The ability to perform comprehensive business process automation is a step beyond the portlet wiring capabilities of Netegrity or the workflow capability of Citrix. When combined with the additional business process automation capabilities provided by the Forte IDE, the Sun ONE architectural platform will begin to approach PAI architecture minus the intelligent agent component.

Vision and direction of Sun ONE Portal Server

Sun's vision seems to be to develop the universal portal platform including a powerful application server and comprehensive EAI capabilities. The vision is best illustrated by Figure 15.4.

Figure 15.4 (Sun, 2001a, p. 7) shows the breadth of Sun ONE's portal vision, including its planned EAI capability, communication services, and portal services. Most portal products do not offer the combination of integration services and business process automation offered by Sun. The evolution of its product in the knowledge management area is a long-term effort, however.

"Touch points" with knowledge processing and knowledge management

Sun offers content-management, "knowledge-management," and collaborative capabilities among its many portal services as described earlier. But its "knowledge-management" and knowledge-processing services are limited. It has, in common with other portal tools reviewed, no specialized support for knowledge claim validation and only limited support for knowledge claim formulation and individual and group learning. Of course, its support for channels and pluggable content providers allows extension of its capabilities to the variety of applications necessary to eventually create the knowledge portal. It remains true, however, that the capability to construct category trees and to collaborate on documents and rate them for importance is only a very small aspect of knowledge processing and knowledge management and is much more properly termed simply content management and collaboration.

Corechange Coreport portal

Corechange Coreport portal (Corechange, 2001) is an access framework specialized to manage the delivery and publishing of content to a single role-based and personalized gateway for knowledge workers. Unlike many portal vendors already reviewed—Plumtree, in particular—Corechange is attempting to offer a flexible, adaptable, and scalable framework, rather than a total systems solution emphasizing EAI and various functional capabilities such as decision support, collaboration, advanced content management, knowledge processing or knowledge management.

Further, the Coreport portal framework is deliverable not only to the desktop, but also to wireless application protocol (WAP)–enabled phones and handheld devices (ibid.). Using Coreport you can access "critical business information—anytime, anywhere!". Corechange has been one of the most active portal vendors in emphasizing this capability. Coreport also claims the following features.

Coreport claims strong scalability as one of its most important features. By adding additional Coreport server scalability the ideal of linearity can be approached (Corechange, 2001a), according to Corechange and Microsoft who tested Coreport at Microsoft's testing laboratory.

Another feature of Coreport is single sign-on capability (Corechange, 2001b). Users can access databases, applications, and password-protected Web sites with this Coreport capability. Coreport manages and encrypts all passwords required for individual applications. Users can log on once per day They don't have to keep "cheat sheets" that make passwords insecure. They are motivated to create passwords that are harder to guess, because they have only one password to worry about. Further, single sign-on capability provides an audit trail for discovering security violations.

One of the most recognized features of Coreport is its role-based based access control and administration feature. Portal products have offered individual-level personalization based on rules. This type of personalization carries with it a heavy administrative burden for portal administrators. It also has not accounted for common patterns of usage characteristic of groups of individuals. One of the current trends in portal software is the capability to support assignment of taxonomic navigational frameworks appropriate for particular "roles." Coreport is one of the first vendors to offer this capability (Delphi, 2000). However, the extent to which roles actually provide the basis for Coreport taxonomies depends on the specific role conceptualization defined in applying the portal framework. Coreport does not provide a definition of corporate role structure users can apply in developing taxonomies and assigning them to roles.

Individual-level rules-based personalization is another feature of Coreport. Specifically, rule-based personalization within a role-based structure can provide individual-level customization of knowledge worker workspaces, including the look-and-feel preferred by a knowledge worker. Since this personalization occurs within the role-based structure of navigation, it does not add a great deal to the administrative burden. In addition, knowledge workers are empowered to perform this personalization themselves, providing another means to reduce the burden of administration.

Coreport has the capability to launch desktop applications from within its framework. Thus common Windows-based applications (MS Word, Excel, Powerpoint, etc.) are accessible from the framework. Thus, their full functionality is accessible, which represents another way Coreport portal solutions get closer to the portal ideal of a single gateway to all enterprise applications, data, and content.

Role-based administration is another feature heavily emphasized by Corechange. Coreport's administrative tool includes a point-and-click/drag-and-drop wizard that allows role-based taxonomies to be easily modified and maintained.

Most of the portal products surveyed have provided "plug-in" access to applications and sources not integrated into the portal. Coreport is no exception. It provides "connectors" to provide framework-based access to data, content sources, and applications. Coreport connectors have the following features (Corechange, 2001c, p. 1):

- "Content is not limited to simple, static HTML. Connectors support DHTML, plug-ins or ActiveX controls.
- Connectors provide the same look-and-feel and full functionality of the native application.
- Functionality is limited only by the capabilities of the client device.
- Connectors run in parallel without intermediate server bottlenecks.
- Users get content as soon as it's available, rather than waiting until all connectors are completed.
- Connectors are completely independent so they can't interfere with each other.
- Nontechnical users can create connectors to Web applications and content, so they are virtually limitless in numbers and possibilities.
- Connectors can optionally interact, if appropriate for a given application.
- Connectors can be created with any development tool, on any platform, using the tools best suited for the task at hand.
- Customers are not locked into a specific platform or SDK.
- Connectors do not have to be rewritten for future versions of the portal, resulting in less maintenance."

This is a powerful set of connector features, unexcelled by any other portal product. Particularly notable are the ability to use any development tool to create connectors, the ability for end users to create connectors, and the ability to access full functionality of applications in the portal framework. This last is an advantage over Plumtree, Citrix, and a number of other Coreport competitors.

A full range of connectors is available for Coreport even though it is a relative latecomer to the portal space (Corechange, 2001c). Connectors include major applications in the collaborative, content-management, decision-support, productivity,

ERP, content, Palm, and WAP connectors. In addition, connectors are available both to Autonomy and Verity search and content-management applications.

In sum, Corechange Coreport is a full-featured, flexible, and easy to administer portal framework aimed at filling the front-end niche of portal systems. It provides no application servers or EAI tools or other applications beyond portal content-management functionality, but it excels at providing connectivity to middleware application servers that provide functionality to the portal system that it does not provide.

Corechange Coreport architecture

Coreport 5.0 components include Coreport data, the Coreport Web Application, Coreport Administrator, and Coreport Server. The data used by Coreport to provide the portal interface (Corechange, 2001) is stored in XML format in Windows Active Directory (AD). This data is transformed into DHTML using XSL Transformations (XSLT). Personal settings for portal users are stored in a separate file system in XML format.

The Coreport Web Application produces the portal interface, provides user authentication and access to the portal, and displays portal content through an Active Server Pages application running under Microsoft Internet Information Server 5.0. It has two components: Coreport portal, and Coreport Web administrator, a browser-based administration tool that lets administrators perform basic configuration tasks through a browser interface. Coreport Web administrator enables an administrator to maintain the portal from any location.

Coreport Administrator is a Microsoft Management Console (MMC) "snap-in." It enables an administrator to assign Persons and Connectors to Organizational Units, Group, and Group Policy objects within Active Directory. It adds property pages to Active Directory objects. These pages are accessed by using tabs on the property sheet of each object. Hierarchies built in Active Directory with these objects provide the taxonomies necessary for Coreport's role-based delivery of portal content.

Coreport Server is a DCOM Server providing access to Coreport personal settings data and to data in Active Directory. It functions in the middle tier and mediates between Active Directory and the Coreport Web application. Coreport Server forwards authentication requests to Active Directory and then returns the query results stored there to the Coreport Web application. Coreport provides dynamic load balancing across distributed Coreport Servers, and also failover. Web farms may be created using two or more connected servers. Windows Load Balancing Server (WLBS), a component of Windows 2000, Advanced Server is used to balance loads in these Web farms. Each server operates as a node, and each node can perform failover for any other node in the farm.

Connectors define data, content, and application sources displayed in the portal. Some are displayed as portal window frames. Others are displayed as text links and/or icons and launch Windows-based or Web-based applications. Connectors are assigned to objects in Active Directory called Operating Units (OUs), Groups, or Group Policies, which are then assigned to an OU. There are two types of Connectors: Portal Connectors and Desktop Connectors.

Portal Connectors deliver Web-based content to the portal interface. They link to the URL address of the content. They can also link to ASP files in the Web application. These do the necessary processing to display portal content. Portal

Connectors can be displayed as separate frames within the portal, or as selectable icons that open to larger display frames. Connector icons are grouped in the *All Web Links* frame in the portal.

Coreport runs not only just on the Microsoft platform. There is also a Java version available, running on a J2EE application server platform. It is supported by a number of available J2EE application servers. Finally, though Coreport is an extremely flexible and open front end to a portal system, it must be noted that it is also a paradigmatic instance of an architecture exemplifying the PAC approach. Coreport's connectors are largely isolated applications being plugged into a small portion of the browser interface. The result may bring much that is useful to the knowledge worker's role to the desktop, but it does not integrate what it brings and still leaves the "islands of information" and "islands of automation" problems to be solved.

Vision and direction of Corechange Coreport portal

Corechange Coreport is following a strategy of providing an excellent portal-only platform that delivers content to PDAs and wireless devices as well as to desktop platforms. On the functionality and EAI dimensions, it relies on third-party products, and its strategy seems to be to develop portal systems having functionality of various kinds by allying these third parties. Its close allies now seem to include Autonomy in the area of search technology and automated taxonomy creation and Stellent (formerly Xpedio) in the area of content management. Corechange has an aggressive program of adding connectors and partners. In the near future it will undoubtedly move into every major horizontal application area in the portal space. In these areas its success will probably depend a great deal on its partners and on its skill in integrating its partners into effective implementation teams for its clients.

"Touch points" with knowledge processing and knowledge management

Corechange Coreport provides little in the way of knowledge-processing and knowledge-management support to date, beyond the support it provides by supplying a presumably relevant role-based taxonomy to each knowledge worker. Its connectors focus more on content management than on collaboration or knowledge processing. Its most advanced collaborative connector is eRoom in the project-management area. Knowledge management activities, finally, are not supported by Coreport.

The above does not mean that Coreport cannot be useful for KM applications. What it does mean is that such applications must be built on Coreport as a foundational application. Not only does specific collaboration, knowledge processing, and knowledge management need to be added, but EAI functionality would need to be provided to this rather pure case of a PAC architecture portal.

Conclusion

Content management portals are still the most plentiful types available, but as with decision-processing portals they are destined to disappear as decision-processing capabilities are added to their basic functionality. Exceptions to this rule may be Verity and Autonomy. Their portal products are defensive offerings that supplement their primary thrust in providing search and content-management technology to other portal product companies. Companies such as Oracle, Sun, and Netegrity already are oriented to providing plug-ins that manage structured data. Plumtree offers gadgets that provide for decision processing. Others have available portlets that are addressing structured data management needs. It will not be long before most vendors in this category move to the decision processing/content management category.

References

Autonomy (2002), at www.autonomy.com/products/portal-in-a-box.html.

Autonomy (2002a), at www.autonomy.com/products/PortalTechSpecs.html.

Autonomy (2002b), at www.autonomy.com/products/PortalFeaturesBenefits.html.

Autonomy (2001). "Technology White Paper," Autonomy, Inc., San Francisco, CA.

Autonomy (2001a). "Technology Brief: Autonomy Content Infrastructure," Autonomy, Inc., San Francisco, CA.

Autonomy (2001b). "Technical Brief: Autonomy Content Infrastructure," Autonomy, Inc., San Francisco, CA.

Citrix (2002). "Citrix XPS," at www.citrix.com/products/default.html.

Citrix (2001). "Citrix Acquires Sequoia Software" at www.citrix.com/news/citrixsequoia.html.

Citrix (2001a). "Citrix XPS™ Technical Overview," Citrix Systems, Inc., Fort Lauderdale, FL.

Convera, Inc., "RetrievalWare Architecture," at www.convera.com/products/retrievalware/converaw_arch.html.

Corechange, Inc. (2001). "Coreport 3G: Next Generation e-Access Framework for All Kinds of Portal," Corechange, Inc., Boston, MA.

Corechange, Inc. (2001a). "Coreport 3G Scalability," Corechange, Inc., Boston, MA.

Corechange, Inc. (2001b). "Coreport AD 5.0 Reference Guide," Corechange, Inc., Boston, MA.

Corechange, Inc. (2000). "Coreport Connectors, Corechange, Inc., Boston, MA.

Cox, Earl (1995). *Fuzzy Logic for Business and Industry* (Rockland, MA, Charles River Media).

DataChannel, Inc. (2001). "DataChannel 5.0 Architecture," Netegrity, Inc., Waltham, MA.

DataChannel, Inc. (2001a). "DataChannel Server 5.0", Netegrity, Inc., Waltham, MA.

DataChannel, Inc. (2001b). "DataChannel Server EAI Framework", Netegrity, Inc., Waltham, MA.

DataChannel, Inc. (2001c). "DataChannel Server 5.0: Portlet Wiring," Netegrity, Inc., Waltham, MA.

The Delphi Group, Inc. (2000). "Centering the Business Desktop," The Delphi Group, Inc., Boston, MA.

Enfish Corporation (2002). "Enfish Corporation Formation Q & A," at www.enfish.com/merger_qa.html.

Enfish Corporation (2002a). "Features," at www.enfish.com/features.html.

Enfish Corporation (2002b). "Infomediary," at www.enfish.com/portal_infomediary.html.

Enfish Corporation (2002c). "Enfish Enterprise Portal Architecture," at www.enfish.com/portal_architecture.html.

Enfish Corporation (2002d). "Portal Technical FAQ," at www.enfish.com/ktrachportaldoc.html.

Enfish Corporation (2001). "Enfish Enterprise," Enfish Corporation, Pleasanton, CA.

Level 8 Software, Inc. (2002), at www.level8.com.

Netegrity, Inc. (2002). "The Netegrity Interaction Server 5.1" (a Graphic). Netegrity, Inc., Waltham, MA.

Netegrity, Inc. (2002a), at www.netegrity.com.

Oracle (2002). "Oracle9iAS Portal," at www.oracle.com/products/portal_fov.html.

Oracle (2002a). "Build Your Own Portlets," at www.oracle.com/products/qt_frm.htm.

Oracle (2001). "Oracle9i Application Server Portal Features," Oracle Corporation, Redwood Shores, CA.

Open Market, Inc. and Sun Microsystems, Inc. (2002). "The Content-driven Portal Solution,"Open Market Inc. at www.openmarket.com/binaries/iPlanetBrief.pdf.

Plumtree Software, Inc. (2002), at www.plumtree.com.

Plumtree Software, Inc. (2001). "The Plumtree Corporate Portal Technical White Paper: Revised to include Plumtree Corporate Portal 4.5 Features" Plumtree Software Inc., San Francisco, CA. Available at www.plumtree.com.

Plumtree Software, Inc. (2000). "The Plumtree Corporate Portal 4.0: Technical White Paper," Plumtree Software Inc., San Francisco, CA. Available at www.plumtree.com.

Plumtree Software, Inc. (1999). "Corporate Portals: A Simple View of a Complex World," Plumtree Software Inc., San Francisco, CA. Available at www.plumtree.com.

Sequoia (2000). "XPS Technical Overview," Sequoia Software Corporation, Columbia, MD.

Sun Microsystems, Inc. (2002). "White Paper—Using a Portal to Gain Strategic Advantage," at http://www.iplanet.com/products/iplanet_portal/whitepaper_2_1_1_3g.html.

Sun Microsystems, Inc. (2002a). "iPlanet Portal Server Personalized Knowledge Pack: Overview," at http://www.iplanet.com/products/iplanet_portal_pkp/home_portal_pkp.html.

Sun Microsystems, Inc. (2002b). "iPlanet Portal Server Instant Collaboration Pack: Overview," at http://www.iplanet.com/products/iplanet_portal/home_portal_icp.html.

Sun Microsystems, Inc. (2002c). "iPlanet Application Server: White Paper Technical Reference Guide," at http://www.iplanet.com/products/whitepaper_2_1_1_3n3.html.

Sun Microsystems, Inc. (2001). "iPlanet Portal Server Enterprise Edition: Overview," at http://www.iplanet.com/products/iplanet_portal/home_2_1_g2.html.

Sun Microsystems, Inc. (2001a). "A Deployment Platform for E-Business in the Net Economy," Sun Microsystems, Inc., Palo Alto, CA.

Sun Microsystems, Inc. (2000) "E-Business," Sun Microsystems, Inc., Palo Alto, CA.

TIBCO Software, Inc. (2002) at www.tibco.com.

Verity, Inc. (2002). "Verity Portal One," at www.verity.com/products/portal/index.htm

Verity, Inc. (2001). "Verity K2 Architecture," Verity Inc., Sunnyvale, CA.

Verity, Inc. (2000). "Verity Launches Portal One," at www.verity.com/press/2000/
    20000626b.html.
Verity, Inc. (2000a). "Verity Search," Verity Inc., Sunnyvale, CA.
Verity, Inc. (2000b). "Verity Intelligent Classification," Verity Inc. Sunnyvale, CA.
Vitria, Inc. (2002) at www.vitria.com.

CHAPTER 16

Collaborative Portal Products

Introduction

The third type of basic portal tool is the collaborative portal. This portal has been the least common of the three basic types. The cases I will analyze include BrainEKP, Open Text, Intraspect, and IBM/Lotus.

TheBrain enterprise knowledge platform (BrainEKP)

In Chapter 5, I pointed out that the "islands of automation" problem is about the need to integrate today's desktop environment of disparate, program-by-program, task-isolated IT applications. It focuses on replacing the Windows desktop's unrelated application icons with a new interface that emphasizes a personalized combination of subject matter (content) categorization, networking, and workflow patterns. So, it emphasizes three different types of EASI. (1) UI subject-matter integration (2) application integration through workflow, and (3) Information integration through ad hoc navigation. BrainEKP (TheBrain Technologies Corporation, 2002) attempts to address the first two but not the third of these problems.

When users see their personalized enterprise portal interface they should see a reflection of the portion of their cognitive map or semantic network (sometimes also referred to as a concept network or a" knowledge map"), relevant to their interpretation of the various roles they play in their enterprise. One aspect of this "cognitive map" is its hierarchical classification of subject matter. Hierarchical classification of subject matter is an essential feature of the first and second generation of EIP products, but only BrainEKP also incorporates the nonhierarchical network relationships found in the cognitive apps of users.

It does this by tracking users' execution of routine business processes, incorporating a representation of these processes in a "knowledge model," and by allowing knowledge workers to associate (TheBrain Technologies Corporation, 2002a)

... words called "thoughts" in a diagram that uses lines called "links" to show how everything fits together. This interface is called "TheBrain." Like your mind, selecting a thought triggers related thoughts, so that connected information is immediately available when you need it. This simple metaphor enables a rich network of connections that lets people access information, share understanding, and communicate effectively.

An illustration of TheBrain interface is shown in Figure 5.5 (2002b). You can see from the illustration that TheBrain is a representation of the cognitive map or network idea illustrated in Figure 7.1. In a cognitive map, as in BrainEKP, the network represents the *context* of the nodes and links that are the network's components. So, a cognitive map or a semantic network representation of information such as TheBrain automatically places information in context in a way that other representations of structured and unstructured information do not. The words, thoughts, nodes, or subjects in the map are thus *integrated* in the context formed by the relationships and the map representation taken as a whole.

When a user navigates TheBrain and selects a subject node as the focus, the view presented to the user is dynamic. With the change in the subject selection or focus, the relationships defining the context that one sees also change. Therefore, the integration of subjects through the BrainEKP interface is also dynamic. At the interface or "islands of automation" level, BrainEKP solves the dynamic integration problem first mentioned in Chapter 2 and emphasized later in Chapters 5, 6, 10, and 13, but it doesn't solve it at the middle-tier level. That is, it doesn't solve the "islands of information" problem, because it does not provide for application integration of portlets or gadgets in the middle tier.

An interesting aspect of TheBrain's visual interface is that its search technology is very different from others surveyed thus far. In BrainEKP a keyword query returns a result as long as the word has been previously related to a piece of information and the relationship is recorded in some repository or directory that TheBrain is able to search. BrainEKP has no capability to extract relationships from documents themselves through use of machine-learning algorithms. Another implication of this inability is that the network-generating capability of TheBrain is completely dependent on the ability of people who feed the system to produce conceptual relationships. TheBrain's visual interface however, may well stimulate people to accelerated knowledge claim formulation in this area.

The Visual User Interface is only one of four components in BrainEKP's "comprehensive knowledge platform" solution. The other three are (1) "The Knowledge Model", (2) universal data access, and (3) integrated collaboration.

"The Knowledge Model" (2002a) is a tool for representing and automating routine, complex, nonlinear business processes. Knowledge workers using BrainEKP can capture representations of such processes simply by executing them. By using The Knowledge Model, BrainEKP can integrate content, information, and applications into workflows. In this way, BrainEKP also addresses application integration at the interface level through workflow, the second aspect of EASI associated with the "islands of automation" problem.

In addition, the process-modeling capability built into The Knowledge Model component enables knowledge workers to model their knowledge-producing and knowledge-integrating processes. It also enables them to model their best practices insofar as they are embodied in procedures and processes.

Universal data access (ibid.) "integrates a broad range of existing systems providing a synchronized view of multiple data sources within one interface." BrainEKP has a data-access layer that employs connectors to establish communication between TheBrain and any information repository such as an ERP system, a relational database, or a document warehouse. BrainEKP can map relationships in each repository and integrate these into the picture it creates for the visual user interface. Relationships among items in different repositories are mapped by knowledge workers using BrainEKP.

Integrated collaboration (ibid.) refers to BrainEKP's capability to enable knowledge workers to collaborate while using TheBrain interface to access the full range of content in the enterprise. There is no separate application involved, no gadget or portlet, only TheBrain itself. Collaboration occurs in the same place that content is created, accessed, retrieved, and published—in the workspace provided by BrainEKP. Knowledge workers may collaborate by creating additional links; sharing summaries of topics in notes; exchanging comments and viewpoints; attaching previously created documents, spreadsheets, files, and Web links supporting a particular "thought," concept, or subject; and creating process models using the knowledge-modeling capability.

One capability BrainEKP does not have is gadget or portlet integration. Its ability to provide universal access to data and content stores is not the same as the ability to provide access to the application functionality of Business Objects, Microstrategy, SAP, Peoplesoft, or any of the hundreds of applications available to portal solutions through gadgets or portlets. So BrainEKP in spite of its breakthrough interface features and its capability to support many aspects of knowledge processing, is not able to fulfill the Shilakes and Tylman requirement of serving as a single point of access to all enterprise data, content, and application functionality. It falls short of being a full-blown EIP in this last area.

BrainEKP architecture

BrainEKP's architecture has not been described by the company in a white paper or other publication, but its major features may be inferred from published descriptions. Figure 16.1 illustrates BrainEKP architecture. BrainEKP is based on J2EE-based Web application servers. These host the BrainEKP platform with its visual user interface, knowledge modeling, universal data access and collaboration components. Collaboration application functionality is tightly integrated into the platform; as is the functionality producing the TheBrain's cognitive maps and their dynamic adjustments. BrainEKP connectors provide access to the data and content tier and to information stored in applications, but this type of connection is one of loose coupling providing for the mapping of nodes and relationships in the information repositories. The connectors do not provide access to the functionality of the applications themselves.

The form of integration in BrainEKP platform is portal interface–based integration, and the underlying architecture is passive access to content (PAC) architecture, but without even the capability to provide access to the functionality of each application in isolation. The J2EE Web-based architecture allows for transactional multithreading and load balancing. But there is no middle-tier layer synchronizing and managing changes in objects, components, workflows, business rules, and metadata across the enterprise. Instead, synchronization is restricted to

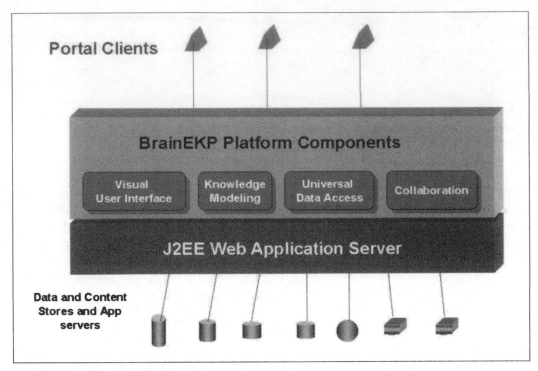

Figure 16.1. BrainEKP components.

the visual composition layer itself, leaving the "islands of information" badly integrated, at least with respect to application functionality.

BrainEKP architecture raises the issue of scalability. The product is very new at present, and TheBrain Technologies has not supplied very much information about load balancing and scalability or, for that matter, about fault tolerance. If BrainEKP is to succeed as an enterprise solution, the company will have to address these issues as well the issue of integration with other enterprise applications at other than the data and content levels.

Vision and direction of BrainEKP

TheBrain Technologies has made an appreciable impact with its technology. It has a patent in the area of using networking interfaces in portal products, and its visual user interface is finding applications in major consulting firms and corporations. But the company's entrance into the portal marketplace as a primary vendor, rather than just a supplier of technology to such vendors, raises the question of whether its future direction will be further development of TheBrain interface, or a matter of concentrating its development efforts on its BrainEKP platform and developing it into an "industrial-strength" portal product that integrates fully with other applications. As a start-up, even a relatively well-funded one, the company probably does not have the resources to do both.

The development of BrainEKP as an entrant into the portal market may signal a commitment on the part of the company to bet its future on the enterprise solution marketplace. If this is the case, TheBrain Technologies will need to develop (1) automatic network construction technology and (2) a more comprehensive EAI integration platform, including the capability to use portlets in its platform.

"Touch points" with knowledge processing and knowledge management

The BrainEKP is billed as an "enterprise knowledge *platform*" not an "enterprise knowledge *portal*" (TheBrain, 2002). One reason for that careful labeling by the company may be its recognition that the product is not yet integrative enough to be properly labeled a portal and that it is more properly viewed as a collaborative, knowledge-generating application falling into the general area of knowledge-management software solutions. Whatever the reason for the product's characterization, the name "enterprise knowledge platform," raises the issue of its comprehensiveness in supporting knowledge processing and knowledge management.

First, according to the development of the EKP concept provided in Chapters 7–10 and Chapter 13, the BrainEKP, would not qualify as an EKP (whether "portal" or "platform,") based on its ability to provide "information in context" in the cognitive map interface. Information in context is, in the first place, just information; whether it is also knowledge depends on how well it has survived knowledge claim validation, and neither a platform nor a portal that fails to provide both facilities for testing and evaluating knowledge claims and facilities for tracking the history of these efforts can reasonably be called an EKP. Further, though the BrainEKP supports collaboration as well as access to data and information sources in the same workspace, that functionality has only limited implications for supporting the idea that it is a knowledge-processing or knowledge management-application.

Second, when we look carefully at the functionality of the BrainEKP, it seems to support formulating concept networks both individually and collaboratively as well as collaborating in problem solving of all kinds, but without specialized functionality in modeling, forecasting, planning, and many other areas of knowledge formulation. Now I do not wish to minimize the importance of supporting activities of individual and collaborative cognitive map construction, distribution, refinement, and recreation. This capability is a strong support for individual and group learning and for knowledge claim formulation. But knowledge claim formulation and individual and group learning are not all there is to knowledge production and knowledge management. Even in the area of concept map/network development, the BrainEKP provides only a generalized ability to do this with only certain types of relatively informal cognitive maps. And as I indicated previously, beyond provision of workspaces in which knowledge claim validation can occur, the BrainEKP provides no specific support for testing and evaluating knowledge claims or for tracking the results of such testing.

Third, the BrainEKP also provides no specific support for leadership, external relationship-building, rule-changing, resource-allocation, and negotiation activities. It may, however, provide more important support for crisis handling through its collaborative workspaces.

In short, to label the BrainEKP as an enterprise knowledge platform, rather than a collaborative platform or portal is a stretch. It may be less of a stretch than the EKP claims of other vendors who don't even provide very much support for knowledge claim formulation focused on concept networks. But the fact still remains that the BrainEKP falls far short of either a platform or a portal of the EKP type. In the end, it does not have nearly enough touch points with the KLC and KM value networks to justify such a label.

Open Text myLivelink

Open Text myLivelink (Open Text, 2001) is not itself a collaborative portal, but when used as a gateway to Open Text's Livelink it becomes a collaborative portal. In fact, Open Text calls it a "collaborative knowledge portal" (2001a) in that context, though as I will show later, this designation is mistaken. Let us first look at the features of myLivelink and then examine the additional functionality that Livelink adds to it. The features of myLivelink highlighted by Open Text (2001b) are (1) brokered search, (2) profiling by job title and industry, (3) support for multiple sets of isolated user communities, (4) single login access; (5) an XML-based infrastructure, (6) application and metadata integration, and (7) interface personalization.

myLivelink provides unified search across structured and unstructured data through its brokered-search capability. Brokered search provides users with a convenient single interface for searching multiple information sources. myLivelink sends the user's query to search engines on various sites, including Livelink's own search engine, and aggregates the results. According to Open Text, "no other brokered search product can search as many different types of data sources, while respecting the authentication required by certain systems" (ibid.).

myLivelink performs profiling by job title and industry and delivers differing role-based portal "views" of information drawn from a variety of sources to users with different profiles. Administrators can structure these views and their content based on predefined user profiles. myLivelink uses these profiles to allow organizations to filter and categorize information according to the demands of different jobs, such as sales, development, management, or physical location, situation and various other criteria.

myLivelink supports multiple sets of isolated user communities by enabling administrators to create multiple "domains" of users on the same myLivelink installation. This capability makes it ideally suited for deployment in any application that needs to keep its user communities separated (e.g., ASP applications, some CRM applications, and applications involving multiple suppliers).

When users log into myLivelink they are automatically logged into Livelink 9.0 and later, and vice versa. This automatic single sign-on applies even when a directory service is not used.

myLivelink and Livelink (ibid.) have implemented an XML-based infrastructure as part of Open Text's support for open standards. Content from multiple sources is presented to myLivelink in a standard XML format, and then delivered through myLivelink widgets as HTML to browsers.

myLivelink runs on a number of back-end servers and accesses both structured and unstructured information across large, multiple and disparate enterprise information systems. It supports Windows 2000, Windows NT 4.0, and Solaris 2.7/2.8 and connects to multiple legacy and more recent enterprise-class applications, including SAP, Lotus Notes, Microsoft Office, and other popular enterprise systems.

myLivelink supports extensive interface personalization, including users adding, editing, and deleting information sources from their portal interface. Configuration commands for colors, display formats, refresh rates, and other display attributes are also available.

Though this set of myLivelink features is extensive, the features of this portal product are not directly supportive of collaboration. When the features of Livelink are added to those of myLivelink, however, the picture changes radically. Livelink features include those discussed in the following paragraphs (Open Text, 2001c).

Enterprise, personal, and project workspaces through which work is organized

Enterprise workspaces are used for "knowledge" sharing rather than active collaboration—sharing best practices, policies, procedures, business critical news, and all projects. Personal workspaces are areas individuals can organize to optimize their own work. From their personal workspaces, individuals can subscribe to information sources, organize schedules and task lists, monitor notifications, and have information pushed to their desktops. Finally, project workspaces are collaborative environments shared by individual members of each project. Each project in Livelink has its own workspace. Every participant in a project workspace shares and accesses project-related information including source documents; project participants and their roles; and an overview of projects, workflows, steps, and tasks. Threaded discussions are a feature of project workspaces and support knowledge claim formulation. Missions, objectives, and goals may also be defined within project workspaces to connect project teams to departmental and corporate goals.

Document and content management

Livelink stores and manages documents and content as objects. Object versions, category and attribute metadata, document relationships, workflow maps, and change histories are all managed by it. It provides predefined user access to objects, it can search and reserve/unreserve them, and it can provide a complete history or audit trail of each object.

Virtual team collaboration

Livelink provides an organized workspace to store information objects of each project. All types of projects can be accommodated. Subprojects can cross functional, organizational, and extranet lines. Every aspect of a project or subproject can be managed using Livelink library, workflow, and task list capabilities. Knowledge claim formulation, individual and group learning, and knowledge integration are facilitated by project news channels and multithreaded discussions. Virtual team collaboration is further supported by Livelink's polling capability (new in Livelink 9.1) (Open Text, 2002a) and by its optional Livelink MeetingZone™ application (It will be described in greater detail subsequently).

Information retrieval and search services

Livelink provides search and retrieval tools enabling "pull" of information from heterogeneous sources and publishing of that information to targeted users. Livelink's search engine and facilities enable building searchable databases by indexing textual objects (documents, files, XML chunks, HTML, PDF, other formats) as well as simultaneous full-text and metadata searches featuring relevance ranking, Boolean searches, and unique indexes of categorized information called "slices." These narrow searches ensure focusing of results, and results and frequently used queries may be saved for reuse. Livelink Spiders™ enhance "pull" technology by automatically crawling documents, files, and the Web. Livelink LiveReports™ display an in-depth picture of the progress of processes and workflows. Livelink Channels™ broadcast information in real time through subscriptions. "Livelink Change Agents™ continuously monitor user-specified activities within a Livelink database and generate reports, informing users that events of interest have occurred". (Open Text, 2002b).

Enterprise group scheduling

Livelink provides access to calendar information with scheduling functionality enabling coordinating meetings and synchronizing work schedules. Calendar information may be updated from a browser at home or on the road. Livelink's real-time scheduling functionality allows an accurate view of everyone's available time.

Business process automation (Open Text, 2002c)

Livelink provides a graphical Java-based workflow designer enabling (1) dragging and dropping workflow steps and participants, (2) attaching documents or other objects, (3) designing sub–workflows, (4) defining conditional loopbacks, (5) setting milestones, and (6) specifying project details such as deliverables and due dates. Livelink also provides a capability to monitor the status of workflow steps in a process from the desktop and to drag and drop workflow objects on the workflow map to modify and update business processes. "Forms can be integrated into automated business processes using the optional Livelink PDF™ module" (ibid.).

Other features

There are many more features of Livelink Workflow too numerous to mention here. But the full set of its workflow capabilities are among the most extensive offered by portal companies.

The recent introduction of the Livelink MeetingZone™ application (Open Text, 2001c) is a significant addition to Open Text's "Collaborative Knowledge Portal" suite of products. Open Text's earlier virtual team collaboration application primarily provided repository-based sharing and collaboration on documents and tasks involving time delays—so-called asynchronous collaboration (ibid. p. 2). But it does not provide synchronous collaboration—real-time collaboration involving communication between individuals who can respond to one another without time delays, because they are in direct contact with one another either in the same physical or "virtual location using audio-video conferencing, instant messaging, application sharing, and electronic whiteboard technologies" (ibid. p. 3).

Livelink MeetingZone™ introduces synchronous collaboration to the Open Text product line in the form of virtual meeting capabilities. It provides not only the technology for such meetings but the ability to capture all that transpires in these meetings in the Livelink repository. The virtual meeting is somewhat similar in concept to an Intraspect workspace, and the interactions captured in the repository are like Intraspect's group memory. But an Intraspect workspace does not provide synchronous (real-time) collaboration, as does MeetingZone, unless Intraspect is integrated with further capabilities such as those of its ally Groove Networks (Intraspect, 2001).

Livelink's virtual meeting application is organized around meeting and meeting session objects rather than the project, as is virtual team collaboration. Therefore, while Livelink meetings can be associated easily enough with projects and project workspaces, they also represent a departure from support for project-based collaboration, the previous focus of Livelink functionality, into the area of support for executive meetings, communities of practice, and more ad hoc collaborative activities of many kinds. The important features of Livelink Meeting-Zone™ include (ibid. p. 5) "tight integration with Livelink, including:

- Ability to set meetings up via the Livelink interface
- Ability to invite attendees from the Livelink user directory
- Integration with Livelink indexing and searching
- One-click access to Livelink content during real-time meeting sessions
- Ability to save the results of a meeting back to Livelink
- Integration with Livelink permissions to control access to meeting objects and their contents
- Operation through a Web browser with no client download or configuration
- Accessibility by attendees through a firewall without special configuration
- Ability to invite external, non-Livelink users
- Provision of application sharing, electronic whiteboard, textpad, group chat, and private instant message capabilities during real-time meeting sessions
- Ability to create and modify tasks, notes, agenda items, and reference links during real-time meeting sessions
- Support for up to 25 concurrent attendees connecting to real-time meeting sessions"

Livelink MeetingZone enables real-time synchronous collaboration in virtual meetings, and it integrates the record of this meeting in Livelink's repository and through the repository within its larger project-oriented collaborative framework. All meetings and meeting sessions are treated as objects by Livelink, and, just as with other Livelink content objects, Open Text's search and retrieval technology and all its other capabilities (e.g., content management, virtual collaboration, business process automation) can be fully applied to them.

Open Text architecture

Open Text's (2002d) open interchange architecture (OIA) is three-tiered and based on industry standards (e.g., CORBA, XML for data interchange, SQL, LDAP, TCP/IP, HTTP, HTTPS, HTML, SMTP, ODMA, PDF, Java and ActiveX). Open Text

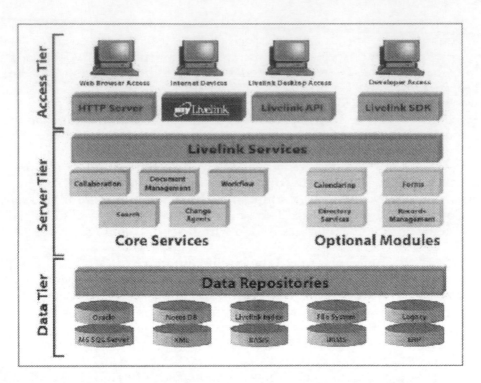

Figure 16.2. Open Text conceptual architecture. (Source: Open Text [2001b], p. 44.)

(2002e) distinguishes an access tier, a server tier, and a data tier. This conceptual architecture is illustrated in Figure 16.2

The access tier supports user access through Web browsers or the myLivelink portal. There is a Livelink API (LAPI) for programmer access to application services of the access tier. There is also an software development kit (SDK) supporting customization across all architectural tiers.

The data tier connects to relational databases (e.g., Oracle, MS SQLServer), information repositories (e.g., Notes DB, Livelink index, XML) file systems, ERP applications, and legacy systems. The server tier delivers virtual team collaboration, document and content management, workflow/business process automation, search and retrieval, change agents, calendaring, directory services, forms, record management, meeting, and other services.

The physical architecture is illustrated in Figure 16.3. It depicts a cluster of Livelink collaboration and myLivelink portal/Web servers, associated databases, RDBMS clients, a Livelink indexing host, a load balancer, and user workstations. Note that the Livelink collaboration server tightly integrates the various services listed above offered by Livelink. The architecture integrates no other application servers within the Livelink system and does not provide extensibility through a J2EE application server. myLivelink also does not provide PAC-based integration of applications into the portal interface. There are no portlets or channels within myLivelink that provide for integration of third-party applications. Instead, myLivelink connects to Livelink, which itself provides extensibility.

That extensibility is provided by the Livelink SDK and by Livelink Activators (connectors produced by using the SDK to CORBA, SAP R3, COM, etc.). These

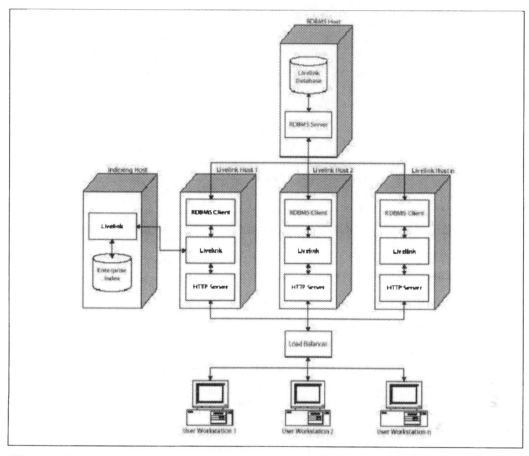

Figure 16.3. Open Text physical architecture. (Source: Open Text [2001b], p. 50.)

enable one to integrate Livelink's functionality with other enterprise systems. The Livelink API (LAPI) also supports extensibility by exposing all collaboration server functions, enabling integration through using C, C++, Visual Basic, and Java. Further extensions to LAPI for DCOM, CORBA, and SAP's BAPI are also available.

While Open Text does not provide for PAC-based integration into myLivelink, it does provide "portal bridges" for other portal products (Oracle, Epicentric, and Plumtree) (Open Text, 2001d) to integrate myLivelink/Livelink collaborative functionality into their portal products. This provides an integrated collaborative application to other portal front ends but not a way for them to integrate other applications (as distinct from content) into the collaborative work space.

In sum, the architecture of myLivelink/Livelink, while open in many respects, does not provide portal interface integration through channels. Instead it provides middle-tier application integration with Livelink service applications through repository sharing and workflow capabilities. Its collaboration capabilities, therefore, are somewhat integrated, but extending myLivelink/Livelink and integrating it with external applications involves more work than is the case with other portal products.

Vision and direction of Open Text

Open Text's product vision seems to be a combination of content management and broad-based collaboration. Open Text (2001, p. 2) presents myLivelink as essentially "a corporate portal interface to the content and services from multiple Livelink systems as well as to information from external non-Livelink data sources." Open Text goes on to say (ibid. p. 3–4),

> Open Text believes that any implementation of a Portal, especially across an enterprise, requires a high degree of customization options. Customization in user interfaces, customization in access to sources of information, and customization in the structure of how information is stored, managed, and displayed. Our job is to provide you with versatile tools that can be deployed "out-of-the-box," are easily configured, and can be managed to meet the needs of your company, your departments, and your end-users. With myLivelink, Open Text accomplishes this by providing the software, services, content, and presentation designed to establish a successful Portal in a minimum amount of time. . . .

> Using myLivelink as the point of access, Livelink can be used as the foundation for structuring and accessing projects, discussions, calendars, and enterprise information. myLivelink incorporates a more universal front end that accesses information outside of Livelink, as well as information from within Livelink or other Document Management repository. In this manner, Livelink applications can be used without restricting the implementation or deployment of the expanded interface.

From a portal point of view this is not a very expansive vision for a portal product. It reflects none of the orientation toward knowledge production and knowledge management implied by the label "collaborative knowledge portal" that Open Text occasionally uses to describe its product. Instead, taking into account Livelink's orientation toward project-based and more recently more expanded forms of collaboration, it suggests, in effect, that Open Text intends to develop further its present collaborative portal solution including strong content management capabilities, with expanding access to diverse information, but not necessarily to applications external to Livelink.

This, in fact, is the direction in which Open Text has been moving. Its latest version 9.1 develops enhancements in improved XML import/export capabilities, new administration capabilities, new user administration features, new collaboration features (including workflow and polling enhancements), enhanced search functionality, enhanced navigation (tree-view), support for classifications, and new optional modules (not one directly related to knowledge processing). While this is an impressive list of enhancements, it is clearly focused in the collaboration and content management areas and not in knowledge processing or knowledge management.

"Touch points" with knowledge processing and knowledge management

Livelink's emphasis on providing support for collaborative project management provides some touch points with *knowledge processing*, particularly with knowledge claim formulation and individual and group learning. myLivelink supports KM in the sense that many KM activities involve collaborative activities. Livelink's emphasis on recording the history of all electronic exchanges that occur in its Meeting zones and virtual team collaborations also suggests that its technology might be used to support knowledge claim validation (which requires historical tracking of testing and evaluation of knowledge claims), provided that its tracking could distinguish the record of testing and evaluation from other aspects of the history of collaborative events. However, with its present capabilities, Livelink supports neither structured data-related techniques of knowledge claim formulation nor historical tracking of validation events; therefore, in these very important respects it falls short of providing comprehensive support for knowledge processing.

Further, as with the BrainEKP and Intraspect (see below), when we look carefully at the functionality of Livelink, it seems to mainly support content-management and project-based collaboration but without specialized functionality in modeling, forecasting, planning, and many other areas of knowledge formulation. So its collaborative capabilities, while certainly supportive of problem solving and knowledge claim formulation, where these activities involve relatively informal knowledge claims about projects, are not sufficient to support these activities where the knowledge claims in question are more formal in character.

In the area of knowledge management, moreover, myLivelink/Livelink does not support most of the KM activities discussed in earlier chapters. Crisis handling, resource allocation, negotiation over resources, and rule changing are not explicitly supported, though insofar as these activities involve collaboration they implicitly support KM. In short, myLivelink may provide a platform that could be developed toward the EKP concept presented in Chapter 13 and earlier chapters, but presently it falls far short of the conceptual standard represented by the EKP.

Intraspect

Collaboration and collaborative commerce are important "buzzwords" in information technology today, and Intraspect (2002) has been at the center of activity in these areas since its inception. In Chapter 12, I offered the following list of specific collaboration functions: (1) prioritization, (2) planning, (3) project management, (4) distributing expertise, (5) training, (6) problem-solving, (7) knowledge production, and (8) workflow as important horizontal categories of collaborative processing functionality. Intraspect (ibid.) offers the following features as "collaborative":

C-space construction and maintenance of secure collaborative workspaces

This is the core of the Intraspect application, a Web-based workspace/place in which any digital object expressing data, information, and knowledge (e.g., discussions, e-mails, Web pages, documents, structured data) either acquired for or produced in the workspace may be organized into a knowledge base and stored in the workspace/place context in which it was developed. Each object in the knowledge base has its data stored in XML and is assigned a unique e-mail address, and a permanent URL.

Collaborative extranet construction and maintenance

This refers to C-spaces with external as well as internal users. Their look and feel may be designed to accommodate all collaborating companies. Users control access and security constraints so that access is role- and company-based.

Availability of workspace templates and custom workflow development capabilities

C-spaces need to be designed and set up as workspaces. Intraspect application modules provide workspace templates and enable creation of custom workflows that may be mapped into new templates. Knowledge workers use these templates, including forms, methods, procedures, techniques, best practices, and patterns, to facilitate design and set up C-spaces.

Enablement of e-mail, Web, and desktop contributions

Any participant in a C-space can publish any piece of information to a URL in the workspace using a desktop, e-mail, or Web browser application. "Users can email electronic information including attachments, upload it through a web browser, or copy it from the desktop using web folders. Since each workspace has a unique email address, all correspondence is captured in its original business context. No client plug-ins or interfaces are required" (ibid.).

Calendaring capability

Intraspect allows users to create calendars for milestones, meetings, other shared events for project teams, or events of the foregoing type for other types of enterprise or cross-enterprise agents and communities. This is a key capability for project management.

Task management capability

Capability is provided for users to create tasks with "owners." The tasks have priorities and due dates, and are linked with collaborative activities in workspaces. Intraspect provides automatic e-mail notifications to users of assigned tasks and links to the workspaces that provide context for these tasks. Task management, of course, is another capability important for project management.

Polling

Polling enables voting and quick collective decisions on topics of interest and commenting on reasons for particular votes. Polling originates from workspaces and is available to all types of workspaces, including extranets. Polling results are tabulated and displayed by Intraspect. Graphics and tables help to establish a history and rationale for collective decisions).

Capability for creating "dashboards"

Users can create activity dashboards from workspaces. These display the status of key business activities such as project plans, tasks, project issues, customer requests, sales and marketing opportunities, and conferences, along with links to these activities. Dashboards can display all activities and updates for individuals, teams, or groups, whether these are in-process or completed or whether the agents are within or across enterprises. Dashboards, therefore are important for monitoring all activities, tasks and projects.

Creates offline folders for mobile use

C-spaces can be saved to laptops so that they may be used while knowledge workers are away from the office. They can keep working on projects, documents, and business activities by using e-mail and web browser applications. Later they can upload their C-space changes to the workspace.

Custom search agents

Intraspect enables users to create persistent search agents customized with any combination of topic, phrase, document type (including Web site), workspace location, contributor, and/or time frame. These monitor updates and changes to any of the information sources they search.

Originating threaded discussions from workspaces

Each discussion thread is stored in the workspace knowledge base in XML and is full-text indexed, creating an easily searched history of work-related discussions, the progress of these across agents of different types, and the relationships among discussions and the chunks of XML that comprise them. Users may subscribe to discussion threads and receive alerts when new content is added to any thread.

Enables notifications

Users can subscribe to any workspace or piece of electronic information in that workspace and be notified of any changes in what they have subscribed to. Daily, weekly, monthly, or immediate notifications through e-mail, messages sent to wireless devices, or communications to or through their own personal workspaces, are available. Notifications enable users to track changes to workspaces, Web sites, or any activities carried on within workspaces (e.g., discussions, tasks, calendars, meetings, workflows).

Document management capability

Document versioning, commenting, approval, and locking are available to all users through the workspaces they participate in.

Synchronous collaboration capability

This capability is not from Intraspect alone, but is provided through integration of it (through a connector built by Intraspect) with Groove Networks's (2002) peer-to-peer collaboration. The integration adds a real-time, person-to-person interaction layer to its other collaboration applications. The combined solution will enable enterprise knowledge workers within an Intraspect community to launch Groove from an Intraspect workspace and to interact in real time, while

Intraspect captures the interactions in the correct business context in its repository, making it available for easy reuse in later asynchronous collaboration.

Personal page workspace creation and maintenance

Intraspect provides a personal page on which users can create and maintain a private workspace to capture and create private information. They can also link this page to public workspaces they use frequently where they share the work they are creating with others. They can be notified on their personal page of any changes to information in the workspaces they share. They can also establish group links to publish information from their personal pages using e-mails and uploads to the workspaces they share with teams, groups, and cross-enterprise communities.

These features provide basic collaborative support through C-spaces, which include some support for collaborative project management, collaborative problem solving, knowledge production, and workflow. But the features, while more extensive than those provided by BrainEKP and most other collaborative portal products, are not extensive enough to make the Intraspect 5 platform an advanced collaborative portal. That is, systematic support for planning, prioritization, training, distributing expertise, those aspects of problem solving and knowledge production involving knowledge claim validation, those aspects of project management involving simulation of alternative project plans, and the aspect of workflow involving workflow management and synchronization are not provided in Intraspect 5, and must be provided through integration with other products or future development.

The Intraspect platform provides a variety of integration capabilities (Intraspect, 2002a) that open the way to development of more comprehensive collaboration capabilities. These include: integration with e-mail, the Web, the desktop, business applications, and other sources of electronic information.

Integration with e-mail is accomplished by providing every object in workspace memory its own e-mail address. An SMTP server manages e-mail to and from workspace memory. Intraspect also includes a Lightweight Directory Access Protocol (LDAP) server. It publishes the Intraspect namespace to the enterprise. Knowledge workers can then search and browse Intraspect e-mail addresses. Since these are fixed, SMTP becomes another way that users can publish enterprise information directly to Intraspect workspaces.

Integration with the Web is done through a built-in hypertext transfer protocol (HTTP) server for communication between Intraspect and users' browsers. Any application that uses HTTP as a communications protocol can communicate with the Intraspect server.

Integration with desktop applications is accomplished through a Web-based distributed authoring and versioning (WebDAV) server. The server enables Intraspect folders to have the appearance and functionality of file system folders. WebDAV is also available as a programmatic API for use by other applications. Intraspect also includes an FTP server that allows information transfer between applications that use FTP as a communications protocol.

Integration with business applications is accomplished through extensive use of standards and rich APIs. Virtually any business application can be integrated. Any application using e-mail can be configured to place information into various C-spaces, both shared and individual.

Integration with other sources of electronic information is done in a variety of ways. Intraspect 5 includes an LDAP client. Existing enterprise personal profile information (e.g., user IDs or e-mail addresses) is stored in LDAP and re-used. Intraspect also includes an HTTP client. It collects and monitors the content of external Web pages. In addition, Intraspect offers as an option modules for connecting to Lotus Notes, Microsoft Exchange public folders, Windows NT file systems, and other enterprise sources.

Intraspect applications

These are in three areas: professional services collaboration, customer collaboration, and product collaboration. "Intraspect applications provide specific features that are core to the business functions, workflow and processes within these disciplines. They are built on the open, extensible Intraspect 4 platform, and are easy to deploy and use. Intraspect Applications complement existing PSA, CRM and SCM tools and applications currently in use to manage business functions, by providing a place to engage a workspace to actually 'do the business.'" (Gruber, 2001, p. 15).

The professional services collaboration application (ibid. p. 15) adds the following features to the basic collaboration platform on Intraspect 5: client engagement workspaces for managing projects, resources, and effective practices and methods for delivering projects; opportunity workspaces for working on potential business, including tools for tracking progress, preparing proposals, and collaborating on strategy; workspaces for managing large accounts, issue tracking and reporting; tools to identify experts and manage staffing of projects; extranet workspaces for negotiating issues, approving deliverables, and managing tasks with clients; tools for managing development and integration of best practices and methodologies; and customizable "executive dashboards" providing a global view across departments and projects.

The product development application (ibid. p. 16) has the following features in addition to the basic Intraspect 5 platform: secure, collaborative workspaces for product development and marketing professionals; tools and data types for managing collaborative creation and review of requirements specifications, functional specifications, and design documents; collaborative workspaces for product development projects; project workspaces for managing product launch activities; tools and data types for issue tracking and management; product dashboards enabling development teams to track product status and issues and their resolution throughout the product lifecycle.

The customer collaboration application (ibid. p. 17) has the following features in addition to the basic Intraspect 5 platform: co-branded extranet workspaces with customizable interfaces incorporating one's brand, one's customer's brand, or partner brands; account management workspaces in which account teams synthesize resources and experience to accelerate sales; spaces in which sales teams collaborate around customer responses, references and pricing; support for capturing and responding to customer requests and input; dedicated workspaces to align local and global teams for integrated interactions with that customer; and capturing all interactions in a central workspace in a "living history."

These three Intraspect custom applications illustrate what is possible using the Intraspect platform's collaborative application framework—a development feature to be covered later.

Intraspect 5 architecture

Intraspect (2002b) uses a three-tier architecture to deliver its services. The presentation tier delivers Intraspect applications to users. The data tier provides persistent repository storage, using either Microsoft SQL Server or Oracle; other databases may also be accessed through JDBC connectivity. The middle tier is composed of a number of application server components including a Web server, an HTTP client, an SMTP server, an LDAP server and client, an FTP server, a Web distributed authoring and versioning (WebDAV) server, the Intraspect collaboration server, and connectivity modules. In addition, Intraspect 5 supports integration with Microsoft Web parts and J2EE application/integration servers. This release has made integration with more comprehensive enterprise application platforms practical and opens the way to much wider adoption of Intraspect. But Intraspect does not yet offer an EAI capability based on its own J2EE server or one of a close ally.

The collaborative server uses object technology configured in a database layer, a services layer, and a customization layer. The database layer manages the mapping from the Intraspect object model to the persistent data stores used by it. The services layer integrates services necessary for creating collaborative applications. These services include: data management, message handling, security, information retrieval, and subscription services. They also include APIs and a development environment for application building, customization, and integration called the collaborative application framework. This framework is the customization layer referred to previously.

Intraspect's search engine retrieves information from anywhere in workspace group memory and displays it in context. It provides full-text indexing, a retrieval engine, and proprietary pre-processing, which enables high-performance retrieval by textual content, custom metadata, information type, author, date, or location in group memory. Intraspect transparently combines relational queries using structured attributes and information retrieval queries referring to documents or XML content. This is a significant feature integrating the use of structured data and unstructured content.

The collaborative application framework/customization layer, by removing much of the necessary programming, enables developers to build secure, "extranet-ready" custom collaborative solutions and user-interface customizations faster than using other development environments. By using Intraspect APIs along with the templates provided in the framework, developers can integrate collaboration into existing enterprise solutions such as portals, CRM, SCM, ERP, document management, and other horizontal applications.

The customization layer includes the following key technologies: a user interface (UI) library, core workspaces and objects, a workflow manager, a template engine, and a documented set of APIs along with support for server-side scripting. The UI library is a complete collaborative application using a Web standards user interface. Using it, changes to the UI can be made without disturbing underlying system operations. Its support for HTML standards allows development of user interfaces, customer branding, and support for specific work processes. It also allows elements of the Intraspect user interface to be inserted into other applications such as portals.

The framework also provides core workspaces and objects. These provide the foundation for developers to use in creating more specialized objects that map to business processes and vertical domains such as professional, product development or financial services. The Workflow Manager is another part of the framework, this one directed at allowing easy creation and deployment of workflows using the specialized objects and customized workspaces previously defined.

The Intraspect 5 Template Engine is a library of HTML templates that constitute its user interface. The template engine supports fast graphical customization compared with previous versions. Business logic is separated from graphical elements of the templates. The template architecture enables user-specific multiple views of the same group memory. By including business logic encoded in a tag-language, the template engine can control Web interface functionality. Templates from the default library can also be used to produce specialized application functions. New templates can also be added and integrated into other applications, and many additional applications of the template engine are also possible. In addition the template engine includes templates for creating and customizing a personal portal interface.

Finally, the Intraspect platform has a set of APIs and tools for developing robust, scalable solutions using server-to-server interactions. XML-based APIs support integration into an enterprise infrastructure. Standard scripting languages may be used to enhance installations by moving specific operations to the server.

The Intraspect architecture is well-rounded and robust and growing increasingly so with each version of the product. Its ability to interface with Microsoft Web parts and J2EE servers now opens its integration potential still more. Intraspect may be used to construct a collaborative portal, or it may be used to integrate with other portal products such as the many others reviewed here. Since there are relatively few collaborative portal products and since Intraspect's basic collaborative capability is extensive and its object-based workspace/group memory design is so full of potential for gradually increasing the functionality of the basic platform, it is likely that other vendors will adopt Intraspect as they migrate from content management to more comprehensive portal solutions.

Vision and direction of Intraspect

The vision and direction of Intraspect is directed at the idea of collaborative commerce, the idea that business transactions are triggered by collaborative relationships that cross the enterprise boundary—relationships with external parties such as customers, partners, and suppliers. Intraspect's vision is to be the leading software vendor in this area.

The company was founded on the philosophy that the best way to add collaboration to e-business is to build a (Pflaging, 2001, p. 2)

> . . . web-based, collaborative workspace . . . inside an existing enterprise application environment . . . that extends throughout an enterprise's business ecosystem (employees, customers, partners & suppliers) . . . acting as an enterprise knowledge source . . . to facilitate many-to-many collaboration . . . and generate ever-greater value as it integrates, manages and, through reuse, constantly upgrades the value of the ecosystem's accumulated intellectual capital . . .

And that statement, in a more specific nutshell, describes Intraspect's vision and direction.

"Touch points" with knowledge processing and knowledge management

From its beginning, Intraspect has been identified with knowledge processing and knowledge management, and some have considered it a KM as well as a collaboration vendor. Intraspect's emphasis on providing support for communities and on collaborative workspaces provides some touch points with *knowledge processing*, particularly with knowledge claim formulation and individual and group learning. Intraspect also supports KM in the sense that many KM activities do involve collaborative activities.

Intraspect's emphasis on recording the history of all electronic exchanges that occur in its C-spaces also suggests that its technology might be used to support knowledge claim validation (which requires historical tracking of testing and evaluation of knowledge claims), provided that its tracking could distinguish the record of testing and evaluation from other aspects of the history of collaborative events. However, with its present capabilities, Intraspect supports neither structured data-related techniques of knowledge claim formulation nor historical tracking of validation events. Therefore, in these very important respects it falls short of providing comprehensive support for knowledge processing.

Further, as with the BrainEKP, when we look carefully at the functionality of Intraspect, it seems to support formulating concept networks both individually and collaboratively as well as collaborating in problem solving of all kinds, but without specialized functionality in modeling, forecasting, planning, and many other areas of knowledge claim formulation. So Intraspect's general collaborative capabilities, while certainly supportive of problem-solving and knowledge claim formulation where these activities involve relatively informal knowledge claims, is not sufficient to support these activities where the knowledge claims sought are more formal in character.

In the area of knowledge management, moreover, Intraspect does not support most of the KM activities discussed in earlier chapters. Crisis handling, resource allocation, negotiation over resources, and rule changing are not explicitly supported, though insofar as these activities involve collaboration they implicitly support KM. In short, Intraspect may provide a platform that could be developed toward the EKP concept presented in Chapter 13 and earlier chapters, but presently it falls far short of the conceptual standard represented by the EKP.

IBM/Lotus

IBM recently (IBM, 2001) decided to merge its WebSphere Portal Server and Lotus K-Station Portal products into a single portal platform combining the horizontal and developmental strength of IBM's WebSphere Portal Server (WPS) with the portal interface and collaborative processing strengths of Lotus's K-Station and its recently integrated (with K-Station) Knowledge Discovery System. "Interoperability" of WPS and K-Station was scheduled for 4Q 2001, and full integration of the two products for 2Q 2002 (ibid.). The integrated product will provide one of the more advanced collaborative portals available.

The "WebSphere Portal Family"

IBM (2002) is offering the WebSphere Portal Family in three packaged solutions:

- The WebSphere Portal Enable Solution
The WebSphere Portal Extend Solution
- The WebSphere Portal Experience Solution

The WebSphere Portal Enable solution is a horizontal foundational framework platform for implementing a variety of portal types supporting personalization. Like other portal frameworks, it makes use of portlets to provide functionality. WebSphere Portal Enable uses IBM WebSphere Portal Server and WebSphere Personalization to provide basic functionality in many areas. It integrates "enterprise applications, syndicated content, Web sites, e-mail, and more through a wide variety of portlets" (ibid.). It personalizes portal content dynamically through use of business rules and collaborative filtering. It provides connectivity, integration, administration, and presentation services that are common across portal environments. Finally, it provides a portlet API that may be used to extend the portal framework broadly and incrementally with a variety of information and application sources. The portlets available, moreover, include enterprise resource planning (ERP), customer relationship management (CRM), supply chain management (SCM), content management, and host applications.

In August, 2001, IBM (2001) announced the addition of twenty application and content providers who are developing portlets to its Partner Program. The partners include: Crystal Decisions for business intelligence; AltaVista, Fast Search & Transfer, and Inktomi Corp. for search; Verity for intelligent portal infrastructure software; Autonomy for automated infrastructure; OnePage for portlet and Web service building tools; PlumDesign's ThinkMap® visualization and navigation software; Kivera and Webraska for location services; Netonomy for wireless; LexisNexis, Mediapps, NewsEdge, and YellowBrix for content; Atomica for answer delivery; Correlate for information mapping; Interwoven and IntraNet Solutions for content management; and EN technologies for cross-portlet functions. These agreements supplement IBM's previously announced partnerships with Hoover's Online, iSyndicate (recently acquired by YellowBrix), Factiva, and ScreamingMedia.

The WebSphere Portal Extend solution extends the Portal Enable Solution mainly by adding integrated collaboration and Web site analysis capabilities. The collaboration capabilities include out-of-the-box portal "Places,"—workspaces equipped with tools including: discussion areas, document libraries with check in and check out, group calendars, task and milestone tracking, and online people awareness and instant messaging. These capabilities integrate K-Station portlets into the WebSphere Extend framework. In addition, certain capabilities of Lotus Domino Extended Search, Lotus QuickPlace, and Lotus Sametime are also included in the Portal Extend solution. Web site analysis capabilities include Web reporting, and come from integration of WebSphere Site Analyzer. In addition, the Portal Extend solution provides federated searches that initiate multiple search engines across multiple repositories and content and data sources including relational databases (e.g., DB2 and Oracle, Lotus Notes and Domino databases), various Web search engines, and text or HTML documents.

The WebSphere Portal Experience solution is IBM's most advanced and complex portal offering. It adds more advanced collaboration, enterprise content-management, and enhanced security features to the Portal Extend solution. For collaboration it integrates further capabilities of Lotus K-Station, Knowledge Discovery System (KDS), QuickPlace, and Sametime technologies (e.g., support for e-meetings, application sharing, and whiteboarding). These allow users to share screen frames, desktops, presentations, and applications; in addition to the content, tasks, and discussions they can already share with the Portal Extend solution. For enterprise content management it provides capability from IBM Content Manager to "index, store, search, and distribute digital content, including business documents, printed reports or statements, and audio/visual, text, XML, and HTML files" (IBM, 2002). It also incorporates IBM Enterprise Information Portal Client Kit for Content Manager. For enhanced security it provides capabilities of Tivoli SecureWay Policy Director for centralized security across all existing resources and applications including single sign-on and authentication.

WebSphere portal architecture

The WebSphere portal is based on a three-tier architecture similar in general outline to Oracle's and Sun's. The first tier, of course, is the Web browser. The second tier is composed of the IBM WebSphere Application Server and other application servers associated with portlets. The WebSphere Application Server hosts WebSphere Portal Services, HTTP Services, and Transaction Management as well as LDAP Directory, Access, Authentication, and Security Services. The WebSphere Application Server "is actually a family of products that makes it easy to build Java server pages, write applications, manage performance, and data mine portal click streams" (IBM, 2002a). It can also host a large number of other Web services as well. The third tier in the architecture is that of data and content stores. The data stores that service portal metadata are DB2 or Oracle. WebSphere Portal is therefore a bit more open than Oracle in its requirement for a metadata repository.

The WebSphere Portal Server does not provide a parallel-page engine such as Oracle's or an MPPE-like capability such as Plumtree's. Performance must be scaled through the addition of more WebSphere Application (and portal) Servers.

The WebSphere Portal Server itself provides portal interface integration (Chapter 12) and PAC architecture (Chapter 5) through its hosting of portlets and their wide-ranging functionality. The integration of portlets into the WebSphere Portal is integration at the interface level only. The architecture does not provide for more comprehensive integration of the islands of information and application entering the portal. Even in its most extended form, in which wide-ranging collaborative and knowledge claim production capabilities are integrated, the applications in the WebSphere Portal do not necessarily work together, and dynamic integration of these applications with one another and of changes in the portal system with one another is not provided.

Vision and direction of the IBM WebSphere portal

IBM's market strategy is to use WebSphere Application Server and WebSphere Portal Server to integrate and deliver many of its other enterprise applications. WebSphere portal can provide an incremental framework for delivering EAI, collaborative, content management, data warehousing, OLAP, data and text mining, AI, transaction processing, workflow, and e-business applications. WebSphere Portal is, for the most part, an open platform, and third parties are being mobilized to offer their software applications through the software framework, thus greatly increasing the applications capability IBM can offer. In every major application area, however, IBM itself has a leading product it can offer. WebSphere Portal therefore cannot help but add to IBM's competitive position in enterprise software systems integration.

More important, perhaps, IBM's merger of its WebSphere and K-Station Portal Products is producing a mature and highly capable example of a collaborative portal with substantial integrative potential that is poised to evolve further into an advanced collaborative portal and, eventually a knowledge portal product of the sort envisioned in Chapter 13. Such an evolution is likely not IBM's conscious direction, since it evidently believes that it already offers a knowledge portal in the form of the WebSphere Portal Experience. Nevertheless, as it further advances its collaborative and knowledge-mining software applications and as it participates in competition with other vendors, it will most likely be led toward the more comprehensive knowledge-processing portal providing support for the full range of knowledge claim validation, knowledge-processing and knowledge-management activities.

"Touch points" with knowledge processing and knowledge management

The IBM WebSphere Portal product platform has substantial content-management, text-mining, collaborative, and enterprise application integration capabilities. But it lacks the kind of broad-ranging formal knowledge production; structured data management; collaborative enterprise data and application integration, comprehensive knowledge validation; workflow; knowledge claim object; knowledge processing; and knowledge management processing specified earlier for knowledge portals supporting knowledge processing and KM.

As I indicated earlier, IBM's product has recently begun to approach the middleware foundation and broad integrative capability necessary for an EKP. But it still lacks the automated synchronization, change management, knowledge production, and cumulative knowledge validation capability of an EKP. In particular, it lacks the IA and inference engine capability necessary for the EKP, and it does not provide a validation framework for people, intelligent agents, and artificial knowledge servers.

Conclusion

The collaborative portal category is one of the more interesting in the portal space. IBM provides the platform with the greatest capability for evolution into the knowledge portal. Its architecture provides a structure that will support evolution. Its ability to attract strategic allies along with its own broad range of technical capabilities suggests that its gradual development into an advanced collaborative portal and a comprehensive knowledge-processing portal is quite likely. Among the other collaborative portals, Intraspect has a technical architecture that can support evolution, but its vision and direction suggest that it will develop its collaborative commerce technology and market it through primarily other vendors' portal products rather than through its own offering. Open Text has good collaborative capabilities but lacks the architecture to provide a generalized portal platform. I believe, consequently, that it, too, will emphasize integration of its capabilities into other portal products.

Finally, BrainEKP is attempting to extend its visual interface technology and collaborative capabilities into a full-fledged portal platform. However, its weakness in the middle tier suggests that it faces an extensive development/integration effort to reach the point where it can offer a platform that can evolve into either the advanced collaborative or comprehensive knowledge-processing type.

References

Gruber, T. (2001). "Enterprise Collaboration Management with Intraspect," Intraspect Software, Inc., Brisbane, CA.

IBM Corporation (2002). "WebSphere Portal Family," at www-3.ibm.com/software/info/websphere/solutions/offerings/portalfamily.jsp.

IBM Corporation (2002a). "WebSphere Portal Server Components," at www-3.ibm.com/software/webservers/portal/architect.html.

IBM Corporation (2001). "IBM Merges WebSphere Portal Server and Lotus K-Station into single portal, announces new portal partners," at www-3.ibm.com/software/info/websphere/kstatwebsphereannc-81401.html.

Intraspect Software, Inc. (2002). "Intraspect Core Collaborative Features," at www.intraspect.com/products/corefeatures.html.

Intraspect Software, Inc. (2002a). "Enterprise Integration with Intraspect 5 Applications," at www.intraspect.com/products/cbusiness-standards.html.

Intraspect Software, Inc. (2002b). "Intraspect Offers the Platform for Enterprise Collaboration," at www.intraspect.com/products/cbusiness-arch.html.

Intraspect Software, Inc. (2001). "Intraspect Software and Groove Networks Partner to Deliver Comprehensive Collaboration Solution," at www.intraspect.com/news/releases/oct29_01.html.

Open Text, Inc. (2002). "You Need to Work in Context," at www.opentext.com/mylivelink/details.html.

Open Text, Inc. (2002a). "Introducing Livelink 9.1," at www.opentext.com/livelink/news.html.

Open Text, Inc. (2002b). "Information Retrieval and Search," at www.opentext.com/livelink/details/information_retrieval.html.

Open Text, Inc. (2002c). "Business Process Automation: Livelink Workflow," at www.opentext.com/livelink/details/business_process_automation.html.

Open Text, Inc. (2002d). "Livelink's Open Information Architecture," at www.opentext.com/livelink/details/architecture.html.

Open Text, Inc. (2002e). "Livelink's Three Tiers," at www.opentext.com/livelink/details/architecture_tiers.html.

Open Text, Inc. (2001). "White Paper Corporate Portals: An Introduction," Open Text, Inc., Waterloo, ON, Canada.

Open Text (2001a). "Create Your Own Space," Open Text, Inc., Waterloo, ON, Canada.

Open Text (2001b). "Livelink® Product Summary," Open Text, Inc., Waterloo, ON, Canada.

Open Text (2001c), "Real-Time Collaboration and Livelink," Open Text, Inc., Waterloo, ON, Canada.

Open Text (2001d). "White Paper myLivelink™ Portal Bridge: Livelink®
Interoperability with Other Portal Livelink® Interoperability with Other
Portal Frameworks," Open Text, Inc., Waterloo, ON, Canada.

Pflaging, J. "C-Business: Intraspect's Vision for Enterprise Collaboration,"
Intraspect Software, Inc., Brisbane, CA.

TheBrain Technologies Corporation (2002), at www.thebrain.com.

TheBrain Technologies Corporation (2002a). "Key Features," at www.thebrain.com/
four.html.

TheBrain Technologies Corporation (2002b). "esolutions," at www.thebrain.com/
images/d_esol_screenshot.gif.

CHAPTER 17

Decision Processing/ Content Management and Advanced Portal Products

Introduction

The products I have reviewed up to this point have been targeted at decision processing, content management, and collaboration. These are three basic types of functionality characterizing first-generation portals as well as newer entrants into the portal space that prefer to specialize in a single area of basic functionality. Some later entrants into the portal space along with companies with more comprehensive perspectives have created products that combine basic areas of functionality. The first combination category of this type is the decision processing/content management category. In my view, there are no current portal products in the advanced collaborative, structured information, or structured or comprehensive knowledge-processing categories as yet.

Decision processing/content management portal products

The products I will review here include Hummingbird EIP, Viador, CleverPath, Brio.Portal, Sybase EIP, TIBCO, Hyperwave eKnowledge Infrastructure, and SAP Portals (formerly TopTier).

Hummingbird EIP

Hummingbird was neither an early entrant nor a latecomer to the EIP market. It began its entry in the Spring of 1999 when it acquired PCDOCS/Fulcrum, one of the leaders in the document/content management field (Hummingbird, 1999). Amidst great fanfare it announced plans to synthesize its considerable connectivity, legacy, and decision-processing know-how (it had acquired Andyne, a DSS/ reporting tools company, before PCDOCS/Fulcrum) with its newly acquired content/document/"knowledge" management capability to develop an enterprise knowledge portal, even trade-marking the term. But since 1999 it has wisely de-emphasized its "knowledge portal" orientation and focused most heavily on establishing its identity as the vendor of the most comprehensive EIP product on the marketplace.

In this respect it has followed a distinctly different strategy from Plumtree, Corechange, and other vendors, which have emphasized arriving at portal solutions through the integration of third-party products. While Hummingbird has emphasized the openness of its own architecture and its interoperability with the document- and content-management systems of others, it has also emphasized its own capability to offer something much closer to a single-vendor solution than many of its competitors. As Hummingbird states (2000, p. 11),

> Hummingbird EIP is a culmination of internal core competencies of Connectivity, Data Integration and Reporting, and Knowledge and Document Management. Hummingbird's proven market and technology leadership in each of these areas contribute to an unprecedented EIP offering.

Thus, Hummingbird (2002) provides not only one of the more comprehensive document-/content-management capabilities along with its portal, but also frontline connectivity and decision processing, including reporting, OLAP, and data warehousing, as well as formidable structured data management, data mining, and packaged analytical capabilities. In addition, of course, Hummingbird also provides a wide range of generalized portal capabilities.

Let us begin with a review of Hummingbird's portal capabilities and then proceed to its more specific content-management, decision-processing, and collaboration features. The generalized portal capabilities include (Hummingbird, 2000) the portal engine, security, caching, unified search, taxonomy, multi-repository support, personalization, application integration, metadata dictionary, collaboration, plug-in architecture and APIs, XML-based infrastructure, and connectivity.

The portal engine

At the core of Hummingbird EIP is a Java-based portal server engine that delivers both information (data and unstructured content) and applications to the portal interface. The channels of delivery are connections called "e-clip" plug-ins. These provide the capability for portal interface integration of any number of information sources and applications.

Security

Hummingbird provides single sign-on access to all content and applications through its common authentication proxy server. This product works in tandem with the EIP architecture but is not dependent upon it. It respects the individual security models of each of the components of an EIP solution and provides single sign-on through an overlay method that does not modify the security arrangements of the component applications.

Caching

Caching, the retention of previous results in memory, is used in the Hummingbird EIP to produce network, response, and performance efficiencies in the context of delivering the results of searching and querying. It is not used for managing and synchronizing objects, components, workflows, etc. across applications.

Unified search

Hummingbird EIP can search all structured, unstructured, external, and/or internal information sources and produce aggregated, unified results in a manner transparent to users. It can "broker out searches to external search engines and return a unified result." (ibid. p. 7). Hummingbird supplies its SearchServer™ product to perform these services.

Taxonomy

Like Autonomy and other portal products mentioned previously but unlike the manual approach taken by Plumtree, Corechange, and others reviewed, Hummingbird (2000a) uses an automated taxonomy generating engine—Fulcrum Knowledge Server™—to produce taxonomies. These are then used for categorization of documents and navigation in the Hummingbird EIP. The engine uses neural network clustering technology to arrive at the hierarchical concept maps comprising the taxonomies. It does this without need of any preexisting taxonomy by analyzing the document base of an enterprise.

Multiple taxonomies may be developed using the engine. All that needs to be done is to vary the document base used to generate the taxonomy according to domain. This will generate taxonomies specific to domains, which, in turn, can be selected for relevance to particular organizational roles. As a practical matter, the engine can handle up to 100,000 documents per analysis. But it need not analyze more than 10 percent of the documents in any domain to produce a useful categorization.

After creating a taxonomy, Hummingbird EIP can automatically categorize documents by using it. The taxonomy can also be edited manually and its categories renamed according to interpretations of them made by humans following examination of documents categorized by the hierarchy.

As new documents are added to the EIP repository, the taxonomy used for categorization becomes dated, because it is based on automated analysis of the initial set of documents used to generate it and not on the original plus the new documents that have been categorized with it. To keep the taxonomy and its categorizations current, therefore, it is necessary to update the automated taxonomy-generating analysis periodically.

Multi-repository support

Many other vendors refer to this feature as connectivity to multiple information sources. In any event, Hummingbird EIP claims to provide access to the broadest range of sources of any product including groupware and e-mail sources; document management, records management systems, and unstructured content; line-of-business systems including ERP and packaged applications of various sorts; data warehousing systems and other structured data sources; network file systems; and Web sources.

Personalization

In the area of personalization, Hummingbird EIP offers a "theme" capability supporting multiple levels of user personalization. Themes are Hummingbird EIP's way of enabling customizing the appearance of the portal interface for categories and subcategories of users or for individual users.

Application integration

Hummingbird provides portal interface–based integration. That is, one can access all applications through a single, unified, consistent environment provided by the portal interface. Further, one can use the functionality of various applications, coupled with information provided from various sources accessible through the interface, to add information and data, make changes in various organizational systems, publish documents or reports, interact with other knowledge workers, or perform various other activities.

Hummingbird provides a plug-in architecture called e-clip for integrating third-party applications into the portal interface. It uses similar means to provide interfaces to its own applications. What it does not provide is a middle-tier EAI capability based on a J2EE application server with an inference engine and a development environment or an alternative server of equal or greater capability. Therefore, its integrative features are limited to portal interface integration and to the integrative features (not inconsiderable) already built in to Hummingbird's component content and document-management, decision-processing, structured data management/ analysis, and connectivity applications.

Metadata dictionary

The metadata dictionary is stored in a repository that aggregates data and information from all enterprise sources. It provides data about all such sources, regardless of where the data is stored and the application that produced it; about the users who generate and use these sources; and about their preferences and interests. Its importance is that it provides a comprehensive and unified view of all of an enterprise's information and therefore greatly enhances searching and retrieving information within an enterprise. The metadata repository is object oriented but resides on any RDBMS.

Plug-in architecture and APIs

As indicated previously, Hummingbird EIP provides "e-clip" plug-in architecture—Hummingbird's version of portlets, channels, gadgets, and CDAs. This architecture is the basis of Hummingbird's ability to provide portal interface–based integration. But it carries with it no additional capability of relating e-clip-based applications to one another.

XML-based infrastructure

Hummingbird uses XML to exchange data between the components of its EIP. It is also used by the portal to communicate with other applications integrated with the EIP through e-clip channels. Hummingbird intends to make its XML document type definitions (DTDs) available on its Web site to facilitate users building extensions for integrating additional data sources and other applications.

Connectivity

Host access and network connectivity solutions are an area of strength for the Hummingbird EIP. They provide Windows-based, Web-based, and e-based technologies host access and network connectivity solutions necessary to access information and resources on legacy systems.

These include: support for Microsoft® WindowsXP™, a Connectivity Security Pack™ providing "a Secure Shell TCP tunnel for communications between clients and hosts on a network, protecting corporate assets" (Hummingbird, 2002a), the Exceed family enabling "desktop, Web, and remote users to easily access UNIX applications from Windows 2000/NT, Windows 95/98/ME, and Windows 3.x-based personal computers" (ibid.), the NFS Maestro™ offering quick "access to file and print resources in a mixed PC and UNIX network" (ibid.), and the HostExplorer™ Family which includes Windows-based host access, Web-to-host publishing and host printing from enterprise desktops.

That completes my review of Hummingbird EIP's general portal capabilities. A central fact should be clear from it. Hummingbird's EIP product is one of the most well-rounded portal offerings reviewed so far, even apart from the more specific content management and decision-processing capabilities still to be discussed. However, it is also a clear instance of portal-interface integration and does not provide middle-tier EAI application integration for disparate applications. I will come back to this point once more in the discussion of architecture. Let us now turn to the features of Hummingbird EIP in the areas of document and content management, decision processing, and collaboration.

Document and content management

Hummingbird EIP (2002b) provides Search Server, Fulcrum Knowledge Server and CyberDocs™ in the area of document and content management. I have already described the role of the first two servers in providing some of the generalized capabilities of Hummingbird's EIP. CyberDOCS (PCDOCS 1997) is a comprehensive Web-enabled document management solution that provides organizations with full document management functionality through a Web browser. CyberDOCS provides a front end to a content/document management subsystem architecture containing DOCSFusion Server (an object-oriented document management business process engine) and DOCS Open™ Repositories, which stories documents in their native formats. CyberDOCS is one of the more capable document-management products on the market and brings that capability to Hummingbird EIP.

Decision processing, business intelligence, data management and integration, data mining

Hummingbird EIP (2002c) provides a suite of tools in this area as comprehensive as any competitor's offerings. Thus, the portal provides an interface to BI Suite™, Genio Suite™, and Genio Miner™ and analytical applications. BI Suite provides desktop- and Web-based query, reporting, and OLAP capabilities, all tightly integrated. Genio Suite is a data exchange solution. It provides ETL services across all structured data applications including decision support systems, data warehouses, data marts, and other enterprise applications. Genio Miner integrates data mining with data acquisition, an innovative combination of product functionality shared with few others. It connects to any data source(s) and then can transform and load data into any target data store, where it can then mine the data using a variety of neural network and other technologies.

Finally, Hummingbird also offers various packaged analytical applications that plug into its EIP. These include: "risk management, profitability reporting, customer analysis, sales forecasting and quality standards compliance" (Hummingbird, 2000, p. 13). Initial domains of focus of these applications are financial services, telecommunications, and health services.

Collaboration

PD Accord (2002d) is Hummingbird's Web-based project- and document-centric collaborative framework. It is applicable both within and across the enterprise and supports continuous collaborative activities of employees, customers, suppliers, and other agents related to the enterprise. PD Accord offers the following features: customizable project folders and templates to pre-structure the collaboration process and facilitate sharing of best practices and creation of new project workspaces; document- and folder-level security; a security model allowing project administrators to delegate authority to manage documents and folders; the ability to have discussion threads related to each document or folder; status flags allowing users to easily determine the status of documents and folders; automatic notification of users about addition of new documents or updating of old ones; audit trails track actions taken on folders and documents; a customizable user interface using XML/XSLT; and secure collaborative communications using 128-bit secure socket layer (SSL) encryption as well as database encryption.

PD Accord, a new offering, represents Hummingbird's entrance into the collaborative segment of the portal space. The offering is strong in its document and content management aspects, but it is clearly much less comprehensive than Open Text's or Intraspect's offerings in the same area. Also, it offers limited project planning and management and no synchronous collaboration capability compared with more comprehensive collaborative portals. Thus, even with its additions Hummingbird EIP remains primarily a content-management, decision-processing portal at the beginning of its move into the collaboration area.

Hummingbird architecture

As I indicated in the description of its features, Hummingbird's architecture (2000b) is an instance of the PAC architecture first described in Chapter 5 (see Figure 17.1). In spite of the variety of features and components it offers and the integration it provides within its content-management, decision-processing, and collaborative components, the fact remains that functionality provided by these three components and any third-party add-ons is isolated from functionality provided by the others. Beyond portal interface integration through e-clips, providing access to role-based content and applications in the same interface and the feature of unified brokered search allowing querying across structured data and

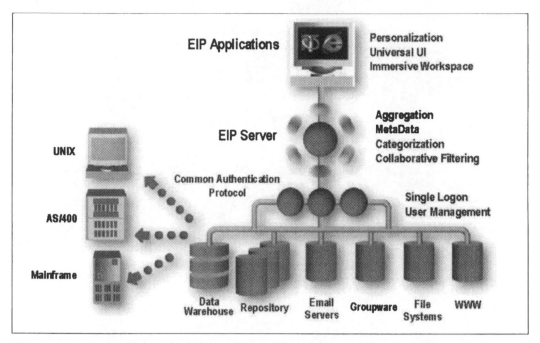

Figure 17.1. Hummingbird EIP functional architecture. (Source: Hummingbird, Ltd. [2000b].)

unstructured content repositories, little integration is provided by workflow functionality or in the middle tier through EAI. No information integration or knowledge integration of the kind described in Chapters 5, 6, 20, and 13, is provided by the Hummingbird EIP.

On the other hand, Hummingbird has been gradually developing the capability to provide artificial information integration (see Chapter 5) in both the content-management and structured-data realms. Its CyberDOCS product applies object technology in its application server. Its Genio Suite is based on a metadata repository employing an object model that has some change adjustment capabilities. The next generation Genio platform (Hummingbird, 2000c, p. 13) promises more extensive support for automated synchronization and for distributed intelligent agents that will be able to: react to events; transform and transport transactions and information directly to defined targets; and transform and transport transactions and information via Genio's information broker.

Vision and direction of Hummingbird

The vision and direction of Hummingbird's EIP is reflected in the architectural changes being planned, in the XML capability being added, in the implementation and further development of Genio architecture, and in the development of new collaboration capabilities. Figure 17.2 illustrates the Genio architecture (Hummingbird, 2000c). Note the similarity between it and the SAI architecture of Chapter 5. Genio is not an instance of SAI architecture yet, since its business process engines do not supply the process-control services required. But this technology development is a natural extension of Hummingbird's present direction in developing its Hummingbird Enterprise Repository (HERO) architecture. When

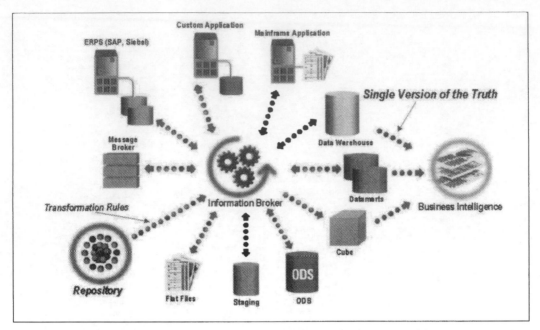

Figure 17.2. Hummingbird's Genio architecture. (Source: Hummingbird, Ltd. [2000b] p. 7.)

Hummingbird also adds further collaboration capabilities it will be approaching the model of the Advanced collaboration portal with PAI architecture.

"Touch points" with knowledge processing and knowledge management

Hummingbird evidently believes that its Fulcrum Knowledge Server provides advanced knowledge-management capability because it has the capability to build "knowledge maps" and "cluster maps" from documents and text and then to use such cluster maps as the basis for hierarchical navigation schema for portal interfaces. In addition, Genio's data mining capabilities are viewed as knowledge-producing capabilities of considerable sophistication and power. Finally, PD Accord's collaboration capabilities provide some support for group problem-solving activities.

While these capabilities are impressive, they are more knowledge claim generation and information-organization capabilities than they are knowledge-production and knowledge-management capabilities. As is true of the other EIP products reviewed earlier, they provide no formal support for knowledge claim validation and no means of telling whether the "knowledge" or "cluster maps" or data-mining results or plans produced are information or knowledge. Nor do they provide any support for the various knowledge-management activity categories specified in Chapter 9.

Viador E-Portal 6.4

Viador was among the first EIP products. In fact, its original name was Infospace and its original focus was business intelligence and data warehousing. Soon after the release of Merrill Lynch's portal report in November of 1998, Viador (1999) changed its name, gave its business intelligence reporting products a face-lift, and—voilà—one of the first decision processing EIPs was born. But Viador is much more than a decision processing portal product. It is also a product that is based on a portal framework.

The framework (Viador, 2000) follows the now familiar pattern of providing a basic set of tightly integrated portal services supplemented by other applications that may be integrated as "portlets." (A portlet (Viador, 2002) is an object that can use the basic services of the portal framework, is registered with the portal, and can function as a well-behaved application in the portal framework.) In fact, its initial classification as a decision-processing portal was based on its integration of its own e-business intelligence suite including its report-server, OLAP, data-management, data-warehousing and charting capabilities as portlets. Since Viador is a framework offering portlet integration, it can more easily evolve from a decision-processing portal to a product with more comprehensive functionality, simply by defining additional portlets. But in this respect it does not differ from Hummingbird, Plumtree, or any of the many portal products already reviewed that can add functionality through portlets or similar mechanisms.

This line of reasoning raises the issue of how Viador and other portal framework products should be classified. I have called Plumtree a content-management portal because even though it is capable of integrating decision processing applications well enough, it is not prominently associated with solutions involving decision processing and provides content management capability through its own portal framework. I have called Hummingbird a decision-processing/content-management portal in spite of its portal framework and use of e-clip architecture, because it has products of its own in the decision-processing, content-management, and document-management categories it features in seeking solutions.

Going back to Viador, I classify it, also, as a decision-processing/content-management portal, because it provides considerable content-management capability through its basic portal platform services and also provides its own e-business intelligence applications. It does not have document-management capabilities but can integrate Documentum, Open Text, or PCDOCS through portlets in order to supply that capability (Viador, 2001, p. 2).

In addition to its lack of document-management capability, Viador also lacks extensive collaboration services. It can however integrate other collaboration applications (e.g., Open Text Livelink, Lotus Notes, Sitescape, and Intraspect) through its portlet capability (ibid.).

Viador's basic portal services include

- *Security services*—including authorization by individual, role, and group; authentication with support for LDAP and other industry standards; and extranet security services including URL, data encryption, SSL, and HTTP tunneling.
- *Search services*—includes the Inktomi search engine; it can also integrate others such as Autonomy and Verity.
- *Data access services*—including a federated architecture of distributed repositories, a repository API, a Java-SQL bridge, all major RDBMS access, non-RDBMS including multidimensional OLAP access, and access to ninety legacy databases through Enterworks VirtualDB data access platform and XML services.

- *Portal object management services*—including facilities to add, delete, modify, organize, navigate, search for, retrieve, and archive portal objects. Viador provides automatic categorization services by integrating Inktomi technology in its e-portal framework. Autonomy can also be used for this purpose.
- *User management services*—including profiling and management of users' relationship to the portal.
- *Development facilities*—for creating, modifying, and managing portal pages.
- *API facilities*—for creating, modifying, and managing composite portal pages.
- *Repository management services*—provides repository management services open to use of customer's database and search technology in installing repository.
- *Workflow services*—supports event triggers allowing for e-mail alerts and pager notifications and allows integration of third-party workflow engines in EIP solutions.
- *Rules engine*—allows integration of third-party rules engines in support of workflow.
- *XML import/export services*—enable translation of content into XML for storage in the repository, communication within the portal, and communication with XML-enabled applications.
- *Event management services*—provide the ability to tag events and determine alerts that users may subscribe to.
- *Scheduling services*—provide a scheduling engine for business processes.
- *System infrastructure services*—managing multithreading, load balancing across distributed services, and audit and logging services to track interaction with and performance of the portal).

Viador portal components (2000, pp. 5–7) that deliver the LISTED services include the Portal Explorer, the Page Builder, the Publish and Subscribe Framework, the Security Management Framework, and the Portal Builder. The Portal Explorer manages the portal objects. It organizes objects into taxonomies; searches; enables navigation; handles subscriptions; and copies, deletes, and executes objects in the repository. The Publish and Subscribe Framework publishes objects to the portal repository for users and publishes objects to the portal interface for administrators. The portal Page Builder allows users to personalize their portal interface. Users can add objects they think will be helpful in their jobs and modify and delete other objects they do not want to work with. The Security Management Framework handles the security services described earlier.

Finally, the Portal Builder is the template component supporting the Viador Portlet Development Kit (PDK). The PDK provides: access to open, published portal APIs that enable developers to manage portal objects (create, modify, retrieve, or delete them, and assign security profiles to them); design and build composite portal pages; integrate third-party applications through a set of APIs and applications that portal developers use to quickly and easily add new applications and portal content; and manage session security.

Viador architecture

The basic architecture of Viador is another instance of PAC architecture. Viador provides a portal server that manages the basic portal services and the portlet objects providing connectivity to the application servers and business-process engines driving portlet applications. The portal framework incorporates all portlet applications as objects, even Viador's own business-intelligence applications. Thus, integration of portlets is primarily through the portal interface. Integration of content occurs through federated search. Integration of structured data occurs through Viador's business-intelligence applications and the federated (DFI) architecture (see Chapter 5) internal to the business-intelligence portlets. But integration across portlet applications is not provided for directly by Viador's architecture and capabilities. To produce that sort of integration, portlet applications need to be tied together through business-process automation/EAI. Such automation can be produced by integrating workflow capabilities and creating process models (see Chapters 5 and 6), but these capabilities must be integrated into Viador through additional portlet integration. Until the development of these capabilities for Viador, it will remain an instance of a decision-processing/content-management portal with PAC architecture.

Vision and direction of Viador

The vision and direction of Viador from its beginning have been to gradually increase the capability of its portal suite to the point where it supports creating the most comprehensive EIP solutions available. Viador began its product development with a decision-processing portal product. It then added its E-Portal Framework, providing a flexible infrastructure for integration of applications of unlimited diversity and also providing a substantial advance in its own content-management capabilities. In its latest Viador E-Portal 6.4 release, it provides (Viador, 2001)

> compatibility with leading J2EE Application servers including BEA Weblogic, IBM Websphere, and Macromedia JRun. Using any of these application servers totally customized Java Server pages (JSP) pages can be quickly and securely published using the point and click Portal Express interface. In E-Portal 6.4 Viador is releasing three new JSP tag libraries for open standards based access to portal page design, user and document metadata and real time reporting. Lab results have demonstrated that Viador's new JSP technology provides open-ended customization without sacrificing performance or scalability.

Even more important, by introducing integration with J2EE application servers, Viador also more closely approaches the architecture it will need to support business-process automation models and workflow and business-process–based integration. In other words, the addition of J2EE servers to the Viador portal architecture brings it a step closer to PAI architecture.

"Touch points" with knowledge processing and knowledge management

Viador has never strongly emphasized its relevance for knowledge management as opposed to information management and business intelligence. This may be because the roots of the company are in the decision-processing/data-warehousing/structured data–processing field, in contrast to the document-management/content-management/search-technology field. It is the latter that has been more closely associated with knowledge management, while the former has been much more closely associated with data and information management. Nevertheless, there are touch points with knowledge processing and knowledge management in the areas of information acquisition, knowledge claim formulation, and knowledge integration.

Viador is, in fact, as relevant for knowledge management as the other decision-processing/content-management portals we have examined. While it supports the above subprocesses and also supplies better support for knowledge claim formulation in the structured data–processing area than most competitors, it provides little explicit support for the knowledge claim validation aspects of knowledge production and the various activities characteristic of knowledge management.

Computer Associates CleverPath Portal 3.5

CleverPath Portal has reached its present state by a somewhat circuitous route. It originated as one of the pioneering portal products in the industry, produced in late 1998 by a DSS/data warehousing/reporting/business intelligence company called Information Advantage. Information Advantage's MyEureka product focused on decision processing, supplemented by a publishing capability and, of course, search technology it licensed from a third party. In early 2000, Information Advantage was purchased by Sterling Software which, itself sold out in a matter of a few months to Computer Associates (CA) (2000).

The purchase of Information Advantage by Sterling Software naturally produced much speculation about the fate of the MyEureka portal. This speculation was further magnified by CA's purchase. CA soon announced that the portal would be integrated with its OO technology and specifically with its Jasmine*ii* O-O database/tool/development/application integration platform and its Neugent agent-based predictive technology (Computer Associates, 2000a). It also promised further development of the content management aspects of the portal. This, in fact has been done. Today, after a name change to Jasmine*ii* portal, a more recent name change to CleverPath Portal, further development of its application/integration server technology, Neugent predictive technology, Aion business rule inference engine, and the release of its new Advantage Integration and CleverPath Enterprise Content Management products to go along with the Information Advantage business-intelligence products, CA has released a portal product with diverse capabilities providing strong support for both decision processing and content management and open to integration with various application/integration server platforms including its own Advantage line. The features of CleverPath Portal 3.5 (Computer Associates, 2002) follow.

- *Application and information integration into role-based, personalized workspaces.* In a manner similar to Netegrity, CleverPath Portal 3.5 enables construction of workspaces through drag-and-drop placement of information and application sources from "tree views" on to the workspace template. Multiple personalized workspaces and views may be created by users. Roles and user profiles are defined in portal-based LDAP structures that can also be linked with security applications.
- *Security.* Security is provided through a number of alternative means representing different levels of security, but the most secure is single sign-on through CA's e-Trust security suite.
- *Broad international support.* CleverPath Portal supports English, French, Spanish, Italian, German, Japanese, traditional Chinese, simplified Chinese, and Korean.
- *Dynamic personalization.* Content is formed dynamically to fit individual preferences at the time of access. CleverPath can use the predictive capability of Neugents to predict individual preferences for purposes of dynamic personalization.
- *Wireless capability.* This is provided "out of the box."
- *Content management.* CleverPath's Enterprise Content Management application is integrated into CleverPath Portal. It provides capability to manage diverse media assets, including data, images, multimedia, presentations, spreadsheets, documents, e-mail, and text. It supports third-party document-management solutions as well. In addition, it does versioning, check-in, check-out, workflow administration, and business-process automation. Its repository is "collaborative." It is built on an OO–based application/integration server that supports XML (Computer Associates, 2002a).
- *Real-time collaboration.* CleverPath Portal provides discussion forums in which users can collaborate in real time and have their interactions tracked and stored in a knowledge base and later used in communities of interest and practice. It also supports integrating third-party collaboration portlets of diverse kinds.
- *Publish and subscribe.* Users share information by publishing and categorizing content and subscribing to automatic delivery of relevant updates. "The Portal Repository instantly 'recognizes' when an item has been added or changed and matches this event to the appropriate agents for notification and delivery." (Computer Associates, 2002).
- *Support for integration and connectivity standards.* CleverPath Portal provides native XML as well as EJB, CORBA, COM, COM+, HTTP, DHTML, TCP/IP, Java, JMS, JND, JSP, among others.
- *Web server support.* Support is provided for Apache Tomcat (ships with CleverPath), IBM WebSphere, Sun ONE, BEA Web Logic, NES, and JRUN; others may be integrated.
- *Searching and spidering.* A search engine enables examining both metadata describing documents and the contents of documents themselves. Autonomy is embedded in CleverPath Portal, but Verity and Convera are also supported, and other search engines may be integrated through a CleverPath Portal API. Queries and results can be added to workspaces

as Portlets. Through search agents, users can define queries, schedule them, and be notified about new or updated content.

- *Visual templates.* Administrators can create such templates for different user role profiles. The templates can then be personalized further by users.
- *OLAP capability* CleverPath Portal integrates CleverPath OLAP 5.0.
- *Reporting capability.* CleverPath Portal integrates CleverPath Reporter 4.0.
- *Analysis capability.* CleverPath Portal integrates CleverPath Forest and Trees 6.5.
- *Predictive analysis capability.* CleverPath Portal integrates CleverPath Predictive Analysis Server 2.0. The server uses CA's patented Neugents technology to develop predictive neural network models from raw data. These "dynamically detect, predict and respond to changing business conditions." (Computer Associates, 2002b). The new version has upgraded profiling capabilities and also is tightly integrated with CleverPath Aion Business Rules Expert (Computer Associates, 2002c) so that predictions may be coupled with rule execution when a condition specified in a rule is fulfilled.
- *Business rules inference engine capability.* CleverPath Portal integrates CleverPath Aion Business Rules Expert 9.1. It provides a business-rules inference engine, along with a component-based development environment that allows organizations to build and deploy rules-based applications.
- *Visualization services,* CleverPath Portal provides enhanced ability for users to interact with data and understand its structure and relationships through visual images.
- *J2EE support.* CleverPath Portal can interoperate with J2EE Application Servers such as IBM WebSphere, Sun ONE, and others. This means that the CleverPath Portal platform is open to other application/integration servers apart from CA's Advantage Server.
- *Application/integration server support.* CleverPath Portal supports CA's Advantage Integration Server (a business process engine), formerly Jasmine*ii* Application Server. This server supports session pooling, asynchronous communications, exception handling, data conversion, messaging, protocol bridging, event management, an object request broker (ORB), XML, distributed object caching, peer-to-peer architecture, Neugents, connectivity to various relational and hierarchical databases, legacy systems, SAP, Peoplesoft, LDAP, and other sources through "providers."

CleverPath Portal architecture

CleverPath Portal 3.5, viewed as a front end, is another instance of PAC portal architecture providing portal interface integration through portlets, but a CleverPath portal system including the CleverPath Portal, plus CA's Advantage Server (Computer Associates, 2002d), Neugents, the Aion Rules Inference Engine, Jasmine ODB, the eTrust Internet Security Suite, and decision processing and enterprise content management applications is something else entirely. A comparison of the features of such a system with the requirements specified for portal application integration architecture in Chapters 5 and 6 indicates that a CleverPath

Portal system approaches PAI architecture very closely, with the possible exception of providing partial instantiation of objects.

That is, the architecture provides the capability for distributing changes in the object model across the portal system through the functioning of the Aion rules engine. The distributed object cache provided by the Advantage Server is, in effect, a virtual In-memory database (IMDB), maintaining the state of the system as reflected in its objects and agents across the portal system. Changes are propagated through the system by rule execution in response to events constituting the initiation of the changes. In short, the capability for management and synchronization of objects, components, workflows, business rules, and metadata is there.

In addition, the system including the components named above supports event-driven behavior, a system-wide object model with shared representation and a unified view of the enterprise across distributed Advantage Servers, declarative and procedural business rules, caching of the object model, a persistent object store in Jasmine ODB, and reflexive objects. Finally, the Advantage servers provide the wide-ranging connectivity to back-end sources required for PAI architecture, including C, C++, Java, XML, CORBA, COM+, text, relational, ODBC, JDBC, OODBMS, hierarchical, network, flat-file document sources, etc.

Vision and direction of CleverPath Portal

CleverPath Portal is one of a "portfolio" of solutions (Computer Associates, 2002e) developed by CA to support managing e-business. My view is that, from the CA point of view, the basic pattern of the portal component of this portfolio is probably set. It is a portal based on object technology with an open architecture supporting a range of open standards and providing navigation based on tree-like views and distinct segments of portal interface real estate. It is easily integrated with J2EE application servers, with CA's own Advantage Server, and with various capabilities available from complementary CA products, including all of those mentioned in the previous section on architecture.

Increases in portal system capability are, from a CA point of view, likely to come from enhancements to these complementary products rather than to CleverPath Portal itself. The reason for this is that CA's interest is in enhancing the integration capabilities and functionality of its e-business platform as a whole (ibid.). The portal is only the front end of that platform, but the key to winning the competitive battle over e-business market share is in an integrated platform with wide-ranging functionality, rather than the features of the portal front end itself. Those must be competitive, but, I think, not really "leading edge."

In particular, pursuit of increased integration and functionality may lead to enhancements in predictive analysis coming from advances in its Neugents, Aion, and Predictive Analysis Server in the area of addition of fuzzy rules and genetic algorithm capability. In addition, upgrades in Advantage Server XML capability relating to XML topic maps and DAML+OIL Ontology (see Chapter 11) are likely, because these will facilitate interaction across the extended enterprise, and enhance the ECM capability encompassed by the portal system. Further, upgrades in workflow and process modeling and integration of these with Aion capability in both ECM and the Advantage platform are likely, because these will lead to enhanced integration through business process automation. And enhancements in collaborative capability are very likely considering that CA would like to be a leader in the critical area of e-business called collaborative commerce.

The end result of these changes will be to maintain CA's position as one of the leaders in the EIP field. In particular, CA is not far from developing an advanced collaborative portal with substantial decision processing and content management capabilities. I believe that movement toward this type will be its direction over the next year.

"Touch points" with knowledge processing and knowledge management

CA states that one of its major areas of focus is "portals and knowledge management." It is also distributing an IDC White Paper by Brian McDonough and Henry Morris (2001) called "Building a Strong Foundation for Knowledge Management." This paper defines KM as (p. 1)

> ... a formal "process" that evaluates a company's people, organizational processes, and technology and develops a solution to get the right information to the right people at the right time to improve productivity.

It then proceeds to describe the content-management, decision-processing, and collaborative functionality present in Jasmine*ii* that might possibly support the process of getting information to people in the enterprise in a timely way, and concludes that CA's Jasmine provides a good foundation for KM. The pattern of their argument (ibid. p. 2) follows.

> Knowledge management access builds on the KM infrastructure to provide individual and group access to a knowledge base. It consists of EIPs and advanced searching and Web-based query for providing access to both structured and unstructured data, augmented by KM tools. Intellectual capital management software builds and manages employee competencies inventory; supports process improvement, definition, and capture; and monitors and measures improvements in process. Other KM tools provide insight into how individuals and groups access information and monitor what information they create for the purpose of profiling sources of tacit knowledge.

The problem with this analysis and with CA's products from a KM point of view is that the (now) CleverPath Portal has no facilities for distinguishing "right" from "wrong" information. Therefore, whether its portal is connecting to a knowledge base as opposed to just information or databases is not ascertainable through use of CA's products. Moreover, the 'KM tools" referred to above are not KM tools simply by virtue of the label IDC places on them To show that they are indeed KM tools one would have to show that they support recognizable KM activities.

Thus, there is not much argument that CA CleverPath Portal solution provides plenty of support for information acquisition, knowledge claim formulation, information sharing, broadcasting, teaching, and searching/retrieving, but no explicit support (unless one thinks that reporting, analysis, predictive analysis, and collaboration are synonymous with knowledge production) for knowledge claim validation and, therefore, in the end for knowledge production or individual and group learning. Also, because there is no recognition of the kinds of activities that constitute knowledge management, it is not surprising that very few of the nine classes of KM activities distinguished in Chapter 9 are supported by CleverPath Portal.

Ultimately, the claims made in the IDC White Paper are not demonstrated by its analysis. As with other EIPs, the foundation for knowledge management provided by CA CleverPath Portal inadequately supports knowledge processing and knowledge management. That is not to say that CA CleverPath Portal is not an excellent product. Indeed, it is one of the most advanced, if not the most advanced, EIP product I review here, and it may provide the best available foundation for moving further down the path of developing the EKP itself. But a comparison of the features and architecture of the EKP specified in Chapter 13 with the features of CA's portal reviewed earlier indicates that CleverPath must undergo considerable further development to become an EKP product and provide "a strong foundation for Knowledge Management."

Brio.Portal

Brio.Portal, previously Sqribe EIP and Brio One, began as a first-wave portal product focused in the area of decision processing based on structured data. Sqribe/Brio leveraged its DSS/enterprise reporting/data warehousing/OLAP/business performance measurement expertise to achieve and maintain a position of EIP leadership in this segment along with Viador, and CA. Brio (along with Viador and CA) more recently enhanced its portal product with features providing content-management capability as well. The company has done this largely through a development alliance with Autonomy leading to incorporation of Autonomy's "knowledge server," (see the earlier review of Autonomy) within Brio.Portal, which now incorporates Autonomy's search, concept-matching, and automated taxonomy technology. With the addition of Autonomy's capabilities to its own Java-based portal framework architecture and extensive decision-processing features, Brio.Portal (Brio, 2001) is another capable entrant in the decision-processing/content-management segment of the portal product space. Brio.Portal's particular emphasis is on personalization and providing specific personalized information that enable end users to drive the business from their desktops in real time. Here are the main features of Brio.Portal (Brio, 2001, 2002, 2002a, 2002b).

Portal pages

The portal page is the Java-based framework within which portal objects may be embedded. Portal objects, Brio's version of portlets, bring all content and applications—external, internal, and embedded—to the portal interface. The kind of content contained in portal pages includes exception alerts, charts, gauges, syndicated content, and business events. But exactly what content and applications portal objects bring to the individual depends on individual and group-level security and access control, personalization, and customization. Thorough end user and administrative customization of the portal is an important feature. Content, layout, text appearance, styles, tab interfaces, and colors are all controllable by end users and administrators. Administrators can also control the number of portal objects allowed on a page and the number of personal pages available to an end user.

Enterprise reporting

A primary Brio differentiator has always been its enterprise-reporting capability. Sqribe built its original EIP product around ReportMart, its industry-leading enterprise reporting product. Today, Brio.Portal offers highly scalable and customizable enterprise reporting with parameter-driven reports providing information to users in real-time. Reports are also delivered applying granular security so that portions of reports are distributed to users in a personalized fashion based on their security and access profiles. Brio also provides for automated report delivery and alerts based on user profiles.

Business-critical performance metrics delivered through personalized dashboards

Brio.Portal's enterprise-reporting capability is further enhanced by business-critical performance metrics delivered through personalized dashboards in real time based on end user role-based profiles (personalized profile-based delivery). Brio Performance Applications™, embedded in portal pages, help users drive enterprise performance by providing interactive business metrics displayed through charts, graphics, and gauges. These metrics are deigned to provide an immediate understanding of the degree of progress toward established goals. The metrics are available on a "24/7" basis. Brio.Portal allows users to drill down into the details behind any observed pattern and to take action (publication, alerts, etc.) based on the results found.

Delivery of real-time information from enterprise applications

Brio.Portal delivers information in real time from ERP, CRM, SCM, and other enterprise applications and production systems, databases, and data warehouses. It provides the connectivity to these sources needed to extract information and place it into the Brio's reporting, performance measurements, analytical, and other business-intelligence applications for continuous real-time delivery to end users.

Wireless markup language (WML) support for PDA and wireless device connectivity

Brio.Portal provides outbound exception, subscription, and alerts to remote users.

Content management features

These rely heavily on Autonomy's Knowledge Server. They include automated document retrieval; aggregation and categorization of content; personal content agents providing alerts; refresh of information; and targeted delivery, crawl service agents and search service agents. The crawl service agents crawl and index portal, internal, and external (to the enterprise) content. They automatically catalog and categorize content to support searches of greater relevance and portal navigation. The search service agents provide full-text search capabilities with concept matching technology and natural-language interaction. Search agents can be trained by entering sample text phrases or attaching relevant documents.

Trained search agents make it more likely that search results will answer end user queries.

Brio.Portal architecture

The architecture of Brio.Portal (Brio, 2002b) is illustrated in Figure 17.3. The architecture distributes portal functions across a number of servers and service agents. Brio provides a WebClient service for browsers that controls what users can access and see through the portal. The WebClient running on a Web server or Windows NT and integrating Macromedia's JRun Pro Servlet engine delivers portal pages to the browser and communicates with the Service Broker, a service agent that performs session management and brokering between other service agents and the WebClient. Other service agents include

- *The Administrator.* A client-side agent running under Windows or in a Web browser and providing a GUI provides the ability to publish content, to perform user and group administration, category (including definition of Brio.Portal categories), and object management (including report), and to perform Brio.Portal services, configuration management, and job factory and database services.
- *The Name Service Agent.* This provides directory lookup and configuration for other service agents resident on the Brio.Portal Information Delivery Server.
- *The Authentication Service Agent.* Not illustrated in Figure 17.3, this feature is also resident on the Information Delivery Server.
- *The Job Factory Service Agents.* This feature requests services (received from the Service Broker) from external DBMS, enterprise application systems, data warehouses, etc. and then delivers the results of its requests to the Service Broker and the Repository for future distribution. Job Factory

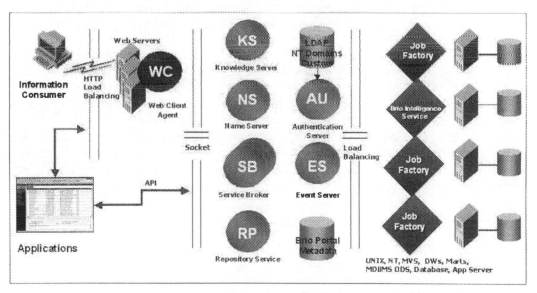

Figure 17.3. Brio.Portal architecture. (Source: Brio [2002a].)

service agents are resident on distributed application servers. The ability to distribute jobs across the enterprise is an important element in providing for Brio scalability.

- *The Repository Agent.* This feature services requests to store or retrieve objects from the object repository or to search and browse through it. It is resident in the Information Delivery Server.
- *The Event Server.* This offers scheduling services to Job Factory Agents and a notification service for end users. It is resident in the Information Delivery Server.
- *Integrators.* These are service agents integrating application servers with Brio.Portal through Java APIs. Developers can use Java APIs to access Brio.Portal from other programs. Integrator also ships with the OO language JPython, a language written in Java. JPython can be used to quickly deliver integrator applications that can be run on distributed application servers.

In addition to service agents and the Web Servers and Information Delivery Servers, Brio.Portal standard systems architecture includes: production databases, various application servers that interact with the Job Factories (including the Brio Report Server), and an Object/Metadata Repository resident on a commercial relational database platform such as Microsoft SQL Server, DB2, Oracle7, Oracle8, or Sybase. The optional systems architecture adds the Knowledge Server with its Crawl and Search Service Agents and its ability to automate retrieval, search, aggregation, and categorization.

Brio.Portal architecture is a flexible and distributed infrastructure for processing and analyzing structured data from enterprise application sources. The architecture is scalable, Java-based, and capable of integrating the full range of structured applications through portal objects. In Brio.Portal 7.0, content-management capabilities have been added through a strategic alliance and use of Autonomy's knowledge server. Document-management capabilities and collaborative capabilities are not featured in the portal and need to be integrated through the portal objects or Java API integration facilities.

Brio.Portal is another example of PAC architecture. It has recently evolved from a pure decision-processing portal to a decision-processing/content-management (DP/CM) portal, but this evolution has not produced architectural development toward greater EAI in the middle tier of the portal system. There is no integration in the Brio.Portal system with a J2EE application server supporting an inference engine, EAI, rapid integration with enterprise applications, and business process automation. Each of the other examples of DP/CM architecture—Hummingbird, Viador, and CA's CleverPath Portal—are more advanced in middle-tier EAI than Brio.Portal.

Vision and direction of Brio.Portal

According to Brio (2002),

Brio.Portal is a complete information reporting and delivery system. At its heart is a secure repository that manages information objects and accesses permissions by users and groups. Brio.Portal acccpts information of all types including business intelligence tool output, Word documents, Excel spreadsheets, graphics, video clips, and custom data formats. Users can easily search Brio.Portal, and view or run the reports they need, when they need them.

Brio's vision has, in addition, clearly been one of providing a portal solution that would provide excellent real-time business intelligence and business-performance metric support for the enterprise. It is among the leaders in fulfilling this part of its vision. But in fulfilling its broader vision it falls short of providing a complete information reporting and delivery system, if by that we mean one that will manage unstructured content at the sub-document level. Brio has just begun to enter this area with its Autonomy-derived capability. Its future will probably focus on strengthening its content-management capability while continuing to maintain its excellence in decision processing. There is no indication of development toward integrating collaborative processing capabilities or EAI capabilities. It is likely that without new strategic alliances it will continue to lose ground in these areas to its other DP/CM competitors.

"Touch points" with knowledge processing and knowledge management

Brio has never claimed knowledge management functionality for its portal product. The closest it comes in this direction is using the name "knowledge server" for the Autonomy component it has integrated into its portal offering. Nevertheless, as is the case with the other DP/CM portals there are touch points with knowledge processing and knowledge management in Brio.Portal, primarily in the areas of information acquisition, knowledge claim formulation, and knowledge integration.

Brio.Portal, is, in fact, as relevant for knowledge management as the other DP/CM portals examined. While it supports the afore-mentioned subprocesses and also supplies better support for knowledge claim formulation in the structured data processing area than many other portal products, it provides little explicit support for the knowledge claim validation aspects of knowledge production and the various activities (see Chapter 9) characteristic of knowledge management.

Sybase Enterprise Portal (EP) 2.5

Sybase was a relatively late entrant into the portal space. It, like Sun, Oracle, BEA, TIBCO, and other late entrants, viewed the EIP as not merely an interface but as a standards-compliant integration platform or portal system, with the interface constituting only one component. In discussing previous portal offerings we have clearly identified a pattern in which many of the early entrants have evolved their own portal offerings into integration platforms. They have done this either by creating alliances with third parties, who supply EAI capabilities in the form of application and integration servers, or by developing their own application servers. In general, the idea that EAI is an essential capability of a portal solution has become increasingly widespread. Sybase's EP 2.5 is one of the more comprehensive offerings recognizing the importance of this trend and attempting to fulfill the need for portal integration with an underlying enterprise architecture that is at its foundation. A review of Sybase's key features follows.

In the area of *portal foundations* (Sybase, 2002), security and access control, range of component support, scalability, availability, and Web services support are all offered by Sybase EP 2.5. Security and access control features include single sign-on access to multiple applications; role-based access, ensuring that groups of users see only what is relevant for their roles; a secure business-object abstraction layer to provide secure and simple developer access to back-end applications; and support for integrating with an existing LDAP directory server. The range of component support for developers in addition to Java includes Active X, C, C++, COM, CORBA, and PowerBuilder.

Scalability features include clustering of servers running on different platforms distributed over remote geographic areas as well as multithreaded transaction management. Availability features include automatic failover of both stateful and stateless components and servlet session information. Web-services features include support for major Web services–related standards such as simple object access protocol (SOAP), web service description language (WSDL), and universal description, discovery, and integration (UDDI) registry, development of Web services-applications from existing business components, and connection of portlets to Web services for e-business–based collaboration.

In the area of *integration features* there are business-process management (Process Server), integration servers (e-Biz Integrator and Web Services Integrator), adapters, EDI, and mainframe features. Business-process management enables workflow-based integration and management of new and existing IT systems. Integration server features include the ability to route and transform messages based on their content while translating their content from one format to another and Web-services integration across the boundary of the enterprise. Adapters provide access to off-the-shelf or customized enterprise applications (including ERP, CRM, financial, technology, and XML adapter types), while EDI integration extends legacy EDI systems to current e-business environments. Finally, Sybase EP 2.5 can incorporate previously developed integration products that save the expense of new development by providing connections to mainframe and legacy applications.

In the area of *portal services,* Sybase EP 2.5 features include a "ready to deploy presentation layer," personalization, navigation, a common look and feel, search and categorization, agent search, channel search, indexing, "ready-to-use" portlets, a portlet development framework, mobile and wireless connectivity, and end-to-end content-management support. The presentation layer is built on a Java-based template framework that supports the other presentation service features.

Personalization includes the ability to direct information to users' desktops, targeted toward their job roles and individual preferences. Sybase EP 2.5 provides role-based, automatic, and explicit methods for personalizing the portal. Any combination of these methods can be used to provide the right level of personalization for each user. Other features include the ability to add as many personalized pages as the user wishes; add and configure portlets providing content and applications; and control the appearance of portal pages by determining layout, styles, colors, and number of portlet windows, among other things.

Navigation features include intuitive navigation allowing rapid access to specific portal pages. "Look-and-feel" features of the portal are intended to provide a consistent end-user experience. Search and categorization features include concept-based, fuzzy, Boolean, and proximity natural language searching along with indexing and searching external content sources including both databases and

Web sites. Content and data are automatically indexed. Agent searching uses both organization agents and agents created by users. User-defined agents can search both structured and unstructured data. Channel Search lets users predefine channels that automatically search structured and unstructured data.

An important category of portal service is portlets. Sybase EP 2.5 provides "ready to use portlets," which, in turn, provide "interaction windows into information and applications." "Multiple portlets in a page provide unified access to multiple systems." In addition, a toolkit for developing portlets supplies a Portlet Development Framework for rapidly integrating portlets. Sybase portlets include enterprise software applications handling structured data such as ERP and financial applications as well as content-management portlets along with some beginning to address issues of collaboration.

Recently Autonomy (2002) and Sybase announced the availability of

- An agent-based personalized information channel portlet that can be created by users and that continually monitors and alerts them in real time to new information
- A community portlet that allows users to view and copy relevant agents created by others
- A profile portlet that automatically profiles each user based on concepts in documents users have been tracking with their agents
- An expertise locator portlet that finds experts based on users entering descriptions of subject matter
- A retrieval portlet allowing content to be searched in any language or format, wherever it is stored, with automatic retrieval in real time of hyperlinks to similar information

Mobile and wireless presentation services for extending the enterprise portal system to mobile devices are provided by Sybase EP along with both WAP and WML support. In the area of content management (CM), an infrastructure supporting the content life cycle from conception through approval and publishing with version control is provided. Authors may submit, edit, review, and approve content using the tools they normally use to generate it. The CM capability includes a list interface for completing tasks. Distributed workflow processes with e-mail notifications may be formulated to support collaborative efforts at content generation. The CM infrastructure may be applied to e-business applications and content as well as internal CM processes. It also supports content categorization and scheduled launch and expiration of content.

Sybase portal architecture

The architecture of Sybase EP 2.5 is another portal architecture that exhibits the now familiar pattern of a portal server hosted by a J2EE-compliant applications server (the Sybase EA Server), (Sybase, 2001) relying on a wide range of open computing standards including Java, XML, HTTP, and many others, but Sybase, like Sun offers strong EAI capabilities. The specific architecture of Sybase EP portal systems is illustrated in Figure 17.4.

The Sybase EP platform, again, like Sun ONEs, provides a greater ability to automate business processes and business logic across both J2EE application servers and enterprise legacy systems than other portal products. Sybase uses its New

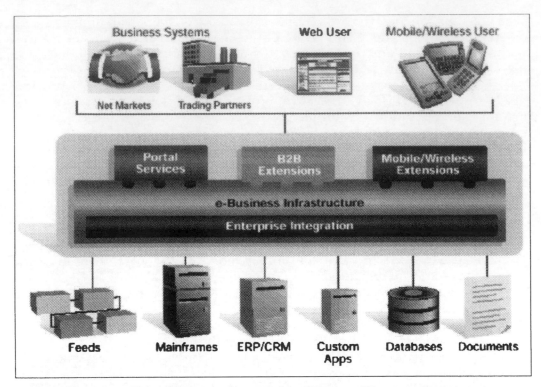

Figure 17.4. Sybase EP architecture. (Source: Sybase [2001, p. 2].)

Era of Networks Process Server (Sybase, 2002b) for designing, deploying, and managing business processes in conjunction with the J2EE-compliant EA Server.

Integration with multiple back-end information systems is provided by various integration products, Enterprise Adapters (including the Enterprise Adapters Workbench and an XML adapter), and its Web Services Integrator (WSI) that extend the application and data assets for enterprise application environments into dynamic Web services based on standards such as XML, SOAP, WSDL, and UDDI. In fact, Sybase EP integrates with Sybase's (2002c) business process integration (BPI) suite containing: BizTracker (a tool for intelligent monitoring of messaging in infrastructure or applications), Process Server, e-Biz Integrator (for routing and transforming messages based on content), EA Server, Web Services Integrator, and Adapter for XML.

The ability to perform comprehensive business process automation and integration provided by BPI Suite is a step beyond the EAI capabilities of most other portal competitors. When combined with the additional business-process automation capabilities provided by Sybase's development platform (Sybase Power-Designer, PowerJ, and PowerSite™) included with EP 2.5, the Sybase EP architectural platform approaches PAI architecture minus the intelligent agent component.

Vision and direction of Sybase EP

Sybase's vision is that "the portal is the platform." This is another way of saying that the portal is not merely a front-end interface tool but rather a system for comprehensively integrating the enterprise and its business processes. Consistent with that vision, Sybase has hosted its portal services on EA Server, integrated EA Server with its BPI suite of tools supporting EAI, and supplemented the suite with substantial developmental capabilities provided by its line of Web-based and Java-based development tools. In addition, however, since there is no reason to view the portal as restricted to the enterprise alone, Sybase added both B2B and mobile/wireless extension to EP. The B2B extensions provide for B2B collaboration on transactions and e-marketplace integration. At present, Sybase's further development of Web services capability seems designed to provide it with a leadership position in extraprise and interprise e-business integration.

The direction of Sybase appears to be to strengthen its portal platform's integration capability further by focusing on Web services and developing a market-leading implementation of this new functionality. Sybase EP does not seem heavily focused in the collaborative-portal or knowledge-portal segments of the portal space. Rather its direction seems to be to provide the leading DP/CM portal consistent with an open standards–based operating systems platform-neutral architecture.

"Touch points" with knowledge processing and knowledge management

Sybase EP is not as strongly oriented toward knowledge processing and knowledge management as it is toward information processing and information management. It has strong content-management capabilities derived from Autonomy's technology. It has strong structured data management capabilities derived from its own products and from acquisitions. Finally, it has incorporated industry-leading EAI capabilities through its acquisition of New Era of Networks (Sybase, 2001a) and its technology. All this means that Sybase EP supports information acquisition, knowledge claim formulation, broadcasting, and sharing very well. But it has no special capability for supporting knowledge claim validation and knowledge management.

TIBCO Active Portal™

TIBCO is a 13-year-old company with a long commitment to EAI. Its portal product reflects that commitment. It is essentially an overlay on TIBCO's extensive line of EAI products with portal plug-ins added. TIBCO (2002) Active Portal platform has three components: TIBCO PortalBuilder™, TIBCO Alert Server™, and TIBCO PortalPacks™. TIBCO PortalBuilder is a Java-based portal framework of services with the following features:

- Provides complete J2EE compliance and runs on well-known Web and application servers such as Sun ONE
- Provides search, content, and document management; e-mail; and ERP/CRM enterprise applications in a mix of decision-processing/content-management functionality
- Provides customized but consistent look and feel
- Supports "plug-in" functionality to rapidly integrate content and applications
- Provides out-of-the-box support for multilingual deployment

- May be integrated with any or all of TIBCO's EAI, B2B and business process management (BPM) solutions, and, more generally with TIBCO's EAI framework
- Provides native single sign-on, authentication support for leading security vendors
- Provides Web-based, centralized administration, supporting delegation
- Enables multi-level individual and role-based personalization and customization by users as well as administrators

TIBCO Alert Server (2002a) is event driven. It delivers alerts to wireless devices when it is triggered by e-business events such as changing market prices or messages generated by internal billing, inventory, and other enterprise applications. TIBCO Alert Server manages millions of event triggers and large data sets. It contains a Profile Manager that allows users to define trigger events and to specify alert preferences. It provides alerts based on both text and numeric data as well as load balancing and fault tolerance. Alerts can be delivered to multiple gateways through integration with TIBCO PortalBuilder (2002b). Finally, a TIBCO Hawk™ (a system of agents for monitoring and managing enterprise systems and applications) (TIBCO, 2002c) micro-agent can monitor and manage the entire alerting system.

TIBCO PortalPacks (2002d) are prebuilt interfaces to applications and content—TIBCO's version of portlets. TIBCO currently offers PortalPacks for Microsoft Exchange, Lotus Domino, Verity, Interwoven, PeopleSoft, Siebel, Documentum, and SAP Workplace. TIBCO's partner program attempts to encourage development of new PortalPacks.

TIBCO architecture

TIBCO's architecture is comprehensive. It provides support for J2EE application servers to either host the portal or provide transaction management as the case may be. It also supports an extensive list of adapters to packaged applications, databases, and networking technologies; an adapter SDK; and integration with TIBCO's full line of integration products. These include TIBCO Rendezvous™ messaging software, TIBCO BusinessWorks™ (a process design and modeling tool providing support for business integration technologies and standards such as XML, J2EE, JMS, SOAP, WSDL, and Web services), TIBCO Hawk™, TIBCO Integration Manager™ (provides business-process definition, coordination and management for cross-application operations integrated using TIBCO Active-Enterprise™, CORBA, and/or Enterprise Java Beans (EJB)), TIBCO InConcert™ ("models, manages and monitors in real time the tasks performed as part of customer-oriented business processes), and TIBCO MessageBroker™.

TIBCO's array of EAI capabilities, when integrated with its portal framework, provides EAI and business-process automation capabilities to TIBCO Active Portal solutions comparable to the capabilities offered by Sybase EP and Sun ONE Portal. That is, TIBCO Active Portal approaches the PAI standard for EIPs.

Vision and direction of TIBCO

TIBCO seems to have entered the portal space as a way of marketing its integration products. Its public statements lack a clear vision of what its portal product is supposed to accomplish beyond providing decision support and application and process integration within enterprises and in e-business. Based on TIBCO's commitment to EAI, process integration, and Web services, it is clear that TIBCO will continue to invest in its integration platform and to approach PAI portal architecture more and more closely. In addition, more functional capability resulting from new PortalPacks will probably be added to TIBCO's portal, but given that TIBCO is a niche player in the portal space, the growth of capability in this direction will probably be slower than it is for TIBCO's competitors.

"Touch points" with knowledge processing and knowledge management

At one point in its promotional material TIBCO claims KM functionality for TIBCO Active Portal. This claim, however, seems to arise from the casual use of "knowledge management" in marketing material, when what is really meant is content or document management. TIBCO PortalPacks include Documentum, Interwoven, and Verity PortalPacks, three applications that support either content or document management, but not KM in the sense I have discussed it in previous chapters. TIBCO still must integrate collaborative and community-of-practice support in its portal offering and, of course, support for knowledge claim validation. Further, the KM activities identified in Chapter 9 are not explicitly supported by TIBCO Active Portal.

Hyperwave eKnowledge Infrastructure

Hyperwave, Inc. has long viewed its Hyperwave Information Server as an ideal platform for an EKP (2001). And it is one of the few EIP vendors that approaches its product line from the viewpoint that it should be evaluated as a tool for supporting the social/business process of knowledge management. In fact, currently it calls its family of products an "eknowledge infrastructure." This infrastructure (Hyperwave, 2001a) consists of

- Hyperwave IS/6, version 6 of the core "KM" engine with functionality required for document management, Web content management, workflow, collaboration, e-learning, information discovery, and enterprise information portals
- Hyperwave eKnowledge Suite (Hyperwave, 2001b), which exposes the functionality of Hyperwave IS/6 in the areas of document management, content management, and information retrieval using Autonomy and/ or Verity. The suite contains two optional modules: the Hyperwave Team Workspace and the Workflow option
- The Hyperwave eLearning Suite (Hyperwave, 2001, 2001c) provides a platform for delivering "eLearning content and advanced functionality for collaborative learning, as well as administrative functions" (2001, p. 14)
- "The Hyperwave eKnowledge Portal is an Enterprise Information Portal with the usual portal functionality (i.e., a personalized, role-based user interface and connectivity to other information systems), but with the added benefit of an underlying DM and CM system that maintains the integrity of the information shown, and with 'tracks' that consolidate information from Hyperwave applications (eKS, eLS, and options) and

from external sources (e.g., databases, data warehouses, ERP system the Internet) on one screen." (2001, p. 14)

Hyperwave views the eKnowledge Infrastructure as a comprehensive, integrated KM application but also maintains that the individual pieces have been constructed so that they can work standalone or in combination with applications from other vendors. Later on, I will review Hyperwave's ideas about knowledge management and consider the relationship of these ideas to its products and to the views on knowledge processing, knowledge management, the AKMS, and the enterprise knowledge portal presented in Chapters 7–10 and 13. First, however, I will review the primary features of Hyperwave's interrelated line of products and then proceed to describe its architecture and vision and direction.

Hyperwave IS/6

IS/6 is the platform on which other Hyperwave applications are built. It provides support for open standards and single sign-on security and also:

- Document/content management (version control, hierarchical document management, support for more than 200 file formats, user-transparent publication capability, customizable and fully expandable metadata, capability to modify and add to classes underlying document object model, and link management/object synchronization
- Information retrieval for documents stored both in the IS/6 repository and in external sources—IS/6 features include support for both Autonomy and Verity search technology, full-text search, search agents with push technology for notification, finding similar documents, document summary, concept-based search, search in any indexed metadata, search in external sources including Web spidering, and automated categorization of documents
- An application framework to facilitate development of "tracks" and applications adding functionality to the infrastructure
- "Knowledge Management" functionality (features include expertise location and trained agents)

Hyperwave eKnowledge Suite

The eKnowledge Suite is the front-end application designed to deliver the functionality of IS/6 to users. Therefore, eKnowledge Suite's features have already been given in the preceding section, with the exception of the features of Hyperwave's Team Workspace and Workflow options.

Hyperwave Team Workspace is a user-friendly environment for collaborating project team members at distributed locations. TeamTabs are role-based portal tabs that provide organized access to and consolidate all information sources and applications related to a given project. TeamTabs enable navigation to discussions, documents, group calendars, task lists, notes, and, in addition to other objects associated with a project, provide complete e-mail integration for collaborating teams and team members separated in time and space. Hyperwave Team Workspace also stores dialogs from integrated discussion forums and online chat rooms for future recall, analysis, and use.

The workflow option makes it possible to model document-based business processes in the system. Procedures such as quality assurance and complex ordering processes are automated by modeling step-by-step protocols for later tracking and understanding.

Hyperwave eLearning Suite

Hyperwave's eLearning Suite is a learning content management system (LCMS) rather than a first generation learning management system (LMS). The difference is that LCMSs combine the features of LMSs, focused on delivering off-the-shelf courseware, with the features of Content Management Systems, enabling delivery of any enterprise content stored as informal learning objects in corporate repositories. In the Hyperwave case, eLearning Suite is built on the content management system provided by Hyperwave IS/6. Consequently, the learning management features of eLearning Suite are an overlay on the more fundamental content-management system and its document, content-management, workflow, publication, and object-management capabilities.

The features of eLearning Suite (Hyperwave, 2001c) address the limitations of traditional learning systems through its assured information delivery (AID) methodology and the support the suite provides for it. The steps in AID are as follows:

- Assessment—prequalification by evaluating skill profiles of attendees or through questionnaires
- Consumption—uses outcome of assessment to ensure that only content providing a personalized view of course content is delivered
- Practicing of acquired skills and/or knowledge
- Testing comprehension
- Creation of new content
- Feedback for continuous improvement of skills and course material

As part of the eKnowledge Infrastructure, the eLearning Suite can utilize all enterprise data, information, and captured knowledge to facilitate learning. The suite is a virtual training center. It has

- A "foyer" for registration and general course information
- A study room for course enrollment, discussion, and performance statistics
- Course rooms for the structured course material
- A "café" for meeting with other people for general discussion and interaction
- An administration room for controlling the training environment

Any desired content, new or existing, can be incorporated using Virtual Folders or other means provided by the eLearning Suite. Learners communicate and collaborate with both colleagues and human tutors. The suite provides both classical classroom training features (e.g., personal attention, interpersonal community, and comprehension testing) and computer-aided training features (e.g., content delivered any time and to any place).

Hyperwave eKnowledge Portal

The Hyperwave eKnowledge Portal (2001d), as I stated previously, is a portal inter-face and server layer exposing the functionality of Hyperwave IS/6, eKnowledge Suite, and eLearning Suite to knowledge workers. It also allows integration of other applications through "tracks." Unlike Plumtree or other portal vendors that primarily provide a portal front end and attempt to integrate "best-of-breed" applications in most application areas, Hyperwave's portal is based on a founda-tion of products built on the tightly integrated object-oriented content-manage-ment system Hyperwave IS/6. The portal's collaborative and content management features are themselves tightly integrated into the portal system. However, the decision-processing capability supplied by "track-based" integration with Cognos BI programs is less well integrated with the underlying CM/DM structure.

Important features of the Hyperwave eKnowledge Portal are as follows:

- Role-based organization of content for controlling the flow of informa-tion to individuals, groups, and communities and for reducing "info-glut"
- Expertise location based on implicit and explicit development of user profiles
- Collaboration, both synchronous and asynchronous, based on docu-ment-management, publication, messaging, workflow, Groupware, TeamTab, and other collaboration capabilities
- Integration of both Hyperwave and other applications through portal "track" feature
- Provides Hyperwave Track Development Kit to facilitate creation of new tracks
- Continuous learning through integration with eLearning Suite
- All features provided by the other three applications in Hyperwave's eKnowledge Infrastructure

Hyperwave architecture

The architecture of Hyperwave eKnowledge infrastructure is based on IS/6. It is an application layer based on a distributed object model functioning on multiple physical application servers. Servers may be pooled to provide a common view of enterprise objects and links across servers.

IS/6 incorporates metadata, search, taxonomy, personalization, security and access, document-management, and link-management services through various engines provided in the operational object models of the application servers. Object relationships are maintained by IS/6's link-management capability. Each piece of data and content in the enterprise is stored as an object with attributes. Metadata and meta-information attributes and values are specified by adminis-trators or users publishing to the system. As objects are changed, deleted, or added, all related objects are synchronized. Either objects are added or deleted or they and their relationships are updated, as the case may be. Any data or content and any object may be tracked, indexed, and retrieved throughout the history of the object.

In addition to the object/component model and its related services, the eKnowledge Infrastructure and, specifically, IS/6 provides Oracle or MS SQL and content repositories to handle both structured and unstructured content. IS/6 also provides connectors to structured databases and legacy and ERP applications. eKnowledge Suite, and eLearning Suite are both built on IS/6 and use IS/6 functionality to fulfill their requirements, including document processing, workflow, and some business-process automation capabilities.

IS/6 also provides an application framework for developing new applications and for integrating other applications through an API or through use of "tracks." Finally, the eKnowledge Portal provides a portal interface for IS/6, eKnowledge Suite, eLearning Suite, and other applications integrated into the IS/6 framework through its API or through "tracks."

Hyperwave's architecture is both object technology–based and very comprehensive. However, it is not J2EE-based and therefore will be less attractive than other portals to some enterprises, even though it has many characteristics of PAI architecture along with a wide range of content management, decision-processing, and even collaboration capabilities.

Vision and direction of Hyperwave

Hyperwave expresses its vision as the "convergence of knowledge management, corporate portals, and eLearning." (Hyperwave, 2002) It further expresses it as providing "the Swiss Army Knife of KM tools" (Hyperwave, 2001, p. 14). But the specifics of its vision are provided in its account of how Hyperwave supports a multistage process of knowledge sharing by acting as a corporate knowledge base (ibid. pp. 17–31). In fact, Hyperwave views knowledge management as knowledge sharing, and therefore implies that its portal products are eKnowledge Portals. Specifically, Hyperwave says (ibid. p. 17).

> . . . as more and more of Hyperwave's customers implement knowledge management projects with Hyperwave's software, it has become clear that its real strength is to support Knowledge Sharing, by acting as a corporate knowledge base.

"Touch points" with knowledge processing and knowledge management

Among all EIP vendors, Hyperwave currently makes the most emphatic claims about providing a broad-ranging knowledge-processing/knowledge-management portal. Its claims are based on the functionality of eKnowledge Suite in supporting knowledge sharing. I will now examine these claims in some detail. First, Hyperwave assumes that "knowledge bases" as distinct from data and information bases may be captured and stored by the eKnowledge Infrastructure. However, the Suite of products has no way of distinguishing knowledge from information, or information bases from knowledge bases, so that assumption is unjustified.

Second, the first step in knowledge sharing is "capture," the process of transforming information into data so that it can be stored and processed in computer networks (ibid. p. 17). Information, here, is viewed as different from data, as if data were not information. Further, there is an implication that only data can be processed in computer networks, as if bits and bytes define only data and not information.

Third, "store" is the process of publishing "the knowledge (that by now has been transformed to data) in the corporate knowledge base" (ibid. p. 18). Here again, it is assumed that what Hyperwave stores was in some sense "knowledge" as opposed to information, before "it" (the knowledge) was transformed into "data." However, there is absolutely no justification for making this assumption provided by Hyperwave.

Fourth, "organize/refine" is the process of putting the "information" stored in the knowledge base into context and "enriching it with additional knowledge" (p. 21). Note that suddenly, in conflict with the statement just above, the "data" stored in the knowledge base is "information" and is enriched with "additional knowledge" that, of course, is only data anyway, according Hyperwave's statement about the "store" step in the knowledge sharing process.

If the reader is confused at this point by Hyperwave's reasoning about the transformations of knowledge into data and into information, he or she is not alone. It is hard to imagine a more cavalier, arbitrary, and inconsistent use of the terminology of data, information, and knowledge than appears in the pages cited.

Fifth, the objects stored in the "corporate knowledge base" are, in Hyperwave, stored along with metadata attributes and their values, structure, hyperlinks, and annotations. This rich object structure must then be disseminated and accessed. Hyperwave supports extensive and sophisticated search technology from both Autonomy and Verity to aid dissemination and access. It also provides categorization and taxonomic capability to support these functions. Hyperwave thinks of this as knowledge retrieval. But since it has never been shown that the Hyperwave "knowledge base" is in fact a knowledge base, it is not clear whether such retrieval is knowledge or information retrieval. The application of search technology to expertise location, further, does not make this step a knowledge-processing one any more than the application of such technology to text. The problem is that neither information nor persons located through search functions have been validated as either knowledge content or knowledge sources as the case may be.

Sixth, "Access is the step of the knowledge sharing cycle, where the data (the bits and bytes) is converted back into information and presented to the users, i.e., the user interface." (ibid. p. 29) Here again is the assumption made earlier that "bits and bytes" are data.

This 6-step "knowledge-sharing" cycle is one that represents knowledge sharing as a process in which individuals convert their individual knowledge into data existing in "the knowledge base," which they then access and retrieve in the form of information presented to them by the "eknowledge portal." Clearly, there is nothing in this "knowledge sharing" that justifies the use of the term "knowledge base" to describe the contents of the repository. That is, there is no guarantee that what I put into the portal that gets transformed into "bits and bytes" is reflective of my "knowledge." Also, there is no reason to think that what I receive from the portal at the end of any cycle corresponds in any meaningful way to the knowledge that was originally put into the portal, if any, or to the knowledge I arrive at after interaction with the information presented to me by the portal. In addition, there is no reason to think that any "knowledge" has been shared in this interaction at a distance, mediated as it is by the portal and the computer network underlying it. Finally, there is no indication that knowledge, other than simply information or data, is managed throughout the above process.

So, finally, what are the touch points of Hyperwave with knowledge processing and knowledge management? In short, they are similar to the touch points of the other portals reviewed with knowledge processing and KM. As is true with many of them, Hyperwave provides fairly generalized support for information processing, including support for collaboration. However, it provides no specific support for knowledge claim validation, and it is not clear that it provides strong support for knowledge claim formulation.

What of the eLearning component of Hyperwave? This component may begin to provide specific support for knowledge claim formulation if the eLearning software can support specific activities of problem solving rather than generalized educational activities. While it is clear that eLearning can be more specifically targeted at individual problem solving than conventional learning, it is doubtful that the eLearning application can be as flexible as the portal itself in providing the sort of ad hoc access to information that is necessary to solve many business problems.

When it comes to KM, moreover, Hyperwave seems to provide no discernible advantages over other portals, except that it supports the obligation of managers to provide for the training of knowledge workers, but the other KM functions (see Chapter 9) receive no specific support from Hyperwave.

SAP Portals Enterprise Portals (formerly TopTier)

SAP, AG, made a great leap into the portal fray by acquiring TopTier, Inc. (SAP Portals, 2001), an early entrant into the portal space. TopTier had grown to $20 million in sales revenue and was known for its "HyperRelational" technology and strong orientation toward EAI. TopTier was one of the first portal vendors to "get" the importance of EAI to portal systems and to approach portal systems through a comprehensive object/component oriented approach. By acquiring TopTier for $400,000,000, SAP immediately propelled itself from an outsider to one of the leaders among EIP vendors. In fact, SAP Portals, Inc., the wholly-owned subsidiary created by SAP to pursue the portal business, is considered by the Gartner Group the top-ranking portal vendor in completeness of vision and ability to execute.

SAP Portals Enterprise Portals (2002) offer a very broad range of features and capabilities. They are discussed in the following paragraphs.

Unification

By unification, SAP refers to an object model that provides an integrated description of relationships both within and across all information (data and content) sources and applications within the portal system's area of e-business application. This object model serves as the foundation for SAP's "patented Drag & Relate™" "HyperRelational" technology. This technology allows portal users to move (by dragging and dropping interface objects) from one application to another in an ad hoc fashion while relating objects (such as customer) in the first application to classes such as orders in process and to the attributes of these orders, in a second application. In Chapter 5, I characterized this type of EASI as *information integra-*

tion through ad hoc navigation. It enables users to navigate across multiple data, information, and application sources as though they were all incorporated into the same virtual application. SAP Portals, Inc. is the only portal vendor offering this integration feature aimed at eliminating islands of automation. I will discuss the basis of HyperRelational technology later on in the section on architecture.

iViews

An iView is a self-contained presentation element based on XML. A well-defined set of interfaces is responsible for displaying the content of the iView, and personalizing the content elements presented in a Web browser as part of a portal page. An iView abstracts the underlying source of the content, such as a customer relationship management application, for example. iViews can be implemented in any language on any platform as long as they adhere to the interface description of iViews. (SAP Portals, 2001 p. 17)

iViews, thus, are the SAP Portals version of portlets and are essentially XML-based wrappers for content and applications. Portal pages are composed of iViews. iViews provide role-based content along with personalization for individuals. Applications may be accessed by the portal directly in full screen views as well as through iViews. When accessed in this way, the entire functionality of the application and its native look and feel are presented to the user through the portal.

Business intelligence

The business intelligence capability provided by SAP Portals is quite comprehensive and flexible. First, BI applications native to the portal support the full life cycle of data warehousing (ETL, data modeling, maintenance processing) along with OLAP, reporting, performance measurement and monitoring, and packaged analytics applications, including financial analytics, human resources analytics, customer relationship analytics, supply chain analytics, product life cycle analytics, and e-analytics. Second, SAP's Business Explorer provides portal interface–based analysis, visualization, and reporting. Third, BI information may be accessed through iViews, and through third-party BI tools. Fourth, a Microsoft Excel–based interface is available for intensive analysis and investigation. Finally, all BI information may be integrated with information from non-BI, including OLTP applications through ad hoc HyperRelational–based navigation.

Knowledge management

This misnamed category of features includes content management (including publish and subscribe features), retrieval and classification, and collaboration capabilities. These "cover the entire lifecycle of content production." These features in SAP Portals allow knowledge workers to transform unstructured content from multiple sources into a network of information. Content is accessed by using intelligent search features provided by Convera's search, retrieval, and semantic networking technology. Capabilities include concept matching, pattern search, and federated search. Information may be integrated with transactions. Content may be processed through the kinds of planning, structuring, filtering, and content-processing capabilities described in Chapter 2. Expertise location and publication capability is also included. Publishing control is achieved through online collaboration and editorial workflow. Classification capabilities automate production of hierarchically arranged taxonomies to provide access to information by subject from a repository.

SAP Portals provides repository synchronization to manage change in the content of multiple repositories. All content-management, retrieval, and classification features are accessed through an interface conforming to the Web-based distributed authoring and versioning (WebDAV) standard for collaborating on documents.

Internet content integration

SAP Portals connect to external Web content through a direct connection to Yahoo's servers. Thus, changes in the structure and content of Yahoo are immediately reflected in SAP Portals. Yahoo also provides a wide range of content packages to SAP Portals and integrates the information in them with information from enterprise sources.

Role-based content delivery

iViews and/or application user interfaces may be grouped according to their relevance to completing a task. Such a grouping is called a work set and may be incorporated into the portal. Work sets, in turn, are incorporated into folders and folders into sub-pages and pages defining the various aspects of a role. Therefore, in SAP Portals a role is a navigational hierarchy beginning with pages or tabs and ending with iViews and/or application user interfaces. SAP Portals provides more than 300 industry-specific and cross-industry role templates, organizing pages, sub-pages, work sets, iViews, and application interfaces. These may be tailored and then used to deliver content. Role hierarchy–determined content, in turn, constitutes the navigational display for users in the portal. Roles can be project based, group based, enterprise based (e.g., employee), or user based (defined in terms of favorites, personal pages, and specialized applications).

Personalization

Users can subscribe or unsubscribe to preferred content and, as indicated above, can define their own user-based roles. They can also determine page layout, format, and the look and feel of their portal interface. Administrators can also personalize portal interfaces for users. Finally, automated predictive technology can be used to personalize the portal.

Security

SAP Portals provides single sign-on security, authentication, secure communication, mapping of users to different security profiles for different applications, and LDAP support.

Syndication

SAP Portals enables delivery of content and iViews work sets and roles to other enterprise systems.

Collaboration

SAP Portals provides two types of collaboration among users in a distributed environment: synchronous collaboration and asynchronous collaboration. Synchronous collaboration involves sharing live information and in the portal includes instant messaging and online meetings. Asynchronous collaboration incorporated into the portal includes threaded discussions, document rating, workflow, feedback, and shared folders. Collaboration in the portal can encompass interaction with respect to any type of portal object, not simply documents.

Process-centric collaboration and integration

This area covers workflow and collaboration in the context of rule-governed business processes, both within and across enterprise boundaries. SAP Portals does not provide process-centric integration and collaboration capabilities in its infrastructure. Instead, it provides process integration through two add-on mechanisms. The first is SAP's Exchange Infrastructure (SAP, 2001b), designed to ensure "the coherence and consistency of transactions between operational applications" (p. 15). The exchange infrastructure does this by incorporating integration and business-process control engines in an integration server and by synchronizing information across applications related one another through process flows. It manages the end-to-end performance of rule-governed collaborative business processes by using shared knowledge relevant to collaboration resident in an object model contained in an integration repository and a related integration directory. The second add-on supporting process-based collaboration is Documentum. TopTier and Documentum (2001) integrated TopTier Portals and Documentum's e-business platform prior to the acquisition of TopTier. Among the available iViews produced by their integrative effort is My Workflows iView, which provides connectivity to Documentum's workflow application.

Integration with a broader SAP platform

An account of the features of SAP Portals would not achieve balance if it failed to mention that Portal Infrastructure is part of a broader vision and family of products being implemented by SAP Portals (2001a). This family of products implements a comprehensive infrastructure (mySAP Technology for Open e-Business Integration) for enterprise and e-business collaboration. It includes

- SAP Portal Infrastructure
- Web Application Server
- Exchange Infrastructure
- Security
- IT Landscape Management

The ready integration of SAP Portals with the other aspects of this infrastructure implies that the capabilities of an enhanced SAP Portal system including all components of the infrastructure would approach a solution to the "islands of automation" and "islands of information" problems.

SAP Portals architecture

SAP Portals architecture is perhaps the most comprehensive in the portals field. It is illustrated in SAP (2001a, p. 8). SAP's architecture is very similar to the PAI architecture illustrated in Chapter 5, the DKMS architecture illustrated in Chapter 10, and the EKP architecture illustrated in Chapter 13. The similarity among these architectures is suggested even more clearly in a previous illustration of the architecture by TopTier (2000, p. 14) prior to its acquisition by SAP.

TopTier's illustration provides more detail about the "Unification Server" component of the architecture and the "Unifiers" component. The Unification Server contains presentation components, a unified object model, and "digital doorways" providing connectivity to marketplaces, applications, databases, the Web, EAI/B2B systems, "knowledge management" applications and repositories, and collaboration applications and repositories. This structure is similar to that of the artificial information and knowledge servers discussed in previous chapters, with some differences to be discussed subsequently. In addition, TopTier (2000, p. 14) illustrates the portal personalization features also represented in SAP (2001a, p. 8) along with the multiplexor component, not represented there. The multiplexor component of the portal infrastructure is significant, because it provides for parallel processing of iViews and for the capability of SAP portals to display iViews on the portal page as they are delivered by iView servers, rather than having to wait for all iView processing to be completed.

There are important ways in which SAP Portals differs from PAI architecture. First, of course, the SAP architecture does not provide a layer of intelligent *cas* agents to supplement server functionality and, when combined with the artificial information server, to create the artificial information manager. So the processing power of SAP's architecture is less than that of PAI architecture. Second, SAP's portal and unification servers do not provide process-control, synchronization, and management capabilities for transactions and business processes, nor do they provide an inference engine to manage business processes as specified by the artificial information servers. These capabilities are provided in SAP architecture by the Exchange Infrastructure, but that infrastructure is not tightly integrated with the portal infrastructure. There is no common object model integrating the two components of SAP architecture. Instead, the Exchange and Portal Infrastructures have separate object models and are loosely coupled by messaging mediated by the Web application server infrastructure. Given that the combination of all three infrastructures along with the security and landscape management components is undeniably powerful, the separation of the unification and process management components in different infrastructures is inefficient. This inefficiency will probably be remedied by SAP as time passes, leading to a more comprehensive integration server that provides a single object model foundation for both business processing and unification.

Vision and direction of SAP Portals

The vision and direction of SAP Portals is integrated with SAP's overall vision for e-business and extraprise integration. Clearly, this vision is to provide comprehensive integration of all applications, data, information, unstructured content and e-business processes within and across enterprise boundaries. SAP Portals is the user interface and first level middle tier infrastructure supporting this overall vision. It provides functional capabilities such as decision processing content management and basic collaboration. In addition, SAP Portals supplies the information integration through the ad hoc navigation or unification capability mode of EASI. The portal infrastructure, however, will increasingly be integrated with the Web Application Server and Exchange Infrastructures to provide Web services applications and process collaboration/integration within an enhanced portal system solving both the "islands of information" and the "islands of automation" problems.

"Touch points" with knowledge processing and knowledge management

As advanced as SAP Portals is in many areas, it exhibits the familiar pattern already observed with other portal vendors. Although SAP Portals claims to support knowledge management, its account of what it means by KM (SAP 2001a, pp. 11–12) suggests that it considers content-management (including publish and subscribe features), retrieval and classification, and basic collaboration capabilities to be the equivalent of knowledge management. As we have seen, this is a position popular with the software vendor community, because vendors are, increasingly, capable of providing these various aspects of functionality. But, as I have shown through the analysis in Chapters 2, 5, 7–9, 10, and 13, information technology support for knowledge processing requires much more specific functionality than is supplied by content-management, retrieval, classification, and basic collaboration capabilities alone. In addition, knowledge management requires both knowledge-processing capability and support for the interpersonal and decision-making functions of knowledge managers. SAP Portals does not supply this full range of support, so at best it may be characterized as a highly capable enterprise information portal. Furthermore, the vision and direction of SAP, while comprehensive with respect to its focus on systems integration, provides no evidence that the primary problems of knowledge processing and knowledge management are even perceived by SAP.

Additional considerations

Advanced collaborative-processing portal products

No products are available yet., but IBM, Hyperwave, CleverPath Portal, and Sun ONE are approaching this category.

Structured information-management portal products

No products are available at this time.

Structured knowledge-processing portal products

No products are currently available.

Comprehensive knowledge-processing portal products

No products are available at present.

Conclusion

This ends my review of EIP products in the four portal segments that currently have representation. The survey and analysis of the last four chapters suggest the following conclusions about where the EIP space has been and where it is now.

Most vendors entered (and still enter) the portal space on the strength of a specific type of basic functionality—namely, content management; structured database decision processing, and basic collaborative processing.

After their entrance and capture of a niche, they proceeded to expand their functionality in other directions. Much of what we've seen so far is a merging of decision processing and content management capabilities, such that the more advanced vendors meet in the decision processing/content management segment. But we have also seen collaborative processing vendors adding content-management and decision-processing capabilities as they move toward the advanced collaborative portal (ACP) segment.

To get to the more advanced segments, the segmentation scheme requires a movement away from PAC architecture toward SAI, DCM, or PAI architecture (see Chapters 5 and 6) by the vendors. In fact, the importance of integration of data, information, content, and applications in the portal system going beyond portal interface integration is increasingly recognized by vendors and companies such as IBM, SUN, CA, and SAP. They are well on the way to PAI architecture (with SAP Portals being perhaps the most advanced, since it supports both some workflow functionality and ad hoc information integration in the portal), while others such as Netegrity and Citrix are certainly striving in that direction. Indeed, many companies now consider the integration problem to be the primary problem in portal development and seem to have adopted the idea of the "enterprise integration portal" as their goal.

Many portal products offer collaborative capabilities to varying extents. Yet the full list of such capabilities stated in Chapter 12 has not been nearly implemented by anyone. Therefore, many developments in collaboration are still to come.

One of the things that emerged most clearly from the case studies in the last four chapters is the gap between claims to support knowledge processing and knowledge management and actual support for these processes, at least in terms of the analysis provided for these concepts in Chapters 7–9 and in terms of the requirements for an IT application supporting knowledge processing and knowledge management described in Chapters 10 and 13.

The various analyses of touch points with knowledge processing and knowledge management showed little support for KM activities and in the area of knowledge processing found support for those aspects of knowledge processing that are as much information processing as knowledge processing. The analysis showed that none of the portal products provided any particular support for knowledge claim validation or evaluation either in knowledge production or in individual and group learning. It also showed that among the various vendors there was not even an awareness of the validation issue and the need for portal products to support the validation subprocess of knowledge production. In addition, the analysis of the vision and direction of the various portal vendors further reinforces this lack of awareness. Support for all the functions in the KLC, including validation, plus support for the knowledge management activities is not yet even on the "radar screen" of portal vendors. Still, many of them claim to be already delivering knowledge portals and knowledge-management functionality. The fact that they can make such claims with a straight Web interface is symptomatic of the cavalier use of the language and imagery currently existing in the "professional" field of knowledge management. More important, it also means that if they think they are already offering knowledge-processing and knowledge-management functionality and if end users agree, the result will be that knowledge-processing and knowledge-management functionality will never be offered, and the benefits of greater competitive advantage, effectiveness, ROI, and accelerated innovation will never be produced by investments in the portal space.

Which vendors are likely to actually produce a knowledge portal first? I will consider this question in Chapter 19, along with consideration of which vendors are likely to be the first to produce advanced collaborative portals.

References

Autonomy Corporation, PLC (2002). "Autonomy Announces Integration With Sybase® Enterprise Portal" at www.sybase.com/Autonomy0122.shtml.

Brio Software, Inc. (2002). "Technical Briefs: Brio.Portal Overview," at www.brio.com/products/portal_overview.html.

Brio Software, Inc. (2002a). "Delivering Enterprise Information Across the Extended Enterprise," at www.brio.com/products/portal/wp_brio_portal.html.

Brio Software, Inc. (2002b). "Technical Briefs: Architectural Overview," at www.brio.com/products/portal/portal_architecture.html.

Brio Software, Inc. (2001). "What's New in Brio Portal 7.0," Brio Software, Inc., Santa Clara, CA.

Computer Associates, Inc. (2002). "CleverPath Portal Features and Benefits at-a-glance," at www3.ca.com/solutions/Collateral.asp.

Computer Associates, Inc. (2002a). "CA Cleverpath Enterprise Content Manager Delivers Point-And-Click Control Of Enterprise Digital Assets," at www3.ca.com/press/PressRelease.asp?ID=1825.

Computer Associates, Inc. (2002b). "CA Launches New Cleverpath Brand Of Portal-Based Business Intelligence Solutions," at www3.ca.com/press/PressRelease.asp?ID=1824.

Computer Associates, Inc. (2002c), "CleverPath Aion Business Rules Expert—Features, Descriptions, Benefits," at www.ca.com/solutions/Product.asp?ID=250.

Computer Associates, Inc. (2002d). "Advantage Integration Server," at www.ca.com/solutions/overview.asp?ID=261.

Computer Associates, Inc. (2002e), "Computer Associates Announces Strategic Realignment of Industry's Broadest Portfolio of e-Business Information Management Solutions," at www3.ca.com/press/PressRelease.asp?ID=1824.

Computer Associates (2000). "Sterling Software Acquisition," at http://ca.com/sterling/index.htm.

Documentum, Inc. (2001), "Portal Partnerships Persist," Documentum, Inc., CA.

Hummingbird Communications, Ltd. (2002). "Hummingbird EIP," at www.hummingbird.com/products/eip/index.html.

Hummingbird Communications, Ltd. (2002a). "Hummingbird's Host Access and Network Connectivity Solutions," at www.hummingbird.com/products/nc/index.html.

Hummingbird Communications, Ltd. "Hummingbird's Document Management and Content Management Solutions," at www.hummingbird.com/products/dkm/index.html.

Hummingbird Communications, Ltd. (2002c). "Hummingbird's Business Intelligence and Data Integration Solutions," at www.hummingbird.com/products/dirs/index.html.

Hummingbird Communications, Ltd. (2002d), "PD Accord: The Hummingbird Collaboration Framework," at www.hummingbird.com/products/hcf/index.html.

Hummingbird Communications, Ltd. (2000), "Hummingbird EIP," Hummingbird, Ltd., Toronto, Ontario, Canada.

Hummingbird Communications, Ltd. (2000a). "Automatic Document Categorization," *Hummingbird, Ltd.* Toronto, Ontario, Canada.

Hummingbird Communications, Ltd. (2000b). "So You Want to Build an Enterprise Information Portal." Presentation to Knowledge Management: An e-Gov Conference, April, 2000 by Gilles Mousseau, Hummingbird, Ltd., Toronto, Ontario, Canada.

Hummingbird Communications, Ltd. (2000c). "The Future of Genio Suite: A Product Roadmap," Hummingbird, Ltd., Toronto, Ontario, Canada.

Hummingbird Communications, Ltd. (1999), "Hummingbird to Acquire PC Docs Group," at www.humminbird.com/press/1999/pcdocs.html.

Hyperwave AG (2002). "Hyperwave eKnowledge Infrastructure," at www.hyperwave.com/c/products/eki.html.

Hyperwave AG (2001). "Knowledge Management with the Hyperwave eKnowledge Infrastructure," Hyperwave AG, Munich, GDR.

Hyperwave AG (2001a). "Hyperwave IS/6: The Knowledge and Portal Infrastructure," Hyperwave AG, Munich, GDR.

Hyperwave AG (2001b). "Hyperwave eKnowledge Suite," Hyperwave AG, Munich, GDR.

Hyperwave AG (2001c). "Hyperwave eLearning Suite," Hyperwave AG, Munich, GDR.

Hyperwave AG (2001d). "Hyperwave eKnowledge Portal," *Hyperwave AG* Munich, GDR.

McDonough, B., and Morris, H. (2001). "Computer Associates: Building a Strong Foundation for Knowledge Management," International Data Corporation, Framingham, MA.

PCDOCS, Inc. (1997). "CyberDOCS," PCDOCS, Inc., Burlington, MA.

SAP Portals, Inc. (2002). "SAP Portals Solutions: Key Capabilities," at www.sapportals.com/index.html.

SAP Portals, Inc. (2001). "SAP to Acquire TopTier," at www.sapportals.com/company/press/press.asp?ID=2.

SAP Portals, Inc. (2001a). "mySAP Technology for Open E-Business Integration— Overview," SAP AG, Munich, GDR.

SAP Portals, Inc. (2001b), "mySAP™ Technology Exchange Infrastructure: Process-Centric Collaboration," SAP AG, Munich, GDR.

Sybase, Inc. (2002). "Sybase EP Highlights," at www.sybase.com/products/detail/ 1,6904,1017287.00.html.

Sybase, Inc. (2002a). "Sybase Enterprise Portal," at www.sybase.com/detail/ 1,6904,1011806.00.html.

Sybase, Inc. (2002b). "New Era of Networks Process Server," at www.sybase.com/ detail/NeonProcessServer1,6904,1012635.00.html.

Sybase, Inc. (2002c). "Sybase BPI Suite Highlights," at www.sybase.com/products/ BPIHighlights.html.

Sybase, Inc. (2001). "Sybase EAServer 4.1," Sybase, Inc., Dublin, CA.

Sybase, Inc. (2001a). "Sybase Agrees to Acquire New Era of Networks, Accelerates Potent e-Business Strategy," at http://my.sybase.com/detail?id=1011783.

TIBCO Software, Inc. (2002). "TIBCO ActivePortal™," at http://www.tibco.com/ portal.html.

TIBCO Software, Inc. (2002a). "TIBCO AlertServer™," at http://www.tibco.com/ prtl_as.html.

TIBCO Software, Inc. (2002b). "TIBCO PortalBuilder™," at http://www.tibco.com/ index.html.

TIBCO Software, Inc. (2002c). "TIBCO Hawk™," at http://www.tibco.com/ Hawkindex.html.

TIBCO Software, Inc. (2002d). "TIBCO PortalPacks™," at http://www.tibco.com/ prtl_pac_data.html.

TopTier, Inc. (2000). "An eBusiness Unification Platform for Enabling the Virtual Enterprise," TopTier, Inc., San Jose, CA.

Viador, Inc. (2002). "What is a Portlet," at http://portlets.viador.com/overview/ overview.html.

Viador, Inc. (2001). "E-Portal Express," Viador, Inc., Mountain View, CA.

Viador, Inc. (2001a). "Viador Announces E-Portal 6.4 Available Now," at www.viador.com/news/2001/oct11_64rel.htm.

Viador, Inc. (2000). "Viador E-Portal Framework—An Enterprise Information Portal Architecture," Viador, Inc., Mountain View, CA.

Viador, Inc. (1999). "Infospace, Inc. Changes Name to Viador and Closes $8.5 Million Round of Funding," at www.viador.com/news/1999/ jan25_umbrella.htm.

CHAPTER 18

Portal Technology, E-Business, Knowledge Processing, and Knowledge Management

Introduction: The migration of EIP technology into e-business

Portal technology is currently in full migration to the field of e-business. EIP technology is equally applicable to internally-facing, trading community, trans-enterprise, and externally-facing portal enterprise applications of all types. In Chapter 1, I introduced the notions of the extraprise information portal (ExIP) and the interprise information portal (IIP) as two portal-based e-business categories of software applications supplementing the basic classification of portals first introduced in the early days of portal activity. Both categories of e-business portals, in common with EIPs, provide an integrative workplace environment through which knowledge workers may fulfill their job roles.

Eventually, when true enterprise knowledge portal (EKP) products and solutions are implemented, they too will be used in e-business. This is especially applicable in trading communities and in communities of practice in medicine, pharmacology, architecture, engineering, science more generally, and other areas where the distinction between true and false information is critical to decision making.

E-business is not the same as e-commerce. E-commerce is about selling over the Internet. E-business is about using Web technology to support a set of related business roles and, ultimately, business processes including sales. Examples of other e-business processes are as follows:

- *e-CRM*—Web-enabled customer relationship management
- *e-SCM*—Web-enabled supply chain management
- *e-ERP*—Web-enabled enterprise resource planning
- *e-KP*—Web-enabled knowledge processing
- *e-KM*—Web-enabled knowledge management

I will discuss each of these later in this chapter.

Here are the prevalent types of Web-enablement related to e-business.

- Custom—use of programming languages to generate Web enabled applications supporting business processes and e-business.
- EIP technology—use of enterprise information portal tools to generate such applications. The use of EIP technology in preference to custom programming is a pronounced, even dominant trend in e-business.
- EIPs—use of EIP tools primarily targeted on producing enterprise facing applications.
- eIPs—use of EIP tools primarily targeted on producing ExIP (extraprise information portal) and IIP (interprise information portal) applications (see Chapter 1 for ExIP and IIP definitions).
- EKP technology.
- EKPs—use of EKP tools primarily targeted on producing enterprise facing applications.
- eKPs—use of EKP tools primarily targeted on producing extraprise and interprise applications.

In short, the core e-business characteristic of Web-enablement leads to consideration of portal technology as an increasingly effective means to achieve this goal. And, increasingly, at least for the moment, the dominant types of Web-enablement are in the eIP category.

Information portals and e-business applications

What should be the role of information portals in e-business? The answer is that EIP technology should provide the knowledge worker's "workplace" and the single gateway to all the resources needed by the knowledge worker to perform his or her role(s) in e-business processes (see SAP, AG, and PriceWaterhouseCoopers, LLP, 2001, p. 2). We have already seen that, in fact, EIPs, *unless they are also EKPs*, cannot fulfill the above objective if we mean by "resources" all the information, knowledge, and application support needed for producing, integrating, and managing knowledge in the service of problem solving. However, EIP technology can provide support for many aspects of e-business processing including content management, structured data management, and collaboration.

EIP technology supports structured data management, including querying, analysis, and reporting. It supports information acquisition through search technology. It supports collaborative commerce through collaborative applications of various kinds, including planning, project management, and community-of-practice applications as well as publication.

EIP technology also supports e-business processing through supporting transaction processing, which in turn enables both noncommercial and commercial transactions to be implemented. EIP technology also supports easy access to enterprise data, content, and knowledge, though without distinguishing among them. EIP technology, further, supports collaborative forecasting, information sharing, and information broadcasting (application of "push" technology) and can support knowledge claim formulation through use of analytical modeling software of various types.

In Chapters 12–17, I presented the full range of features of enterprise information portals and indicated products (e.g., SAP Portals and Computer Associates

CleverPath Portal) that were specifically targeted on supplying support for e-business. These features also apply to e-business information portals. Content management, decision processing, collaborative, and combinations of any two or more of these basic types may all be featured in eIPs.

The difference in how these features are applied to e-business is in their organization into a workplace whose purpose is to allow knowledge workers to perform e-CRM, e-SCM, e-ERP, and e-commerce transactions. The reason portal technology is so vital in supporting such activities is that the portal workplace provides an environment that knowledge workers may use to execute workflows, business processes, and ad hoc business decisions in whatever sequence seems necessary to perform their roles in e-business activity.

Though eIPs are increasingly important in e-business, as in the case of inward-facing EIPs, they do not support key aspects of social system activity related to knowledge production, knowledge integration, knowledge management, and their outcomes. For that kind of support for e-business, we must look to eKPs.

Knowledge portals and e-business applications

eKPs, once again, are themselves e-business applications that Web-enable knowledge processing and knowledge management within the enterprise. An eKP uses EKP technology to support e-business processes that transcend the enterprise. In Chapter 13, I introduced a six-category classification of knowledge portals. The classification included four types of eKPs: structured knowledge-processing ExIPs and IIPs and comprehensive knowledge-processing ExIPs and IIPs.

eKPs provide all the support for e-business provided by eIPs. In addition, eKPs provide unique support for e-CRM, e-SCM, e-ERP, and e-commerce. Figure 18.1 illustrates the idea that EKPs and eKPs integrate and support a number of e-business processes.

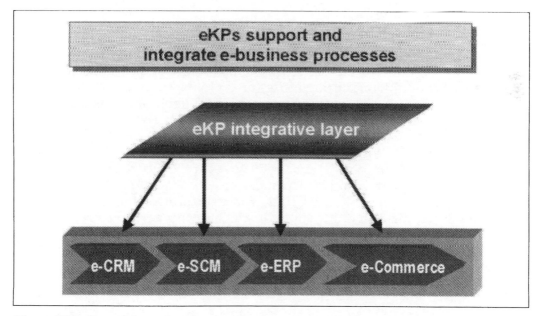

Figure 18.1. Integrating e-business processes.

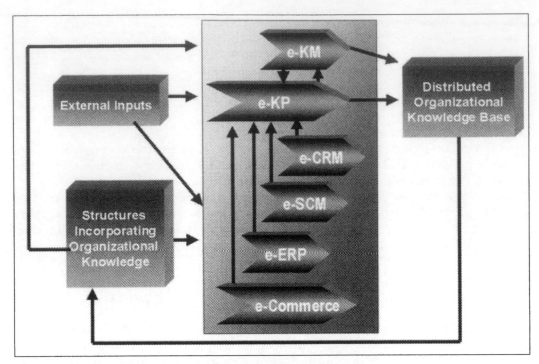

Figure 18.2. The KLC framework and e-business processes.

Figure 18.2 further illustrates the idea that business structures and external inputs impact on e-business processes and that these, in turn, produce problems for e-KP and e-KM, which produce new knowledge for the distributed organizational knowledge base (DOKB), in the context of e-business processes. The DOKB impact then feeds back to business structures and so on. Here are some ways in which the EKP/eKP impacts the various e-business processes.

The eKP and e-CRM

eKPs provide generalized support for e-CRM decision making by customers, marketing, sales, and customer-service personnel simply by providing access to a DOKB that, by definition, distinguishes among knowledge claims according to their track records of previous performance in the light of testing and evaluation. This is immediate support for using knowledge in arriving at better e-CRM decisions.

eKPs also provide knowledge-based personalization of e-CRM Web clients through the interaction of the Avatar and the AKM. That is, the validated (from the user's point of view) cognitive map of each user is available to the eKP system through the Avatar. The system can thus provide information to each user based on such cognitive maps. In other words, the eKP provides a personalized focusing of the DOKB for the user and knowledge worker in searching and retrieving knowledge appropriate to the role of the customer, knowledge worker, company representative, or any other user of the eKP.

The eKP and e-SCM, e-ERP, and e-commerce

Support for these e-business processes is similar to that provided for e-CRM. eKPs provide generalized support for decision making by agents performing e-SCM, e-ERP, and e-commerce by providing access to a DOKB that distinguishes among knowledge claims according to their track records of previous performance in the light of testing and evaluation. This provides immediate support for knowledge use in arriving at better decisions in all three of these e-business processes.

eKPs also provide knowledge-based personalization of e-SCM, e-ERP, and e-commerce Web clients through the interaction of the Avatar and the AKM. Once again, the validated (from the user's point of view) cognitive map of each user is available to the eKP system through the Avatar. The system can thus provide information to each agent based on such cognitive maps that provides a personalized focusing of the DOKB for the user and knowledge worker in searching and retrieving knowledge appropriate to the role of the customer, knowledge worker, company representative, or any other user of the eKP.

The eKP and e-knowledge processing

Knowledge-based personalization of e-knowledge processing Web clients is provided by eKPs through the interaction of the Avatar and the AKM in a number of areas of knowledge processing. First, eKPs provide knowledge-based personalization of c-knowledge–processing Web clients through the interaction of the Avatar and the AKM. As in the case of the other e-processes, the validated (from the user's point of view) cognitive map of each user is available to the eKP system through the Avatar. The system can thus provide information to each user based on such cognitive maps. That information can serve as the foundation for knowledge-based navigation or for further knowledge production of any sort.

Second, individual and group learning is supported by the eKP through the individual and collaborative knowledge production facilities it provides to agents that are part of the e-business system. That is, all agents performing e-business processes on occasion encounter problems for which there is no answer in the DOKB. That launches the agents involved into problem-solving activity and more specifically into knowledge production through information acquisition and individual and group learning.

Third, support for knowledge claim evaluation (validation) would be available in eKPs in such areas as

- E-CRM–related knowledge production:
  - Strategic and tactical CRM planning (the eKP has planning facilities)
  - Customer acquisition (the eKP provides analytical modeling and validation support in this area)
  - Customer retention (the eKP provides analytical modeling, validation support, and service facilities)
  - Customer lifetime value (the eKP provides analytical modeling, measurement, validation, and forecasting support)
  - Monitoring and evaluating CRM initiatives (the eKP provides database, analytical modeling, and validation support)

- E-SCM-related knowledge production:
  - SCM planning and process modeling (the eKP has planning facilities)
  - Raw material development (the eKP provides analytical modeling and validation support for new acquisition processes)
  - Ingredient forecasting (the eKP provides analytical modeling and validation support for such forecasting)
  - Manufacturing process control (the eKP provides planning, analytical modeling, validation support and process control facilities)
  - Inventory forecasting and control (the eKP provides planning, analytical modeling, validation support and inventory control facilities)
- e-ERP-related knowledge production:
  - Budgeting (eKPs provide planning, analytical modeling and validation support)
  - Accounting (eKPs provide planning, analytical modeling and validation support)
  - Asset Management (eKPs provide planning, analytical modeling and validation support)
  - Human Resources (eKPs provide planning, analytical modeling and validation support)
  - Shipments (planning, analytical modeling and validation support and shipment control facilities)
- E-commerce-related knowledge production:
  - E-commerce planning (eKPs provide analytical modeling and validation support)
  - Sales forecasting (eKPs provide analytical modeling and validation support)
  - Billing (eKPs provide database, analytical modeling and validation support)
  - Collection (eKPs provide database, analytical modeling and validation support)
  - Orders (eKPs provide databases, analytical modeling and validation support)
  - Deliveries (eKPs provide database, planning, analytical modeling and validation support)

The eKP and e-Knowledge management

The kind of support that eKPs provide for e-knowledge processing also applies to e-knowledge processing at the knowledge-management level. This includes support for knowledge-based personalization of the eKP workplace, support for individual and group learning related to knowledge processing, and support for knowledge claim formulation and for knowledge claim evaluation in areas such as strategic and tactical planning related to knowledge processing; knowledge worker recruitment; monitoring and evaluating knowledge-processing efforts; causal, systems; and measurement modeling, forecasting, and benefit assessment.

The targets of KM-level knowledge processing are not problems in e-CRM, e-SCM, e-ERP, and e-commerce. Rather, they are problems arising in e-knowledge processing including accelerating innovation, enhancing knowledge life cycle events, changing knowledge claim evaluation criteria and practices, changing knowledge-processing rules, implementing changes in knowledge-related infrastructure, and recruiting knowledge workers as well as many other problems related to the functioning of an organization's KLC.

The eKP also supports e-knowledge management by providing applications in such areas as resource allocation, negotiation, and leadership (including recruiting, hiring, training, motivating, monitoring, and evaluating staff).

Conclusion: Portal applications and the future of e-business

As portal technology makes advances in the areas of distributed content and knowledge management, enterprise application systems integration, enhanced retrieval technology, and especially agents that can learn, the workplace foundation of e-business will increase in capability to support collaborative commerce and other interprise and extraprise activity. Such an increase in capability will include not only an enhanced capacity to manage content, structured data, and collaboration but also the ability to support knowledge processing and knowledge management. Portal technology in e-business, then, will evolve from its current EIP-technology–based character to EKP technology. This will not happen during the next two years, which will see the generalized diffusion of EIP technology in the form of ExIPs and IIPs. But once the first EKPs appear the need for: support for knowledge claim evaluation; distinguishing knowledge from information; supporting KM-level knowledge production, knowledge integration and knowledge management; accelerating innovation; KM resource allocation and negotiation; and other KM-level functions, will motivate a rapid shift from EIP to EKP technology as the foundation for e-business.

References

SAP, AG and PriceWaterhouseCoopers, LLP (2001). *The E Business Workplace* (New York: John Wiley & Sons).

PART SEVEN

The Future of the EIP

Part Seven contains the final chapter on the future of EIPs. It covers: pathways of development; increasing vendor consolidation; increasing multi-functionality of portals; verticalization of EIPs/EKPs/eKPs; more comprehensive integration of EIP systems; collaborative commerce; increasing focus on knowledge processing and KM; and concluding remarks about the bright EIP future.

CHAPTER 19

EIP Development: Pathways to the Future

Introduction: pathways of EIP evolution

The guesses that follow about likely pathways of EIP evolution assume that vendors will follow a "path of least resistance" in evolving their products to more advanced stages of development. Further, it is assumed that the path of least resistance is determined by (1) the kind of technical capability inherent in an existing portal product type and (2) industry views about what customers want.

Figure 19.1 illustrates these pathways of least resistance. From it, one can arrive at the following hypotheses about portal product development.

Decision processing portals will evolve into structured information management or into combined decision processing/content management portals

These are the most likely immediate development paths for decision processing portal vendors. DP vendors began by incorporating BI and DW capabilities into their products. Now they are incorporating access to SAP, PeopleSoft, Baan, and other OLTP sources. Also, since I first pointed out this trend in 1999 (Firestone, 1999, Ch. 9), DP vendors such as Viador, Computer Associates, Brio, and others have incorporated CM capabilities into their products and have begun to populate the DP/CM segment of the portal space.

Content management portals will evolve into combined decision processing/content management portals or into advanced collaboration portals

The leaders in CM portals, such as Plumtree, have either worked to integrate DP capabilities into their offerings or have at least provided the means of integrating third-party DP capabilities into their frameworks through gadgets, portlets, or similar "plug-ins."

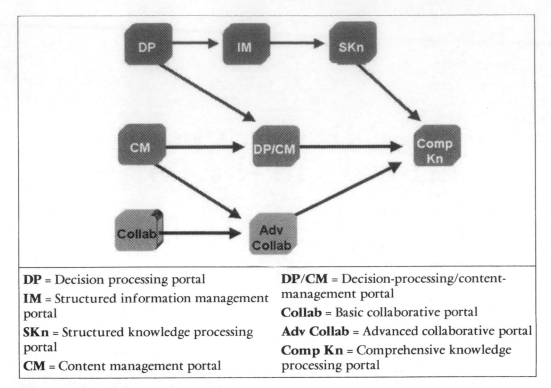

DP = Decision processing portal

IM = Structured information management portal

SKn = Structured knowledge processing portal

CM = Content management portal

DP/CM = Decision-processing/content-management portal

Collab = Basic collaborative portal

Adv Collab = Advanced collaborative portal

Comp Kn = Comprehensive knowledge processing portal

Figure 19.1. Pathways of portal evolution.

Basic collaboration portals will evolve into advanced collaboration portals

Examples of this trend are Open Text and IBM, which have incorporated collaboration capabilities on a content management foundation and are now focused on extending their collaboration capabilities further.

Structured information management portals will evolve into structured knowledge processing portals

This will occur naturally as the distinction between information and knowledge portals enters industry consciousness and software companies figure out what needs to be done to incorporate formal knowledge production and knowledge claim validation, KM processes, and validity information into their portals. Cognos and Business Objects are candidates for evolution in this direction, but first they must reach the structured information management stage.

Combined DP/CM portals will evolve into comprehensive knowledge processing portals

To accomplish this they need to add Advanced collaborative capabilities and incorporate formal knowledge-processing and KM capabilities. It will be at least one year before any software company approaches this synthesis, and that assumes they're thinking about it right now. It is more likely that knowledge portals will not appear for another two years, since most portal vendors seem focused on e-business support without recognition of the importance of distinguishing knowledge from information.

I believe the companies most likely to proceed along this path rapidly are SAP, Sun, Computer Associates, and Sybase. Each has a portal platform well grounded in an object/component integrative layer; each has sufficient resources to manage the development of the knowledge portal; and each has a chance of understanding the character of the knowledge portal early enough to be among its developmental leaders,

Advanced collaboration portals (ACPs) will evolve into comprehensive knowledge-processing portals with KM as well as knowledge-processing capabilities

ACPs need to add knowledge-processing and KM capabilities to evolve into Comprehensive knowledge processing portals. Again, it will be at least six months to a year and probably two years, before we see the first of these products. The company that is likely to be the first down this road is IBM. It has the platform, the resources, and the possibility of understanding the knowledge portal necessary to be an early leader.

Structured knowledge processing portals will evolve into comprehensive knowledge processing portals

This requires incorporating collaborative and content-management capabilities. Provided a company is at this stage to begin with and has previously made the more difficult transition from information processing and management to knowledge processing and management, this change should not be difficult—particularly since by this time, content-management and collaborative processing capabilities should be widespread in the portal space. The companies most likely to follow this path are, again, Cognos and Business Objects, but only after they produce structured knowledge-processing portals.

These pathways of development will be accompanied by key trends that characterize and define progress in the EIP field. The trends are as follows:

- Increasing vendor consolidation
- Increasing EIP functionality
- Verticalization of EIPs and EKPs
- More comprehensive EIP systems integration through active object/component layers, supplemented by "clouds" of intelligent agents with the capacity to learn, utilizing XML data streams, and Web services along with semantic networking, workflow, and ad hoc information integration technology for "front-end" integration
- Collaborative commerce "workplace" applications

I will review these trends subsequently, and then I will end with some concluding remarks about the bright EIP future and its increasing focus on knowledge processing and knowledge management.

Increasing vendor consolidation

It has been a dizzying ride to closely watch and try to understand the EIP space. EIPs burst upon us suddenly at the end of 1998 with Merrill Lynch's declaration of a new investment space. There followed a burst of furious activity with many small companies quickly entering a space then inhabited only by Plumtree and Brio, including Viador, Information Advantage, Netegrity, Sequoia, Knowledge Track, Autonomy, Epicentric, Open Text, IntegrationWare, Glyphica, SageMaker, and many others. Today (about 3.5 years later), many of the early entrants are gone, having been acquired by others or having withdrawn from the portal space to sell technology to portal vendors.

Most of the products reviewed previously are from newer vendors, many from larger companies (SAP, Oracle, Sun, IBM, Computer Associates, and Sybase). It is likely that the future of the EIP space is with these vendors, and that continuing consolidation will occur. As I write this concluding chapter, DataChannel has recently been acquired by Netegrity, reducing the number of independent portal pioneers still further. It is doubtful that the remaining small portal players have the resources to sustain the marketing and platform development burdens that still lie ahead. In addition, they no longer have decisive technology advantages over larger companies that have entered the space.

Competition and over-investment has caused consolidation among EIP vendors, but one of the most important reasons for that is the perception that a key, and perhaps the central, issue in EIP development is enterprise application integration (EAI). Portal users recognized the limitations of PAC architecture early on, and, in reaction, vendors recognized that the portal is not just a pretty interface but an enterprise system requiring substantial EAI capabilities.

It has become the fashion to view the portal as a framework supplemented by an integration platform—increasingly a J2EE application server. This, in turn, has meant that companies offering such servers, along with portal front-end tools and the most recent development environments, appear more robust to portal customers than smaller companies offering a front-end along with gadget server technology. The end result is that the larger companies named above are increasingly tough competitors, and smaller portal companies are either acquired by them or seek the shelter of acquisition by middle-sized companies that still retain the ability to compete. In this category, we find firms such as Netegrity, Citrix, and Hummingbird.

The future of EIPs and the likely development of the EKP must be viewed against this backdrop of consolidation, the relative collapse of the technology capital markets, and the trends discussed earlier in this chapter. The convergence of these suggests that the pathways of development—increasing multi-functionality, increasing verticalization, more comprehensive integration of EIP systems, further development of collaborative e-business workplaces, and, eventually, development of the EKP—will be accomplished by major vendors who in the 3.5 years since its emergence are now in a position to determine its future.

Increasing multifunctionality

The discussion of pathways of development expresses the central expectation that EIPs will become increasingly multifunctional. From EIP applications focusing on either structured data management or unstructured content management (in

1998) and adding publication and distribution applications, there have now developed applications combining these and either adding or beginning to incorporate collaboration, knowledge processing, information management, and knowledge management. The trend, simply, is to add more and more applications to EIPs through portlets or other wrappers of external applications. This trend highlights the nature and promise of EIPs (including EKPs) as the integrator of *all* enterprise processing. EIPs are the leading edge of a developing distributed knowledge management system (DKMS) (Firestone, 1997) for the enterprise, the extraprise, and the interprise. Their culmination in comprehensive EKPs will mark the emergence of the DKMS as the platform providing computing support for organizational knowledge management (Firestone, 1999a).

Verticalization of EIPs/EKPs/eKPs

In their initial report on EIPs, Shilakes and Tylman (1998) pointed to the trend of a likely increasing focus of portals on integrating applications packaging vertical market content such as: accounting applications, specialized analytical applications, and applications involving an industry content focus. This has also been a trend in DSS and business intelligence (BI), and in ERP applications. Packaged applications offer compelling economies as long as they can be integrated in portals. "Widgets," "gadgets," or "portlets" allow more rapid integration of all types of applications, including vertical applications. Their development and deployment has accelerated the trend toward incorporating vertical applications in enterprise portals.

More comprehensive integration of EIP systems

The third important trend in EIP development is increasingly comprehensive integration of EIP technology-based systems. As I indicated in Chapter 5, enterprise artificial systems integration is concerned with both of the "islands" problems. EIP applications highlight ten types of integration in the information islands area and three types of integration (subject matter, work flow, and information integration with ad hoc navigation) in the automation islands area. As EIPs develop, we are seeing and will continue to see the following integration trends:

- Interface integration around cognitive maps (e.g., TheBrain EKP) and personalized workflow (e.g., SAP, Sun, and other portal vendors) for ending islands of automation
- Increasingly effective and comprehensive data and content store integration through XML-assisted universal connectivity to back ends and to the Web, and through representation of data and content in integrative object/component models (using standards such as RDF, XML topic maps, and DAML+OIL) mapping and representing the content of XML-data streams
- Increasingly effective and comprehensive application and process integration through integration servers, business process engines, and increasingly intelligent agents (the components hosting object/component models and creating the object/component integrative layer pro-

viding the basis for both workflow and information integration through ad hoc navigation), and Web services (using simple object access protocol (SOAP), Web service description language (WSDL), and universal description, discovery, and integration (UDDI) registry). As time passes, and they acquire the capacity for *cas*-style learning, the role of intelligent agents in automated management of change will become increasingly significant.

When these trends have run their course, EIP applications will have evolved into platforms solving both of the "islands" problems, and will be integrating every data, content, information, and knowledge store, every application, and the user's window on the virtual modern enterprise.

Collaborative commerce and e-business "workplace" applications

The migration of portal technology to e-business is characterized by attempts to conceptualize the roles of agents in e-business and the construction of portal-based workplaces that will support these roles. Roles are composed of activities and tasks, the components of business processes and workflows. A specific role may enter more than one business process or be expressed in more than one workflow. Roles are at the heart of collaborative commerce- and business-oriented EIPs, because collaborative roles that support e-commerce and e-business provide the basis for determining the content and applications that should be pushed to the agents engaged in collaborative commerce and e-business. The trend to define roles and to construct personalized portal workspaces composed of customized roles will, therefore, only strengthen as time passes and will increasingly determine navigation in portal applications and knowledge worker productivity in e-CRM, e-SCM, e-ERP, e-commerce, e-KP, and e-KM processes.

Conclusion: knowledge processing, KM, and the EIP future

The future is bright for the EIP or, to be more precise, for integrated computing platforms, which provide portal access to knowledge workers in enterprises, extraprises, and interprises. Such platforms are becoming the standard in organizational computing, and they are growing and will continue to grow increasingly sophisticated technologically. Soon, everyone will have access to portal workplaces to do both their internally- and externally-facing work, and no one will think of providing access to computing resources through a means other than a portal interface (whether desktop, mobile, or wireless). Thus, the EIP revolution will be complete in the sense that everyone will use a portal to perform their work.

At that point the focus will shift to evolution within the portal space. First, attention will focus on development of advanced collaborative portals. In fact, that focus has already grown in intensity during the past twelve months. Second, the realization will come that collaboration is not in itself knowledge production, knowledge integration, or knowledge management. At that point the focus on the nature and development of EKPs will increase and, finally, the year of the EKP will be here.

At a number of places in this book I have mentioned the connection between the benefits of EIPs and their success in producing and integrating knowledge, rather than mere information, into the enterprise. I have also emphasized, at various points, the distinction between portals aimed at achieving the sort of success that emphasizes the knowledge claim evaluation or validation process and those that have no explicit emphasis on the distinction between knowledge and information or on KM.

I think the distinction between information and knowledge along with an explicit emphasis on KM are both crucial elements in determining the long-run success of portal applications. Ultimately, it comes down to having the highest quality information it is possible to have to support one's decisions. Again, knowledge is information whose value or quality has been enhanced by a competitive testing and evaluation process and, more specifically, *by the contextual information about the result of that testing process.* This contextual information tells us whether we can rely on the knowledge claims it describes for decisions.

Given a choice between having such enhanced information and having mere information, it is a reasonable guess that the market will choose the enhanced information produced by enterprise knowledge portals and eKPs and the support for knowledge production, integration and KM they provide, rather than the mere information produced by EIPs. So, once again, the EIP future is the EKP, provided only that people begin to understand the issues of information quality and risk involved in the choice between EIPs and EKPs.

We are already seeing the move toward EKPs in the marketing of some software companies. But the truth is that if we apply the criteria used in this book (see Chapter 13) for distinguishing EKPs from EIPs, and also accept the analysis of touch points with knowledge processing and knowledge management provided in Chapters 13–17, then we must conclude that no existing company is close to producing an EKP. So the EKP future is not quite now.

The enthusiasm that greeted the introduction of enterprise information portals was little short of overwhelming. Every area in information technology is now seeking a seat on the portal bandwagon. But from the first introduction of the concept by Merrill Lynch, a special connection between EIPs and KM was envisioned. Sarah Roberts-Witt (1999, p. 37) in a survey of the exploding EIP marketplace completed some time ago, referred to portals as "knowledge management's killer app." I have said enough in earlier chapters and just above to indicate that I share her view, but only with respect to the EKP. But why is this so? What is the factor that makes the EKP/KM connection feel so right?

I think the answer to this question is the broad integrative nature of the EKP, along with the absence of any competing IT application of similar scope. Other IT applications claiming to be KM applications or to have KM relevance have all obviously been partial solutions for KM. On the one hand, we have had a broad integrative conceptual framework at the level of KM theory, while at the IT level we have been supplied with image management, record management, document management, workflow, data warehousing, BI, and the like—partial solutions that at best allow us to view only a portion of the KM elephant. With EKPs, we have an envisioned application that at last provides a program of systematic integration of the various tools that each address only a part of the KM problem. The great effort at synthesis that is the EKP may or may not succeed in the end. But it will, at least address the problem of providing IT support for KM—not some other problem, which is then labeled a KM problem in hopes of increasing software or consulting sales.

Amidst all the enthusiasm and high expectations focused on EIPs, and all the opportunity for disillusionment accompanying the EIP movement, this, at least is a great improvement. EIPs, or at least EKPs, are relevant to KM and to the two "islands" problems. If even a part of their promise is fulfilled, we will be much closer to the KM vision and the virtual enterprise than we are today, and perhaps then the vision of the knowledge worker working in an intelligent enterprise, the dream of organizational intelligence, will finally be realized.

References

Firestone, J.M. (1999). "Approaching Enterprise Information Portals," *Executive Information Systems Industry Report, Executive Information Systems, Inc.,* Wilmington, DE, December, 1999.

Firestone, J.M. (1999a). "Enterprise Information Portals and Enterprise Knowledge Portals," *DKMS Brief,* 8, Executive Information Systems, Inc., Wilmington, DE, March 20, 1999. Available at http://www.dkms.com/White_Papers.htm.

Firestone, J.M. (1997). "Distributed Knowledge Management Systems: The Next Wave in DSS," *Executive Information Systems White Paper No. 6,* Wilmington, DE. Available at http://www.dkms.com/White_Papers.htm.

Roberts-Witt, S.L. "Making Sense of Portal Pandemonium," *Knowledge Management* (July, 1999), pp. 37–53.

APPENDIX

List of Acronyms

ACDA	Arms Control and Disarmament Agency
ACI	Autonomy Content Infrastructure™
ACP	Advanced Collaborative Portal
AD™	Active Directory™
AHP	Analytic Hierarchy Process
AID	Assured Information Delivery
AIM	Artificial Information Manager
AIS	Artificial Information Server
AKM	Artificial Knowledge Manager
AKMS	Artificial Knowledge Management System
APCM™	Adaptive Probabilistic Concept Modeling™
API	Application Programming Interface
ASP™	Active Server Pages™
AXE™	Autonomy XML Engine™
B2B	Business-To-Business
B2C	Business-To-Consumer
B2E	Business-To-Employee
BAPI™	Business API™
Bean ML	Bean Markup Language
BI	Business Intelligence
BPA	Business Process Automation
BPI	Business Process Integration

BPM	Business Performance Management
CAS	Complex Adaptive Systems
CBT	Computer-based Training
CDA™	Content Delivery Agent™
CDS™	Content Delivery Server
CKC	Codified Knowledge Claim
CKIM	Certified Knowledge and Innovation Manager
CKIM-G	Certified Knowledge and Innovation Manager-Government
CKML	Conceptual Knowledge Markup Language
CM	Content Management
CML	Chemical Markup Language
Collab	Basic Collaborative Portal
CompKn	Comprehensive Knowledge Processing Portal
CORBA	Common Object Request Broker Architecture
CRM	Customer Relationship Management
CSEE™	Content Server Enterprise Edition™
CSS2	Cascading Stylesheets Level2
CTS	Component Transaction Server
DAML	DARPA Agent Markup Language
DARPA	Defense Advanced Research Projects Agency
DBMS	Database Management System
DCM	Distributed Content Management
DCOM	Distributed Component Object Model
DCS™	DataChannel Server™
DDS	Dynamic Data Staging Area
DEI	Dynamic Enterprise Integration
DFI	Data Federation Integration
DHTML	Dynamic HTML
DIMA	Distributed Information Management Architecture
DIMS	Distributed Information Management System
DIP	Dynamic Integration Problem
DKMS	Distributed Knowledge Management System
DSSSL	Document Style and Semantic Specification Language

DOKB	Distributed Organizational Knowledge Base
DOM	Document Object Model
DP	Decision Processing
DP/CM	Decision Processing/Content Management
DSS	Decision Support System
DTD	Document Type Definition
DW	Data Warehouse
EAI	Enterprise Application Integration
EASI	Enterprise Application Systems Integration
e-Commerce	Web-enabled Commerce
e-CRM	Web-enabled Customer Relationship Management
ECW	Enterprise Content Warehouse
e-ERP	Web-enabled Enterprise Resource Planning
EIP	Enterprise Information Portal
eIP	e-Business Information Portal
EIS	Executive Information System
EIT™	Enterprise Integration Template™
EKM	Enterprise Knowledge Management
e-KM	Web-enabled Knowledge Management
EKP	Enterprise Knowledge Portal
eKP	e-Business Knowledge Portal
e-KP	Web-enabled Knowledge Processing
EPM	Enterprise Performance Management
ER	External Relationships
ERP	Enterprise Resource Planning
e-SCM	Web-enabled Supply Chain Management
ETL	Extraction, Transformation and Loading
EW	Exploration Warehouse
EXIP	Extraprise Information Portal
FTP™	File Transfer Protocol™
GEI™	Geneva Enterprise Integrator™
GIF	Graphics Interchange Format
HERO™	Hummingbird Enterprise Repository Architecture™
HTML	HyperText Markup Language

I & G	Individual and Group
IA	Intelligent Agent
IA	Innovation Acceleration
ICP™	Instant Collaboration Pack™
IDE	Integrated Development Environment
IIP	Interprise Information Portal
IM	Information Management
IMDB	In-memory Database
IR	Innovation Relevance
IT	Information Technology
IV	Innovation Velocity
J2EE™	Java2 Platform Enterprise Edition™
JDBC™	Java Database Connectivity™
JMS™	Java Messaging Service™
JNDI™	Java Naming and Directory Interface™
JPEG	Joint Photographic Experts Group Format
JSP™	Java Server Pages™
KBMS	Knowledge Base Management System
KCE	Knowledge Claim Evaluation
KCF	Knowledge Claim Formulation
KCO	Knowledge Claim Object
KCV	Knowledge Claim Validation
KDD	Knowledge Discovery in Databases
KDS™	Knowledge Discovery System™
KI	Knowledge Integration
KLC	Knowledge Life Cycle
KM	Knowledge Management
KMC	Knowledge Management Consortium
KMCI	Knowledge Management Consortium International
KMP	Knowledge Management Process
KP	Knowledge Production
KPD	Knowledge Production and Delivery
KPI	Key Performance Indicator
KQML	Knowledge Query Markup Language

LAPI™	Livelink API™
LCMS	Learning Content Management System
LDAP	Lightweight Directory Access Protocol
LMS	Learning Management System
MathML	Math Markup Language
MDL	Meaning Definition Language
MMC™	Microsoft Management Console™
MOLAP	Multi-dimensional Online Analytical Processing
MPPE™	Massively Parallel Portal Engine™
MSMQ™	Microsoft Message Queuing™
NASA	National Aeronautics and Space Administration
NKMS	Natural Knowledge Management System
ODB	Object Database
ODBC	Open Database Connectivity
ODS	Operational Data Store
OEM	Original Equipment Manufacturer
OIA™	Open Text Interchange Architecture™
OIL	Ontology Interchange Language
OLAP	Online Analytical Processing
OLCP	Online Complex Processing
OLTP	Online Transaction Processing
OML	Ontology Markup Language
OO	Object-Oriented
O-O	Object-Oriented
OODBMS	Object-Oriented Database Management System
ORB	Object Request Broker
OU	Operating Unit
PAC	Passive Access to Content
PAI	Portal Application Integration
PDA	Personal Digital Assistant
PDF™	Portable Document Format™
PDK	Portal Development Kit
PKP™	Professional Knowledge Pack™
PSA	Professional Services Automation

RDBMS	Relational Database Management System
RDDL	Resource Directory Description Language
RDF	Resource Description Framework
RMI	Remote Method Invocation
RoBoML	Robotics Markup Language
ROCE	Return On Capital Employed
ROI	Return On Investment
ROLAP	Relational Online Analytical Processing
RPD	Report Production and Delivery
SAI	Structured Application Integration
SAI	Software Agent
SDK	Software Development Kit
SFA	Sales Force Automation
SGKM	Second Generation Knowledge Management
SGML	Standardized Generalized Markup Language
SKn	Structured Knowledge Processing Portal
SMIL	Synchronized Multimedia Integration Language
SMTP	Simple Mail Transfer Protocol
SOAP	Simple Object Access Protocol
SORD™	Shared Object Repository Database™
SpeechML	Speech Markup Language
SSL	Secure Socket Layer
SSO	Single Sign-On
TCP/IP	Transmission Control Protocol/Internet Protocol
TIFF	Tagged-image File Format
TNKM	The New Knowledge Management
UDDI	Universal Description, Discovery, and Integration
UI	User Interface
UML	Unified Modeling Language
URL	Uniform Resource Locator
VQL™	Verity Query Language™
W3C	World Wide Web Consortium
WAP	Wireless Application Protocol
WebDAV	Web Distributed Authoring and Versioning

WFI	Work Flow-based Integration
WFT™	Work Flow Template™
WLBS™	Windows Load Balancing Server™
WMF	Windows Metafile
WML	Wireless Markup Language
WPS™	WebSphere Portal Server™
WSDL	Web Services Description Language
WSI	Web Services Integrator
XFS™	XML Foundation Server™
XML	eXtensible Markup Language
XPS	XML Portal Server
XSL	XML Stylesheet Language
XSLT	XML Stylesheet Language Transformation
XTM	XML Topic Map
ZOOBA	eXtended Object-Oriented Broker Architecture

Index

ABOUT THE AUTHOR

Joseph M. Firestone, Ph.D.
Executive Information
Systems (EIS), Inc.

Joseph M. Firestone, Ph.D. is vice-president and chief knowledge officer (CKO) of Executive Information Systems (EIS), Inc. Joe has varied experience in consulting, management, information technology, decision support, and social systems analysis. Currently, he focuses on product, methodology, architecture, and solutions development in enterprise information and knowledge portals, where he performs knowledge and knowledge management audits, training, and facilitative systems planning, requirements capture, analysis, and design. Joe was the first to define and specify the enterprise knowledge portal (EKP) concept, and is the leading writer, designer, commentator, and trainer in this area. He is widely published in the areas of decision support (especially enterprise information and knowledge portals, data warehouses/data marts, and data mining) and knowledge management, and has completed a full-length industry report entitled "Approaching Enterprise Information Portals." He is also the author (with Mark W. McElroy) of *Key Issues in The New Knowledge Management* (KMCI Press/Butterworth–Heinemann, forthcoming, 2003).

Joe is a founding member of the Knowledge Management Consortium International (KMCI), its corporate secretary, executive vice president of education, research, and membership, and the CEO in these areas, directly responsible to KMCI's board. He is also the director of the KMCI Knowledge and Innovation Manager Commercial Certification (CKIM-C) program (see http://www.kmci.org/Institute/certification/ckim_details.htm), director of the KMCI Research Center, and editor of the new journal, *Knowledge and Innovation Management*. Joe is also a frequent speaker at national conferences on KM and portals, and a trainer in the areas of enterprise information portals, enterprise knowledge portals, and knowledge management (KM). He is also developer of the Web site www.dkms.com, one of the most widely visited Web sites in the portal and KM fields. DKMS.COM has now reached an annual visitation rate of 135,200 and an access ("hit") rate of 1,014,000.